Big-noting

Big-noting

The Heroic Theme in Australian War Writing

ROBIN GERSTER

MELBOURNE UNIVERSITY PRESS

First published 1987
First paperback edition, with corrections, 1992
Printed in Australia by
Brown Prior Anderson Pty Ltd, 5 Evans Street, Burwood, for
Melbourne University Press, Carlton, Victoria 3053
U.S.A. and Canada: International Specialized Book Services, Inc.,
5602 N.E. Hassalo Street, Portland, Oregon 97213-3640
United Kingdom and Europe: University College London Press,
Gower Street, London WC1E 6BT, UK

National Library of Australia Cataloguing-in-Publication entry

Gerster, Robin, 1953– .
  Big-noting: the heroic theme in Australian war writing.
  Includex index.
  ISBN 0 522 84501 0.
  1. War and literature—Australia. 2. Heroes in literature.
  3. War in literature. 4. Australian literature—20th century—
  History and criticism. I. Title.
A820.9358

Contents

Illustrations

Every man thinks meanly of himself
for not having been a soldier . . .

SAMUEL JOHNSON

Preface

The war writer's ambition to make 'art' out of historical military events is often subverted by the temptation to manipulate them for the propagation of political, cultural or philosophical doctrine. Though these conflicting impulses are generic rather than national in derivation, the tendency in Australian war writing is so propagandist in promoting nationalistic sentiment and ideals as to make it the object of special literary interest. The word 'promoting' is used advisedly, since Australian war writers – especially from the time of the Anzac landings at Gallipoli in April 1915 – have written more in the manner of publicity agents for the 'Digger' as an exemplar of heroic racial characteristics than as disinterested observers of human conflict. This book examines the literary formulae used to mythologize the Australian warrior. My primary sources are the memoirs and autobiographical narratives of the combatants themselves, as well as novels, stories, journalism and both popular and officially-sanctioned historical accounts. Though the emphasis falls heavily on prose, reference is made to the work of war poets, particularly when it is seen to have contributed to the aggrandizement of the Digger as a national hero.

This book was adapted from a doctoral thesis, which was completed in 1985 with financial assistance from the Australian War Memorial in Canberra. I wish to acknowledge the support and encouragement of Dr Michael McKernan, the Assistant Director of the Memorial's Research and Publications Branch. At no stage did the Memorial attempt to impose restrictions on the nature of my research, or to influence my opinions. The staff at its Research Centre were always tireless and efficient in helping me plough through a mass of archival material to find what I wanted—virtues also of the staff at the La Trobe Library in Melbourne, the other major repository of my primary sources. I am grateful to my colleagues in the English Department at Monash University who assisted me, especially Brenda Niall and Professors David Bradley and Clive Probyn, who all showed great stamina in reading the drafts. Their comments were extremely helpful. I also thank for their support Kevin Fewster, formerly of the History Department at Monash, who kindly permitted me to quote from his research, Laurie Hergenhan, Peter Pierce, Margaret Wyenberg, John Wyenberg and Gail Ward. And I am particularly indebted to Sheila Wilson for her herculean effort in typing up the work from my messy manuscript, and to Jan Bassett for her invaluable suggestions and unearthing of precious documentary material . . . special thanks to Lindsay Van Jager for putting up with it all.

My debt to the war writers themselves, and to published criticism, is acknowledged as fully as possible in the notes. I must single out Paul Fussell's *The Great War and Modern Memory*—an inspiration (and an awesome standard) for anyone interested in the literature of war.

This book is dedicated to my late father, John Bernard Gerster, a veteran of the Second World War.

I

1915 and All That

FANFARE

In 1936 Angus & Robertson – prolific publisher of Australian military literature, from the slim handbook on company drill to C. E. W. Bean's massive *Official War History* – trumpeted its publication of *The Gallant Legion*, a twelve-volume series of personal reminiscences by veterans of the Great War. An advertisement recommending the collection to 'every Australian home' uses language which the prolonged agony of twenty or so years earlier would seem to have rendered redundant. 'EPIC STORIES THAT TOUCH THE HEARTSTRINGS! . . . DEEDS THAT WILL ECHO DOWN THE CENTURIES!', screams the blurb – 'WHAT MEN! WHAT TALES! WHAT INSPIRATION FOR US AND THOSE WILL COME AFTER US!' [*sic*] In case all this exaltation does not suffice, the common Australian 'Digger' is labelled, in big bold type, 'THE MODERN ODYSSEUS'.[1]

Hyperbole is intrinsic to most if not all forms of advertising in all countries, but what is notable about Angus & Robertson's ballyhoo is that it is remarkably faithful to the tone and content of the literary product being promoted. Australian prose writers had in fact been waging a publicity campaign of their own on behalf of the First Australian Imperial Force since the Anzac landings at Gallipoli in April 1915. That, in 1936, their major publisher chose to appeal to the public in such exuberant terms attests to the enormous success of that campaign. Indeed, Angus & Robertson could confidently herald the same series in similar language today. The revival of the heroic theme in fiction of the 1939–45 and even Vietnam conflicts, as well as contemporary fascination with the Gallipoli legend itself,

1

suggest that what was originally a triumph of the art of self-advertisement has developed into an enduring national mythology which has far outlived any transient conquests achieved on the actual fields of war.

Australian prose of the Great War was based on one fundamental premiss: that Australians excel, even revel, in battle. But it was not simply a matter of saying that the A.I.F. was 'good' at war. The force's exploits verified not merely that the national character had survived its first important ordeal of fire, but demonstrated that it was positively galvanized by it. Such was the contention of C. E. W. Bean, whose colossal historiographical enterprise was inspired by the archaic concept that the supreme purpose in writing about the past is to enshrine warlike achievement and suffering. Without a national tradition of battle literature on which they could draw, the war writers cultivated a fresh, home-grown heroic image, while simultaneously exploiting an imported one from antiquity. The Anzacs in particular were portrayed as belonging to a new, vigorous race from the Great South Land, grown strong through generations of combat with the Australian bush; at the same time they were seen as having somehow atavistically inherited the transcendent qualities of the heroes of the legendary Trojan battlefield so tantalizingly close to Gallipoli itself. George Johnston, one of the more articulate 'second generation' enthusiasts of the Anzac legend, was moved to write of them as 'throw-backs to that earlier golden time when gods and men walked the earth together, to the myth-time of the ancient Homeric heroes'. Half a century after the event Johnston dutifully recites what has become the familiar catechism of Australian war heroism. The Anzacs, he claims, were physically imposing (tall, tough, sunburnt), with an 'almost superhuman' spirit to match; they were men with

> stoic and almost pagan attitudes of acceptance of the ordeal as a test of fibre, of gusto for the moment of living, of delight in the comradeship of shared peril, of amused cynicism and irreverent hilarity, of belief in man's individuality and admiration for his resource, ingenuity, cunning, wit and daring.[2]

Perceived resemblances to the Homeric demigods aside, it appears that the Australian soldier also possessed the enormous self-regard of the ancient hero. The classicist Charles Rowan Beye could just as easily have been talking about the Diggers when he remarked of Achilles, Agamemnon, Ajax and company that they, 'like movie stars, can endure anything but being ignored. The glory syndrome demands recognition, approbation, and, in fact, applause'.[3] Sensing their un-diminished hunger for kudos, General Monash motivated his other-wise embittered and exhausted troops in the crucial summer of 1918 by distributing among them press reports signalling their courage and prowess. Prestige, rather than patriotism or political idealism, was the required stimulus.[4] And the men of the First A.I.F. craved favourable notices.

When these swashbucklers came to swap their swords for pens, the glory syndrome that animated their martial performance tended in turn to generate an assertive boastfulness of a blatant and often crude nature. The idiomatic term 'big-noting', signifying the giving of extravagant praise to oneself or the exaggeration of one's own importance, is helpful in defining the fictional character of the Aus-tralian military narrative.[5] The tendency to big-note is everywhere evident in First A.I.F. literature, from the wartime letters and later historical writings of Monash himself, which reveal his 'obsessive trait' of overestimating his achievements,[6] down to the personal records of the most 'humble' Diggers. '*Over There' with the Australians* (1918), a narrative enumerating the adventures of a junior officer, R. Hugh Knyvett, is an exercise in going over the top in both the military and hyperbolic senses. The exploits of the Australians, Knyvett boasts, made 'the deeds of the heroes of past times pale into insignificance. Never were there bred men of such large and heroic mould . . .'. Knyvett indulges in some spectacular name-dropping. Invalided home from France, he claims to have felt 'like the old King of Ithaca [who] had wandered for many years in many lands, but at last had returned home, and soon would have Penelope in [his] arms'.[7] 'The Modern Odysseus', indeed.

Rather than the cultivated Odyssean figure, however, the image the Australian soldier-writer liked to advance was that of an antipo-dean Achilles, a magnificent barbarian unenervated by the ravages of European over-civilization, who could kill mercilessly and with some pleasure. In *Goodbye to All That* (1929) Robert Graves won-dered if the Australian reputation for wilful violence during the war was not perhaps due to 'the overseas habit of bragging and leg-pulling'.[8] Graves has a point: certainly, there is a histrionic tinge to many of the stories told by the Diggers. In many cases the braggadocio verges on the hysterical. Writing home from the Western Front, an Australian described his method of dispatching the Germans thus:

Strike me pink the square heads are dead mongrels. They will Keep firing until you are two yds. off them & then drop their rifle and ask for mercy. They get it too right where the chicken gets the axe . . . Its good sport father when the bayonet goes in there eyes bulge out like a prawns [sic].[9]

One should regard the bluster of the letter-writing combatant with suspicion, of course. The overbold bloodthirstiness of this soldier was perhaps his way of reassuring his anxious family that there was nothing to worry about, that he was safe and in control of battlefield affairs. Then there is the psychological release of bravado, in the unburdening of what was an overwhelming emotional experience for most men. 'I don't suppose you know what a relief it is to brag', admits a Digger in Gladys Hain's *The Coo-ee Contingent* (1917).[10] Yet even a considered narrative reflection on the conflict like 'Over There' with *the Australians* emits an extraordinary pitch of murderous vehemence. R. Hugh Knyvett, who was a clergyman before the war, remembers that

> one of our men, who was champion wood-chopper of Australia before the war . . . drove his bayonet through a German and six inches into a hardwood beam, and as he could not withdraw it had to unship it, leaving a German stuck up there as a souvenir of his visit . . . these Fritzes must have thought us a race of Samsons.[11]

The glory syndrome, furthermore, is manifest in serious works written (after the bellicose chauvinism of 1914–1918 had abated) by professional literary people who did not themselves participate in the conflict. William Baylebridge's *An Anzac Muster* (1921) is indicative of the broad literary base from which the Great War legends were launched. Baylebridge, whose reputation is that of a poet with a marked Nietzschean bent, tried to compensate for a lack of personal knowledge of combat by tackling what he deemed to be a noble subject in a highly mannered, self-consciously 'epical' mode. His ambitions, like those of the combatants, were not modest: he aspired to enshrine the Anzacs in a work as universally significant, as 'virile', as that of 'the old Greeks' or 'the Norsemen of the heroic age'.[12] Unable to boast any martial virtues of his own, he can at least flex his stylistic muscles. He renders the famous Anzac attack on Lone Pine in August 1915 by means of a spurious Anglo-Saxon gusto, unpleasantly violent sexual imagery, and fossilized phraseology:

> Once up and on to that parapet, did these Australians wait? Not so! They tore up the roof from those front trenches; they leapt down into a dark-

ness ripe with death. Then, then, was there bloody work! In and home went their steel; it had a thirst in it, I warrant, for the blood of the Turks . . . now thrusting, now holding off, now twisting, now turning, now wrenching out their bayonets from this crush of flesh . . . now dropping down with their limbs shattered, with their bowels split and torn by the foe . . . the steel of Australia ploughed always a stayless passage through those trenches.[13]

Propaganda hacks, misguided ego-trippers, self-styled modern Homers – whatever their various motivations and aspirations, all were to some degree impelled by the same didactic purpose. From 1915 on, every mode of Australian war prose, whether 'factual', 'fictional', 'historical' or 'imaginative', typically functions either overtly or covertly as publicity for the Australian soldier as a twentieth-century embodiment of classical heroic virtue.

GREAT WAR: GREAT LITERARY EVENT

The assured and aggressive Australian response to the Great War, particularly the primitive focus on the lusty use of the bayonet, seems now, in the nuclear age, to be absurdly old-fashioned. But it was also anachronistic in its own time and out of step with the radical developments in war writing which took place internationally during and after 1914–18, especially in Europe. Before 1914 'most Europeans believed that they could have their wars and enjoy them'.[14] The slaughter and trauma of the next four years changed that for ever. 'Great' in the sense of its being a seismic historical catastrophe which transformed the literal, social, intellectual and political landscape of Europe, the war also caused severe tremors in the literary world. As Samuel Hynes has remarked, the conflict created a major 'literary event'; its scale and intensity compelled writers 'to find new forms for describing the ways in which men kill men'.[15] The mechanized butchery on the Western Front seemed to invalidate any reapplication of the myth of the all-powerful warrior. After all, the most monumental of fictional soldiers, Homer's Achilles, would have stood no more chance against the impersonal force of a high-explosive shell than the most craven weakling. Heavy artillery mocked pretensions to prowess. Pure luck, rather than virtuosity, determined individual survival on the battlefield. Laments Paul Baümer, the narrator of Erich Maria Remarque's *All Quiet on the Western Front* (1929), 'In a bomb-proof dug-out I may be smashed to atoms and in the open may survive ten hours' bombardment unscathed!'[16] Even Ernst Jünger, the German novelist whose imagination dwelt fondly on the mystique of violence, had his expansive confidence shaken by the 'storm of steel' that rained over the European front. Disappointed that it was not a fair test of individual or racial valour, Jünger regarded the Great War as a great letdown, in which the combatant 'exchanged heroism's iridescent mantle for the dirty smock of the day-laborer'.[17]

The common soldier in non-Australian literature of the First World War is 'a passive rather than an active figure . . . a victim rather than a hero; what he does is not so important as what is done to him'.[18] The formal consequences of this volte-face are memorably evident in the work of English war poets (notably Owen, Sassoon and Rosenberg) written after the disastrous Somme Offensive of mid-1916. In his study of the genre, John H. Johnston detects an absence of 'the classic qualities' of the traditional epic narrative, those of 'comprehensiveness, objectivity, and a sense of proportion and restraint, together with a positive, assertive attitude with respect to the values upon which motivation and action are based'. The 'conditions of modern warfare', Johnston argues, made the epic tradition 'impracticable and irrelevant'. In its place emerged a poetic mode which, characteristically, is the intensely subjective lyric registering war's agonizing impact on the private, usually dispirited and disillusioned, sensibility.[19] Man's immemorial boast about his warlike abilities thus modulated into the cry of protest, the shriek of horror, and the despairing effusion about the pity and futility of it all.

Novelists were no less vehement in their expression of anti-war sentiment. The huge popular success of such polemical fictions as Henri Barbusse's *Under Fire* (*Le Feu*, 1916; trans. 1917), and, later, of *All Quiet on the Western Front*, indicates that the war novel was just as influential in shaping the modern revulsion against warfare as the poetry of the Owens and Sassoons. The impact of *Under Fire* was especially dramatic owing to the splendid wartime timing of its publication. To Ernest Hemingway, who thought it the 'only good book' to appear during the years of conflict, the novel proved that one could protest about 'the gigantic useless slaughter' in a form other than poetry.[20] Barbusse, indeed, inspired poets as well as budding war novelists. In hospital recovering from neurasthenia, Sassoon read and was deeply stimulated by *Under Fire*, and later lent the novel to Owen, a fellow-patient. Disgusted by civilian ignorance of the war, Sassoon was encouraged to find that, at last, 'Someone was really revealing the truth about the Front Line'.[21] The choice of a vitriolic passage from *Under Fire* as an epigraph to his controversial collection *Counter-Attack* (1918) confirms the novel's status and influence.

As with the poems in *Counter-Attack*, war itself is the target in *Under Fire*. The work's urgent tone suggests that, like the poets, Barbusse saw his primary 'mission' as that of a 'spokesman' directing the attention of a smug public to the reality of the conflict.[22] As defiantly as anyone, Barbusse drew the anti-war lines from which a literary insurrection against military ideals has raged to the present day. The novel dramatizes the shattering of the warrior's once assured self-image, and implicitly proposes the obliteration of the established literary structures supporting martial endeavour. In the insurgent words of one of his beleaguered *poilus*, Barbusse argues that

> The work of the future will be to wipe out the present . . . to wipe it out like something abominable and shameful . . . Shame on military glory, shame on armies, shame on the soldier's calling, that changes men by turns into stupid victims or ignoble brutes.[23]

Debunking the martial figure, if something of a twentieth-century literary pastime, was not the invention of Barbusse or any other Great War writer. Anti-heroic sentiment is endemic in important eighteenth and nineteenth century writing, from the cynicism of Johnson, Swift and Voltaire, through the novelistic scorn for classical heroic models in Defoe and Richardson ('Of what violences, murders, depredations, have not the epic poets been the occasion, by propagating false honours, false glory, and false religion?'), to Fielding's comical mock epics, and the famous war fictions of Stendhal, Tolstoy and Stephen Crane.[24] The power of Crane's remarkable imaginative leap into the American Civil War in *The Red Badge of Courage* (1895) issues from the collision of his protagonist's fatuous expectations of glory with the prosaic reality of the battlefield. Inflated ambition is sabotaged: Henry Fleming, his mind 'lurid' with 'breathless deeds' and 'Greek-like struggles', struts into his first encounter with the real thing, and scurries out of it 'like a rabbit'.[25] In their treatment of the Napoleonic campaigns in *The Charterhouse of Parma* (1839) and *War and Peace* (1865–69) respectively, Stendhal and Tolstoy signalize the confusion and impersonality of artillery-age warfare by making their ardent young adventurers, Fabrizio del Dongo and Petya Rostov, charge blindly toward the distant smoke of the invisible enemy in a futile attempt to fulfil *passé* warrior-dreams.[26] Fundamental to Tolstoy's mobilization of a complex network of anti-heroic themes in *War and Peace* is his insistence on the redundancy of the posturing man-of-action, whom he reduces to the 'blind tool' of uncontrollable historical forces. 'The ancients have left us model heroic poems in which the heroes furnish the whole interest of the story', he interpolates during his account of the senseless slaughter at Borodino, but 'for our epoch histories of that kind are meaningless'.[27] Moreover, times were tough for the aspiring hero three hundred years before the advent of the machine-gun, the Mills bomb, mustard gas, and all the other torments that made the Great War battlefield unendurable to so many soldiers. In *Don Quixote* (1605), Cervantes' eponymous hero – the greatest of all parodies of the swashbuckler – bemoans embarking on the profession of knight-errantry in a 'detestable' period during which the warrior's individualistic skills were being made superfluous by 'the dreadful fury of these devilish instruments of artillery'.[28]

The fictional ground had long been cleared for the Barbusse juggernaut, therefore. But what is so striking about the novels of the Great War is the virtual uniformity of their hostility to the postures and practices of war heroism. Select a major novel from each of the three nations most involved in the politico-military argument – say, *Under Fire*, *All Quiet on the Western Front* and Richard Aldington's *Death of a Hero* (1929) – and what emerges is not so much a certain similarity of fictional responses as a chorus of dissident voices. In each, a brutally frank portrayal of the formulae of modern battle is given a political and 'philosophical' context through a sort of running authorial commentary which intersperses special pleading on the soldiers' behalf with angry rhetoric against war as a human institution, and specifically against the 1914–18 conflict as a uniquely barbaric, illogical and indefensible historical event. In all three, the heroic and patriotic shibboleths customary to battle literature are either eschewed or attacked. It should be added that a symbolic rejection of the very language of traditional heroism, 'words such as glory, honour, courage, or hallow', triggers the disaffection and ultimate desertion of the great anti-hero of American war fiction, Frederic Henry in Hemingway's *A Farewell to Arms* (1929).[29]

For such stern pacifists, the anti-war novelists evince a curious propensity to luxuriate in violence. Combat is depicted as an unrelieved concentration of mutilated corpses and unhinged minds, as a welter of gorged rats, pestilential vapours, slime, gurgling blood and saliva, and (in two of Remarque's more precise naturalistic flourishes) farting and sweaty feet. In this remorseless enumeration of grisly images, what purports to be documentary realism veers toward lurid expressionism. Viscera spiral gothically from the broken ceilings of ruined buildings, the faces of dead men become 'anthills' with 'rotten berries' for eyes, and wounded soldiers stagger about holding the arteries of severed arms between their teeth.[30] In the long run, this reliance on repulsive physical detail is a kind of self-indulgence, a straining after gratuitous literary effects. The gusto and various grotesqueries with which combat and its consequences are described prove counterproductive: so much 'blood' mixed with the 'ink' etherizes rather than arouses the sensitivities of the reader.

Worse still, the atavistic energy of a novel like *All Quiet on the Western Front* is liable to inflame the militaristic passions it ostensibly strives to extinguish. The very horror of war is part of its enduring attraction for man; and running rivers of blood, carnage and cold steel – all the accumulated shocks that make Remarque's novel such a *tour de force* – are, after all, elements of the archaic view of war as a crucible of human endeavour. The violence and degenerate behaviour extravagantly depicted by the anti-war novelists caused some critics to question their professed authorial ambition to tell the naked truth about war, and led to charges of rank commercialism and the exploitation of a gullible, sensation-loving public. In *The Lie About the War*, for example, Douglas Jerrold granted Remarque the 'legitimate use of poetic licence to crowd the horrors together', but discerned his picture of war to be short-sighted, distorted, sentimental, egocentric, comprehensively invalidated by absurd exaggerations and improbabilities, and downright dishonest.[31] One Australian commentator, writing in 1930 in the *Army Quarterly*, was so alarmed by the 'filthy foreign' war books (in which 'practically all' soldiers were either 'drunkards or beasts') that he demanded the cessation of their publication, and asked for an inquiry into their alleged factuality.[32] This is a ridiculous over-reaction; but it is fair to say that, in the effort to redress the age-old spurious glamorization of the battlefield, another kind of literary monster was created.

'Every battle a defeat, every officer a nincompoop, every soldier a coward'[33] – the anti-war picture is emphatically negative, and perhaps no less vicariously appealing for being so. In 'Inside the Whale' George Orwell observes that most of the Great War books 'that have remained readable . . . are written from a passive, negative angle. They are the records of something completely meaningless, a nightmare happening in a void'.[34] Orwell, not unusually, is right. Of the several British narratives to have endured, for example, very few could be said to have removed the 'nightmare' of the war from the 'void' and to have relocated it in a historical context so that it could be approached in the conventional epic manner.

Significantly, one of these, Frederic Manning's *Her Privates We* (1930), was written by an expatriate Australian who served in the ranks of the British Army. Manning elevates the English Tommy through the use of Shakespearean chapter-headings, notably quotations from *Henry V*; hence his picture of the doings of the harassed soldiers in the Stygian morass of the Western Front is refracted through resplendent cultural memories of the glory of Agincourt. The First World War infantryman is thereby placed in a grand national tradition. Not that Manning is an unqualified traditionalist: *Her Privates We* is really a very 'modern' novel which considers war as an inevitable part of the existential human destiny. Like life itself, the war is an ordeal to be faced with as much grace and self-reliance as the individual man can muster. The supreme effort to come to terms with it brings out the best as well as the worst in Manning's gritty Englishmen. Another celebration of the common British soldier (the central character is named 'Private John Ball') is David Jones's *In Parenthesis* (1937). Jones incorporates the motifs and symbols of Welsh, English and Norse myth and legend, as well as of medieval romance, into his fiction of the distinctly unchivalric warfare on the Somme. Like Manning he does not try to condone the numerous horrors of that notorious theatre. Nevertheless, as Paul Fussell contends in his brilliant investigation into the mythopoeic nature of 1914–1918, *The Great War and Modern Memory* (1975), *In Parenthesis* 'uses the past not, as it often pretends to do, to shame the present, but really to ennoble it'. Fussell, in arguing the inappropriateness of Jones's folkloristic interpretation of the war, makes the important point that the conflict 'will not be understood in traditional terms: the machine-gun alone makes it so special and unexampled that it simply can't be talked about as if it were one of the conventional wars of history'.[35] Tell that to an Australian war writer.

One big novel in particular, Ford Madox Ford's complex tetralogy *Parade's End* (*Some do Not*, 1924; *No More Parades*, 1925; *A Man Could Stand Up*, 1926; and *Last Post*, 1928) is noteworthy for its accommodation of, and deviation from, the heroic tradition. The novel is therefore bound to throw some light on the opposing Australian and European tendencies in modern war literature. Ford's theme, that of the representative Englishman at war combined with a panoramic overview of a civilization at a point of drastic change, bristles with epic promise. The protagonist, Christopher Tietjens, hardly conforms to the prototype of the modern soldier created by Barbusse, the nonentity-cum-victim. With his allegiances rooted in the aristocratic past, he is notionally the last surviving member of the extinct English species of High Tory. Committed to the concept of *noblesse oblige*, he adheres rigidly and ritually to the ethical abstractions 'Honour' and 'Duty' so despised by the Barbusses and the Hemingways as the catchwords of warmongers. In the mould of the ancient epic hero, Tietjens embodies a way of life, a racial attitude, the aspirations and will of a culture.

But although he has no pacifist axe to grind, Ford ironizes his potentially epic theme, turning it into a revelation of the sickness of the man and the civilization he is supposed to personify. In the Fordian landscape, war is truly 'total': clashing armies on the Continent are just the outward expression of internecine friction at home, and within individuals as well. Tietjens bears the brunt of conflict on all fronts. While his integrity is the standard against which moral anarchy, crowned by the Great War, is judged, an antithetical force in the fiction strongly implies the destructiveness of his steely maintenance of a stiff upper lip in the face of tremendous personal and military trials. His code of private probity and public responsibility is founded on a ruinous suppression of the emotions, which Ford in turn relates to the collective arsenal of frustrated passions unleashed in August 1914. It is only when Tietjens begins to strip himself of his inhibiting cultural role that he increases in stature. Under 'the long strain of war', Ford writes, he had 'outgrown alike the mentality and the traditions of his own family and his own race. The one and the other were not fitted to endure long strains'.[36] War, as Ford presents it, is an emotional rather than physical test. By the usual gauge of epic heroism, that of the discharging of martial force, Tietjens's output is feeble to say the least. The source of his triumph lies elsewhere, in his final psychological liberation from the conventional attitudes of the past, and in his belated recognition of an 'under self' propping up the stony public façade. This making of a separate, private peace coincides with the Armistice of November 1918; in both man and civilization, healing and growth are promised.

The rare achievement of *Parade's End* as a novel of the Great War is that it embraces many of the ideas of traditional heroism while undermining much of the heroic ethos itself. Ford subjects the gigantic historical event to his critical and imaginative vision without appearing overly grandiose or overly apocalyptic. By contrast, *Under Fire* and other works of the anti-war school lack the detachment that makes for great art. Full of intense anti-war 'bark', they lack perspective, penetration, 'bite'. An inability to transcend the personal nightmare subverts their didactic intention; what remains is bathetic melodrama. The self-proclaimed role of the narrator of *Under Fire* is that of the soldier (presumably Barbusse himself) taking notes in the trenches in order to record faithfully 'the truth' about the war, and so to guard against the temptation to fictionalize it from memory.[37] But this posture is, in the final analysis, just a pretext for anti-war propaganda.

Those who scour the Australian rendering of the Great War for the degree of disinterested insight achieved by Ford in *Parade's End* are also likely to be disappointed. Like Barbusse, Australian war writers claimed to have defined and illustrated the reality of the conflict. Narratives by members of the A.I.F., for example, are riddled with authorial declarations of a commitment to telling 'the whole truth and nothing but', of a fidelity to fact rather than to fancy. Yet the collective substance of their historical witness could scarcely be more different. More often than not, their asseveration of objectivity is a pretext for the unabashed promotion of Australian ideals. Ion Idriess, in the Author's Note to his Light Horse Memoir *The Desert Column* (1932), asserts that the book— 'this diary'—is the daily record he dashed off and kept (at the expense of his iron rations) in his haversack. And so it is—but not completely. A close check of the published text against the actual, desert-dust encrusted notebooks in the archives of the Australian War Memorial reveals significant emendations and embellishments which appear to have been designed not merely to turn the sketchy original into a more finished artefact, but also to reinforce conventional assumptions about the heroic disposition of the Australian warrior-horsemen.[38] Even a patent fictionist like William Baylebridge claims conformity with truth. Complaining in *An Anzac Muster* about the spuriousness of the national character habitually portrayed in Australian literature, Baylebridge says he aims to depict the 'authentic' Digger, a man 'not sentimental', but 'tough', 'cynical' and 'humorous'. But in fact the figure he finally settles on emerges as a slightly scruffy knight errant who charges across the globe to defend the dubious honour of those two damsels-in-distress, Belgium and France.[39]

The basic Australian literary strategy rested upon the reworking of the most fundamental of all conventions of the battle epic—the proud endorsement, through a 'naturalistic' rendering of action and behaviour, of the fighting prowess and blithe spirit of the national army in confrontation with the frightening odds of combat. While war horrors are often shuddered at, the tendency is to communicate the *thrill*, rather than the terror, of the fight. Like the proverbial theatre critic who thought the play appalling but the acting superb, Australians struggle to enunciate an abhorrence of war's wastage while in the same breath rapturously acclaiming its star performers.

The two distinct and characteristic sets of responses to the events of 1914–1918—European debunking and Australian big-noting—offer what are in effect two biased and contradictory versions of the same 'story'. Taken as a whole, the literature spawned by the Great War validates what Samuel Johnson once said of the power of war writers to generate humbug. 'Among the calamities of war', Johnson wrote, 'may justly be numbered the diminution of the love of truth by the falsehoods which interest dictates and credulity encourages'.[40]

THE REVELATION OF THE AUSTRALIAN WAR HERO

Parochialism slanted, even warped, the Australian military perspective. It should not be inferred from this, however, that there was nothing to feel proud about, or that the A.I.F. stories are mere fables, devoid of historical substance. To some degree, the Australian testimony was corroborated, especially by British observers, who were often generous in their recognition of the Digger's capacity in the art of combat if quick to denounce him as being beyond the pale in more general social and military terms. On odd occasions, the quality of their commendation resembles the self-applause of the Australians themselves. A British major who witnessed the Anzacs advance through heavy enemy shelling and machine-gun enfilading recorded his wonder that they seemed 'at home in hell-fire . . . They laughed at it; they sang through it. Their pluck was titanic. They were not men, but gods, demons infuriated'.[41] Furthermore, it was an Englishman, the Gallipoli correspondent Ellis Ashmead-Bartlett, who established the fanatical tone of Australian war writing with his famous Anzac despatch describing a rampaging 'race of athletes' storming the Turkish cliffs and bayoneting everything in its path.[42]

This fascination with the vitality and virility of the A.I.F. is almost certainly compensatory in nature. While generally eager to portray their fellow countrymen as the hapless scapegoats of forces beyond their capabilities and control, the British saw in the Australian some vestiges of the irresistible hero that modern weaponry had superseded. John Masefield, whose presentation of the Dardanelles campaign in *Gallipoli* (1916) is prettified by extracts from *The Song of Roland*, remarks that the Anzacs 'walked and looked like Kings in old poems'.[43] The reference to physical appearance should be noted, since it betrays the thinly veiled eroticism inherent in some British responses to the Australian soldier. Both C. E. Montague, in *Disenchantment* (1922), and Masefield enthuse about the Digger's looks, though the connoisseur's seal of approval comes from that devotee of heroism, T. E. Lawrence, when in *Seven Pillars of Wisdom* (1926) he casts an appreciative eye over the Light

Horsemen with whom he came into contact in the Middle East.[44] Seen in this light, the palpitations experienced by Compton Mackenzie during a visit to the Australian sector of the Gallipoli peninsula are especially revealing. In likening the Anzacs to the Homeric heroes as embodiments of 'absolute beauty', Mackenzie lovingly details their 'litheness and powerful grace', their 'tallness and majestic simplicity of line', and – startlingly – their 'rose-brown flesh burnt by the sun and purged of all grossness'.[45]

However much support it may incidentally have found from these foreign testimonials, the legend of the pre-eminence of the First A.I.F. was created and propagated by the Diggers themselves, in concert with their civilian Australian publicists. Certainly, most Diggers would have shrunk from the kind of adulation advanced by Compton Mackenzie, perhaps preferring the praise of Frank Richards, a tough and experienced private in the Royal Welsh Fusiliers, who in *Old Soldiers Never Die* (1933) states simply that they were 'very brave men'.[46] It must nevertheless be said that an unchecked narcissism – sometimes (especially in works written by non-combatants) diffused through a lofty identification with the heroic national character – acts as the instigating creative force in the writing of many Australian war narratives. The source of the heroic myth and its relation to historical truth can be deduced by glancing at a piece of dialogue from Oliver Hogue's *The Cameliers* (1919). An officer of the Light Horse asks a captured German, 'Say, old Hun, what do you think of the Australians now?' The prisoner sardonically retorts, 'They are splendid fighters. Still, I do not think they are any better than they think they are'.[47]

In locating the reason why Australians perpetuated man's traditional fanfaronade about his military might while writers elsewhere turned from celebration to condemnation, broad cultural factors must be considered. The collapse of the heroic literary framework in Europe, at least, was just one symptom of a manifest disintegration of old orientations. As Anthony Powell pithily describes it in his novel *The Kindly Ones* (1962), August 1914 represented 'the close of an epoch; the outbreak of Armageddon; the birth of a new, uneasy age'.[48] D. H. Lawrence found the right apocalyptic note when, in 1915, he saw the conflict in terms of a 'great wave of civilization, 2000 years . . . now collapsing . . . the past, the great past, crumbling down, breaking down'.[49] To an emergent nation, participation in the European cataclysm meant something else altogether. Out of the ashes of the thousands of national war dead emerged Australia Phoenix, a country triumphant and newly self-possessed. If the Great War brought on a kind of 'nervous breakdown' in Europe, then it was Australia's 'epiphany'. Writing in the *Official History*, C. E. W. Bean asserts that Australia came to 'know itself' during the war years.[50] Exploits in battle rid the country of its colonial inferiority complex – in the crude, primitive sense of the adolescent's attaining adulthood through a crucial test of strength – and replaced it with the cocky 'superiority complex' admitted by the A.I.F. memoirist G. D. Mitchell.[51] Hence the certain swagger which runs through Australian war prose, transmuting the unpleasant particulars of modern combat into an epic model of national achievement.

As part of his discussion of the 'historical connection' between 'heroic writing and periods of national growth and vigour', Thomas R. Edwards asserts that 'Great deeds are done in great times, in the adolescence or early maturity of cultures, or at least . . . find responsive literary audiences at such times'.[52] The readiness of the Australian public to embrace a distinctively national martial hero is undoubted. It was only too keen to hear of the nation's youth making good in the world arena. It had been waiting a long time: as early as 1895 Henry Lawson expectantly contemplated the day when 'the Star of the South shall rise – in the lurid clouds of war . . . while blood is warm and the sons of men increase'.[53] Prior to the Great War, probably the most-read war book written by an Australian had been W. H. Fitchett's *Deeds That Won the Empire*, a collection of tales which celebrates specifically English courage and daring (a contradiction in terms according to most writers of the A.I.F.). First published in 1897, this work was in its twenty-ninth impression by 1914.[54] 'Almost as much as the English', Bean claims in *Anzacs to Amiens* (1946), Australians 'had been brought up on tales of Crecy and Agincourt, Trafalgar, Waterloo, the Indian Mutiny, and the Crimean, Afghan, Zulu and other British wars'.[55] The case of Charl Bentley, an aggressive young Digger in Leonard Mann's novel *Flesh in Armour* (1932), is possibly typical: along with Fitchett's ubiquitous volume, he had in his childhood devoured such romances of British adventure as Charles Kingsley's *Westward Ho.*[56] Starved of the 'genuine article', Australia took passionately to a work like C. J. Dennis's verse-narrative about the larrikin from Melbourne who improbably becomes a raging patriot and war hero, *The Moods of Ginger Mick* (1916). The tremendous popularity of Ginger Mick, along with the ecstatic response afforded the archetypal Australian soldier's book, *The Anzac Book* (1916), indicate a radical shift in literary tastes, martially speaking, from the meekly colonial to the stridently nationalistic. At the time of Gallipoli, the nation discovered and gloried in what Ginger Mick calls

'Pride o' Race', agreeing with this one-time cynic that 'it's grand to be Australian, an' to say it good an' loud/When yeh bump a forrin country wiv sich fellers as our crowd'.[57]

Before the swashbuckling Digger made his dramatic entrance, the local hero had been the itinerant rural worker, in fitful competition with the bushranger. To borrow the grandiose phrase used by Russel Ward in his inquiry into the genesis of 'the Australian legend', the bushman had been 'the presiding deity' of the national literature since the 1880s.[58] Given that the circumstances of battle seemed to offer an outlet similar to the bush for a manifestation of the bushman's idiosyncratic virtues – a connection argued by historians from Bean to Ward, and more recently, by Bill Gammage[59] – it is not surprising that he was seized by the promoters of military heroism and transposed from his natural environment to the fields of international conflict. It is no accident that perhaps the Digger's most famous eulogy, 'The Australian: "The bravest thing God ever made" ' (1915), was written by a poet, the Scot Will Ogilvie, who had made his literary name writing romantic bush ballads around the turn of the century. The typical soldier of the A.I.F. is actually prefigured over and over again in Australian writing leading up to 1915. Lawson's portrait of a shearer in 'Send Round the Hat' (1902), for example, conforms almost perfectly with the martial stereotype, not just in the simple matter of appearance but in the peculiar kind of benign menace he radiates:

> He was six-foot-three or thereabout. He was loosely-built, bony, sandy-complexioned and grey-eyed. He wore a good-humoured grin at most times, as I noticed later on; he was of a type of Bushman that I always liked – the sort that seem to get more good-natured the longer they grow, yet are hard-knuckled and would accommodate a man who wanted to fight, or thrash a bully in a good-natured way.[60]

A more explicit foreshadowing of the antipodean warrior-hero is evoked by Bernard O'Dowd's mystical engrossment in the Australian countryside in his long poem 'The Bush' (1912). O'Dowd prophesies that the Australian experience will prove to be the apotheosis of all ancient mythologies, in particular the Homeric story. Looking forward to 'Troy tales of old Australia', he sees the bush as 'the scroll on which we are to write/Mythologies our own and epics new'. With admirable prescience, he even predicts the celebration of the urban larrikin soon to be undertaken by C. J. Dennis. From the 'tough blocks strewn o'er our ancient stream', he writes, 'sculptors shall chisel . . . myrmidons of some Homeric dream/From Melbourne mob and Sydney push'.[61]

But perhaps the Digger's most recognizable precursor is found in the small body of literature produced by the Boer War of 1899-1902.

(An earlier peripheral military role in the Sudan in 1885 occasioned the first real Australian war novel, E. Phillips's *Out in the Soudan*. This work, however, evinces virtually no sense of a national awareness. Aside from desultory references to 'the steadiness and valour' of the Australian volunteers – laudatory enough, given the limits of their exertions – most of the patriotism and the praise is reserved for the British.)[62] Though the Australian involvement in Britain's imperialistic adventure in South Africa sparked violent controversy at home – with Henry Lawson, his martial dreaming temporarily behind him, lining up with the anti-war faction against the jingoes – the campaign created no great literary event. On the evidence of their diaries, letters and reports the men of the colonial contingents went into battle 'keen to win golden opinions for themselves and their country';[63] but the public response to their endeavours was one of polite rather than fanatical interest, and even that turned rapidly into disillusionment. And, notwithstanding the longevity of the fascination with the sensational 'Breaker' Morant trial and execution (the generally romantic focus of which has turned a disagreeable rogue into a martyred victim of British military 'justice'), it did not exert a lasting impact on the Australian imagination comparable with that of the Great War. Randolph Stow puts the war in its proper place in *Tourmaline* (1963). In connection with a derelict memorial standing bleakly amid the general decay of his fictional Western Australian town, he writes: 'Some sons of Tourmaline, it seems, patronized the Empire in the days of the Boer War, but not much is remembered'.[64]

Yet there is some reason for suggesting that the heroic myth – its birth doubtless fixed on the rocky slopes around Anzac Cove – may well have been conceived on the African veldt. Certainly, the war consummated the nationalist trend of Australian literature of the 1890s. In his aptly-titled study *The Forgotten War* (1979), L. M. Field claims that the citizen volunteers from the bush 'carried about them the romanticism bestowed on bush dwellers by the literature of the nineties', and consequently were idealized by the popular press.[65] Another recent commentator, Shirley Walker, has illustrated the important role played by the war journalism of A. B. ('Banjo') Paterson in reinforcing the literary 'myth of masculine self-sufficiency and prowess' associated with the last years of the nineteenth century. Paterson, the celebrated proponent of 'The Bush', went to South Africa as a correspondent for the *Sydney Morning Herald* and the *Argus*. Walker notes that his many dispatches repeatedly highlight the rebirth of the old bush virtues in the Australian soldiers.[66] The qualities and talents of resilience and courage, of improvisation and skilled equestrianism, combined to make the Australian a fit opponent for the unorthodox, hardy Boer. As Paterson himself inadvertently reveals in his reminiscences of the war in *Happy Dispatches* (1934), his accounts of the fighting presage the partisan distortions of the battle literature of 1914–18. He recalls the occasion when he 'scooped' the fall of Kimberley, in which operation were involved some five thousand English troops and a mere four hundred Australians and New Zealanders. Following to the letter the earlier instructions of the chief press censor in South Africa, Lord Stanley, to concentrate on the colonials, Paterson's report made it appear that the town had been relieved entirely through their efforts. Never mind, 'the Australians and the New Zealanders got a fine advertisement out of it'.[67]

The soldiers themselves were keenly aware of their glamorous cultural associations and willingly capitalized on them in their first-hand accounts of their encounters with the Boers. J. H. M. Abbott, who was to become a prolific writer of historical fiction, served with the First Australian Horse in South Africa, and his *Tommy Cornstalk* (1902) offers a characteristic picture of the war from the ordinary ranker's point of view. In both appearance and temperament Abbott's characters are in the mould confected by Lawson and other celebrants of a peculiarly Australian type. The 'Cornstalks', the sobriquet of the 'lanky', 'wiry' and 'clean-limbed' volunteers from New South Wales, are described as a 'renewed and reinvigorated reproduction' of their forebears from the Mother Country; men hardened by their long grappling with a hostile environment. Unlike the English Tommy, the Cornstalk is no 'unthinking piece of mechanism' in the military apparatus, no mere 'pawn in the game'. Allied with his free-spirited assertiveness is a 'hardly veiled excellent opinion of himself'. As Abbott says, 'the Australian is at times "flash". He considers himself to be rather a better man than most other men'. Often ingenuously, Abbott provides many illustrations of this aspect of the national make-up – the swollen head atop the long, angular body – in his battle descriptions. These range from an enthusiasm for war as 'a big sport' to a recognition of the 'devilish fascination' of violent action which offers intimations of the shape of literary things to come. One observation might even have made the unflappable R. Hugh Knyvett wince: 'There is no hunting', he enthuses, 'like the hunting of man!' If Knyvett likes to view himself as a modern Odysseus, then Abbott casts himself and his fellow Cornstalks in a chivalric role, as 'knights-errant of no mean order, going forth to wrest the fair maiden of African freedom from the vile clutches of the Boer dragon'.[68]

While Abbott's Cornstalk obviously anticipates the hero of Gallipoli and the Western Front, the importance of the Boer War in the creation of a strikingly Australian war literature should not be overestimated. The big-noting of Abbott and his contemporaries drifts off into inaudibility amid the riotous cacophony of myth-making in 1915 and beyond. It was left to the Great War writers to reinterpret systematically the bush mythology from a military perspective.

Of all the writers involved in this gradual process of cultural definition, none played a more crucial role than C. E. W. Bean. As H. M. Green wrote of the *Official History*, 'no literary product of the Australian nineties and early nineteen-hundreds, not even Furphy's or Lawson's, is more instinct with the fundamental principle of democratic nationalism'.[69] Bean's opus, and indeed the entire canon of Australian First World War literature, can therefore be seen as confirming and accelerating the nationalist tradition begun before 1915 and maintained well after the war by novelists such as Vance Palmer and Katharine Susannah Prichard. While he remained faithful to the historian's primary responsibility to disclose and interpret the past, Bean exploited the mythology of the bush with all the fervour of his fiction-writing predecessors. He calls on the recognizable elements of the prototype to evoke a super-bushman whose virtues and foibles (mostly virtues) he magnifies by amassing a gargantuan catalogue of revealing episodes and anecdotes. Resourceful, self-confident, combative, disarmingly egalitarian and conspicuously 'graceful' under pressure, the Digger according to Bean is more a virile 'noble savage' than, as might well be argued, a rough-and-tumble colonial larrikin. Bean significantly calls him a 'child of nature': an appellation which in itself helps explain the mystique attached to the idealized bushman by the predominantly urban intellectuals of the 1890s.[70] Glimpsed first in *The Anzac Book*, of which Bean was the scrupulously selective editor, this questionable exemplar is recycled in all manner of Great War narratives, in works as varied as Oliver Hogue's grossly propagandistic *Trooper Bluegum at the Dardanelles* (1916) and Frank Dalby Davison's polished memorial to the Light Horsemen, *The Wells of Beersheba* (1933). Even the few which deprecate warlike activity, such as Donald Black's memoir, *Red Dust* (1931), use the bush myth as a basis for strenuously promoting the uniqueness of the Australian soldier.

Of the millions of words expended in praise of the Digger over the years, one short phrase provides the key to the military amplification of the old bushman image. At the end of *The Story of Anzac* (1921), the opening volume of the *Official History*, Bean defines the fatalism of the stalwart Anzacs on Gallipoli as the weeks passed futilely on, by saying that they were sustained by an 'idea of Australian manhood'.

Underlying the various excesses and incongruities inspired by the heroic war myth is the conviction that masculinity is best tested on the battlefield. From Knyvett's somewhat ambiguous insistence on the 'erect manhood' of the volunteers to Baylebridge's bayonet-thrusting supermen, Australian war prose deals obsessively with this outmoded notion of heroic manliness. The much-vaunted virtuosity of the First A.I.F. is that of the Latin *virtus* – a manifestation of pure physical force and energy, of male strength, wilfulness and comradely resolve. As D. H. Lawrence interprets him in his portrait of Jack Callcott in *Kangaroo* (1923), the quintessential Digger is 'the manly man, the consciously manly man'. Indifferent to contemplation, he revels in action.[71]

It is only in the context of such a trenchantly masculine ideology of heroism that the characteristic introspection of the prisoner-of-war memoirist is properly understood. The POW's exclusion from the potent fighting élite did severe damage to his self-image. One former prisoner of the Turks during the Great War, John Halpin, speaks volumes about the national military spirit when he tersely comments that by having given himself up to the enemy, he had in effect 'surrendered manhood'.[72] A further measure of the cultural hegemony exerted by the Great War legends is that the debunking, anti-heroic or demythologizing literary territory has with few exceptions been occupied either by women, like Angela Thirkell, unimpressed by male histrionics; by expatriates dissociated temperamentally, artistically and of course geographically from the mainstream culture, of whom Martin Boyd is the classical example; or by contemporary explorers of the mythological world of 1915, such as Roger McDonald and David Malouf, who are free of the impulse to promote or justify themselves in martial terms.

There is a sense in which C. E. W. Bean is more the godfather than the humble historian of the national hero's fiery baptism on Gallipoli. Or, to put it another way, the Great War writers wrote more in the manner of apostles of a new creed than as mere propagandists in their zealous proselytizing of the Australian people into an acceptance of a heroic cultural identity. Ultimately myths, like religions, have power and veracity only because people actually believe in them. In Randolph Stow's *The Merry-Go-Round in the Sea* (1965), a young country boy confuses the burning of Remembrance Day poppies with the burning of little wooden crosses on Ash Wednesday. To his horrified companion, 'That was a blasphemous idea, anti-Anzac'.[73] The following chapters survey the part played by literature in the creation of this reverential ethos.

II

Spreading the Word

MIGHTIER THAN THE SWORD . . .

War, especially in its early phase, tends to infect any nation with a spirit of bellicose chauvinism. It is not surprising, then, that the Anzac enterprise provoked a rash of heroic works celebrating the first stage of the Australian war effort. Indeed, it would have been strange had this *not* occurred. In the 'total' war conditions of this century, in which the dividing line between the engaged soldiery and the non-participant citizenry has become increasingly blurred, 'literary activity, like any other, is compelled to serve the interest of the community'.[1] Literature, in this sense of 'community interest', becomes a vital weapon in the national arsenal. It operates both as a line of defence and as a motivator of offensive action, buttressing as well as helping to fulfil the aims of the incumbent (and often beleaguered) war government. The First World War, the first of the really modern wars, saw the marriage of imaginative literature and politico-military policy. Governments, notes Holger Klein, had 'to justify the sacrifices demanded of whole peoples, and in the age before the arrival of the wireless and of television the printed word was a key factor. What might be termed the "spontaneous" literary response was thus embedded and often enmeshed in the official propaganda campaigns'.[2]

The primary task of the early-wartime book was to bolster morale within and without the combatant forces, to stimulate recruiting and to manufacture an optimistic picture of the fighting which would encourage widespread national confidence. In Britain, in the days before the Western Front turned into a charnel-house—after which, to paraphrase Barbusse, it would seem like a crime to exhibit the fine side of war, even if there was one—this important function was notably served by the works of two journalists, Ian Hay and Boyd Cable, the latter an Anglo-Australian.[3] Being the 'personal adventures of a typical regiment of Kitchener's Army', Hay's relentlessly cheerful *The First Hundred Thousand* (written in 1915, published in book form in 1916) pushes the prevailing optimism to the point of absurdity. When, for instance, the author's unit is holed up in a French town under heavy bombardment, the reader is reassured that 'nobody seems to mind'. Almost as an afterthought, Hay adds: 'Of course there is a casualty now and then'.[4] In *Between the Lines* (1915, reprinted eleven times within a year) and *Action Front* (1916), Boyd Cable relates the 'inside' heroic stories lying behind the terse official communiqués that gave notice of happenings on the various battlefields. In one of these he describes a group of Tommies who seem to be experiencing the joy of battle with a Julian Grenfell-like intensity. About the trenches they race, 'laughing and shouting noisily, tumbling and picking themselves up and laughing again like children'.[5] Yet the missiles they are scurrying to avoid are not (as appears likely) mud pies, but German heavy mortar bombs.

The First Hundred Thousand, Between the Lines and *Action Front* are transitional narratives: part-fictional and part-factual in content, if entirely propagandist in intention. They contain just enough factual substance to appear to an uncritical audience as accurate reflections of the fighting. But the atmosphere in Britain early in the war was so tinged with hysteria that the public also readily accepted as 'truth' works of a wildly romantic, fictional nature. The ecstatic response given Arthur Machen's short story 'The Bowmen' when it was published in the *Evening News* in September 1914 provides an excellent case in point. In 'The Bowmen', St George sends the spirits of English archers killed at Agincourt into the twentieth-century fray to assist the routed British soldiers withdrawing from Mons. They duly send their 'singing' arrows through the air at 'the heathen horde' . . . the mighty German guns are silenced . . . and the Tommies are saved. It all goes to make a pretty story; but the curious fact is that the tale was widely accepted as the historical reality. The bowmen, whom Machen describes only as 'a long line of shapes with a shining about them', rapidly developed into the avenging Angels of Mons – a national legend not merely believed in, but revered with patriotic fervour. As the amazed author was to write of the reaction to his invention, it seemed that 'the main "facts" of "The Bowmen" must be true, that my share in the matter must surely have been confined to the elaboration of a veridical history'.[6] The retreat from Mons in August 1914 was the first major military setback for the British in the conflict. As the war wore on and turned into an overwhelming human disaster, fictions like 'The Bowmen' and *The First Hundred Thousand* came to be seen as the quaint products of a period of great naivety. And in the popular imagination the Angels of Mons were replaced by the more sinister myth of the martyred millions, a myth, of course, which largely owes its existence to the writing of the pacifist poets and novelists after the débâcle on the Somme in 1916. The 'marriage' of British writers and warlords ended thus in a bitter divorce.

The preaching of a heroic gospel in the incipient stage of the Great War was therefore hardly peculiar to Australia. What *is* unique about this country's wartime response is its sustained enthusiasm for the event – a passion impelled by the manner in which Australians, in frenetic literary activity in the days and months following the April 1915 invasion at Anzac Cove, transformed a charmless patch of rocky terrain into consecrated ground. As early as August of that year, the noted (soon to become notorious) journalist Keith Murdoch mentioned his 'anxiety as an Australian to visit the sacred shores of Gallipoli' when seeking permission to visit the battlefield.[7] Just four months later the Anzacs skulked secretly off the land they had fought so hard to win, as part of a general withdrawal from the peninsula. The English writer Ernest Raymond, author of the Gallipoli novel, *Tell England* (1922), observed that the campaign began in the dawn of a spring morning and ended in a winter midnight; that it 'began with a thunder of guns' and 'ended in a shuffling silence'.[8] Raymond is musing on the tragic aspect of Gallipoli. For the English, the disappointment and unfulfilled expectations of the Dardanelles enterprise crystallized the irony and the disillusionment of the Great War experience itself. Australians were far less dejected in their appraisal of the failed operation's symbolism. The patriotic clamour that greeted the Anzac Landing survived the embarrassment of the eventual defeat. Moreover, the gusto with which Australian war writers continued to celebrate the efforts of the A.I.F. on other battlefields in Europe and the Middle East indicates that no such acknowledgement of 'defeat' had occurred. That this should be so must be attributed largely to the energy and dedication of the original Anzac legend-makers in fabricating a rudimentary body of heroic myth on which later memorialists could conveniently draw.

ANZACS IN THE NEWS

The literary acknowledgement of the Anzac Landing was immediate and intense. The original legend-makers were the men 'on the spot', the intrepid war correspondents, whose rapid-fire despatches informed the Australian public about the doings of the A.I.F. with an immediacy obviously denied the commemorative novelist or memoirist. 'The war correspondent is responsible for most of the ideas of battle which the public possesses', wrote Charles Bean, the official representative of the Australian press, on Gallipoli.[9] The opening stanza of Henry Lawson's 'Song of the Dardanelles' (1916) highlights the role of the pressman in feeding the self-satisfaction of the people at home, who impatiently awaited information about the A.I.F.'s first big engagement:

> The wireless tells and the cable tells
> How our boys behaved by the Dardanelles.
> Some thought in their hearts "Will our boys make good?"
> We knew them of old and we knew they would!
>   Knew they would—
>   Knew they would;
> We were mates of old and we knew they would.[10]

In his unpublished study of Australian military censorship in the Great War, Kevin Fewster points out that 'Australia was well served by her war correspondents'.[11] Infused with a robust nationalism, they demonstrated on Gallipoli and in the campaigns to come a commitment to communicating the martial talents and the heroic demeanour of the A.I.F. If by chance their patriotism failed them, the stringent censorship and the pressing need for further recruitment ensured that the force continued to be shown up in the best possible light. The hegemonical Deputy Chief Censor is quoted in the *Sydney Morning Herald* in August 1915 as saying that, 'There is no better way of stimulating recruiting than the publication of spirit-stirring stories, fresh and unconventional, of the gallant lads now fighting at Gallipoli'.[12]

The censorship authorities debarred accounts which depicted war horrors, and they suppressed references to sickness among the soldiers, particularly venereal disease.[13] No demur, however, was made at Ellis Ashmead-Bartlett's breathtakingly intemperate Gallipoli despatch, the first eyewitness rendering of the Anzac Landing to be published. Ashmead-Bartlett 'electrified the world', Bean was to observe; another journalist who covered Gallipoli, Charles Smith, more accurately asserted that the Englishman did 'almost as much towards bringing Australians into the limelight of world-fame as . . . the heroic deeds of the soldiers themselves'. The despatch, which appeared on 8 May under headlines such as 'AUSTRALIANS AT DARDANELLES: THRIL-LING DEEDS OF HEROISM', contributed significantly to a dramatic upsurge in recruiting. Such was the power of the printed word at that time of high excitement that, as Bill Gammage observes in *The Broken Years* (1974), many of the May volunteers arrived at the enlistment offices armed with the article. Ashmead-Bartlett's tribute to the bold bravery of the Anzacs was material fit for an Australian public which (Bean confided to his war diary) 'only tolerates flattery and that in its cheapest form'.[14]

Bean's own despatch, which to his chagrin was delayed and did not appear until a week after that of his English colleague, is almost insipid by comparison. It is more objective, more stolidly factual. So it should have been: Bean, an inveterate prowler about the front lines, had been the only journalist to go ashore with the invaders on the morning of 25 April. Ashmead-Bartlett, whose eyesight must have been brilliant, had 'watched' proceedings from a battleship out in the Aegean, going ashore for a brief period later in the day. The Australian does not deny himself the occasional stylistic flourish, however. He writes of the third brigade (the first unit to break upon Anzac beach) going up 'those heights and over successive summits like a whirlwind with wild cheers and flashing bayonets'.[15] Bean's version was deemed sufficiently inspirational by the New South Wales Education Department for it to be printed in pamphlet form along with Ashmead-Bartlett's piece, and distributed to senior schoolchildren in that state.[16]

The Gallipoli reportage of Bean and Ashmead-Bartlett, as well as that of unofficial Australian correspondents such as Charles Smith and Oliver Hogue, was the taproot of the burgeoning Australian war myth. It helped to establish a national tradition in an astonishingly short period of time. By 1918 the Australian Government had expanded the War Precautions Act in order to forbid the vulgar employment of the Anzac name for trade and business purposes. Use of the word in the naming of one's residence, boat or vehicle, was also prohibited. After the post-war repealing of the Act, the prohibition continued under the 1921 statute, 'Protection of the Word Anzac'.[17] (The British Parliament, in response to such 'outrages' as an English real estate venture named 'Anzac on Sea', had outlawed use of the word for gain in December 1916.) Within a year or two of the Landing, the novelist Roy Bridges would call his collection of Gallipoli tales *The Immortal Dawn* (1917) with the certainty that such a title would be readily understood; within a year, a popular book for the nation's children, E. C. Buley's *A Child's History of Anzac* (1916), would assert that 'that word' means as much to Australians 'as Bushido does to the people of Japan' – a somewhat unfortunate allusion, in the light of subsequent military events.[18] The 'In Memoriam' notices on the first anniversary of the Anzac Landing bespeak the early entrenchment of the new national tradition, though sometimes to disconcerting effect:

> WHITAKER – In loving memory of Private C.L. Whitaker, who died of wounds at Gallipoli, April 25, 1915
>
> We commemorate Anzac, the twenty–fifth,
> For he was one of the gallant 5th,
> Who rushed to capture Gallipoli Heights,
> And with comrades round him charged left and right.
> The task well accomplished, the 5th went on,
> But leaving behind – what was left of our son . . .
>
> (Inserted by his father and mother, Moonee Ponds)[19]

The success of the stories of the Landing not only set the tone for future reportage of battles in which the A.I.F. was involved, it meant that the appellation 'Anzac' was taken up and applied to all Australian combatants, whether or not they had fought on the peninsula. Thus, in a report of the bitter fighting at Mouquet Farm in August and September 1916: 'The Anzacs leapt over the parapets at dawn, and faced not only shell fire but a cross-fire of machine-guns, yet they raced on with an irresistible dash and gained the enemy's lines'.[20] Boyd Cable draws heavily on the legend of the Landing, and on his own fertile journalistic imagination, in his account of A.I.F. activity on the Somme in *The Grapes of Wrath* (1917):

> . . . there was a wild yell, a shrill 'Coo-ee', a confused shouting, 'Come on, boys . . . at 'em Anzacs . . . Advance Australia', and the dozen went plunging off forward. Out to the right and left of them the yell ran like fire through dry grass, the coo-ees rose long and shrill; as if by magic the dead ground sprouted gleaming bayonets . . .[21]

This free use of the Anzac reputation created embarrassment and even anger among the Australians in Europe. *Aussie*, a magazine written, illustrated and printed in France by members of the A.I.F., contains several barbed references to the predilection of the press for specious glamorization. An anecdote in the June 1918 issue, describing the reaction of a group of Australians to the sound of an errant whizz-bang, wryly comments that they 'forgot the "cool, gallant Anzac" (vide Press) touch, and streaked for the nearest dug-out'. Elsewhere in *Aussie*, however, the derivative noun 'Anzacitude' – as in 'He faced the situation with superb Anzacitude'—is used to denote the sang-froid under fire which, legend has it, characterized the genuine Anzacs and which apparently resurfaced in the diabolical war zones of the Western Front.[22]

C. E. W. BEAN AND *THE ANZAC BOOK*

Bean's involvement in the exploitation of 'Anzac' is ambiguous to say the least. He was trenchantly critical of the practice, but he could also be as prodigal in his use of the legend for propagandist purposes as some of the more unprincipled members of the press corps. While it was no doubt reasonable of him in his later role as a historian to discern 'the tradition of Anzac Beach', in subsequent battles, Bean during the war showed an indecent haste in applying the Anzac label to all manner of troops. His report of a savagely-foiled raid on German trenches near Fromelles in July 1916, for example, cleanses the operation of its tactical futility by applauding the Australian performance as being 'worthy of all the traditions of Anzac'.[23] Bean recognizes in a collection of his Western Front despatches, *Letters from France* (1917), that the men in France did not want to be seen reaping the glory of others, and that they associated the term 'Anzac' with 'highly coloured' and 'imaginative' press stories. Yet precisely that sort of journalistic licence is used earlier in the book when he describes the response of the A.I.F. to the awesome enemy bombardment at Pozières: 'What is a barrage against such troops!', he declaims, 'They went through it as you would go through a summer shower . . .'. And this from the pen of one who, in his diary of about that time, stated that 'soldiers are not the fictions which war correspondents have made of them, but ordinary human men'.[24] Clearly, Bean was perfectly aware of the importance of the journalist's role in the making of war myths.

Whatever the chasm separating Bean's public utterance from his private thoughts, his reportage was relatively circumspect in manner and matter. The comparison with the blustering Ashmead-Bartlett (who once complained that the Australian 'counted the bullets') is proof enough of this, while Kevin Fewster argues that Bean's writing 'contained considerably fewer distortions' than that of his Australian colleagues Keith Murdoch and G. L. Gilmour.[25] Bean's Gallipoli diary records his distaste for the pressman's love of the bayonet charge, and his personal preference for less ostentatious displays of heroism involving the defeat of one's private dread and the simple carrying out of soldierly duties. He laments the fact that war correspondents have 'so habitually exaggerated the heroism of battles that people don't realise that the real actions are heroic'. The public appetite had to be satisfied, and at least in the eyes of certain newspaper proprietors Bean's accounts were less than satisfactory. In September 1915 both major Melbourne dailies, the *Age* and the *Argus*, discontinued publication of his reports, preferring to print what Bean derisively calls the 'beautiful stuff' available through Reuter's agency in Cairo.[26] Bean had other critics. To General Monash, his reportage represented 'the apotheosis of banality' – a charge which led Bean, years later, to counter-attack that Monash's letters, with their 'grandiloquent phrases' and 'efflorescent adjectives', falsely depict the diggers as 'titans', 'demigods' and 'supermen'. The *Bulletin* also attacked Bean's communications for being 'colourless' and thus hindering recruiting, though on other occasions it railed against and also parodied aggressive and optimistic reporting.[27] Obviously Bean could not have pleased everyone whatever line – objective or historionic – he chose to adopt, and his despatches tend to reflect this dilemma.

In spite of his heavy load of official duties, Bean found the time during the war years to write three extended works, though the second of these, *Letters from France*, is little more than an edited selection of his despatches. As its title implies, *What to Know in Egypt: A Guide for Australian Soldiers* (1915) is a *vade mecum* for the large Australian force gathered in the Middle East preparatory to the move to the theatres of war. Among many pieces of advice, the morally fastidious Bean warns the men off the adulterated native 'grog' ('in some cases the colour is obtained in ways too disgusting to be described') and the 'diseased' local women.[28] Judging by the exploits, both bibulous and sexual, of the Australians in Egypt at that time, *What to Know* must be regarded as an egregious failure. Right at the end of the war Bean produced a utopian tract, *In Your Hands, Australians* (1918), in which he expressed his hope that post-war Australia would build upon the freedoms preserved by the men who had fought and died in the previous four years.

But by far Bean's greatest wartime contribution to the building of the Anzac myth came not directly from his own pen, but through his editorship of the collection of poems, prose sketches, anecdotes and illustrations known as *The Anzac Book*. From the time of its appearance in early 1916, *The Anzac Book* probably found its way into more Australian homes than any other war book. Certainly, in terms of pure sales the work far outstripped the six volumes Bean was to write for the *Official History*, upon which his reputation mainly depends.[29] As its editor, Bean called upon all the patriotic conviction he had brought to bear upon his war journalism. Writing about Hay's *The First Hundred Thousand* in *The Great War and Modern Memory*, Paul Fussell observes that modern mass wars 'require in their early stages a definitive work of popular literature' which reassuringly demonstrates 'how much wholesome fun' is to be had in playing the game of war.[30] *The Anzac Book* is such a 'definitive' work. More than that, it is something of a manifesto which sets out a thesis of Australian heroism. It is the first real unveiling of the 'official' literary portrait of the Digger. This portrait has over the years occasionally been revised, but rarely has it been rejected.

The Anzac Book was at first intended as a magazine which would help relieve the tedium and discomfort experienced by the men on Gallipoli during the stalemate of the bitterly cold final weeks of 1915. Contributions from the soldiers themselves were called for, and prizes were awarded for the best items. Bean had completed much of the work of editing before the surprise evacuation of the peninsula on 20 December dramatically altered the nature of the project. As Bean was to remark in his Editor's Note to the final publication, 'it was realised by everyone that this production, which was to have been a mere pastime, had now become a hundred times more precious as a souvenir'.[31] By the unrelenting manner in which he threw himself into ensuring the sales and broad distribution of the book, it is clear that he, at least, did not inflate its potential significance.[32] Moreover, his methodical editing of the mass of raw material at his disposal indicates that he divined that this ostensibly ephemeral work would become a potent literary instrument by which the Anzacs would be commemorated, celebrated and mythologized in the decades to come.

In a study of the editorial process undertaken towards the making of *The Anzac Book*, David Kent argues that Bean was 'an exceedingly selective editor who rejected anything which might have modified his [own] vision or tarnished the name of "Anzac" '. According to Kent, a file of the manuscripts Bean rejected for inclusion in the final text 'could be used to produce an "Alternative Anzac Book" which would be markedly different from that which Bean assembled'. He consigned to oblivion those contributions which dwelt on the extreme dangers of combat; those which dealt with cowardice or malingering; with an intemperate longing for Australian beer (ANY beer!); with bitterness at the relative comforts and privileges enjoyed by the officers; and he especially put aside those pieces which to any degree echoed Owen's famously cynical Great War statement, 'The old Lie: Dulce et decorum est/Pro patria mori'. As Kent concludes, *The Anzac Book* is only 'a partial record'.[33] The blurb on the back cover of the 1975 reprint of the work proclaims that inside is to be found 'the *truth* behind the legend'. That is misleading. The book tenders the legend itself.

Exactly what material, then, did Bean deem suitable for the image he wished the book to transmit? Any discussion of *The Anzac Book* must begin with the comic nature of several of the contributions. A cursory perusal of the contents reveals that they exude a certain *joie de vivre* which seems inconsistent with the savage experience on which they are based. To the young George Johnston, reading the book at home just after the war, it 'made the whole campaign seem like a quixotic romp' which he 'could hardly reconcile with the stark and terrifying picture presented in the *Illustrated History of the War*'.[34] Johnston, the boy, exaggerated the book's good humour, but it is true that it is filled with jauntiness that is disarming. Under the surface fun, however, an element of tension is detectable. The type of laughter it expresses, and provokes in the reader, is that of the cruel Bergsonian kind, the 'froth' with a 'saline base' that is characteristic of the desperate, dark humour of the early novels of Evelyn Waugh. The sagacious A.I.F. chaplain Kenneth Henderson defines the source of *The Anzac Book*'s liveliness when, in connection with the high spirits he discerned among the Australian forces, he writes that humour in war 'is a victorious insurrection against the continual oppression of its horrors'. [35] There is something cathartic about *The Anzac Book*'s comedy. Discomforts and privations, for all the selectivity of Bean's editing, are not overlooked. Rather, they are purged through a comic, usually ironic, detachment – as in the ludicrously formal military language used to describe the hordes of flies and fleas which terrorized the men nearly as much as the airborne metal:

> With the setting sun the flies retire, but operations are simply handed over to their allies, the fleas; and no worthier ally could be found than those pilgrims of the night . . . Advancing in open or close formation, according to circumstances, the enemy attacks on every flank with fixed bayonets, in the handling of which his units are experts. If driven off, they come again in still greater numbers; they appear to have unlimited numbers of reinforcements which can be mobilised on the shortest notice. Their organisation is perfect . . . Keating's Powder is of no avail against the Gallipoli fleas, it requires a still higher explosive to have any effect.[36]

On occasions the irony takes a sharper, more caustic turn, especially when civilian ignorance of the nature of the struggle conducted in the claustrophobic gullies of Gallipoli is involved. The *non sequiturs* uttered by a Sydney girl in a letter accompanying a gift parcel to her Anzac sweetheart expose the complacency of wartime Australia:

> I suppose you have to walk some distance from the firing-line to the nearest shops. No doubt the cigars will be acceptable after dinner, and, later on,

the pyjamas. Don't think me forward in sending the latter. But I know fellows do wear them. I've seen them advertised in the *Herald*... Please don't get shot, dear. We intend to send you lots of nice things for Christmas.[37]

Mock classified advertisements at the back of the book are infused with a kind of raw wit that may be healing rather than merely high-spirited. On Gallipoli there were no lively *estaminets* and no comely *mademoiselles* to offer the soldier a measure of solace after his harrowing time in combat. (The one real pastime, swimming in Anzac Cove, was an activity fraught with danger.) An advertisement in the 'Personal' column expresses the pain of emotional deprivation under a cloak of jokey laconicism:

> Will the girl who smiled at William Tomkins last Boxing Day please write to him at once?[38]

And the sense of entrapment on the tortuous piece of land won by the Anzacs is summed up by the playful escapism of the following entry filed under 'Miscellaneous':

> Man with good memory would like the job of taking messages from the troops to friends in Cairo.[39]

Yet there are few moments of unrelieved gloom in *The Anzac Book* to dim the genial sunniness of the work. Aside from the poisonous barbs at civilians and the cartoons lampooning military authority (the men of *The Anzac Book* are sturdily independent types, unlike the regimental ciphers of *The First Hundred Thousand*), the dominant tone is one of tolerance and stoical acceptance. Even the Turkish enemy is viewed more as an equally oppressed comrade than as a reviled opponent.[40]

The Australian soldiers depicted in the book possess an extraordinarily insouciant attitude to shell and rifle fire. The 'cool, gallant Anzac' image promoted by the press predominates. Only one piece deals in any descriptive detail with the mechanics of battle, A. R. Perry's 'The Landing', which opens the volume. David Kent reveals that Bean's editorial pen mutilated this story of the April invasion, removing references to the savage shell-fire concentrated on the beaching craft, snipers, and so on.[41] He did not want to make the Landing seem too bloody, especially when much of the blood being spilt was Australian. The substance of Perry's account is therefore greatly vitiated. What remains is little more than a sprightly yarn about an exhilarating, if dangerous, adventure. As they eat their final meal before the perilous disembarkation, the men 'laugh and joke as though picknicking'. (The ironic potential of this image is wasted by Bean's cleansing of the ensuing bloodshed.) The invasion itself is registered by means of a plethora of exclamation marks of the 'bang-swish!' variety and by references to bayonets 'scintillating in the sunlight like a thousand mirrors'. Perry ('alas!') receives a nasty wound, and soon finds himself back at sea aboard the troopship, but he 'would not have missed it for all the money in the world'. One need only to refer to the matter-of-fact realism of A. B. Facey's remembrance of the fear, confusion, and shocking slaughter of that morning, published in *A Fortunate Life* (1981) some sixty-five years later, to appreciate the spuriousness of Perry/Bean's fiction.[42]

The Anzac Book does not ignore war horrors completely. Hector Dinning's 'Glimpses of Anzac' contains several illustrations of the randomness of the warfare that prevailed on Gallipoli, of soldiers 'struck down suddenly and unmercifully' while performing the most trivial of daily chores, of men dying with their pipes still steaming in their teeth.[43] Unlike Barbusse, however, Dinning does not employ these vignettes as points of an anti-war argument. His stance is essentially one of grim fatalism. He does not question the Gallipoli operation itself; he does not complain. Only one soldier in the book is shown to fear, and not forbear, the omnipresence of sudden violent death. Going by the apt sobriquet of 'Icy', this 'cold-foot' manages, however, to transcend his anxiety, and redeems himself in the performance of an outrageously reckless act of heroism of the kind Bean privately claimed to abhor. Alone and without orders, he attacks and eliminates a troublesome Turkish machine-gun post, a deed which earns him sixteen bullet wounds; more importantly, he gains the admiration of his formerly scornful mates as well. One or two contributions treat the effects of shell-fire in a way which is positively whimsical. In 'Beachy', a story about a favourably positioned Turkish battery so named because it continually peppered Anzac *plage*, a Digger loses the extremity of his arm in a shell-blast. He records this loss in a manner which is appropriately described as offhand:

> "Feel comfortable?" said the A.M.C. man.
> "Yes, except for the pain in my left hand," I answered.
> He looked down, and I followed his gaze.
> "You haven't got no left hand," he said quietly.
>
> I saw that he was right, and this new illusion struck me as being about the last straw. With a dazed sort of conviction I muttered: "Well, it's a rummy world"– and promptly lay back and drifted out of it for the time being.[44]

The comic nonchalance of the Australian soldier is one of his distinctive trademarks, and A.I.F. slang is one of the richest sources of modern military vernacular. The imagery of many of the First World War 'Diggerisms' is unforgettably macabre – for example 'Anzac soup', denoting shell-hole water polluted by the presence of a corpse, and 'throw a seven': to die. George Johnston felt that this sort of sardonicism as manifested in *The Anzac Book* was 'self-denigrating' and precluded 'heroics and histrionics': '. . . it was something that took the place both of boasting and of grizzling'.[45] Though it is doubtful that it is actually a 'self-denigrating' work (it is too preoccupied with the uniqueness of the Digger for that), *The Anzac Book* does appear to avoid, and often implicitly attacks, heroic posturing. Apart from the stories 'Icy' and 'The Landing', there are only three obvious instances of big-noting in the book. Of these, one is heavily ironical; another, the poem 'The Trojan War, 1915', is a grandiose comparison of modern Australian with classical heroism which was stolen from the *Bulletin* and was written by someone who was not in fact an Anzac – Bean must have been so impressed by its highfalutin sentiment that he nevertheless included it; and the third, the panegyric 'Anzacs', is the work of the English thriller-writer Edgar Wallace.

The ironic piece, 'How I Won the V.C.', by 'Crosscut, 16th Battalion A.I.F.', is a longish narrative poem in which an Anzac recalls his single-handed destruction of a fortified enemy position while armed only with tins of Fray Bentos, the much-reviled meat which was a staple of the troops' diet. In the face of terrible fire, he works his way up the slope towards the post, tosses cans of the notoriously salty meat into the Turkish trenches, and the next morning the occupants are found to have perished from thirst. The exploit, while illustrative of the capacity for improvisation which is part of the Anzac legend, is ludicrous, more a sarcastic comment on the food the men were forced to endure than a boast. Furthermore, the narrator's false modesty, his transparently insincere proclamations of embarrassment at being the one to relate such a glorious achievement, signifies a calculated snipe at the soldier's trait of telling tall stories. One stanza in particular reveals the contradictory impulses that seem typical of the Australian soldier, and which are often unconsciously manifested in his writings. 'Crosscut', fundamentally self-effacing about his great ability for effective individual action, is torn by the opposing desire to let the world know all about his skills, in terms loud and clear. He says to his comrades:

> "I don't want no red-tapey orders,
> And I don't want no kudos nor pelf;
> You get back to your own little dug-outs,
> And I'll tackle the knoll *by myself!*
> I'll lay down my life for my country,

> For old England, the land of the free;
> And you'll find that the bloke called
> Horatius
> Was only a trifle to me!"[46]

CIVILIANS JUMP ON THE BANDWAGON

The impact of *The Anzac Book*, following the galvanizing reportage of the war correspondents, contributed greatly to the elevated status of the Anzacs. By 1916 they had won an acclaim akin to the adulation received these days by the superstars of popular music and film. To extend the analogy, it could be said that while Ashmead-Bartlett, Bean and company 'discovered' the new popular hero, there were many astute civilian promoters back in Australia prepared to cash in on the new phenomenon. The heroic Australian was in vogue, and was duly exploited – just as, one cynically suspects, writers like Remarque noted the *Zeitgeist* and then plundered the European market for disillusionment and a vicarious wallowing in war violence a decade later.

C. J. Dennis's creation of the larrikin war hero in *The Moods of Ginger Mick* is the outstanding example of literary capitalization on the emotional climate created in wartime Australia by the events in distant Turkey. As K. S. Inglis has argued, the tremendous success of *The Sentimental Bloke* in 1915 derived in no small measure from Dennis's perception that 'many Australians shared his hazy romantic attraction to the larrikin type'.[47] *The Moods of Ginger Mick* was a topical reapplication of a winning formula, and predictably it, too, was a triumph, earning Dennis the title of 'the Anzac laureate' to add to his earlier 'laureate of the larrikin'. Published in one form as a pocket edition for the trenches, it was received enthusiastically by the troops, who in H. M. Green's words took it 'to their hearts and haversacks'.[48] This is perhaps the ultimate accolade for a war book, especially for one written by a civilian. 'A rorty boy, a naughty boy, wiv rude ixpressions thick', Ginger Mick had made only fleeting appearances in *The Sentimental Bloke* – most memorably as the best man at the wedding of Bill and Doreen, in which role he distinguishes himself by giving a drunken and highly *risqué* speech. The metamorphosis of this graceless rabbit-vendor from the back streets of inner Melbourne into a teetotalling patriot and nation-builder is truly one of the more remarkable literary events brought about by the war.

Initially, the rebellious and plebeian Mick is sceptical about going to war just 'so toffs kin dine/On pickled olives'. But Mick is a man, after all, and no real man (Dennis implies) can resist a good fight. Quasi-political principles and 'pride o' class' allegiances are soon cast aside when he hears 'The Call uv Stoush!', the ancient impulse that had also driven 'them brave an' noble 'ero blokes uv old': 'The Call uv Stoush! . . . It's older than the 'ills/Lovin' and fightin'—there's no more to tell/Concernin' men'. Dennis is not trying to pose as some sort of Freudian analyst of male behaviour, of course. Rather, he sees loving and fighting as the two paths down which the red-blooded man, redirecting his wayward energies, can travel towards the fulfilment of his potential. The Bloke, rejected by the army on account of his flat feet, opts for the former, and Doreen. Mick goes off to battle, with a determination 'to prove Australia, an' our boastin' uv the breed'.[49]

In the character of Ginger Mick, Dennis modifies the larrikin stereotype to some degree, refining a truculent ruffian into a model of earthy humanity. As a soldier, he becomes a likeable 'man's man' with a broad popular appeal. We are not surprised when (appropriately for a former rabbit-oh) he excels in the fighting on Gallipoli's rabbit-warren terrain, and we are sad when he is killed in action, a victim of C. J. Dennis's desire to reflect the lengthening casualty lists.[50] There is even a touch of a very different First World War culture hero, Rupert Brooke, about Dennis's presentation of Mick. Brooke thought the war offered the promise of personal and national regeneration after the corruptions of a 'sick' peace; memorably, he envisaged it as a chance for the youth of England 'To turn, as swimmers into cleanness leaping/Glad from a world grown old and cold and weary'. As the Bloke expresses it in a letter to his friend, Dennis saw the struggle as Australia's purgative coming-of-age, which would lay the foundation for future vigorous growth: 'So I am 'opin' we will fight to make our man'ood clean/When orl the stoushin's over, Mick, there's 'eaps o' work to do'.[51] Here is an indication of Dennis's equivocal attitude toward Mick. Ostensibly, he applauds his lawless and irrepressible larrikinism, and suggests that such a character is eminently suited to combat. Yet Dennis is also subtly critical of the larrikin disposition, seeing it as frivolous and irresponsible and needing to be tempered by the great testing experience of war. The implication of the letter just quoted is that after the war Mick, as the Bloke had already done, would reject his old urban affiliations and repair to the bush to begin the vital work of nation-building. (The hero of Dennis's 1918 set of verses, *Digger Smith*, is an invalided Anzac who decides to 'go bush' rather than return to his old Collingwood stamping ground.) Dennis's position is therefore a curiously conservative one for a celebrator of what might be called a 'radical' type. War, he intimates, maketh the man.

The wartime fashion in Australian fiction called for novels and stories which typified the Anzacs. It was an age of platitudes and mindless parochialism. Roy Bridges, the popular author of historical romances of bushranging and Tasmanian convict life, tried to transcend the humdrum in his collection of stories, *The Immortal Dawn* (1917). Whereas Dennis communicated his heroic message in a largely invented and exceedingly colourful Australian vernacular, Bridges wrote from the other extreme, in a rhetorical mode that pretends to be cultivated but often ends up as turgid. In his description of the Landing on 'the immortal dawn' of 25 April 1915, pseudo-Homeric imagery clothes the object of prosaic promotion:

> Out of the sea they came, while yet the pale image of the moon trembled upon the waters; out of the sea, when the shores were bloody purple with the dawn; out of the sea as a wave of living fire . . . Splendid hazard dared; splendid hazard lost; and the red libation of their blood drunk up by the sand.[52]

Most self-respecting Anzacs would surely have cringed with embarrassment at such gush. Bridges's application of essentially foreign symbolism to the Australian war myth is again apparent in 'The Fire-Swept Zone', the 'true' story of Neville Ussher, an Anzac killed the day after the Landing. Like Dennis, Bridges sees war as a forcing-house which brings the best out of its participants. But the hero of 'The Fire-Swept Zone' is as recognizably one of those glamorous English Public School heroes as Ginger Mick is proletarian-Australian. Ussher, indeed, is in most essentials an antipodean Rupert Brooke, a handsome young warrior who takes into battle outstanding intellectual, artistic and athletic capabilities. Bridges's pillaging of the Brooke mythology to portray his Gallipoli hero perhaps signifies that he grasped the opportunity to capitalize on the war legends of both Australia *and* Britain. That *The Immortal Dawn* was published first in England by the London-based firm Hodder and Stoughton – and in 1917 when the Brooke cult was by no means dead – indicates that Bridges might well have had an eye on both English and local markets.

Depicted in 'the sunshine of his youth', Ussher is a man 'as fine of mind as of body', with a 'brave high face' and 'serene eyes' looking into 'a future rich in material promise'. This description strongly calls to mind the romantic posed photographs taken of Brooke, in particular the bare-shouldered portrait which served as the frontispiece to the volume *1914 and Other Poems* (1915). Ussher, furthermore, is attributed 'a sense of beautiful things' and the potential to be 'the fashioner of beautiful things'.

Such a refinement of sensibility is rare in Australian Great War literary heroes, who usually excel only in the purely physical domain. Bridges enlists Ussher in the ranks of the legendary 'lost generation' of those years, the Brookes, Owens and Grenfells of martyred youth: 'He might have influenced the thought of his time. He was cut off from life too soon'.[53] Part of the Brooke legend, and the key to the ironic character of the 1914–18 experience as a whole, is the adolescent enthusiasm and ingenuousness with which he and his peers had donned the colours. Anticipating the adventures to come in the expedition to the Dardanelles, Brooke wrote of having 'never been quite so happy' in his life; he looked forward to looting St Sophia's mosaics and eating Turkish Delight, to the sight of Hero's Tower and the proverbial 'wine-dark sea'.[54] The same intensity of innocent excitement is communicated by Ussher in a letter he writes home from Lemnos before the short voyage to the Turkish coast, and his death. The pastoral peace and sensuous imagery of his word-picture of the island, with its air 'scented with wild flowers', its thistles and white clover, its 'silky-haired sheep with bells' and 'ancient picture-book' shepherds, its figs and houses of yellow stone, windmills and 'silky-voiced kiddies', form a dramatic and moving contrast with the Gallipoli hell-fire that follows.[55]

Bridges does adhere to the central tenet of Australian Great War literature – that the war hero is the apotheosis of Australian manhood. Ussher may be 'scholar and student and athlete', but (Bridges hastily adds) he is 'before all, a man'. Rupert Brooke, of course, had died somewhat unheroically, of blood poisoning, on an Aegean island remote from the scene of fighting. His fate is thus in itself a paradigm of aborted British war expectations. Ussher, by contrast, goes on to achieve his martial destiny, 'the end for which he had come into the world – for those who knew him to live as the memory of a joyous figure of youth-heroic!' He is killed leading a raid on a Turkish machine-gun, but his abruptly truncated life is not viewed as a tragedy. His potential 'to give expression to the beauty of the young land about him' becomes insignificant beside the revelation of his heroic death:

> He gave all for his country. He stands with the figures of the Anzacs who shall be the eternal inspiration of the Australian people. Too soon cut off? Bitter destiny? In the ultimate scheme of things, the higher inspirant![56]

Nevertheless, Bridges's dependence on a largely imported iconography of heroism suggests that his support of the notion of Australian superiority is limited. The opening story, 'The Sphinx', celebrates the gorgeous blood sacrifice of a superbly adventurous and capable Australian

generation whose 'red sweet wine of youth' had apparently been fortified by the strong southern sun.[57] Generally, though, *The Immortal
Dawn* effuses imperial rather than parochial sentiment, and gives freer
acknowledgement of English virtues, both martial and moral, than most
Australian war books. It is not for nothing that its title comes from a
poem by the great champion of the Empire, Sir Henry Newbolt. Neville
Ussher himself is said to have 'come of a long line, that had spent itself
in service of England; and the spirit that had inspired his race was enkin-
dled in him'. The 'hot youth' of Australia, says Bridges in 'The Sphinx',
has in it 'the blood of Drake and his men of Devon . . . [and] the intrepidity of Clive and the Indian conquerors'. Ginger Mick had answered
the primal 'Call uv Stoush'; Bridges's Anzacs respond instead to 'the
trumpet call, and the long roll of British drums across the seas'.[58]

To reinforce his point about the potency of Australia's identification
with Britain, Bridges also garbles the classic Great War statement
proclaiming Australian solidarity with the Empire, 'For England', by
J. D. Burns. James Drummond Burns had attended Scotch College in
Melbourne (Neville Ussher was a Trinity boy), and edited the *Scotch
Collegian*, in which publication his famous poem appeared before he
sailed to Gallipoli, where he was killed in September 1915. Burns and
'For England' form the subject of the opening story of Gladys Hain's
The Coo-ee Contingent, a typical wartime pot-boiler containing fictional
sketches of the A.I.F. in and out of battle, at Anzac and in France and
England. It was Burns, argues Captain H—, the narrator of *The Coo-ee
Contingent*, who expressed 'the motive' that drew 'as a magnet' young
Australians into the Old Country's battles:

> The bugles of England were blowing
>   Across the winter sea,
>   As they had called a thousand years,
>   Calling now to me.
>
> They woke me from dreaming,
>   At the dawning of the day,
>   The bugles of England—
>   And how could I stay?[59]

Hain offers a reprise of sorts to this declaration of loyalty in 'The Old
School', the closing story of the collection. The story concerns a brilliant lawyer, Peter Brigden, whose 'historic mania' involves a passion
for his family's genealogy and, conversely, 'an overwhelming ambition
to become a big man and give his children a name to live up to'.[60] He
opts for martial action over the claims of his developing legal career,

and so earns his young son 'a richer heritage of honour and name'. The last man to leave Anzac at the time of the evacuation, Brigden is the first over the parapet at Armentières, where he is fatally wounded. His death is recorded in – it must be said – almost laughably mawkish terms:

> Half his abdomen was torn away – but he stood, staggered and raised his arm. "Advance, Australia, for you can. I'm done, boys, but go on."[61]

What this story illustrates, however, is not so much the 'advancement' of Australia, but a national clinging to the skirts of the Motherland. The action leaps from the Flanders battlefield back to the hallowed halls of the Old School, where we see Brigden's son remarking to the Headmaster, 'Mother says Daddy died for England'. The Head replies with a famous line from Kipling, slightly misquoted: 'Yes . . . and "who dies if England live"?'[62] This kind of glib fiction is as lacking in subtlety as a wartime propaganda poster. Furthermore, it is fundamentally schizophrenic, trying hard to promote identifiably Australian qualities, but ending up as slavishly colonial. Throughout the book, Hain indulges in several boasts about Australian egalitarianism in comparison with pompous British formality and class-consciousness, but makes her Anzac heroes socially 'respectable' by virtue of their strong sense of duty and implied upper or middle-class origins. The working-class soldier is ignored. While it is true that social status was not necessarily consistent with military rank in the A.I.F. (a fact made much of by Bean in his *Official History*), Hain makes it seem as if most Australian privates were either wealthy graziers or professional men. And Captain H – himself is an insufferable snob, for all his professed pride in Australian classlessness. As with Roy Bridges, Hain's divided loyalties detract from the coherence of her fictional vision. We as readers are unsure whether she is promoting an 'indigenous' warrior or a picturesque colonial version of the English paladin.

The war novels by those two enormously successful writers of juvenile fiction, Ethel Turner and Mary Grant Bruce, also amplify the Anzac myth. As Brenda Niall rightly suggests in her study of the two authors, their 'composite portrait' of the Digger corresponds closely with the proudly independent figure later idealized by Bean.[63] For instance John Calthrop, the hero of Ethel Turner's 'Cub' trilogy – *The Cub* (1915) *Captain Cub* (1917) and *Brigid and The Cub* (1919) – is a well-heeled younger son from a New South Wales station who decides to enlist as a private, and then fights in close company with a former worker in a Sydney bottle factory. 'Plain fighting's all I want', he asserts.[64] In his pre-war condition the Cub does not resemble the physical stereotype of the Australian soldier. An indolent, rather weedy figure with more interest in social reform than sports, he is at first rejected as unfit for service. The war transforms him, turning him into a dashing young man guaranteed to appeal to the teenage girls who formed the bulk of Turner's readership:

> He was six-foot-two at least . . . He had lost his stoop; he was burnt to a brick-red colour; there was a long scar seaming his left cheek . . . there was a glow in his eyes, a new look of purpose about his mouth. He had turned from a dreaming stripling into a man, and more than that, a strong man.[65]

So far, so conventional. But there is also a refreshing and relatively sophisticated critical perspective in 'The Cub' books that is missing in many Australian works of Great War fiction whose audience was adult. Ethel Turner makes some attempt to see beyond the successes of the battlefield to the psychological effects of too much 'plain fighting'. In mid-1918 Calthorp suffers a nervous collapse as a result of a year's intensive service and is removed to England to convalesce. The overuse of the A.I.F. as a shock force by the British military authorities was a source of some controversy in the latter months of the war, and no doubt Turner was fuelling those flames; but it was very rare in wartime literature for the Digger to be portrayed as anything other than a man with nerves of steel. Brenda Niall points out an even more daring instance of Turner's departure from the norm, that of her questioning of the boasted democratic nature and composition of the A.I.F. While the Cub progresses rapidly through the ranks, becoming on Gallipoli (where he had fought at Lone Pine) the youngest captain from New South Wales, his equally gallant mate from the Sydney bottle factory is promoted no further than the rank of lieutenant. The reason given for this anomaly is his coarse manner of speech – a preclusion associated rather more with the British Army than the A.I.F.[66]

If the Cub grows into his adopted martial role, the hero of Mary Grant Bruce's *Captain Jim* (1919) was born for it. Jim Linton, from the wealthy squatting family of Mrs Bruce's fictional 'Billabong' station, is a chip off the old British heroic block. Like Neville Ussher, he is Australian proof of Wyndham Lewis's contention that the English Public School system, with its strong sporting emphasis, in effect trained young men for war.[67] A glittering career on the playing fields of Melbourne Grammar leaves him superbly equipped for the winning of military honours. In his poem 'Vitaï Lampada' (in which harried English soldiers are rallied by the remembered cry of a schoolboy cricket captain: 'Play up! play up! and play the game!'), Sir Henry Newbolt made what Paul Fussell calls the 'classic equation' between war and sport.[68] Mary Grant Bruce, with the Newboltian ethos in mind, makes the same analogy many times in her depiction of Linton's soldiering career. 'Captain Jim' and his second-in-command, his old school chum Wally,

> learned their men by heart, knowing each one's nickname and something of his private affairs; losing no opportunity of talking to them and gaining their confidence, and sizing them up, as they talked, just as in the old days, as captains of the team, they had learned to size up boys at football.[69]

The military *noblesse oblige* that is at work here is perhaps to be expected, since the men of Linton's 'team' are not unruly Diggers, but servile Tommies. Despite his personal desire to join the A.I.F., Linton had been commissioned into a British regiment at the instigation of his family. Linton senior had felt that his son might miss his chance for involvement in great actions if he enlisted with a force thought unlikely to be sent to the Front. This was a monumentally inaccurate forecast. At about the same time as Jim and Wally are gassed in France, their compatriots on Gallipoli are making 'the name of Anzac ring through the world'. Nevertheless, their presence in the British Army provides Mary Grant Bruce with the scope to make flattering, if commonplace, comparisons of the Australian soldier with his British counterpart. In appearance, the two young men are straight off the Digger assembly line. Both are tall, 'lean and clean-shaven, tanned to a deep bronze, and stamped with a look of resolute keenness'. They also possess the ability to see great distances and an acute sense of hearing which, developed from their background in the Australian bush, seem 'uncanny' to their merely mortal British comrades. Mrs Bruce goes further, directly relating bush origins and education to soldierly prowess. Jim in particular utilizes his uniquely Australian attributes as a leader of raiding parties: '. . . there was seldom rest for the weary Boche in the trenches opposite [his] section. Some of his raids were authorized: others were not'.[70] Here is Bean's ideal in action. Yet Bruce never properly assimilates Linton's Australianness with her reverence for what is really a British tradition of patrician service. Her hero is a hybrid creation, both thoroughbred and bush brumby. 'It may be Mary Grant Bruce's unique contribution to our literature', writes Ms Niall, 'to have combined in Jim Linton a version of the *Boy's Own Paper* hero with the archetypal Australian squatter'.[71]

A similar uncertainty in the characterization of the Australian war hero can be found in John Butler Cooper's *Coo-oo-ee! A Tale of Bushmen from Australia to Anzac* (1916), a novel published, like *The Immortal Dawn*, in England by Hodder and Stoughton. The story of young Australians who travel from a Victorian bush town (with the Patersonian

name of 'Ironbark') to predictable heroism on Gallipoli constitutes only
a part of the action of this romance. The narrative interweaves the war
with the murder of a despised German settler, the scandal surrounding his pregnant daughter, the inquiry into his death and the consequent
controversy in the small town. War, murder, racial propaganda, mys-
tery, illicit sex, and even a love affair or two thrown in for good measure –
there is something here to appeal to most popular tastes. It must have
been a potent brew to concoct for Cooper, who was predominantly a
writer of municipal histories, such as *The History of Prahran* (1912).
Clearly, it took the overheated atmosphere generated by the war to fire
his otherwise rather limited imagination.

Like Mary Grant Bruce, Cooper applauds the traits and abilities of
the Diggers over those of the Englishmen. He also draws heavily on
the city/country opposition established well before the war in a work
like Paterson's 'Clancy of the Overflow', and so extends his discrimina-
tion to include urban Australians. Stripping for the army medical at
the recruiting centre, 'factory operatives' (obviously from Paterson's
'dusty, dirty city') appal the men from Ironbark with their 'ill-nourished
bodies', 'narrow chests' and general 'weedy' appearance. The bushmen,
on the other hand, 'stripped well', appearing to be 'as hard as nails'.
Cooper also directly links the buoyant Australian spirit to the bush's
effect on the human personality: 'The ozone enveloping the gums in
the forests fills a man's being with the verve and spring of life. In the
presence of the physical glow . . . a sense of depression soon disap-
pears . . .'. The bush thus acts elementally and environmentally as a
positive force for good. Cooper illustrates this further by remarking on
the way in which the inhabitants of the bush look upwards at the trees
and so 'see heaven' (a variation of 'the vision splendid'), while the eyes
of urban dwellers are 'glued to the paving stones' of sunless city streets.[72]

But having defined the Bush and the City as two separates spheres,
as earthly correlatives of heaven and hell if you like, Cooper then confuses the issue by making his hero, the young farmer Jack Danvers, the
most spurious sort of imperialistic ideologue. 'Hard and wiry', Danvers
is labelled 'a typical Australian'. Cooper, however, seems to think that
this is insufficient for a hero of a romantic war novel. His supposedly
quintessential bushman is lumbered with a Public School background
(Melbourne Grammar), the 'best traditions' of which had shaped his
adult character. 'In his school's ample grounds he had learnt to "play
the game" ', Cooper writes. So when 'the cry of the Motherland' stirs
'the bovine-like contentment of bush life', Danvers responds in a fashion
that is natural for a protégé of Newbolt. The war, we are told, 'promised

to be better fun than even a football final'; at Gallipoli, Danvers turns in a best-on-the-battleground performance. After all, as the novel's epigraph – the same Kipling 'Who lives if England dies?' quotation used by Hain – makes clear, the imperial stakes were high. Honourable and upright, courteous and a touch prim, Jack Danvers is about as convincing in his heroic role as Clancy of the Overflow would be if he went 'a drov-ing' down The Mall. Indicative of his atypicality as an Australian war-rior is that he is a staunch advocate of military discipline. Aboard the troopship *en route* to the Middle East, he notes approvingly how the Diggers 'lost their own identities' in 'the greater personality of the brigade'. This pleasure in subsumed individuality, in losing oneself in the Regiment, is inimical to the Australian military ethos, being more akin to the Regular Army mentality celebrated in Hay's *The First Hundred Thousand* than the perversely civilian individualism of *The Anzac Book*. It certainly sits most uneasily with the volatile tempera-ment of a proudly 'mongrel' race sanctioned by Danvers in conversa-tion with an Englishman at another point in the novel.[73]

For a more assured wartime fictionalization of the Australian soldier, one must turn to A. G. Hales's McGlusky books and Steele Rudd's *Memoirs of Corporal Keeley* (1918). Admittedly, the artistic achievement of these novels is slight. But at least they do not suffer from the cultural cringe that ultimately cripples the fictions of Bridges, Hain and Cooper. The enormous popularity of Hales's twenty novels following the world-wide wanderings of the dynamic Scotch-Australian McGlusky was due chiefly to the broad appeal of their charismatic central character.[74] In his day a miner, a shearer, a drover and a sportsman, McGlusky's prac-tical and 'manly' skills and experience mark him out as something of a paragon of Australian talents. Conversely, his altruistic and idealistic nature lend him a magnetism which transcends national boundaries. His adventures, his energies and his enthusiasms are almost mythical in dimension; he is both Ulysses and Dionysius. For all that – and despite his speech, which is a quaint amalgam of Scottish brogue and Australian vernacular – his genuineness as an Australian frontiersman is beyond doubt. In looks, he combines the tensile toughness of the bushman with the inherited visage of a ferocious Scottish chieftain:

> . . . his shirt sleeves were rolled carelessly nearly to his shoulder, display-ing a pair of gnarled, hairy arms, so muscular, sun-tanned and rough, that they looked like twisted rope . . . From his heels to his head he measured well over six feet, and so lean was he that his ribs could be counted through the cotton of his shirt . . .

It was a mighty face, rough, scarred and weatherbeaten. The forehead was immense, the brows craggy and tufted with hair that was grey at the tips. Blue-grey eyes, hard as bayonet points . . .[75]

McGlusky's Great Adventure (1917) begins in New Zealand, where Hales's hero is spending time as a trader. Though well over military age, he tries to join the Maori contingent, but is turned away. He journeys to England, but on two occasions he is rejected for service. Somehow he manages to worm his way into the A.I.F., and winds up on Gallipoli. He sets himself up as a sniper, where his bushman's accomplishments come into full play: '. . . not for nothing had he practised sharp-shooting wild dogs . . . in the Australian wilds when he was a scalphunter'. McGlusky's heroism apart, Hales embellishes his narrative with many metaphorical references to the 'tiger' or 'lion-like' characteristics of the Diggers. At various points, furthermore, they are dubbed 'a breed unto themselves', 'demi-gods', 'heroic invaders', as men on a 'quest for fame', and as 'athletes to a man' (the spectre of Ashmead-Bartlett once again).[76] *Ginger and McGlusky* (1917) takes McGlusky and the Anzacs to France, and more deeds of derring-do. One picture of battle in particular, that of a bayonet charge of 'frenzied . . . stabbing, hacking' Australians at Bapaume, rivals William Baylebridge at his most sanguinary.[77]

Crudely comical and anecdotal, *Memoirs of Corporal Keeley* is a typical Steele Rudd work. The novel's humour derives mainly from the guileless innocence of the narrator, Frankie Keeley, a timid, self-effacing young shearer who is as unsuited to the battlefield as McGlusky is at home on it. Keeley hardly touches on his time at Gallipoli – indeed, his 'memoirs' barely constitute a war novel at all, with only about six of its one hundred and twenty-odd pages dealing with his actual service. All he is willing to say about Gallipoli is that he was in a state of 'constant an' indescribable dread' while he was there.[78] Keeley claims to have eventually subdued his fear, however, and in France he goes into battle with the fatalism that befits a real warrior. This is Australian perseverance at its finest, and reminds us of the grit shown by the pioneering heroes and heroines of Rudd's most famous work, *On Our Selection* (1899), in taming the Australian bush. There is something to be said for the understated brand of heroism celebrated by Rudd. Just as the new nation was not 'made' by cutting one gigantic swathe through the virgin countryside, but by years of unglamorous toil, so the dogged, if undistinguished, striving of ordinary soldiers like Keeley is ultimately as worthy as that of the bayonet-wielding demigods randomly promoted in all modes of Australian war literature.

TALES OF HEROES AND HOOLIGANS: THE SOLDIERS' STORIES

The civilian war writers cannot claim any private compulsions to excuse their worst excesses besides patriotism and opportunism. By contrast, the aggression of the wartime soldier-writers is understandable. They resented being called 'six-bob-a-day tourists' (or, worse, murderers) by non-combatant cynics, and some of them were bitter at having to bear the burden of the national war effort. More crucially, they were justifiably proud of their performance in battle. As a genre, the wartime narratives of the A.I.F. lack the wry critical awareness and sense of proportion that characterizes *The Anzac Book*. Giving every indication of having believed their own publicity, the soldier-writers often seem unaware of any gulf between the ideal (the glorious swashbuckler) and the reality (that of the hard-pressed military journeyman). They were caught in the same propagandistic treadmill as civilian publicists like Roy Bridges.

In considering the wartime stories of the Australian soldiers, it is instructive to refer first to a contribution to *The Anzac Book*, a piece bluntly titled 'Anzac Types', in which two stereotypical Australian personalities are profiled.[79] The first, the bushman warrior, is represented by 'Wallaby Joe'. A Light Horseman who had ridden 'nearly a thousand miles over sun-scorched, drought-stricken plains' to enlist, Wallaby Joe's appearance suggests 'the typical bushman'. He is 'tall and lean, but as strong as a piece of hickory'. Moreover, he is as capable as the typical bushman: 'A horseman from head to toe, and a dead shot'. And, to complete the picture, he behaves as a bushman should, being 'laconic in the extreme'; his beer-drinking capacity is prodigious, and he is 'very shy in the presence of the softer sex'. The resourcefulness and initiative he attained in the struggle for survival in the bush serve him well in his military career. The 'typical bushman' thus becomes an 'ideal soldier'. Anzac Type Number Two, 'The Dag', is a soldier called Henessy, 'a dag if ever there was one'. Henessy, who lacks the munificent virtues derived from a lifetime's contact with Nature, thrives through a baser form of human cunning and ingenuity. By definition, the dag is an eccentric (usually urban) humorist, an irrepressible bane and baiter of authority, a bender of rules, a scrounger and a confidence-man. He is a 'character', a 'hard case'. Certainly, under his brash, vulgar exterior lurks a heart of gold, but the Henessys of the A.I.F. were hardly models of military excellence.

It was the heroic bushman rather than the inglorious dag—the

McGluskys rather than the Ginger Micks – who claimed most of the attention of the Australian soldier-writers during the war. Chief promoter of the rural superman was Oliver Hogue. Hogue, who fought in the usual military repository for up-country Australians, the Light Horse, was himself no bushman. University-educated, and a son of a prominent New South Wales politician, he worked before the war as a journalist for the *Sydney Morning Herald*, where one of his friends and colleagues was Charles Bean. During the war he published several articles under the by-line 'Trooper Bluegum', which were to form much of the material for his three books. At the same time he managed to rise through the military ranks, becoming a Major before dying of illness in 1919. Bean records that on Gallipoli Hogue acted as Colonel Ryrie's 'enthusiastic and devoted' orderly.[80] This enthusiasm and devotion he transferred, in huge quantities, to the literary service of the men of the Australian Light Horse. He was by no means alone in his adoration: the A.L.H. was generally considered to be the élite arm of the national forces. By virtue of their rural background, the horsemen were viewed as the biggest and the best Australians, and consequently even more effective than the infantrymen as fighters. The volume of the *Official History* which deals exclusively with the Light Horse campaigns, Sir Henry Gullett's *Sinai and Palestine* (1923), eclipses Bean's volumes on Gallipoli and France in sheer promotive intent, even allowing for the latter's blinkered concentration on the bush ethos operating within the A.I.F. as a whole. According to Gullett, the Light Horsemen represented 'the very flower of their race'; they were 'a remarkable band of brothers in arms, a capable band drawn from a wide and fragrant countryside, animated by a noble cause'. Despite their relaxed bearing, they were distinguished by 'great physical strength', 'superb athleticism' and a 'love of physical exercise' even more ardent than that of the ancient Greeks.[81]

Such effusive praise reflects the vanity of the Light Horse itself. In *Love Letters of an Anzac* (1916), Oliver Hogue's cavalryman-hero remarks without irony that its members considered themselves 'a cut above the infantry', lending 'tone to what would otherwise be a mere vulgar brawl'.[82] *The Kia Ora Coo-ee*, the magazine of the Light Horse, provides a revealing mirror of this self-esteem. Unlike its sister publication *Aussie*, produced contemporaneously by the infantry in France, *The Kia Ora Coo-ee* cannot resist the temptation to pander to the collective ego of its readership. Whereas *Aussie* was content to serve as 'a laughter-bearer from Digger to Digger', *The Kia Ora Coo-ee* combines humour with strident self-publicity. It evinces all the signs of being the journal of a dominant army, exuding the arrogant self-assurance that T. E. Lawrence observed in the victorious Australians at Damascus at the end of the Light Horse campaign.[83] Harking back to the Anzacs (many of whom were Light Horsemen), the editorial on the front page of the second issue seeks in vain for a historical parallel to their 'tragic heroism'. The legions of Alexander, of Hannibal, of Caesar and of Cromwell all fade into obscurity alongside their courage. The editorial goes on to make a statement about the ennobling, almost sanctifying nature of death on the battlefield which is especially startling for being uttered in the war-weary days of 1918. Describing the 'soul' of the Australian soldier, it states:

> Deep down in their hearts is a conviction somewhat akin to that of the fanatic, who believes that death on the battlefield is everlasting life. They will go out in a blaze of glory . . . Death comes to all of us some day. When it comes on the battlefield, it exalts the humblest to the Valhalla of the Happy Warrior . . . Theirs is the pinnacle of martial glory.[84]

For a close approximation to this grandiose expression of heroic sentiment, it is perhaps necessary to go back as far as the *Iliad*, and Sarpedon's famous rationalization of the warrior's fatalistic philosophy.[85] Elsewhere in the journal, allusions to the unique appearance of the bushman soldier and boasts about his prowess indicate a determination to compensate for what was felt to be a neglect of the Light Horse's achievements. The Light Horse, like any vainglorious creature, perpetually felt ignored. The footslogging infantry in the bloody but 'picturesque' battlefields of Flanders and France seemed to occupy the pressmen's attention. Oliver Hogue, as 'Trooper Bluegum', was a frequent contributor to *The Kia Ora Coo-ee*. In the poem 'Lucky Tim' he ironizes popular misconceptions about the ease of the Middle East fighting:

> When Abdul came with a mighty charge,
> And Romani was fought and won,
> Tim stopped some shrapnel good and large,
> For a while his work was done.
> They packed him off with his blood-soaked gear
> In a ricketty ambulance;
> But the driver laughed, as the shells dropped near:
> "We're lucky we're not in France."[86]

Hogue's prose writings are concerted attempts to redress this perceived bias against the Light Horsemen. His novel *The Cameliers* (parts of which first appeared in *The Kia Ora Coo-ee*), for example, is blatantly didactic. Ostensibly concerned with following a spasmodic love affair between a wounded Light Horseman and the Australian nurse who tends him in a Cairo hospital, the narrative is fleshed out with virtually direct reportage of the deeds of the Imperial Camel Corps, a largely Australian component of Chauvel's all-conquering Desert Mounted Corps. Hogue does make a feeble attempt to merge the divergent strands of his 'plot'. Soon after the nurse, Flora, sends off a letter to her father confessing that she has become 'a bit fond of a young sun-tanned Camelier', the scene shifts to the family home in New South Wales. Her father, having just read her note, chances by a 'curious coincidence' to pick up a copy of the *Sydney Morning Herald* which contains an account of the exploits of the Australian airmen ('Knight-errants of the clouds') in the Middle East. There are no prizes for guessing who penned the article. Hogue the 'novelist' and Hogue the journalist thus combine to form the essential Hogue: a one-man propaganda machine. He is so concerned with the Light Horse's image that he had earlier provided a promotional context for the article by making Flora remark that eighty per cent of the airmen were former Light Horsemen. The credibility of *The Cameliers* as a work of fiction suffers further when Hogue again interrupts the narrative to complain about the Australian Government's 'oversight' in not ensuring adequate press coverage of the Sinai campaign, so as to inform parents 'how heroically their sons had fought and died'.[87]

Paul Fussell has discussed the impossibility of adequately defining many war books which are based on the author's personal experiences. Are they memoirs, or are they really first-person novels? As he says, 'It is finally up to the bookseller alone to determine whether he will position such a book on the table marked Fiction or on that marked Autobiography'.[88] Oliver Hogue's books would provide even the most discerning of booksellers with a problem. *The Cameliers* is usually consigned to the shelves containing novels, yet in reality it is non-fiction of the most artless kind. An epistolary novel which deals with actual public events, *Love Letters of an Anzac*, by contrast, is sometimes categorized as a factual narrative. *Trooper Bluegum at the Dardanelles: Descriptive Narratives of the More Desperate Engagements on the Gallipoli Peninsula* (1916) is even harder to define. This book is composed substantially of Hogue's despatches to the *Sydney Morning Herald*, observations set down, in the finest war correspondent's tradition, 'in dugouts between intervals in the fighting, often with shells screaming overhead, shrapnel bursting, and bullets flying . . .'.[89] As such, it is a journalistic pot-pourri in the manner of Bean's *Letters from France*. Yet *Trooper Bluegum at the Dardanelles* is hardly objective journalism: essentially, it is a typically hybrid piece of wartime ephemera which pays little attention to the presentation of bland historical truth. We follow Bluegum and his fellow 'aspirants for fame and glory'—'sun-tanned bushmen', of course, 'lean and wiry, with muscles rippling'–through the early days of training in Australia and Egypt to the Big Day, the martial Grand Final on that transplanted Melbourne Cricket Ground by the Aegean. Pitted against what Hogue calls the powers of 'Light and Freedom and Civilization' are the Turkish dupes of the dastardly German 'forces of the Devil'. Hogue, in the hysterical manner of a sports commentator, relates that in a ferocious manifestation of heroic virtue the Anzacs 'scaled the steel-lined heights like demons', flailing their bayonets with murderous ingenuity: 'One huge farmer actually bayonetted a Turk through the chest and pitchforked him over his shoulder'.[90] It probably goes without saying that Hogue/Bluegum was not even present at the Landing he describes with so much relish.

The book is littered with shamelessly chauvinistic boasts and with *passé* epical phrases. Early in the book we hear of 'virile young Australians stripped for the fray'; later, of the Anzacs 'making new history' and doing 'big things'. We hear of them being described as 'the best fighters in the world', and we see them fighting 'like Trojans' and 'trusting to the cold steel'.[91] Hogue's attitude to war is simply incongruous. He mealy-mouths some references to the 'wastage of war' and calls it 'a gruesome business'; then in the same breath describes his first week on the peninsula as 'the most wonderful week of my life – full of excitement and hair-breadth escapes'. Like Rupert Brooke, who can be excused because he saw so little of it, Hogue depicts war as great fun. He utters the phrase 'all the fun of the fighting' with a lack of irony which is almost shocking. Even dodging shrapnel is regarded as a *divertissement*. He carries his boyish ardour for battle further than Newbolt. Repeating the term 'playing the game' *ad nauseam*, he draws analogies between war and cricket that are of a refined, almost technical nature. For instance, the men's habit of catching the long-fused Turkish bombs before they explode is called 'slips practice'. With bombs, says Hogue, 'our cricketers excelled', while in 'the wild bayonet charges our footballers were simply irresistible'. The 'sport' of hunting is not forgotten either. Snipers are shown to be on the lookout for what is called 'big game'; one is heard to boast about having bagged 'three Turkeys'. However, the most memorable analogy drawn by Hogue in *Trooper Bluegum at the Dardanelles* is not between war and sport, but war and literature. It is perhaps the finest example of unconscious wit from a writer who is one of its past masters: 'your true sniper, like your true poet, is born, not made'.[92]

Love Letters of an Anzac reproduces most of the themes of *Trooper Bluegum* within the framework of a Light Horseman's excruciatingly sentimental love letters to his sweetheart back in Australia. The correspondent, 'Jim Bluegum', is her 'Soldier Boy' and she is his 'Honey-bunch', his 'Heart of my Heart' and his 'Bonnie Wee Lassie'. Saccha-rine romantic asides ('I can feel your lips on mine now') sweeten Bluegum's rudimentary account of his adventures leading up to and on Gallipoli. Training is 'joy – all joy'; there are references to Byron and to Troy; the Australian love of the bayonet is illustrated ('we who watched were spellbound'); and the Digger's superiority over the Tommy is asserted. Jim Bluegum is an egocentric lover. He postures before 'Honey-bunch', he blusters, he self-advertises. 'I want you to feel and know that when the Empire called, *your* MAN answered', he says in an early let-ter.[93] But let us not be too hard on him: under the threat of being thought effeminate, the pressure on men to do their masculine duty was immense, and often emanated from the women themselves. The coercive methods of women's recruiting groups ranged from the sending of white feathers to those considered fit for battle, to poems which none-too-subtly challenged the masculinity of the 'shirker'. A poem entitled 'The Test' asks of the man who is 'fearful of the bayonet's stabbing bite' . . .

> Will she who is worth the winning,
> She who is yet to be won,
> Take to her marble bosom, one who has turned
> from a gun?[94]

But Bluegum really does respond to the challenge rather extravagantly. When he is evacuated from Gallipoli because of illness, he does so with misgivings, and not only because he is leaving behind his mates, dead and alive. He feels nostalgic at least in part because on Gallipoli he had 'first experienced the lust to kill and the fierce delight of battle'. In a final letter to 'Honeybunch' (who plans to travel from Australia to Lon-don to be with him during his convalescence) he proposes marriage and a rushed honeymoon before he gets back into 'the Big Game' to 'prac-tise anew the gentle art of slaughtering Turks'. When it is all said and done, he adds in a postscript, 'it's the girl behind the man behind the gun that counts'.[95] These are strange and old-fashioned sentiments in-deed! In 1916, however, they may well have appealed to a wide audience, particularly to those women who had husbands, lovers or sons risking their lives overseas.

Very few wartime narratives by Australian soldiers managed to add to the proliferating bushman-warrior legend and at the same time give a balanced account of the fighting. One such work is Sydney de Loghe's *The Straits Impregnable* (1917), a perceptive and stylistically satisfying treatment of one man's war, from the Gippsland wilderness to the Gallipoli hills and gullies. But as the 'Trooper Bluegum' books prove, if the thematic emphasis on the bush character of the Australian forces is strong, then usually the bravado and the jingoism are correspondingly vehement. This is true also of works written by men who were themselves not Light Horsemen, or even especially bush-oriented. R. Hugh Knyvett, for example, was a scout attached to Intelligence – hardly a swashbuckling role, if still a dangerous one. Yet '*Over There' with the Australians*, with its glowing references to the homicidal feats of 'champion wood-choppers' and the like, is among the most exuberant celebrations of the bushman-warrior. Like Hogue, Knyvett would like us to believe that all the men who took up the ultimate challenge to their manhood came from up-country. In *The Cameliers* Hogue describes the great Australian mass migrations of September 1914, when men left 'every' farm, homestead, sheep and cattle station for 'the metropolis' at the beginning of what was to be 'a walking tour to Berlin'.[96] Similarly, Knyvett devotes an entire chapter to the gathering 'human snowballs' of young Australian 'red-bloods' descending on the cities from the inland. When he writes of 'khaki-clad, laughing demons, seeking Turks to kill', one can be assured that he is referring to the rural red-bloods.[97]

Racism of the most grotesque kind is a concomitant of the ideal. At the very bottom of the human register are the Egyptians, encountered on the first stage of the Anzac odyssey. To Knyvett, the 'Gyppo' is an 'animated lump of muck'. Hogue is only fractionally more circumspect, describing Arabs as 'the lowest and most degraded creatures on the scale of civilization. Talk about the Australian aboriginal . . .'.[98] The Turks on Gallipoli are given credit for their bravery and their chivalrous spirit, with most of the bile being reserved for the hated Germans, especially in Knyvett, who fought them in France. Knyvett's tone is always overheated; but whenever he touches on the Hun 'monster', it boils over into outright racist propaganda:

> A woman showed me on an estaminet floor the blood stains of her own baby, butchered before her eyes. These were French women, not ours. But what if it had been? Your sister! Your mother! Your wife![99]

The depth of hatred felt for the Germans is also illustrated by W. J. Denny's *The Diggers* (1919), the memoir of a Light Horseman who transferred to the Artillery and served in Europe. Denny is generally far less belligerent than Knyvett, yet is moved to describe the German as not merely a baby-killer, but 'a blood-lust beast who violates nuns and bayonets guiltless priests' as well.[1] Racism, of course, is intrinsic to warfare; but in some Australian soldier-narratives it is not limited to an antipathy for the enemy. In his *A Handful of Ausseys* (1919) C. Hampton Thorp contrives outrageously artificial dialogues which allow for a full recital of the heroic catechism – but at the expense of the major ally. A baronet's wife at a reception in England asks a wheat-farming Digger: 'Why is it that your men are so different from English Tommies . . . they seem ever so much more alert, bigger in their ideas, able to think for themselves, and their physique is so much better?' The soldier's answer is predictable and long-winded. In short, he argues that the new nation's democratic temper, its freedom from the oppressive constraints of hidebound customs and traditions, its pioneer heritage and the self-dependence learned in the taming of a wild environment, all contributed to the happy state of Australian superiority and to the sublime self-confidence of the A.I.F. The fighting in France may be awful, but 'hadn't [the] boys – many of them – faced appalling odds in their own country?'[2]

Thorp even dares to make an Englishwoman, in answer to an inquiry regarding the large numbers of local girls marrying the Australian visitors, assert the matchless skills of the Digger as a lover. In a passage peppered with *double entendres* which are surely unintended, she catalogues the Australian's 'direct, searching gaze', his 'quick grasp of things and ability to understand any situation', and the 'open', 'natural' and 'very up-to-date' manner of his love-making, especially in comparison with the more careful Englishman, who is 'too stiff and formal'.[3] It is not surprising that a force so enamoured of its murderous abilities on the battlefield should see itself collectively as a lady-killer in the bedroom. Most early Australian war books, however, are decidedly coy about women and sexuality, 'shy', like Wallaby Joe of *The Anzac Book*. One is reminded of one of the London scenes in Hain's *The Coo-ee Contingent*, in which brave Anzacs on leave flee the advances of importunate 'flappers' so as to avoid being 'eaten' by them.[4] And even the flames of Bluegum's burning passion in *Love Letters of an Anzac* are, at best, flickering. *A Handful of Ausseys* provides perhaps the first glimpse of the womanizing demigods glorified by William Baylebridge in *An Anzac Muster*, though it was not until the explicit and self-consciously 'sexy' popular fiction of the Second World War that the Australian warrior-lover was given free rein.

Unlike their brothers-in-arms in other forces, the Diggers were in no doubt as to their genuine heroic status. Whereas Barbusse's *poilus* in *Under Fire* wonder whether they will be remembered as 'heroes' or as 'hooligans', and see themselves as 'murderers' rather than as 'idols',[5] wartime Australian soldier-writers strove assiduously to keep the A.I.F. escutcheon blemish-free. The inhibiting thought that war was a form of

legalized murder – such a prominent theme in European battle literature of 1914–1918 – seems never to enter their head. Indeed, the Australians had a reputation for a willingness to kill which, as Bill Gammage
asserts, had a foundation in fact.[6] The undeniable hooliganism of an
element within the force was, however, difficult to ignore. In *Le Feu*,
the French original of Barbusse's novel, the word translated as 'hooligans' is *'apaches'*, after the Parisian ruffians. The closest approximation
in the Australian idiom is probably 'larrikin'. The éclat earned by the
A.I.F. for its savage effectiveness in battle had a grubby correlative –
that of its infamous wildness, its unfettered larrikinism, out of the line.
This less attractive side of the legend was played down by most
soldier-writers.

From almost the moment of the vanguard's disembarkation in Egypt,
the rampant indiscipline for which the Australians soon became notorious revealed itself. Suzanne Brugger's *Australians and Egypt 1914–1919*
unearths a plethora of misdemeanours, from the minor and essentially
comical (such as the teaching of unwitting Arab news-boys obscene cries)
to various brutalities, including rape, committed on the despised local
population. Drunkenness and degeneracy were common; venereal disease scarcely less so.[7] The problem became so quickly evident that in
December 1914 the authorities requested that C. E. W. Bean, as the official correspondent, write an open letter to the Australian press giving
public notice of the force's misbehaviour and warning the nation of the
imminent return home of the incorrigibles. Significantly, Bean chose
to exclude the Light Horseman from the opprobrium, blaming chiefly
'a certain class of waster' that had found its way into the infantry. (The
truth of the matter is that as many Light Horsemen as infantrymen were
sent home for misdemeanours in the Middle East.) The letter caused
a sensation. It earned Bean much resentment among the troops, the accusation of 'wowseristic whining', and a distrust which dissipated only
when they observed his courage on Gallipoli.[8] The letter, more intensive training and tighter restrictions did little to quell the unruliness:
on Good Friday, 2 April 1915, Australian and New Zealand troops rioted,
looted and burnt a section of one of their favourite haunts, the 'Wasser'
district of Cairo, the capital's brothel quarter. The so-called 'Battle of
Wasser' has passed into legend as the apogee of antipodean military larrikinism, though the behaviour of the A.I.F. later on in France and in
England was also far from exemplary. On the available evidence, Robert
Graves may not have been unduly denigratory in *Goodbye to All That*,
when he sarcastically observed that the Australians were 'only two generations removed from the days of Ralph Rashleigh and Marcus Clarke'.[9]

The English press had been laudatory of the Diggers since Gallipoli. Michael McKernan notes the hero's welcome they received when they arrived in England in April 1916, quoting the *Daily Telegraph*'s description of them as 'super-soldiers'. The extraordinarily high incidence of venereal disease contracted within the A.I.F., the number of English war brides, and a spate of court cases involving a variety of felonies all combined to stain this heroic image. 'In the British imagination the Australians had been transformed from heroes to criminals during their stay in Britain from 1915 to late 1919', writes McKernan, though he is quick to add that their unpopularity 'derived more from differences in temperament between host and guest than from really wicked behaviour'.[10]

Influenced by the line taken by military censorship (which had rejected a set of verses written by C. J. Dennis on the Wasser fiasco intended for inclusion in *The Moods of Ginger Mick*), Australian soldier-writers did their best to exculpate such waywardness. Oliver Hogue, for example, calls the Cairo incident mere 'boyish follies' which had been distorted by 'captious critics', while W. J. Denny defensively rationalizes Australian misfeasance in England by arguing that a soldier's 'supreme test is not [his] behaviour in Broadway or on the Strand, but in a crucial and perhaps unequal contest in Flanders'.[11] Thorp explains away the Australian's notoriety by referring to his 'natural wildness', and makes the dubious claim that most of the trouble-makers were emigrants to Australia anyway. In the case of the charge of immorality, he shifts the blame to the hero-worshipping English girls. The 'Hard-Case Aussey', argues Thorp, is characteristically an infantryman, a man from a humble urban background who had once stalked the mean streets of his neighbourhood as a member of one of the larrikin gangs: 'From his earliest recollection he has been a fighter'. Like the bushman, the larrikin emerged from a home environment that fitted him well for warfare. What he lacks is the former's selfless patriotic commitment. Shrewd and cunning, with 'no strong adherence to regular hours of work', he is 'essentially an adventurer'.[12] It was left to the bushmen to provide the force with its backbone, its iron will and its moral fibre. And it was they, fighting for 'true democracy', who gave the A.I.F. its freedom-fighting impulses.

Paradoxically, writers such as Hogue, Knyvett and Thorp who exaggerate the bush influence and discriminate against the cities when searching for the reasons for the A.I.F.'s singularity, are conservative and even stuffily imperial in outlook. In this they resemble the inherently antagonistic sympathies unsuccessfully melded in the wartime fictions of civilians like John Butler Cooper. Hogue's books in partic-

ular are replete with obsequious references to 'the grand old flag of the
Empire'. Bluegum records his feeling at the beginning of the war that
he had to recompense 'Old England' for his 'priceless British citizen-
ship'. The men of the A.I.F. supposedly were free of snobbery, whether
military or social, but one would not think so from Hogue. Bluegum's
swelling pride as he receives one promotion after another rather deflates
the notion of the egalitarian Digger. Knyvett, as usual, goes further:
'It is not often realised what a purgatory the educated, independent man
who enlists as a private has to go through before his spirit is tamed sufficiently to stand bossing, without resentment, by men socially and educa-
tionally inferior.'[13]

The first substantial revision of the Digger's idealized self-image occurs
in Harley Matthews's collection of short stories published late in the
war, *Saints and Soldiers* (1918). These amusing anecdotes of excessive
behaviour in bar, barrack and on the battlefield expose and even promote the uncouth nature of the A.I.F. At least as dedicated to the financial
conquest as the military, Matthews's soldiers are more like benign urban
hooligans than a golden breed of rural heroes. The collection begins
unpromisingly. The book's sub-title –'With the MEN over there'– gives
promise of yet another celebration of excessive *machismo*. (Knyvett,
Hogue, Thorp and even Gladys Hain all employ a similar capitalization of the noun in their individual manifestos of military and male chauvinism.)[14] Happily, the stories themselves soon dispel this expectation.
Matthews's characters, unlike Ginger Mick, are larrikins unredeemed
and indeed irredeemable. They are 'dags' of the Henessy stamp, in all
ways dissimilar to the earnest jingoists who lurch through the pages of
Hogue and Knyvett.

Matthews is an iconoclast. In *Saints and Soldiers* he is not concerned
with embellishing martial achievements and accomplishments, but with
the animal resourcefulness of men temperamentally incapable of being
pressed into adaption by the military machine:

> When you hear that a man is a good soldier you don't think, do you, that
> he is an angelic individual who is always smart and dutiful, and whose voice
> is loud only when it is singing hymns?
>   A good soldier is one who can keep himself out of clink by the force of
> imagination, and the spoken word.[15]

The Digger's independence and his determination to fight the war on
his own terms frightened the mainstream legend-makers. They scarcely
mentioned, let alone proudly proclaimed, his capacity to get himself

in and out of trouble with the authorities. In one story, 'The Higher Finance', Matthews makes a calculated jibe at the heroic clichés promulgated during the war. He begins the story with praise for the perspicacity of a London *Times* correspondent, who had tagged the men of the A.I.F. 'the hard-bitten Australians': 'He saw further than the lean determined faces, the lithe long limbs, and all the rest of it that correspondents usually affect to see'.[16] According to the simple structural formula followed by Matthews in all his stories, general introductory comment foreshadows episodes of an illustrative kind. So, in 'The Higher Finance', these opening, somewhat barbed, observations prepare the reader for a portrayal of activities that are supremely inglorious – the habitual cadging of money, food and drink from all and sundry by Australian soldiers. The hero of 'Or Vanity' is 'Kiddem', a quintessentially perverse Australian larrikin from Woolloomooloo who absolutely refuses to play the military game. Aided by Matthews's sardonic exposition, he sabotages the entire Newboltian philosophy:

> In those days there were still people who thought that a man only joined the army in the hope of becoming an angel quickly. So when the army showed no signs of sprouting wings, it was lectured and reprimanded and exhorted. "Play the game, men!" the bored army had shouted at it in camp, on the march and at every meal. The army took it all just as a horse does when he swipes the flies away with his tail.
>
> But not so Kiddem the first time. As soon as parade was dismissed he was at the sergeant-major's tent. "Yes, my lad?" said his superior officer.
>
> "Will you give our tent first chance of the cricket set or the football or the marbles or whatever it is, sergeant-major?" Kiddem asked.
>
> "What are you talking about?" the sergeant-major sneered.
>
> "This game!"
>
> "What game, man?"
>
> "The game the captain was talking about to-day. He told us to play it always."
>
> In vain for the sergeant-major to take ten minutes to explain what the captain had really meant. Kiddem would leave him with a you-can't-have-me-I'm-too-clever-for-that sort of air.[17]

Though Matthews was a veteran of Gallipoli and had participated in the April Landing, his stories betray no hankering after personal kudos. The collection opens with 'The Music of Life', which objectifies and summarizes the Digger's war experience, from embarkation in Sydney to the troopship back home. Gallipoli is dealt with, of course, but the Landing itself is ignored. The tense countdown to the invasion is described, then the action leaps forward to an impressionistic rendering of fighting on the peninsula some days later. Moreover, in the following story, 'The Anzac Touch', Matthews treats Gallipoli in a cavalier and almost sacrilegious fashion. This story derives its impact by playing on the ambiguity of its title, and by ironizing the legend itself. The 'Anzac Touch' displayed in post-Gallipoli war days by an original Anzac, Private Tommy Smailes, has nothing to do with the heroic mark stamped on him by his experiences, but concerns his use of his status to 'touch' people for money. 'Anzac Smailes' is thus his 'trading name'—all legislative prohibition against the base use of that sacred name notwithstanding'. Believing himself 'deserving of recompense as well as honour', Tommy's technique is simple but effective:

> "It's like this," Tommy explained. "I'm Anzac Smailes, No. 006, original battalion. While you were back in Australia I was fighting for you. Five francs and I'll call it quits."[18]

'The Anzac Touch' clearly ridicules the canonization of the Anzac in the Australian imagination; nevertheless, there is something attractive about Smailes's amoral craftiness. And when he applies it to the 'touching' of the Prince of Wales (strolling in his captain's uniform in Belgravia Square in the company of two detectives), we like him immensely:

> "What do you want?" the captain asked sharply.
> "Half a note from you, sir" Tommy told him . . .
> "But you can't—do you know who I am?"—the young captain got boyishly flustered. Tommy showed no signs of recognition.
> "I'm the Prince of Wales".
> That meant little to Tommy except he knew that for success now, deference might be necessary. "Your Highness," he said in his best manner—he may use it on you one of these days—"there's only a couple of letters different in our names. I'm Smailes—Anzac Smailes—No. 006—original battalion."[19]

In the Hall of Memory, that impressive shrine of pagan hero-worship within the Australian War Memorial in Canberra, a huge stone warrior looks up at a series of stained-glass windows which depict qualities held to be intrinsic to the Australian serviceman and woman. Included among these are 'Resource', 'Candour' and 'Audacity'. Diggers of the Tommy Smailes type possessed these attributes in abundance. In the view of the Australian orthodoxy, however, they had misapplied and perverted their inherited racial talents, and for their sins they were relegated to a kind of literary limbo.

Matthews's soldiers are drinkers, rabble rousers, and inveterate gamblers. Ginger Mick gives up the booze for his country; these larrikins almost drown in it. Though *Saints and Soldiers* is randomly ordered, with no real progressive thematic development, all the yarns deal to some degree with a group who call themselves 'the Band of Boisterous Boozers'. The band is introduced in 'The Music of Life', carousing and cursing in a Cairo street café. The men are attended by the ubiquitous Arab boot-blacks, who call all Australians 'Mr. Mackenzie'. (There is some inadvertent prescience in this, since Matthews's characters bear a distinct resemblance to the representative 'Ocker' invented decades later by Barry Humphries – the type of Australian embodied by Humphries's 'Bazza' was more acceptable to Australians in the 1970s than it was around the time of the Great War.) Drunken revelry was not unusual within the A.I.F. Indeed, it was an almost venerated activity. Thus, in 'Or Vanity', scenes of Diggers rorting in Cairo at Christmas, including the unedifying sight of a soldier riding up the steps of Shepheard's Hotel on a donkey, present themselves to Kiddem as 'haloed visions'.[20] To be sure, the Boisterous Boozers do drink with a fervour that is religious in its intensity and in its forms. 'The Swan Song' dramatizes the curious ceremony by which would-be boozers are initiated into the band, or sect. The ceremony is replete with chants:

> "For I've been a bit of a boozer in my time,
>   And I see no alteration;
> I don't give a hang if I do go blind
>   Through excessive jollification."

and invocations:

> "Oh, beer, thou art a great influence,
>   And I am a second–class private;
> We've got no money and we can't get tick,
>   Yet never let us be short of beer, beer, beer."[21]

Comic profanity is combined with a satirical attack on the disciplines of the military life. In one story the Boozers set up their own kangaroo court to try one of the members on a charge of 'conduct prejudicial to the maintenance of good order and military discipline in that [he] did come into the camp sober, and with the price of numerous beers concealed on [his] person, thereby deserting [his] comrades in their hour of need'. The defendant is found guilty of the offence, and is fined eighty drinks.[22] The Boozers, it should be noted, augment their capacity for excessive drinking with a strong aversion to paying for it. In 'The Poverty of Riches' they start fights in a café so as to create a diversion for their escape from the premises, leaving behind a gigantic unpaid bill. This kind of knockabout comedy often degenerates into the tiresome, the juvenile and the asinine. On occasions, however, Matthews manages to capture the type of macabre humour that distinguishes *The Anzac Book*, a humour that gives a genuine expression to the laconicism of the A.I.F. In 'A Close Call' a Digger rescues a mate, who had been inveigled into promising to marry an unlovely English girl, by concocting the following note to the fiancée:

> Dear Miss,—
>   This is just to let you know that a German shell came over this morning, and my old cobber, Pte. Huskie, was in the way. He often used to tell me about you, and I'm sure he died happy. I'm sorry I can't send you a memento, but there is not a bit of him to be found anywhere.[23]

The parochialism of the Australian soldier does not escape Matthews's notice. The self-styled 'Dinkum Australian' is lampooned with a sharpness which anticipates Angela Thirkell's extended satire in *Trooper to the Southern Cross* (1934), while the aptly-titled story 'The Power of Imagination' alludes to the bragging that was endemic in the A.I.F. 'Strike-me', the soldier with the power of imagination, is a habitual improver of the truth: 'Strike me if I didn't win 620 piastres, and strike me . . .'. To anyone willing to listen, he boasts that on the first day on Gallipoli he 'killed 230 Turks on his own'.[24] Perhaps it is a little unfair to criticize the man—he had probably spent his spare hours reading Ashmead-Bartlett, or Hogue, or Knyvett . . .

Matthews's attitude to the excesses of the A.I.F. is nevertheless one of amused tolerance rather than satirical reproof. Though it could not be claimed that Matthews offers the 'complete' Digger—his version is in its own way as much a caricature as the official heroic type—he rounds the portrait by supplying much of what had previously been omitted. The graceless, anarchic nature of the A.I.F. was absolutely vital to its singular fighting effectiveness. By 'cleaning up' the force, publicists like Hogue and Bean (in his rigorous editing of *The Anzac Book*) tended to emasculate it. By broaching the A.I.F.'s unconventional side, Matthews, by contrast, succeeds in paying tribute to its dynamism. In any case, one thinks that Matthews's real target is not the Australian Army itself, or even the heroic myth which surrounded it, but foolish sanitizers of the myth like Oliver Hogue. *Saints and Soldiers* is an important bridge in the development of Australian war literature, a work which comically previews the V.D., warts-and-all inclusiveness of Baylebridge's *An Anzac Muster*.

While it was not until the early 1930s that their first genuine military memoirs appeared, old soldiers of the A.I.F. continued to tell their story in the intervening period, mostly in the form of long-forgotten paperback pulp fiction. It is appropriate to glance at their works here, as together they form an adjunct to the wartime soldier's book. One of the major purveyors of the pulp war book in the 1920s was Herbert Scanlon, who produced some fourteen slim volumes of stories from 1919 to 1928. Perhaps the most interesting thing about Scanlon's one-shilling paperbacks was the method of their sale. In order to provide work for unemployed ex-Diggers, they were canvassed door-to-door around the suburbs. This surely amounts to a literal spreading of the heroic word. Scanlon presents to his prospective 'customers' his credentials to write about the war. These are military rather than literary: the majority of his books provide proof of his service record, from a Returned Soldiers' Association Certificate to the King's Certificate issued by the British Government. So as to ensure what he calls an 'impartial hearing' for his writings, he also issues an extraordinary statement guaranteeing the integrity of his salesmen:

> It has always been my proud boast, that no man has ever sold a book written by Herbert Scanlon that is not worthy to represent the book or myself . . .
>
> He is selling a genuine article, an original publication, and a work of considerable merit, that demands tact, and good manners. For that reason, he has been personally examined by me, and found to be desirable in every sense of the word [*sic*] . . .[25]

After such a fulsome attestation, the stories themselves are disappointing – of meagre interest or comic value, and, despite their author's assurances, of little literary worth. To Scanlon's credit, he largely dispenses with bravado; his description of the conduct of Australians in France in *Humoresque* (1922) even harbours a moment of post-war revisionist perception: 'Loving well and fighting well, lying well'.[26] Countless other flimsy pamphlet-like collections plotting the deeds and misdeeds of the A.I.F. emerged in the 1920s. Often they were written and produced with the noble motive of assisting men disabled by their war service, and in some cases identical texts appear elsewhere with different authors, and published by different publishers. And how could any true patriot with a heart resist *Dinkie Di Diggers* (1927), by 'Two One-Legged Anzacs'? Their material is primarily comic and *risqué*, related in a bright and breezy patter more suited to the smoky enclaves of the local returned servicemen's club than to the printed page. The

'Two One-Legged Anzacs' put their heads together and came up with the following characteristically tawdry joke:

> An Australian, Scotchman, and an Irishman were walking down a street in Paris. A pretty French girl passed them. "Oh," said the Scotchman, "I wish 'twas wee Mary."
> "I wish it was Bridget," said the Irishman.
> "Um," said the Australian, "I wish it was dark."[27]

But for the most part the post-war ephemera is inoffensive and relatively low-key. There are exceptions. In *Fragments from Gallipoli and France* (1921), E. Wells, 'A Returned Anzac', describes a bayonet charge with a kind of negligent linguistic energy which harks back to the grand days of wartime big-noting, and which provides a further context for the more polished techniques of self-advertisement used by the soldier-writers of the 1930s. It is a fitting postscript to the obsessions that dominate the literature of war produced in Australia in the years 1914 to 1918:

> . . . we get the order, "Fix bayonets!" This order is the height of a soldier's ambition . . . This is the moment men have waited for since first enlisting . . . It could be fittingly described as the climax of a soldier's life.
> . . . So we fix bayonets and get slightly hot in the head in the doing of it. The heat in the head gradually develops into an all-consuming flame, scorching and scarring refinement, until we emerge different men. Supermen! with a lust to kill . . .[28]

III

Books of the Tribe

THE AUSTRALIAN *ILIAD:* BEAN'S *OFFICIAL HISTORY*
Eulogizing the Anzacs in his ephemeral novel *Coo-oo-ee!*, John Butler
Cooper looked forward to the day when a major writer would com-
memorate their achievements in appropriately enduring art:

> The troops were the virile expression of the young nation. . . Hereafter
> some Australian Homer will tell the story in an Iliad that will rival the
> tale of the siege of Troy . . .[1]

The Anzac story was barely one year old when Cooper wrote these
words; it is implied that some years would need to pass before the
Gallipoli experience could be properly assimilated and given adequate
expression. In essence, his prediction was vindicated. The post-war
period, stretching right through to the next world conflict, saw the
appearance of four works which gave the First A.I.F. some sort of
elevated literary treatment. These are C. E. W. Bean's *The Official
History of Australia in the War of 1914–1918*, William Baylebridge's
An Anzac Muster, Leonard Mann's *Flesh in Armour*, and Frank Dalby
Davison's *The Wells of Beersheba*. Bean, Baylebridge, Mann and Davison added a measure of literary finesse to the crude nationalism of
the war years, and so provided the developing military myth with
the depth and direction it needed. In general authorial intention and
in specific effect they honoured the heroism of the A.I.F. within a
tradition which has its roots in Homer's archetypal war epic. Their
heroes are men of historical consequence and distinction, whose extraordinary feats in combat are lent gravity by being related in a fundamentally ceremonial style. The tone of each of the four works asserts
a proud racial identity, acting as a controlling nationalistic conscious-

ness over narrative structures which are episodic and diffuse. In these essentials, each fulfils what has been described as one of the foremost original functions of the epic, that of being a 'book of the tribe', a chronicle of national tradition.[2]

Bean's *Official History*, perhaps more than any other single text, comes closest to the 'Australian Iliad' envisioned by Cooper. The label can be qualitatively applied only to a limited degree, of course. One guesses that George Johnston was not merely referring to Gallipoli's suitability as a heroic subject when he commented that, 'Homer could have written it better than anyone else'.[3] Perhaps the *Iliad*'s most supreme quality is that it radiates a tragic intensity which transcends narrow historical and communal preoccupations and sympathies. As Paul Merchant has noted generally of the great epics, 'We are confronted not by a man at a moment in history, but by Man in History. We are all involved in what becomes of him'. It cannot be claimed for Bean's opus that it contains such a grandeur of meaning, or that it possesses a universality of relevance. If, according to Ezra Pound's deceptively simple definition, 'An epic is a poem including history', then in Bean there is rather too little 'poetry' and far too much 'history' – and a partisan reworking of history at that.[4]

Bean himself harboured few illusions about the intrinsic artistic value of the *Official History*. Speaking in 1925, he described it as a repository of factual information which might provide future inspiration for 'some great Australian poet', who would 'tell the people of the world, in language that would last forever, the epic story of Australian courage and valour'.[5] That great epic poet has yet to appear. It is ironical that the most enduring literary monument to Australian heroism remains a work which, ostensibly at least, set out to be a mere survey of battlefield events. But the success of the *Official History* finally depends not only on the acuity of its perceptions of past events, but on the modest historian's potent fusion of a visionary spirit with a nationalistic zeal. Like the 'Father of History', Herodotus, who began his seminal war history with the hope that his 'researches' would prevent 'the great and wonderful deeds of the Greeks and Barbarians from losing their due meed of glory', Bean sought to commit to racial memory the actions of the A.I.F. in forging a 'consciousness of Australian nationhood' during the Great War.[6] He succeeded.

In terms of sheer bulk alone, *The Official History of Australia in the War of 1914–1918* is a publication of truly 'epic' dimensions and range. As its general editor and the writer responsible for at least half of the work, Bean at first considered that it would take only two years to complete. In the end, it took twenty-three years of dedication, twelve fat volumes and nearly four million words to put the Australian war story on the public record. The work's continuing distinction rests almost entirely upon Bean's own six-part account of the campaigns of the A.I.F. in Gallipoli and France. This is not to discount the separate volumes on the airmen and the seamen, on the capture of German New Guinea, on the social and political events of the Home Front, and (especially) Henry Gullett's lively account of the mounted campaigns in the Middle East, which all retain their value as sources of historical information. But Bean's own volumes form the imaginative core of the entire historiographical enterprise. The six books together make a single continuous narrative, one complete artefact, and in them is most palpably manifested the patriotic purpose which motivated the whole project.

At their respective dates of publication (1921, 1924, 1929, 1933, 1937 and 1942) Bean's histories were greeted with some acclamation. The notices ranged from the extravagant – the reviewer for the London *Observer* tagged the opening work, *The Story of Anzac*, 'Australia's *Iliad* and *Odyssey*' – to the respectful, as in the considered praise of the eminent British military historian Liddell Hart, who thought the third volume, *The A.I.F. in France: 1916*, 'one of the most absorbing and illuminating of all war books'. Angus & Robertson advertised the series as being 'MORE INTERESTING THAN WAR FICTION – MORE INTIMATE, PERSONAL, FEARLESS, DRAMATIC, THRILLING'. In its promotion the firm quoted several testimonials from local and foreign journals and newspapers which abound in adjectives not usually applicable to an official military history. 'Wonderful vividness and realism', 'intimate personal detail and dramatic colour', 'poignant interest' and 'extraordinary vigour' are some of the terms of commendation. The most telling compliment of all comes from the *New Statesman*, which describes the work as 'Probably the most *readable* official history of the war published in any country'.[7]

The *Official History*'s accessibility derives directly from Bean's historiographical method. It has been remarked to the point of cliché that this is a history of the man at the front lines of the Great War.[8] Bean devotes his narrative energies to the fighters at what he liked to call 'the cutting edge of battle' at the expense of the machinations and chess-board manoeuvres of the politico-military leaders. The relative unconventionality of this approach is evident when Bean's work is placed alongside the British war histories, which are 'official' not merely in patronage but in their intrinsic nature, with technical and emotional sympathies lying with the manipulators rather than the manipulated. Since both the British Official Historian, Sir James Edmonds, and the author of the official history of the Gallipoli campaign, C. F. Aspinall-Oglander, were Regular Army soldiers of exalted rank (both Brigadier-Generals), this is not surprising. Equally predictable, perhaps, is that Bean, a journalist with a mere honorary captain's status in the A.I.F., should be more concerned with the common men at the front than with their commanders at headquarters. Aspinall-Oglander's account of the miscalculated Anzac Landings is terse, almost perfunctory. As he played a major part in the formulation of the invasion plan, his reticence is possibly understandable. But whereas he writes blandly of Australians being 'somewhat badly shelled from Gaba Tepe at 4.45 A.M.' on the morning of 25 April, Bean draws the reader into the deadly immediacy of the situation, simulating its drama with the skill of a novelist. He captures the men's bewilderment at landing at an inhospitable place markedly different from that which had been described to them:

> The firing was increasing fast. A machine-gun was barking from some fold in the dark steeps north of the knoll; another was on the knoll itself or on the edge of the plateau above and behind it. The seaman who, as if he had been landing a pleasure party, was handing Captain Butler his satchel out of the boat, fell back shot through the head.
> . . . The men were ashore and mostly alive, but the place was clearly the wrong one . . . Something was clearly wrong. Everything seemed wrong . . . "What are we to do next sir?" somebody asked of a senior officer. "I don't know, I'm sure," was the reply. "Everything is in a terrible muddle."[9]

Winston Churchill's comments about the Landing in his self-justifying account, *The World Crisis, 1915,* point to the essential differences in the narrative strategies of the British and Australian historians. 'It would not be fitting here', he says, 'to recount the feats of arms which signalized the day. To do them justice a whole volume would be required: each Beach deserves a chapter; each battalion, a page'.[10] C. E. W. Bean adopts the kind of intense focus recommended by Churchill. His proud boast that his volumes furnished 'more detail than has been put into a war history, at least in modern times', seems justified, though he readily admits that this comprehensiveness was facilitated by the limited nature of the colonial involvement. The small scope of the activities of the A.I.F. in comparison with those of the mammoth British and European armies made it possible 'to record with more than usual certainty the play of strains and stresses at the actual point where battles are won or lost'. This methodological consideration aside, Bean's reliance on the viewpoint of the ordinary soldier over that of the war lords stemmed from an egalitarian scepticism about the value of the despatches of generals and statesmen, and from a Tolstoyan cynicism about the concept of the godlike military genius.[11]

An almost excessive faith in the factual worth of the eyewitness testimony meant that Bean's historiographical task was as concerned with the selection and ordering of first-hand data as with general descriptive exposition. The result of the incorporation of so much material illustrative of individual experience into the texture of the narrative is that the *Official History* has the intimacy of a military memoir and the variety and dynamism of a good war novel. Doubts could be raised about the wisdom of such prodigal use of highly coloured (and dubiously documentary) personal accounts, such as those by G. D. Mitchell, H. R. Williams and E. J. Rule, as primary sources. But despite suspicions about their veracity, there is no doubting the vitality and the sense of occasion personal records instil into a war history—even when, as in the case of G. D. Mitchell's quoted observations about preparing to ambush German armoured cars near Hébuterne in 1918, Bean's motives appear to be the exploitation of 'colour' for colour's sake:

> Part of our battalion moved to their trench positions. The 47th marched out. [Colonel] Imlay commandeered a lorry and sent it down . . . to block the road. We waited lined up. The strained feeling vanished, and we all licked our lips in anticipation.[12]

While Bean's journalistic background, training and impulses occasionally get the better of his judgement as a historian, they usually work to his positive advantage. In the manner of an investigative journalist, he weighs and balances his sources, supplementing the personal narrative and the diary with regimental records, interviews with the participants, quotations from war correspondents (including, naturally, himself) and—most importantly—his own copious notes taken during the conflict. Aware that after the war he would be writing the official Australian history, it was as a researcher as well as a professional journalist that he went about his reporting duties.[13] Heedless of personal risk, he made a point of visiting all the battlefields, observing, listening, learning. The author Frederick Loch ('Sydney de Loghe'), who bumped into him on Gallipoli, noted that the journalist had 'the face of a student'.[14] It is Bean's intimate acquaintance with 'what actually happened' which gives the *Official History* its special flavour. That it was allowed to be written virtually free of any form of censorship ensured that Bean could attain his desired level of fidelity without the worry of treading on the tender toes of officialdom.

Bean's biographer, Dudley McCarthy, often alludes to his subject's 'capacity for hero-worship'.[15] Though Bean may have felt impelled to write a new kind of war history by concentrating on the battlefield itself rather than on the conference-room back at Headquarters, in truth it was his almost undiscriminating reverence for the Australian soldiers which shaped his narrative. Just as he had moulded *The Anzac Book* according to his idealized notion of what constituted proper publicity for the A.I.F., the *Official History* was constructed as 'a memorial' to the men who had fought.[16] It is worth speculating whether he drew on any particular literary source when pondering how best to achieve the aim of commemoration. Certainly, his scholastic grounding fitted him well for the task. Educated partly at Clifton College, the old school of Generals Haig and Birdwood and also of Sir Henry Newbolt, Bean won a scholarship to Hertford College, Oxford, where he read classics. Some of his youthful studies must have remained with him during the war and after. Remarking upon his first voyage to Gallipoli from Egypt, McCarthy notes that Bean 'knew these seas, though he had never sailed them before, for the *Iliad* and the *Odyssey* were open books to him as Homer had written them'.[17]

Surprisingly, however, the obvious military and geographical connections linking the stories of Troy and Anzac are unexploited by Bean in his two volumes on Gallipoli. The only clearly Homeric allusion is inadvertent, a reference to a soldier who happens to be named Troy—a man who is no hero either, being recorded only as having been 'knocked senseless by a bomb'.[18] Yet on the evidence of the narrative organization of the *Official History*, Bean, as George Rawlinson said of Herodotus, had 'drunk at the Homeric cistern till his whole being [was] impregnated with the influence thence derived'.[19] He structures a succession of primarily small-scale engagements so as best to illustrate the battle virtuosity of the Australians, without ever losing sight of the need to provide the necessary strategic and tactical context for the particular actions. The monolithic conflict is broken down battle by battle, skirmish by skirmish, ultimately to that degree of fine detail indicated by the quoted observation of a soldier (E. J. Rule) at Pozières, who proclaimed that 'Each Aussie seemed as if he was having a war all on his own'. This Homeric technique of concentrating on brief anecdotal descriptions, including dialogue, of a few men in combat surrounded by a swirling free-for-all provides 'the perfect context for the creation of notions of heroism'.[20]

Homer, in his admittedly much shorter work, picks out relatively few glorious figures for special attention in the *Iliad*, and in keeping with traditional practice these men are aristocrats, the heroic chieftains. There are heroes by the hundred in Bean's epic, and the spotlight is directed as often on the Myrmidons as on the Achillean favourites. It is surely more by design than by chance that among the first words spoken by a member of the Anzac Landing party on the morning of 25 April are those of a 'Private Smith', of Bendigo. In the Homeric manner, Bean catalogues his host of heroes, either integrating their biographical details into the main text or providing footnotes for the relevant information. Convinced that 'the true credit for famous achievements in war, as in politics, lies often with unknown subordinates', Bean admitted that he chose his radical historiographical technique not only 'to give a true picture of the test of battle', but also 'to distribute the credit as widely as possible among those who deserve it'.[21] At times he stresses the innate courage of ordinary Australians by juxtaposing their feats in battle with their unheralded civilian existences. During the counter-attack at Lone Pine, a certain obscure Captain Scott leaps on to narrative centre-stage:

> Scott, who in private life was a clerk in Dalgety and Company's Sydney office, was a cheerful and dashing soldier. He at once called to the men: "Who'll come with me?", and leaping over the new barrier without the least knowledge of what was in front of him, ran straight past the junction of the Traversed Trench to Lloyd's old barricade. There he came upon a party of Turks busily throwing bombs over the barrier . . . He shot three or four, causing the rest to draw back round the bend of the trench.[22]

One trusts that the swashbuckling Scott behaved a little more circumspectly in the company office than he did on the battlefield. In the case of R. L. Leane, leader of an audacious raid on Gaba Tepe in May 1915, Bean makes it plain how far ordinary men can develop as soldiers: 'Leane, who at the beginning of the war was working in a large store in Western Australia, was before the end of it the head of the most famous fighting family of soldiers in Australian history, and the fighting general *par excellence* . . . His tall square-shouldered frame, immense jaw, tightly compressed lips, and keen, steady, humorous eyes made him the very figure of a soldier.' Three members of Leane's renowned family served under his command with the 48th Battalion in France. Bean, always on the alert to provide examples of the wry wit of the A.I.F., tells us that the unit's sobriquet became the 'Joan of Arc Battalion' – Made of All-Leanes.[23]

The inclination to apportion praise where it is due without deference to rank does not preclude the commanders of the A.I.F. being given their proper prominence. Bean provides biographical and character sketches of all the major figures, portraits which are detailed and usually respectful. According to the modern international literary convention, all common soldiers are helpless pawns and all senior officers are egomaniacal fools and murderers. Bean dissents on both counts. The degree of careless intrepidity epitomized by Brigadier-General H. E. ('Pompey') Elliott, whose infantry brigade played a vital role in the crucial counter-attack at Villers-Bretonneux in April 1918, is in fact the romantic standard by which Bean assesses soldierly accomplishment. Elliot is portrayed as an antipodean Ajax. Tempestuous, wildly independent and contemptuous of battle skills that fall short of the superhuman, he is the quintessential happy warrior, a man who revels in his temporary military incarnation. For Elliott (a lawyer in civilian life) the dreary *Field Service Regulations* was 'alive from cover to cover, each paragraph illuminated by some scene from military history with himself as the central player; his dearest ambition, far beyond hope during most of his life, was to conduct an advance like that of Clive on Arcot or a retreat like that of Moore to Corunna'.[24]

The perceived deficiency of John Monash in this critical area of personal example is the reason for the lukewarm appraisal given him by the historian. Monash is fulsomely praised for his supreme administrative and organizational skills, his incisive brain and his cultural refinement, but on Bean's scale these talents rate well below raw courage. His leadership as a divisional commander is criticized as suffering badly from his 'insufficient experience of the firing line'. War correspondents, Bean cuttingly remarks, observed that Monash was 'the best leader from whom to seek information before a fight but the worst to go to afterwards'. Unlike the Englishman General Birdwood, who is said to possess 'the quality, which went straight to the heart of Australians, of extreme personal bravery', Monash 'took no delight in running bodily risk'.[25] Dead commanders, of course, provide no command at all, but Bean seems oblivious to this. He approvingly refers to the courage of the commander of the 1st Australian Division, General Bridges, in taking his meals in the open with shells bursting in the vicinity, arguing that this devil-may-care attitude permeated the behaviour of his staff and helped create the strong *esprit de corps* of the entire division.[26] That Bridges's recklessness virtually guaranteed his eventual fatal wounding on Anzac does not impinge, in Bean's view, upon his efficiency as a leader.

Bean's antipathy to Monash surfaces most clearly in his contemptuous barbs at the General's ignorance of sporting traditions and his youthful inability at games as a student at Scotch College, where, intellectually, he had swept all before him. (Having distinguished himself with the Clifton Second XI Bean felt qualified to pontificate on such matters.) And in stark contrast with the beloved Brudenell White, for whom Bean in concert with the ever-conspiring Keith Murdoch intrigued against Monash to be appointed commander of the new united Australian Corps in 1918, Monash is shown to have been tainted by vaulting personal ambition. White is esteemed as a 'magnificent man . . . with a heart as great as his body', but is infuriatingly indifferent to his own advancement; Monash, on the other hand, is implied to be a bit of a prima donna. Bean was a team man. He felt that Monash's colossal ego was inimical to the best interests of the men under his command. If Napoleonic in all-round accomplishment, Monash is also reminiscent of 'that great prototype' in haughty temperament, having 'an almost Napoleonic skill in transmitting the impression of his capacity'.[27]

Integral to this churlish appraisal of Australia's most renowned Great War soldier is the feeling that Monash's surpassing intellect, overweening ambition and—a sad comment on Bean—his Jewish heritage and loyalties rendered him incompatible with the ethos of the A.I.F. Throughout the history Bean stresses that the superiority of the A.I.F. as a fighting force lay in its egalitarian character and composition. Referring to the fact that for the most part the rich and the poor, the educated and the unschooled, went into the ranks of the A.I.F. unconscious of distinctions, Bean asserts that the Digger 'knew only one social horizon, that of race'. The rigid, semi-feudal forms and suppressions of the British Army (reflective of the stratified society it represented in war) are invoked to explain what are viewed to be enervated energies and a tendency towards despondency in tough situations. By contrast, the efficacy of the A.I.F. 'was not in spite of the Australian Jack's being as good as his master, but because of it – or, more accurately, because in the A.I.F. Jack and his master were the same'. Against the British aristocratic model, the Australian Army was a military meritocracy. As in the civilian society of the nation, 'men passed for what in themselves they were worth'. The force drew its strength in battle from the principle that the sole criterion for the selection of officers from the ranks was individual ability, and gained its 'unity of spirit' from the harmony created by the absence of any real social demarcations.[28] One result of the 'honours system' operating within the A.I.F. was a continual desire on the part of the officers and men to prove themselves. A cynical interpretation of the high death rate of newly-commissioned second lieutenants[29] suggests that this compulsion was inherently counter-productive. Indeed, the pages of the *Official History*, like those of the *Iliad*, are littered with would-be heroes who tried too hard to justify themselves in the eyes of their fellows.

The best example Bean provides of the inspirational qualities of the Australian ideal of leadership comes in the form of the deeds of the Sixth Brigade, A.I.F., the 'baby' of the Tasmanian apple-grower, John Gellibrand. Bean's portrait of Gellibrand oozes admiration and affection. Paramount among the virtues Bean discerns in Gellibrand, besides his sense of humour and his 'standard of quixotic honour', is his ability to motivate his men. Somewhat fastidious himself, Bean writes approvingly of Gellibrand's eccentric taste in dress, especially his habit of going about in the same old 'Aussie' tunic worn by privates even after he became a general commanding a division. The historian also delights in the 'Bohemian simplicity' of his headquarters at the front, where he and his staff 'lived together as one family'. Gellibrand is further praised as being the finest trainer of young officers in the A.I.F. Through his direct influence he manufactured a unit 'which pulled together like a crew in an eight-oared race'.[30] The 'instrument' Gellibrand had 'forged' met its great 'test' during the night of 3 May 1917, at the Second Battle of Bullecourt. Alone and outflanked following the failure of its supports, the Sixth Brigade faced murderous German opposition at the Hindenburg Line. Bean begins his account of its stalwart determination to maintain its position with the arrival of a single young remnant of the withdrawn Seventh Brigade, Captain Jack Roydhouse, who 'half in tears' tells the men of their exposed and vulnerable situation. Roydhouse, who had once served on Gellibrand's staff, insists on staying to fight with the old brigade. The historian, in celebratory detail and with characteristic vividness, then describes how Gellibrand's men, like a collective Horatius defending the bridge, go about maintaining their seemingly untenable post. His emphasis is on the cohesion and tenacity they evince under extreme pressure:

> Whenever there appeared . . . signs that the enemy might attack, the call to "stand-to" came from the men themselves. Captain Savige [adjutant of one of the brigade's battalions] tells of two whose bayonets had been blown off their rifles, running from one post to another to replace them—they must have bayonets for this work! Another was firing from German rifles and ammunition, with a collection of German bombs beside him and his own rifle carefully covered for use in an emergency. Men could not be spared for stretcher-bearing—the wounded made their own way to the rear "unless absolutely mangled." One man with a fragment of shell in his lung reached the railway before he fainted; a corporal with a piece of metal in his knee carried another man out . . . the firing line became crowded with men with ghastly wounds. Savige tells of one whose entrails were showing through a gash in his abdomen, but who lay smoking a cigarette. To Savige's "Stick it out, lad," he answered "Don't worry about me, sir, but give the bastards hell!" Afterwards he shot himself by placing a rifle between his feet. "The men (says Savige) had one notion only—'it doesn't matter at what cost, we're going to beat them!' ' Officers . . . were consciously working to the standard their brigadier had set them.[31]

The qualities shown by the men of the Sixth Brigade at Bullecourt are all vital elements of the 'Identikit Australian' Bean strives to promote throughout the *Official History*. They exude independent action, improvisation and unbounded resourcefulness, courage, physical strength, comradeship, and pride in their own abilities. Bean's volumes begin and end with general commentary explaining why Australian conditions produced such a distinctive people and such a superior army; the body of the text elucidates and particularizes these remarks. Specifically, Bean is anxious to stress how colonial life had improved the racial stock. Large-framed, wiry-bodied and thin-lipped, the Digger was 'in the main the British "worker" perhaps two generations removed, but developed . . . to nearer the Briton's natural stature'.[32] The relatively poor physique of the Tommies, especially those bred in the slums of the manufacturing areas, is held responsible for the apparently questionable fighting capacity of the British Army. Bean observes a group of representative Tommies gathered in Egypt before 'the test', in late 1914:

As they walked among the Cairo crowds, the little pink-cheeked lads from the Manchester cotton-mills, who had had the pluck to volunteer in the East Lancashire Division, looked like children when compared with the huge men of the Australian regiments.[33]

Despite Bean's severe assessment of the Tommies' prowess but taking into account his infatuation with soldiers and soldiering, it is intriguing to wonder what Paul Fussell would make of such references to 'pink-cheeked lads'. Fussell's provocative examination of the homoerotic strain running through British literature of the Great War reveals that the term 'lad' signifies the pinnacle of comradely affections, above 'boy', the appellation usually preferred by Bean.[34] We can safely assume that Bean's attitude here is one of condescension rather than erotic tenderness. In this he conforms with the Diggers themselves, who as C. E. Montague observed in *Disenchantment*, regarded the Tommies 'with the half-curious, half-pitying look of a higher, happier caste at a lower'.[35] An Australian medical officer at the Second Battle of Villers-Bretonneux touchingly captures the essence of the Digger/Tommy relationship:

> A little Tommy corporal came stumbling in, weeping like a kid and holding his arm. "Pain bad," says I. "No, Sir," he squeaked, "this is nothing, but I can't get the boys to go forward." He had evidently been trying to rally a very young platoon with a bullet in his arm. A wounded digger soothed him. "Never mind, kid," he said, "the boys will hunt Fritz without yous [*sic*] kids."[36]

Pseudo-sociological analysis cannot hide the fact that Bean's habitual juxtaposition of Australian virility with English effeteness is really little more than an indulgence in colonial one-upmanship. The assertive Digger—whose autobiographical writings reveal a remarkably insular human creature—is improbably described by Bean as 'a man of the world'. By sad comparison, the Tommy, stultified and stunted by various forms of military and socio-economic repression, is pitied for being 'pathetically modest'. Can there be any wonder that the docile Englishman 'instinctively looked up to the Australian private as a leader'?[37] Bean's idolatry of the 'peculiar independence of character' and 'unfettered initiative' of the Australians sometimes endangers the credibility of his historical argument. He is fond of celebrating the Digger's 'colourful' and 'incorrigibly civilian' temperament, which even after years of subordination the army was unable to tame. But when that individualism manifests itself rather too grossly, as in the

'Wasser' mêlées, Bean stumbles into an unconvincing whitewash of his behaviour. The first Wasser battle and its successor some months later were 'not heroic', Bean admits, 'but they also differed very little from what at Oxford and Cambridge and in Australian universities is known as a "rag" '. Bean shifts the blame for the wild scene to the presence of the British military police, 'always a red rag to the Australian soldier'. In a footnote near the end of the sixth volume, he bitterly attacks 'some Australian caricaturists', presumably writers such as Harley Matthews, who reduced the 'rich types' of the A.I.F. to the figure of 'a slouching "dag", intent only on beer, thieving, "skirts" and scoring off nincompoop officers'. A 'false legend' was thus established which 'travestied' the whole force. Bean likes to have it both ways. He lionizes the worldliness, the energy and the sense of adventure of the Australian, and then carps when the more extreme manifestations of his character are played upon.[38]

The Australian Bush, more than any other cultural force or factor, is seen as the generator of A.I.F. supremacy. (Lloyd Robson has observed that Bean glorifies bush virtues to the exclusion of other important historical influences, such as the nation's convict heritage and the impact of Irish immigration.)[39] Bean, who venerated the Australian countryside for its almost mystical capacity to invigorate both body and spirit, saw the Australian soldiers as 'fundamentally the shining products of the wide open spaces, cleansed by the burning winds and the simple strengthening lives of those spaces'.[40] The *Official History* is the consummation of a process of idealization begun before the war in *On the Wool Track* (1910) and *The Dreadnought of the Darling* (1911), the products of two reporting assignments for the *Sydney Morning Herald* which took Bean to the far west of New South Wales. Time and time again in *On the Wool Track* the pastoral country beyond the Great Divide is called 'the real Australia'. Out in the bush, men – 'real Australians', by logical extension – develop a versatility which is intrinsic to the Anglo-Saxon breed, but which is in Englishmen retarded through living in 'water-tight compartments'. And in *The Dreadnought of the Darling* he argues that, as boys, up-country Australians learnt the 'spirit of improvisation' from the constant effort to outwit nature, and they had additional valuable training in shooting and riding.[41] These ideas are cultivated in the *Official History*, which affirms the belief that the home environment ensured the military success of what was basically an untrained group of individual volunteers. Bushfires (the fighting of which, 'more than any other human experience, resembles the fighting of a pitched battle'), floods, even the concentration of sheep for shearing, are said to simulate the conditions of warfare. Bean adds droving to this list, though not in the metaphorical, 'cattle to the slaughter' sense often applied to war since 1914–18. The Australian therefore went into battle well-trained; in effect, he was 'half a soldier before the war'.[42]

For much of the time Bean would have his readers believe that the A.I.F., almost to a man, was composed of all-round virtuosi from the bush. But on the evidence he himself provides, it is hard to see how such a claim can be justified. Gellibrand's renowned Sixth Brigade, for example, was mostly town-bred. While Bean largely attributes the Sixth's effectiveness to its exceptional commander, it is interesting to note that the two officers whom he describes performing so brilliantly at Bullecourt, Captains Roydhouse and Savige, were respectively a Perth schoolteacher and a draper from the inner Melbourne suburb of Hawthorn: men who probably had more in common with 'Ginger Mick' than with 'Wallaby Joe'. Even the most legendary Anzac of them all, John Simpson Kirkpatrick, the human part of the 'Simpson and his donkey' combination, was a ship's fireman from Melbourne. Furthermore, as some spoil-sports have pointed out, Simpson was a Britisher anyway. Bean's helpful footnote informs us that he hailed from unsalubrious Tyne Dock in England's industrial north.[43] (That about one in four Australian soldiers were British-born is a fact overlooked by Bean.) And, to mention just a few of the more acclaimed Australian warriors, 'Pompey' Elliott was a Melbourne solicitor, Iven Mackay a lecturer at Sydney University, and Charles Rosenthal a Sydney architect. Monash, of course, was very much a man of the city – though perhaps Bean would hold that this proved his thesis. There really is little excuse for the historian's single-minded celebration of the bushman at the city man's expense. As early as September 1918 the irreverent A.I.F. magazine *Aussie* had tellingly debunked the myth of the super-soldier from the bush. A cartoon depicting a pipe-smoking Digger chatting to a young Englishwoman has the caption:

> The Romantic Young Thing (with visions of Bushrangers, Explorers, Boundary Riders, Prickly Pear Estates, etc.):
> 'And what were you in Australia before the war?"
>
> Truthful Aussie (V.C., D.C.M., M.M.):
> "I was a Clerk in an office in Melbourne!"[44]

Inevitably Bean, under the weight of simple fact, is forced to qualify

his emphasis on the bush character of the A.I.F. Near the end of
the sixth volume, he reluctantly admits that 'the percentage of Australian soldiers who had acquired their powers of determination,
endurance, and improvisation from country occupations was probably not much more than a quarter'. In any case, as he somewhat
desperately argues, the urban Australian's familiarity with the bush
(through cultural inspiration, holidays and upbringing) 'undoubtedly
modified' differences in quality between the country and the city soldier.[45] This belated blurring of distinctions comes after thousands
of pages containing the prodigal use of bush imagery to exemplify
the special nature of the national force. Illustrating its egalitarian
policies and procedures in the opening volume, for instance, Bean
says that subalterns at the front line conversed with their men 'as
freely as a manager with the old hands at an Australian sheep-station,
and the men talked equally naturally with them'. In Volume II a coolly
courageous Anzac fires at targets as casually 'as if he were shooting
in the paddocks at home'. And the comradeship with their fighting
brothers of the non-combatant, but plucky, transport drivers is given
a special colouring by their being referred to as 'usually bush-bred
men, perhaps the cream of the infantry'.[46]

Bush-bred mateship, that hoary old chestnut of the nationalist literary tradition, is crucial to Bean's heroic vision. Mateship, as David
Kent has observed, was a 'commonplace reality' of the Great War,
as palpable in the British, German and French trenches as the
Australian—even the otherwise inconsolable Englishman Richard
Aldington fondly remembers wartime comradeship, the 'undemon-
strative exchange of sympathies between ordinary men racked to
extremity under a great common strain in a great common danger'.[47]
Yet Bean would have us believe that it was an A.I.F. monopoly, a
quasi-religious enthusiasm embraced by a chosen race. Irreligious
in the conventional sense, the Digger's 'prevailing creed' was 'a romantic one, inherited from the gold-miner and the bushman, of which
the central article was that a man should at all times stand by his
mate'.[48] Mateship bonded men together in shared endeavour, accomplishment, and pain; it was also the factor which influenced the
individual Digger's view of himself. In a memorable and often quoted
passage at the end of the first volume, Bean explains that the original Anzacs on Gallipoli were impelled by other factors than 'love
of a fight' (though they 'loved fighting more than most'):

To be the sort of man who would give way when his mates were trusting to his firmness; to be the sort of man who would fail when the line, the whole force, and the allied cause required his endurance; to have made it necessary for another unit to do his own unit's work, to live the rest of his life haunted by the knowledge that he had set his hand to a soldier's task and had lacked the grit to carry it through—that was the prospect which these men could not face.[49]

Heroism, even that of the most primitive and bloodthirsty variety, involves more than being dependable and courageous. It involves an attitude, an egocentric commitment to heroic ideals and a corresponding willingness to confront the pitfalls that await those who prize the glories of the battlefield. It requires morale. As a knowledgeable student of warfare and, more importantly, as a celebratory historian, Bean was acutely aware of this; hence the *Official History* is one long tribute to high Australian military morale. He studs his narrative with episodes in which the self-confidence of the Diggers triumphs in tight situations. The 'elated' Australian response to the order to stem the German advance through routed British opposition before Amiens in March 1918 is an example. 'What! Let a bloody Fritz lick me!', a Digger sneers. Amid cries of *'Vive l'Australie!'* from the deliriously grateful local population, a soldier assures a Frenchwoman: 'Fini retreat, Madame . . . Fini retreat—beaucoup Australiens ici'.[50] One burst of bravado, borrowed from G. D. Mitchell's narrative, contributes an Australian entry to the international lexicon of famous battlefield utterances. Legend tells us that at Waterloo the commander of the French Imperial Guard, General de Cambronne, responded to a call to surrender with a pithy *'Merde!'*; and at the siege of Bastogne in December 1944 the U.S. General McAuliffe retorted 'Nuts!' to a similar demand. The defiance of Australians on the Somme in 1918 is equally memorable, if enfeebled in impact through being expurgated:

> A big German officer climbed out of his trench and roared, "Do you want to surrender." "Surrender be – – –," was chorussed back in pure Australian.[51]

The sang-froid of the Diggers in the heat of battle also illustrates their buoyant morale. Indifference to fire, as we have seen in *The Anzac Book*, was one Australian trait Bean was keen to advertise; he exercised the same policy in the *Official History*. During the Gallipoli landing Private Smith points out to his mate the Turkish bullets whizzing by overhead: 'Just like little birds, ain't they, Snow?' The 'outstanding readiness to risk danger' of the Australians resurfaced in the even harsher war conditions of the Western Front. In the midst of bitter fighting around Bullecourt during April 1917 we are confronted by the sight of a certain Captain Mott of the 48th Battalion incongruously 'laughing' as he charges through machine-gun fire. Months earlier, on one of the deadliest of all battlegrounds encountered by the A.I.F., Pozières, Australians are observed strolling about 'as if they were in Pitt Street, erect, not hurrying'.[52]

Bean's Digger is not merely laconic and relaxed; when roused he is also extremely dangerous. The *Official History*'s aggregation of what Bean calls 'dramatic and effective acts of individual audacity' not only includes famous feats, such as Albert Jacka's Victorian Cross-winning rampage on Gallipoli, but less celebrated displays of bravery as well. Here, in terse blow-by-blow detail, he commemorates the courage of a junior officer at Villers-Bretonneux:

> Captain Sayers leapt among three of the enemy in a shell-hole; he hit one of them on the head with the man's own steel helmet, strangled the second, and the third escaped.[53]

Bean's strategy for the promotion of the Australian warrior depends upon the cumulative effect of such incidents. Sensibly, he tries to avoid big-noting of the overt kind, cunningly framing his heroic boasts in the form of the accolades of foreigners, whose words of praise often appear in footnotes to the main text. For instance he uses the impeccable source of General Haig to confirm the battle discipline of the A.I.F., thus countering charges that the force was impossibly anarchic. To one such British cynic, Haig is reported to have rejoined, 'When they are ordered to attack they always do so'.[54] When Bean himself directly assesses Australian achievements, he falls prey to the use of purple, almost Churchillian phraseology, what H. M. Green rightly called 'romantic fag-ends'.[55] His addiction to the application of sporting imagery to the battlefield is a good example of this tendency towards rhetorical obsolescence. As 'a sign' of their 'native mettle', the despondently-entrenched Anzacs during the Gallipoli stalemate of July 1915 are said to 'chafe' for the impending offensive 'like racehorses approaching the starting-gate'. When battle comes, at Lone Pine on 6 August, Bean again turns to the sporting arena to define the disposition of the troops. As the men of the 1st Brigade excitedly congregate in the bays just prior to the attack, they are said to have 'chaffed each other drily, after the manner of spectators waiting to see a football match'. During the countdown prior to going over the parapet, the officers give final words of advice to their men, while keeping an eye on their watches 'as though they were starting a boat-race'. Bean's Newboltian Public School background and sensibility emerge in such analogies between warfare and rowing (it will be remembered that Gellibrand's staff in responding to 'the test' teamed 'like a crew in an eight-oared race'), and also in his references to cricket. The first wave of attackers at Lone Pine stand alongside the edge of the enemy's trench upon reaching it, thus appearing to observers as 'a crowd not unlike that lining the rope round a cricket field'.[56]

But for the most part Bean manages to keep his enthusiasm in check. His style is lucid and direct, though not incapable of making the odd arresting image, such as his description of a procession of tanks rolling across the Somme countryside 'like elephants accompanying an Oriental army'.[57] In fact, like the dissembling 'Crosscut' of *The Anzac Book*, Bean at times seems to be unsure just how far to extend his heroic theme. The discipline of sober historical accounting inhibited the unfettered heaping of praise upon the Diggers. H. M. Green applauded the balanced realism of the historian's account of the conflict, noting how he avoided 'extremes' in assessing the horrors and the heroisms of the various battles before giving them their due.[58] This may be so, but it should be recognized that Bean's account is striking as much for its uneasy marriage of conflicting impulses as for its balance and perspective. Bean is ambivalent about war: he is seduced by its vestigial glamour, and he is repelled by its effects. As many men die ingloriously in the *Official History* as heroes are born. But if the tragedy and pathos of his descriptions of random death constitute a melancholic vision of human destruction which counterpoints the celebratory vigour of the general battle narrative, then it must also be said that the mood of the *Official History* is seldom anything other than excited. Bean shows an old-fashioned preference to look at the positive, the 'bright', the heroic side of war.

The equivocal treatment of the slaughter at the Anzac ridge known as 'The Nek' the morning after Lone Pine illustrates Bean's ambivalence. Like Lone Pine, the attack on The Nek was essentially a feint to decoy the Turks away from the scene of the landing of the British New Army troops at Suvla Bay a mile to the north of Anzac. But it resulted in perhaps the most appallingly pointless expenditure of Australian lives in the whole war. Some justification can be argued for Bean's use of sporting similes in his account of the battle at Lone Pine—the sense of exhilaration in the attacking troops was real; the battle involved intimate man-to-man conflict (Alan Moorehead likened it to 'a vicious street-fight in the back alleys of a city');[59] and the operation, in the short if not in the long term, was a success. The Nek, on the other hand, was an unmitigated disaster, not even a Pyrrhic victory. Confusion about the timing of the preliminary artillery bombardment enabled the Turkish machine-gunners to be in position and at the ready when the Australians leapt over the top to make the twenty-metre dash to the enemy trenches. The victims were inexperienced but confident Light Horsemen, anxious to emulate their comrades at Lone Pine, and eager for free and open warfare after weeks of a troglodyte-like existence in the trenches. Line after line of these young men were relentlessly mown down, many barely taking a step from their own parapet. Well over two hundred lives were lost in this exercise, while at nearby Suvla the 'assaulting' Englishmen, owing to the procrastinations of their leadership, loitered on the beach.

In the abysmal depth of its futility and in its terrible irony, The Nek is what Paul Fussell would call a 'Satire of Circumstance' to rival Haig's 'Great Fuck-Up' on the Somme on 1 July 1916, when British soldiers by the tens of thousands were machine-gunned to death, also following the ineffectiveness of the pre-battle artillery.[60] But while Bean is critical of the local command for causing such a 'needless loss of lives' when it was immediately apparent that the operation was a failure, he concentrates on highlighting the 'sheer bravery', 'devoted loyalty' and 'self-discipline' the Light Horsemen irrefutably displayed in going to their vain sacrifice. Several times he asserts how they went unhesitatingly into 'the tempest' when it was clear that they would be killed. The affecting sight of 'mate . . . saying good-bye to mate' adds a poignant touch to this solemnization of the fatalism of the Anzacs. Bean summarizes the human loss of the third wave of attackers with a characteristically picturesque catalogue of doomed warriors:

> The 10th went forward to meet death instantly, as the 8th had done, the men running as swiftly and as straight as they could at the Turkish rifles. With that regiment went the flower of the young of Western Australia, sons of the old pioneering families, youngsters – in some cases two and three from the same home – who had flocked to Perth at the outbreak of war with their own horses and saddlery in order to secure enlistment in a mounted regiment of the A.I.F. Men known and popular, the best loved leaders in sport and work in the West, then rushed straight to their death. Gresley Harper and Wilfred, his younger brother, the latter of whom was last seen running forward like a schoolboy in a foot-race, with all the speed he could compass; the gallant Piesse, who

had struggled ashore from the hospital ship; two others, who had just received their commissions, Roskams and Turnbull—the latter a Rhodes scholar.[61]

There is no more stunning image of fierce and impetuous Australian courage in the entire canon of the national war literature than Bean's picture of the schoolboy sprinting headlong to his extinction—a romantic tableau which was eventually to be exploited so effectively by the makers of the movie *Gallipoli* (1981), in the closing frame of that film. But Bean shrinks from giving 'The Nek' the thoroughgoing analysis it warranted. He closes his chapter on the feints of 7 August with a scene of battlefield carnage in which the tragedy is melodramatically implied rather than directly presented:

> During the long hours of that day the summit of The Nek could be seen crowded with their bodies. At first here and there a man raised his arm to the sky, or tried to drink from his waterbottle. But as the sun of that burning day climbed higher, such movement ceased. Over the whole summit the figures lay still in the quivering heat.[62]

Bean is forced to be less equivocal when he comes to tackle the mechanized carnage on the Western Front. His account in *The A.I.F. in France: 1916* of the shell-fire at Pozières is pregnant with horrors, reminding us that this particular volume appeared in the same year (1929) as three of the great post-war exposures of the Western Front nightmare, *Death of a Hero*, *Goodbye to All That*, and *All Quiet on the Western Front*. Bean points out that under such conditions as existed at Pozières, 'the will to persist' of even the finest soldiers could become undermined, and their self-control 'deranged'. He refers to the vivid narrative of a junior officer of the Sixth Brigade, a former Melbourne journalist: '. . . courage does not count here. It is all nerve—once that goes one becomes a gibbering maniac . . . Poor wounded devils you meet on the stretchers are laughing with glee. One cannot blame them—they are getting out of this'. The officer describes the condition of himself and his comrades with a Barbussian loathing and disgusted realism:

> . . . We are lousy, stinking, ragged, unshaven, sleepless . . . I have one puttee, a dead man's helmet, another dead man's gas protector, a dead man's bayonet. My tunic is rotten with other men's blood, and partly spattered with a comrade's brains . . .[63]

Yet the abundant vignettes of Australian courage, prowess, and jaunty self-pride Bean provides throughout his volumes on the Western Front suggest that he sees modern impersonal warfare and traditional swashbuckling self-assertion as being far from incompatible. Certainly, mechanization makes it more difficult for the potential hero; but by its very harshness it forces him to draw on his reserves of courage. It brings out the best in him. Assessing 'the measure of Australian mettle' exhibited during the dreadful French winter of 1916, Bean remarks that the Diggers were 'sustained' by a 'determination that no one should hold them inferior to those around them'.[64] As manifested in battlefield practice, it is this sublime sense of superiority which remains Bean's primary interest. Even the occasional sporting simile finds its way into his narrative. The rendering of the disastrous Battle of Fromelles (in which the A.I.F. lost well over five thousand men in one day) contains this bold juxtaposition of German and Australian valour:

> The crisis called for instant action, and Sergeant Stringer of the 54th rallied a few badly shaken men and boldly assaulted—the Germans tossing stick-bombs from the shelter of the trench, while the Australians, up on the parapet, flung their missiles like cricketers throwing at a wicket.[65]

Given that the *Official History* is such a generous effusion of this kind of appealing testimonial, it is hardly surprising that it has been instrumental in securing for the Digger a supreme place in the pantheon of Australian heroes. The work exemplifies the paradox that, in the end, it is the hero who is dependent upon the artist, and not the reverse. 'Many heroes lived before Agamemnon', Horace mused, 'but all are overwhelmed in unending night, unwept, unknown, because they lack a sacred bard'.[66] Bean not only helped insure the men of the A.I.F. against obscurity, he thrust them into the cultural spotlight; he, of all Australian war writers, deserves the status of 'sacred bard'.

CHEERFUL LIES: *AN ANZAC MUSTER*

One of the more intriguing tales in *An Anzac Muster* is 'The Cheerful Liar', in which two military censors derisively discuss 'the art' exhibited by the Anzacs in their letters to the families and friends back in Australia. Among the 'conceits' they list as being examples of the Anzacs' imaginative skills are such flights of fancy as 'the great quarrels put up to remain in the hottest parts of an engagement', and 'the most astonishing and flesh-puckering escapes: the hair, to the scalp itself, parted by the foe's bullets'.[67]

It is the common epistolary habit of soldiers on active service to distort the truth of their time in the front line. That most assiduous bender of battlefield facts, Oliver Hogue, genially acknowledged that most Anzacs 'told cheerful lies about the good time they were having, the romance of war, the excitement of battle, and the exhilaration of victory'.[68] While the desire to protect the feelings of worried loved ones and plain soldierly bravado are the two reasons usually provided to explain this practice, William Baylebridge in 'The Cheerful Liar' suggests something fundamental about the Australian literary communication of the war experience. The bulk of the story is taken up by a paper issued to the men by the two censors which mischievously exhorts them to maintain their fictionalization of their activities, and offers advice on how best to modify those 'inane' facts which, unmythologized, appeal only to 'limited imaginations'. Called 'The Art of Lying', the paper is a heavily ironical lampoon of war literature as a genre, and of the apocryphal A.I.F. yarns in particular. Indeed, the list of suggested themes for the Anzacs' future attention playfully tacked on to the end of the paper includes a few, such as 'great kills firing under the crutch, backwards' and 'catching bullets as they fly', which look as if they have been lifted directly from books like *Trooper Bluegum at the Dardanelles*. Only by 'lying fitly', the censors suggest, can the Anzacs 'secure justice for those experiences, hairraising and splendid, and perhaps never before met with'. And only by lying will 'Valour be brought forth with his due flourish; only thus will your several reputations be exalted and secured; thus only will the lustre of this great army be increased, confirmed and held in honour till the remotest times'.[69]

Albeit facetiously, Baylebridge has divined the guiding literary principle of Australian First World War writers. While others before him had gently gibed at Australian military boastfulness, Baylebridge's insight is the more penetrating. Amid all the drollery he has something significant to say about the birth and formation of national mythologies in general:

> Look closely into the origin of all noble speeches, proclamations, poems, and outgrowths of spirit whatsoever. Examine carefully the things by which nations without end have been comforted and promoted. You will find these have sprung up where but in the mud, the vital mud, of some abounding lie? Indeed, without lies, would not the world have been lost long ago in the sheer flatness of common sense?[70]

Baylebridge is cutting with a double-edged sword. His strong suggestion is that the Australian war legends, created to meet the wish fulfilment of the nation, emerged out of the mythological mire of historical untruth. At the same time the author is self-consciously aware of his own part in this process. To be sure, there is no more energetic miner of the 'vital mud' in Australian war literature than William Baylebridge. He saw the mythologization of the war as a challenge to his own creative powers, and *An Anzac Muster*, which was available only in its 1921 private printing until Angus & Robertson published a revised edition in 1962, is the result. P. R. Stephensen, who edited and prefaced the revised text, writes of Baylebridge's 'sense of high mission' as a teller of Anzac tales, and alludes to Horace's meditations upon the 'unknown' and 'unwept' pre-Homeric heroes to stress his determination to lionize the Australian soldiers in 'enduring literary art'. *An Anzac Muster* is therefore more than 'a contemporary definition of the Anzac spirit and a description of the men themselves'; it is 'an offering rather to their posterity than to the men of that time'.[71]

With a stronger sense of artistic design than most Australian war writers, Baylebridge set out to contribute to the expanding war myth. *An Anzac Muster* consists of twenty-seven tales, linked by passages of communal chatter and framed by a prologue and an epilogue, told over a sequence of three consecutive Saturday evenings by a band of nine returned servicemen. The inherent tripartite structure of the work is crucial to Baylebridge's myth-making purpose. As Paul Fussell illustrates in *The Great War and Modern Memory*, the 'empirical principle of three' in military procedure and experience—triads such as front, reserve, and support trenches; infantry, artillery, and cavalry; and training, battle and review—bears an intimate relationship with 'the magical or mystical threes of myth, epic, drama, ritual, romance, folklore, prophecy, and religion'.[72] Baylebridge's muster of story-tellers is brought together on the idyllic Queensland grazing property of a Colonel of the A.I.F., in response to a request made by his brother, known throughout the book only as 'the Squatter'. Injury had prevented the Squatter from participating in the war, and he is eager to learn about the Gallipoli saga. The host is the apotheosis of the bushman-warrior:

> a moderately-proportioned but well-knit man, with the confirmed countenance of those who have been tried in many fires, and who have come through as conquerors; his eyes, small but direct in vision, were alert and searching without being aggressive; in short, his face carried that

mark upon it which sealed him as being one of the elect breeds . . .
He looked what he was—his own man.[73]

The 'reporting stock' of chroniclers the Colonel selects to fulfil his
brother's wish are workers on his property. With characters to match
their bizarre nomenclature, they form a varied and eccentric group:
'the Pilot', a former clergyman; 'Hoppy Joe', a typical bushman ('a
piece of ironbark that has learned to think'); 'Monoculus', a big
bearded one-eyed Cyclops, 'primitive and untamed'; 'the Ram', bawdy
and mirthful, and resembling 'certain pictures of medieval monks';
'the Crow', the Ram's 'yoke-fellow in the unsavoury'; 'the Sergeant';
a tall, long-haired, rat-like writer; 'Ink-Finger', also a man with literary pretensions, shifty-eyed and emaciated ('to quote the local jest
. . . by Toothpick out of Splinter'); and 'the Captain', a more conventional 'good soldier', tall, erect and impartial. By popular association and by literary pedigree, their characteristics are both Australian
and classical-European. The influence of Chaucer in particular—
not exactly common in Australian war books—is detectable in the
personality of 'the Ram' and to a degree in the content of his tales.
As has been noted by T. Inglis Moore, the device of the band of
story-tellers itself recalls *The Canterbury Tales*, as well as Boccac-
cio's *Decameron*.[74] With its Gallipoli-like setting in a rocky gully
illuminated by dip-lamps, with the communal partaking of cheese
and 'a multitude of small loaves', the ready keg of beer and the plugs
of tobacco, and with the Colonel etching the order of the raconteurs
on a rough sheet of bark, the entertainment takes on a primitive and
folkloric aspect. The group toast made at the conclusion of each of
the three sessions adds the final touch of ritual, and captures the
celebratory tone of the entire literary enterprise: 'To the men we have
here told and heard of, to the men who returned, to the men who
returned not!'[75]

Baylebridge's commemorative aim is inseparable from his own literary ambition and his inflated image of his stature as a writer. His
friend John Kirtley, noting how proud Baylebridge was of the work,
remarks upon his aspirations for everlasting fame and his sure belief
that he would join, '*in absentia*, the stream of future lives, that he
would remain with each generation of good Australians until the end
of civilization'.[76] *An Anzac Muster* would help guarantee this immor-
tality. When, late in the book, the Squatter looks forward to the
coming of the supreme soldier-poet who would 'enrich the nation,
and not less the world, with his testimony', the deluded Baylebridge

is not expressing a disinterested hope for the future.[77] He is referring to himself, and to *An Anzac Muster*. Yet his own involvement in the Great War was obscure to say the least. When the war broke out he was in England, where he had published several slim volumes of his poetry between 1908 and 1914. At little more than thirty, he was of fighting age; but he did not enlist in the Australian or any other force, though it does appear that he spent some time in Egypt concurrent with the Gallipoli campaign. Certainly, he tried hard to create an impression of a participation of sorts in the conflict, claiming to have performed some mysterious 'special literary work' for the British Secret Service.[78]

Baylebridge combined his inordinate pride in *An Anzac Muster* with an almost paranoic sensitivity to criticism. His determination to protect and promote the reputation of his writings is pitiably revealed by his distribution of letters of self-praise, letters written under the heading of his own printing press and 'signed managerially in his handwriting though modestly under a name invented for the purpose'.[79] His anxiety is manifested in *An Anzac Muster* in the Author's Preface and the Author's Protest which are tacked on to both ends of the revised edition. (The 'Protest' was in fact not written until 1932, and so is missing from the original work.) Both discourses deal with anticipated and perhaps actual critical attacks through the medium of a fabricated 'friend' who discusses, defends and defines the stories contained therein. The ventriloquist Baylebridge is therefore able to indulge in disguised self-justification. More importantly, the Preface and the Protest set out his strategy and aesthetic goals for *An Anzac Muster*. Describing the work as 'a sort of epic in prose', the friend enunciates Baylebridge's belief that the work transcends the ephemeral contemporaneity that is the abiding limitation of most Australian war literature. 'There is a largeness of outlook here', he asserts; the stories are intended to be read as 'human documents', not mere war narratives.[80]

The grandiloquence of Baylebridge's own vision of *An Anzac Muster* is based on a confidence in the mode of expression he used to relate his idiosyncratic version of the Australian war story. His style is formal and elaborate, designed to dignify the Anzacs themselves, and also to elevate the whole endeavour to that sublime level where nationalistic allegiances and associations are stripped of their tawdry chauvinistic meanings. *An Anzac Muster* is a sustained epic pastiche that is uninhibited by 'trivial' mimetic considerations. Baylebridge totally rejected the *Bulletin* bardic style that was then fashionable; his diction is as lofty as that of Steele Rudd or Henry Lawson is down to earth. Unfortunately Baylebridge's literary adventurism proves his undoing. His extravagantly sonorous prose virtually sabotages the work's credibility not only as a mythopoeic 'lie' but in the wider aesthetic sense applicable to all literature. The reworking of classical styles becomes an exercise in literary showmanship; any heroic message Baylebridge hoped to convey gets lost in the meretriciousness of his chosen medium. The 'final impression' of *An Anzac Muster*, writes Brian Elliott only slightly harshly, 'is rather like the narrative of *Beowulf* being declaimed by a stentorian sergeant to a gathering of high school cadets—bogus, bogus and bogus'.[81]

The Colonel, discussing the import of 'The Cheerful Liar' at the conclusion of its telling, makes the confirmatory remark that, 'To some of our men . . . the redundant thing was the choice thing'.[82] This insight could just as easily be turned on the bloated rhetoric of *An Anzac Muster*. A sample from the Captain's tale, 'Lone Pine', illustrates Baylebridge's characteristic use of obsolete diction in combination with syntax which is insufferably tortuous:

> Like hounds loosed from a leash, off raced our men: with bayonets fixed, up and over the parapet they leapt, and charged. Well might that have stirred the blood up in any man! There raced these men, spat hard upon by fire from every loophole, cut down by machine guns, torn through by a rain of shrapnel, and not one who could but held on. Thick they fell here, thick there; but they cared not. Believe me, it was no hard thing later to see what way they had gone by: heavy-sown it was with men dead.[83]

At least these lines are propelled by a certain primitive rhythmical verve which stimulates the swift ferocity of battle. More unpalatable, perhaps, is the nature of his characters' speech. A major dining at a palatial Cairo hotel chastises three English subalterns, who are sneering at the gaucherie of an Australian Other Ranker falsely uniformed as a captain, with the rhetorical question, 'Is this not an ill jest—to think a man less than his clothes? to find virtue and its converse in the way he takes his food?'[84] Ever his loyal defender, P. R. Stephensen argues that Baylebridge's style is 'startling only in its application to Australian "diggers" at a time when they were being conventionally presented . . . as larrikins'.[85] But the simple fact is that the stilted speech patterns and the periphrastic language he forces his characters to utter sound so unnatural as to be absurd. Baylebridge's Australians are not inclined to call a spade a spade. It is simply inconceivable that one bushman would greet another with

'So your affairs here . . . stand well with the capricious gods?'

—as the Squatter does in greeting his elder brother at the beginning of *An Anzac Muster*.[86] Baylebridge rationalizes the artificiality of his dialogue by alluding to his professed aim of breaking down the barriers of native realism. He insists that his characters are not 'the stock figures of convention', but 'elemental shapes', and that he had imposed 'the illusion of a higher reality' upon 'the everyday and the common'. But his rejection of 'the lesser verisimilitude for the greater' is inconsistent with his other stated aim of presenting the 'authentic' Australian, a figure which he sees as having hitherto been reported 'falsely' in tales professing to express the national spirit. While he does succeed in cleaning much of what he calls 'the viscidity of sentimentalism' from the Digger's popular portrait, what he offers is not the elusive 'real Australian', but a cipher for his own stylistic excess.[87]

In matter as in manner, *An Anzac Muster* is an unusual Australian First World War book. In a more extreme way than Harley Matthews in *Saints and Soldiers*, Baylebridge launches a full-frontal assault on the wholesome image of the Digger promoted by conservative publicists like Oliver Hogue and C. E. W. Bean. Snubbing what he saw as a pusillanimous public morality, Baylebridge aimed to produce a work in which 'the Australian soldier would at once find himself and not some travesty of himself, and least of all a travesty of the sort that pleases mincing quacks and convention-mongers'.[88] Though it is doubtful whether most Diggers would have recognized themselves in *An Anzac Muster*, particularly in so far as their speech is concerned, it does at least remedy the commonly prim idealization of their attitudes and activities. In this lies the value of *An Anzac Muster* as a desirable development in the national war literature.

Some of Baylebridge's stories must have made the puritanical Bean recoil in horror. The Ram's 'The Remount', for example, deals in salacious detail with the chance sexual encounter of a rakish Australian on furlough in Edinburgh and the wife of a local soldier who is away serving in France. Yet whereas the unadorned simplicity of Harley Matthews's style is perfectly attuned to the activities of his uncouth 'Band of Boisterous Boozers', Baylebridge typically goes in for rhetorical overkill in handling the facts of Australian licentiousness. In 'The Remount', an equestrian metaphor for sexual intercourse culminates in the following laboured *double entendre* uttered by the Australian upon hearing that his prospective 'mount' is seeking revenge for her husband's past infidelity:

> 'All this . . . is well put. I'll now make this track out easy enough. And, though a man ride in a saddle the gods lent to another, is the going, then, the harder for that?'[89]

When a soldier and a girl grapple in carnal combat in another of the Ram's tales, 'The Mopoke', the ribaldry is given even freer rein:

> The couple began now to play. Opening his neighbour's blouse, the man bit, now here, now smartly there, on the smooth flesh. She would titter, and then squeal like a pig. It did not stop there either: there was biting enough, and in queer places enough, before he got done with that business. Then they got catching at one another. Then, giving over awhile because of their heat, they sat quiet.[90]

The calculated perversity of Baylebridge's aim and method is crowned by the third in the Ram's lewd trilogy, 'The Three Symbols', in which the rituals of a Cairo brothel as witnessed by two engrossed Diggers are strongly imbued with Christian symbolism. The ablutions of the whores before and after their couplings with their clients, for instance, are linked to an act of baptism.[91] Baylebridge elsewhere implies that Australian profanity cannot in any case be judged according to the strictures of conventional Christianity. To the men of the A.I.F., remarks the Pilot in prefacing his tale 'Bill's Religion', 'the creeds known to the conclaves and synods' were 'dead things'. These they had replaced with a mixture of egocentric idealism and patriotic commitment. Asked the question 'What religion?' at the time of his enlistment, the bushman who is the subject of the tale responds with certainty: 'Australian. That's my religion'. At the interview he rattles off an Australian 'decalogue' which makes explicit the Digger creed, a creed to which pettifogging questions of personal morality simply do not apply. The decalogue begins with the commandments:

> Honour thy country; put no fealty before this.
> Honour those who serve it.
> Honour thyself; for this is the beginning of all honour.[92]

Baylebridge is as much at home in the area of scatology as in sexuality. The Crow's 'Of a Very Private Matter' is an especially Rabelaisian piece about the misadventures which befall the victims of dysentery. Here again, as the title suggests, 'prohibited' material is exploited primarily for its comic potential and its scope for clever wordplay. The accentuation of such a singularly unheroic aspect of the soldier's common experience goes some distance to correct widespread romantic illusions about the way men live and die on the battlefield:

> Lives have not seldom been saved, and lost, too, upon the whim of a man's entrails. Such small affairs as going off to do a known thing, or to wash up, have many times meant the whole difference between life and death.[93]

Baylebridge's naturalistic humanizing of the sentimentalized Digger, however, serves only to advance the superman image that was at the heart of the mainstream legend from the beginning. Virtuosity in battle combined with strong human appetites makes a heady mix. Like the traditional Herculean hero, the Australian soldier in *An Anzac Muster* is 'excessive in everything', both the self-confident strong man and the indefatigable seducer.[94] Contrary to Stephensen's belief that Baylebridge 'contradicted the loutish legend' propagated by popular literature, he actually pays homage to it, differing only in his determination to break through the suppressions that had constrained his predecessors in the field of war writing. The bravado that typically pervades the conversations of soldiers is converted in *An Anzac Muster* into boozy and lecherous one-upmanship. Relaxed by the convivial atmosphere, the raconteurs become their own appreciative audience, both encouraging and trying to eclipse one another. The Ram in particular wins admiration and applause for his story of adultery in 'The Remount'. Guessing that he had spoken from personal experience, the listeners marvel not merely at his narrative skill, but at his own 'part in the affair'.[95]

'Ink-Finger', a chief rival of the Ram in bawdry, strives to outdo the others in 'The Full Battalion'. This tale deals amusingly with the ignoble parades of cases of venereal disease conducted in the Australian camps in Egypt. Venereal disease, the 'salacious scourge that has stalked so largely through the ranks of all armies', does not rate highly on the list of priorities of most publicists of the A.I.F. Baylebridge gives the subject the full uncensored treatment – maybe it was this story which prompted Miles Franklin to remark that *An Anzac Muster* exposed 'the ravages of the fiery crutch as well as of the Fiery Cross'.[96] But 'The Full Battalion' is no cautionary tale. Rather, the men greet it with the amused recognition which bespeaks a kind of communal egotism:

A laugh went round . . . More than one of the company there had a
first-hand acquaintance with the subject; and tales by the score on it,
with the ease that comes of matured knowledge, could have been furnished at short notice.[97]

As Patsy Adam-Smith remarks in *The Anzacs* (1978), venereal disease,
while a stigma to some soldiers, was to many others 'a joke, a comment on their virility, almost another feather in their larrikin head-
dress'.[98] Clearly, Baylebridge is in the business of making – and not
breaking – 'loutish legends'. In his Preface he rejects anticipated
charges of obscenity with a contemptuous shrug of the shoulders,
arguing that his tales were written 'to entertain soldiers, and not for
young women'. But surely this confession is at odds with the grand
universal theme he claims for his work. And his assertion that *An
Anzac Muster* possesses a 'masculinity of tone which makes the reading of it a sure test of the masculinity in the reader' is a boast of
the most crass and limiting kind.[99]

The Digger promoted by Baylebridge is a potent man-of-action
whose appeal to women is magnetic. The vengeful wife of 'The Remount' is aroused almost to the point of orgastic rapture by the close
proximity of her Australian lover: 'Turn down the lamp, you great
savage', she pleads.[1] C. J. Dennis's folksy dictum, 'Lovin'' and
fightin' – there's no more to tell/Concernin' men', is postulated as an
article of national faith in *An Anzac Muster*. Baylebridge is careful
to give the two great male talents equal weight. So as to avoid the
possible charge of wanton poltroonery, he concludes the tale of the
Digger's debauch in 'The Remount' with the provision that the Australian fought afterwards in France – as if feeling it necessary to confirm that the latter was eager and proficient in *both* pursuits. In the
description of the fighting at Lone Pine, sexual aggression and the
lust for combat are brought into even closer correlation. Unpleasant
scenes of 'thrusting' Australian bayonets 'twisting' and 'turning' and
being 'wrenched' out of a 'crush of flesh' as they 'plough' a 'stayless
passage' through 'dark and stinking' Turkish trenches, create a canvas
more connotative of a pack rape than a hand-to-hand military
encounter.[2]

Baylebridge's evident attraction to the Dionysian type is no aberration. Critics have long noted the Nietzschean echoes that resound
in both his prose and his poetry, T. Inglis Moore going as far as
to dub him the 'Australian Nietzsche'.[3] In *National Notes* (1913),
published just one year before the outbreak of war, he promoted a
vitalistic figure which, by way of the Greek demigods, is strikingly

akin to the *Ubermensch*. Wilful, unrestrained individualism is the key to his nationalistic vision. Anticipating his assertion in *An Anzac Muster* that the Australians on Gallipoli 'strove like gods', Baylebridge in one of the many aphorisms in *National Notes* opined that, 'Every man, by the inviolable law of his own being, is an adventurer, a warrior, a god'. In line with what he saw as the direct connection between the intellectual, artistic and physical greatness of ancient Greece and its participation in a series of bloody wars, he presciently argued that Australian 'aggression abroad' would act as a national tonic: 'The sooner Australia wins her spurs in battle, the better in every way for her national being'. But would Australia be ready to take on the world before the implementation of Baylebridge's proposed programme of eugenics to raise the quality of the race? Baylebridge's *Weltanschauung* as set down in *National Notes* reaches a final nadir of absurdity with the ludicrous vision of 'the overrunning of Earth by Australians, strong, hot-necked, natural men'. Varying his heroic physiognomy in *An Anzac Muster,* he replaced the 'hot necks' of the rumbustious antipodean conquerors with 'primitive jaws and the straight-looking eyes that turn aside for nothing known to man'.[4]

In the Epilogue to *An Anzac Muster* Baylebridge offers a critique of the Australian performance in 'winning her spurs'. The Squatter, acting now as a sort of intertextual mouthpiece for the reader, has returned to his own property some weeks after the gathering. Reviewing his recent 'communion' with the Anzac chroniclers, he believes himself to be 'a better man' for his contact with men who had 'so marvellously proved themselves', men whose 'self-consciousness was small', but whose 'racial consciousness was anything but'.[5] Some lip-service is paid to the freedom-fighting knight-errantry of the Diggers, who had ventured abroad so as to preserve the fundamental human liberties endangered in Western Europe. Like Beowulf's quest to Denmark to free the land of monsters, and like the Greek expedition to Troy to recover the abducted Helen, the A.I.F. was on an errand of deliverance. But as the Squatter's meditations centre on Gallipoli in particular, this hotchpotch of heroic notions coalesces into what has been called 'a long passage of Nietzschean nationalism'.[6] In retrospect the Gallipoli undertaking might well be regarded as a calamitously wasteful undertaking; but Baylebridge does not like dwelling on 'inane facts'. This literary alchemist transforms a futile military defeat into a priceless heroic legacy bequeathed to the young nation:

If Australia had been given an impossible task on that battleground, had she not reaped it in the first-fruits of her valour, of her resolution, of all her best qualities – had she not gathered from it, even at a price so bitter, a glory great enough to herald her to the world, great enough to confirm her place in it? If the affair was a tragic error, in which all the virtues of heroic men were pitted against the impossible, and, indeed, not seldom achieved this, if a final triumph was betrayed, as many hold, by the irresolution of lesser souls, not Australian – well, and what then? Out of that high grappling with the impossible we had plucked things richer than victories in the field: we had proved greatly our blood in it; we had set, thus, an immortal seal upon our race.[7]

No wonder 'Inky' Stephensen, interned during much of the Second World War because of his involvement in the quasi-fascist Australia First movement, was such a champion of *An Anzac Muster*. Baylebridge's position on armed conflict is basically analogous to that of Nietzsche's Zarathustra, who, in response to the maxim, 'a good cause halloweth even war', retorted that 'a good war halloweth any cause'.[8]

Paul Fussell's discussion of the fictionalization of the war experience in *The Great War and Modern Memory* alludes to Aristotle's view that a poet is 'one who has mastered the art of telling lies successfully'.[9] On the evidence of *An Anzac Muster*, at least, it cannot be said that William Baylebridge is a particularly convincing 'liar'. One tends to concur with the assessment of those detractors resentfully cited in the Author's Protest, who call it 'mendacious', 'over-confident', and 'too rich a fancy'. Baylebridge's euphuistic grandeur of phrase is inapplicable to his essentially parochial subject. Indeed, even the claim that his sophisticated approach raised the work above 'transient topicality and chauvinistic fustian' cannot be accepted without some reservation. The cocksure nationalism of stories such as 'Lone Pine' and 'Bill's Religion' remind us of Bean at his most pedestrian – as does his requisitioning of foreign military praise (snuck in amid the philosophical bluster and exalted tones of the Squatter's final thoughts) in order to buttress his heroic theme.[10]

Nevertheless it is true that, even in its obscure original edition, *An Anzac Muster* became something of an 'underground' Australian classic. For all its faults, it deserves this status – it is an often hugely entertaining work which both extended and cultivated the restricted terrain covered by Australian war writing. Baroque and bizarre, the book remains, to borrow E. Morris Miller's appropriately ambiguous assessment, 'an outstanding production of war fiction in Australia'.[11]

A HALF-HEARTED HERESY: *FLESH IN ARMOUR*

Flesh in Armour, which won for Leonard Mann the Australian Literature Society's Gold Medal for the best book of 1932, is often regarded as being the finest work of fiction about the First A.I.F.[12] There being very few Australian Great War novels of real quality, it is only marginally unjust to Leonard Mann to suggest that this accolade has been won largely by default. Regrettably, most Australian novelists who were technically well-equipped to fictionalize the war did not fight in it, and so tended to remain silent. For someone like Joseph Furphy, who had died in 1912, the war had of course come much too late; for young novelists who started to make their mark after the war, such as Xavier Herbert (born 1901), it had occurred too early. Others, such as Martin Boyd and Frederic Manning, were expatriates who fought with the British Army, and confined their fictions to that military organization. Another novelist who also fought with the British but wrote about the Australians, Frank Dalby Davison, opted for the short story form rather than the full-length novel. Vance Palmer, who was in the vanguard of the resurgence of Australian fiction in the 1930s (and an advocate of the spirit of literary nationalism to which war literature was an important contribution), was perhaps a likely heroic war novelist. Palmer, however, was essentially a pacifist, and campaigned vigorously against the two conscription referenda in 1916 and 1917. His late enlistment in the A.I.F. in March 1918 meant that he saw no combat: his troopship, indeed, arrived in England three days after the Armstice.[13] Though Palmer did not attempt a war novel in the strict sense, he tackled the problem of military service in *Daybreak* (1932), which portrays the psychological collapse and eventual suicide of a decorated returned soldier afflicted by war neurosis.

Leonard Mann, a barrister who worked for a time in the Commonwealth Arbitration Court and then for employers' organizations, in industry and finally in farming, was essentially an amateur writer. His literary career, as he himself described it in an aptly titled article, 'A Double Life', was 'sporadic'.[14] He followed *Flesh in Armour*, his first book, with six novels and the occasional volume of verse over the next half-century until his death in 1981. Unable to secure a publisher for *Flesh in Armour* either in England or Australia, Mann decided to bring the book out himself, and it was in this limited edition that it remained until the more favourable climate of the Second World War, during which Robertson and Mullens published it by arrangement with the Commonwealth Literary Fund. As is attested by the Australian Literature Society medal, the novel met with immediate critical recognition, but even then it was refused by Angus & Robertson on the basis that it could not be put 'into everyone's hands'. What an odd assessment – the entire first edition had quickly cleared, and the journal *All About Books* recorded the novel in the best-seller listings, albeit in the 'Novels for Popular Reading' section rather than as one of the 'Novels of Literary Merit'.[15]

1932 was a good year to publish a novel which, as *Flesh in Armour* does, rejoices in the uniqueness of the Australian character. Though the Depression had constricted the literary market, the general gloom had turned people's hearts and minds back to the inspirational days of warlike achievement, to the golden Gallipoli days of April 1915, and to the European summer of 1918, when the unstoppable A.I.F. had smashed through the Hindenberg Line and 'won the war'. Importantly, Mann's novel appeared at a time when Australian literary nationalism was beginning to regain some lost momentum. Mann saw his literary generation as being the heir to the pre-war tradition fostered by the *Bulletin*. Late in his life he wrote of feeling at that period a part of 'a considerable and palpable body of serious Australian writers, drawn together by a natural common feeling, who . . . were conscious of the separate identity of the Australian people and [who] were not unaware that what they were largely about was to show their people to itself'.[16]

The timing of the appearance of *Flesh in Armour*, then, was both fortuitous and appropriate. Certainly, Mann was not exploiting a revival of public sentiment about the war. Injured in a bomb explosion at Passchendaele in October 1917, Mann suffered a 'trauma, physical and mental', from which it took virtually the rest of his life to recover. Thus, in his specific case, Marjorie Barnard was speaking the literal truth when she observed that the tardy appearance of many novels about the Great War was due to there being 'a period of shocked silence' before potential soldier-writers could become articulate.[17] The depth of Mann's war experience and the lengthy period of gestation before it was transformed into fiction undeniably contribute a certain plausibility to *Flesh in Armour* as an account of Western Front warfare. William Baylebridge tried to hide his ignorance of war behind a dazzling stylistic veneer. By contrast, Mann's generally subdued and understated style (which, admittedly, tends toward stodginess) and his fastidious attention to detail (which likewise is liable to become tedious) proclaim his intention to give a

studied, authentic picture of the conflict. 'Authenticity', or one of
its synonyms, is the description habitually favoured by commentators on the novel. Marjorie Barnard recommends the book's 'authentic
ring of truth', as does Cecil Hadgraft; H. M. Green sees the novel
as 'lifelike', John Laird as 'realistic' and 'objective', and Miles Franklin praises its 'quiet realism'. When a debate raged in the pages of
All About Books over *Flesh in Armour*'s alleged immorality in depicting
the 'sordid mentality' and 'unsavoury morals' of some Australian soldiers, a veteran leapt to its defence, ingenuously calling it 'a fair and
accurate portrayal' which brought back the war 'in a way no other
book has done'.[18]

Mann's adherence to the disciplines of realism suggests that his
affinities lie rather more with the British and European Great War
literary model than with the heroic Australian genre. The novel can
be seen as heavily revisionist, even heretical, correcting the obsessive idealism of so much Australian war writing. Mann tells the fundamentally tragic story of an introverted A.I.F. infantryman, Frank
Jeffreys, who is isolated and psychologically crushed by the intense
pressures of active combat and by his temperamental incapacity to
match the intrepid warrior-ideal he sees in action around him. Jeffreys
nurtures a developing sense of personal unworthiness which he
resolves by committing suicide on the battlefield in the last days of
the war. In character, personal predicament and the manner of his
death, Jeffreys's closest literary relation is George Winterbourne,
Richard Aldington's protagonist in *Death of a Hero*. But whereas Aldington screams his theme of war waste and futility with all the anger
he can muster, adopting a tone which is often as hysterical as the
unhinged Winterbourne himself, Mann plots the process of Jeffreys's
crack-up with a careful precision, which, if relentless, is restrained.

The First A.I.F. no doubt contained within its ranks many warriors as unhappy and as ineffective as Frank Jeffreys, but they seldom
appear in the literature. Several things proclaim his singularity as
the hero of an Australian war book. When we are first introduced
to him as he strolls about the Tower of London while on leave, we
are immediately directed to observe his 'perpetually anxious look'.
Shining self-confidence, that stamp of the classical Digger visage,
is missing. Suffering has evidently superseded swagger. When he
laughs at the comment of his companion, he does so 'in a spasmodic,
painfully self-conscious way' which is antithetical to the wild, Homeric mirth usually associated with the Diggers both in and out of
battle.[19] A former schoolteacher with socialistic political leanings and

a strong aesthetic sense, Jeffreys fits uneasily into the broad character types promoted by the Australian war publicists. He is neither a conservative, flag-waving imperialist nor an urban larrikin, and he is most certainly not a rough-and-ready bushman. To complicate matters further, he is also a teetotaller. For all their reinforcement of the legend of Australian eccentricity, very few Australian war writers were prepared to contemplate such renegade behaviour.

What really makes Frank Jeffreys so different is his almost complete lack of personal courage and self-esteem. More inclined to duck for cover than to dart after the foe, he is a member of that most rare species of Australian fictional warriors—he has a poor opinion of himself. With an intensity reminiscent not only of George Winterbourne but also of that other exemplar of the introverted, oppressed modern soldier, Ford's Christopher Tietjens, Jeffreys is a 'worrier'. He is burdened by thoughts and incapable of effective action. He thinks too much to be a good soldier. Anxiety, as with Winterbourne and Tietjens, is his habitual condition.[20] His tentative hold upon his self-control is lost when, in a clearly autobiographical incident, he is caught by a bomb blast at Passchendaele. Buried in 'the thick stinking ooze' of the apocalyptic Flanders landscape, he emerges unscathed physically, but with his nerve broken, weeping uncontrollably while his horrified mates try to conceal their embarrassment. In a similar circumstance in *Parade's End*, Tietjens emerges from the symbolic mire reborn, transmogrified from a meek victim of social and political corruption into 'a man' at last willing to take charge of his own destiny. No such deliverance is afforded Frank Jeffreys. He is paralysed by fear in all future combat, and his self-image is further eroded by the 'derision' he senses in his comrades.[21] He allows himself to become a military leper.

Jeffreys had always possessed what Mann's narrator calls an 'impulse toward isolation'. Early in the novel, when his battalion is making an improvised camp somewhere on the Menin Road, he wanders off alone, 'hither and thither in a sort of dementia'. He curses his 'wretched solitariness of mood', which prevents him from joining the others and causes him to transgress the Digger creed of mateship. Seeing himself as both cowardly and incompetent—and therefore, according to the A.I.F. doctrine outlined by Bean, unworthy—he eventually decides to throw in his corporal's stripes. In the very next battle, he lingers in a trench while his companion makes a fatal charge at the enemy. This final disgrace delivers the *coup de grâce* to his failing self-esteem. He had 'played the coward, deserting his mate'.[22] He walks along a trench, halts, and draws the pin of a Mills bomb pressed against his chest. (George Winterbourne ends his life much more cleanly by deliberately exposing himself to enemy machine-gun fire.) Jeffreys therefore commits perhaps the ultimate military sin. Mann records his demise tersely, with an admirable lack of melodrama. And with an unmistakable message for those believers in the idea that all death on the battlefield is in the nature of a noble sacrifice . . .

> Jack Skipton, when, after the explosion, he came along to look around and saw the body in the trench, imagined that a small sudden shell had got poor Frank when he had gone off for a crap. He called to Harry Mullane, who came around the corner and stood alongside his officer . . . The body was very much mutilated. The chest was torn away and the head half off. When Harry's eyes wandered for a moment, they caught sight of the lever of the bomb. With a casual seeming movement he covered it with his foot and ground it into the mud. . . Between them the survivors made a cross for the grave, on which, as there were no identification marks, Harry carved, "Frank Jeffreys, Corporal, Nth. Bn., A.I.F. Killed in action."[23]

The source of Frank's trauma had not stemmed from the battlefield alone. In love, as in war, he is a rank loser such as one rarely encounters in Australian war fiction. While on leave or convalescing in Britain he engages in a scarifyingly unhappy love affair with an English girl, Mary Hatton, which proves as damaging to his fragile ego as his flirtation with the martial life on the Western Front. Here again, Mann appears to have been influenced by *Death of a Hero* and *Parade's End*, the two major British fictional attempts to correlate the world politico-military crisis with private domestic despair. As with Winterbourne and Tietjens, troublesome private affairs compound the agonies Jeffreys has to endure in combat. Out of a combination of sexual repression, timidity and chastity, Frank and Mary—a lugubrious couple whose scenes together are best described as mawkish—do not consummate their relationship. Frank asks her to wait for him until after the war has ended; but the romance is thwarted by a fellow member of his platoon, Charl Bentley, who had a fleeting sexual encounter with Mary while himself on leave in London. While guilt gnaws at the woman, the dawning awareness of Bentley's intimacy with her eats away at Jeffreys, complicating and magnifying his battle neurosis. Like Winterbourne, he lives in 'a sort of double nightmare—the nightmare of the War and the nightmare of his own life. . . . His personal life became intolerable because of the War, and the War became intolerable because of his own life'.[24]

Uncomplicated and little given to self-examination, Charl Bentley is the antithesis of Frank Jeffreys, and his smooth progress from military and sexual immaturity to seasoned manhood contrasts with the gradual breakdown of his antagonist. Bentley's ego is as robust as that of Jeffreys is diseased. He had snared Mary as a kind of trophy of war. Believing that one brief sexual skirmish had given him a proprietorial hold over her, he is bitter at news of her developing friendship with Frank, even though their relationship had long concluded and he had stopped corresponding with her: 'It was the shock to his vanity which hurt. She had chucked him for the corporal. She had made a fool of him'. Eventually the simmering resentment between the two men erupts into open violence, with most of their comrades roaring encouragement for Bentley. It appeared to them that the 'bastard' Jeffreys had done Charl out of his 'bit of skirt', a 'mean', 'indescribably base', and 'putrid' act.[25] The squabbles of soldiers over women are as old as war and war literature; this particular fracas has the quarrel between Achilles and Agamemnon over possession of Briseis as a venerable literary context. But the incident is far from heroic. The crude allegiances of the onlookers and their inability to recognize the depth of Frank's genuine feelings for Mary connote an attack on the coarseness of soldierly sensibilities and on the idea of heroic conquest itself. Moreover, the conflict between Jeffreys and Bentley makes *Flesh in Armour* a major statement of the fundamental opposition of the sensitive misfit and the conforming man-of-action in Australian literature of the First World War. The weight of Mann's own sympathies being directed to Jeffreys, the novel casts a shadow on the dominant A.I.F. philosophy of masculine self-assertion.

Mann, however, is the victim of his own iconoclasm. By so pointedly making Jeffreys as inadequate as a lover as he is inept as a soldier, he in effect embraces the same dubious and archaic connection between sexual activity and military prowess made by Baylebridge in *An Anzac Muster*. Only the emphasis is different. Furthermore, as if to compensate for his listless, morose central character, Mann conceives a host of heroes who meet the accepted Australian standards of versatility and capability. Mann's cross-section of orthodox antipodean manhood comprises the dashing, patrician Colonel Gilderoy; the irrepressible 'old dag' Johnny Wright, who has the habit of going on benders every so often; Ted Marshall, 'the roughest and most genuine diamond', a Sydney wharfie; the two bushmen Dingo

Williams and Jack Smith, the latter a man who hails from Kelly country and who appropriately finds his military niche as a sniper; sports-
men such as Blue McIntosh, a celebrated footballer; the classically
untamable Digger, Artie Fethers, a Geelong Grammar reprobate who
delights in subverting authority; and the articulate university graduate
who often appears to act as Mann's spokesman, Harry Mullane.[26]
Most of these characters are barely developed sketches only, flitting
into the action when there is a German to be bayoneted, a *vin blanc*
to be scoffed, or a wisecrack to be made. More detailed treatment
is afforded Private Jim Blount, who functions as something of a buffer
between Jeffreys and his *bête noire* Bentley. Like Frederic Manning's
enigmatic Private Bourne, the 'sombrely magnificent' Blount is a man
of superior sensibility (with literary tastes which run to Shakespearean
tragedy, Cellini, and Byron's *Don Juan*) who declines promotion because he values the freedom to express his own individuality. An
ex-Anzac with a bush background, Blount is 'enriched', in a vastly
more profound manner than Charl Bentley, by his war experience:
'In the midst of war he had made a discovery. He had discovered
himself'.[27] By no mere coincidence, Blount's confirmed self-assurance
is paralleled by his emergence as a superlative warrior. Fittingly, it
is his superb self-sacrifice which shames Jeffreys into suicide.

Flesh in Armour is a confused and confusing novel. Leonard Mann
bravely commits an act of literary heresy by having as his protagonist
an Australian soldier who simply *cannot fight*, then has second
thoughts by throwing into the narrative a plethora of Diggers who
can, and brilliantly. He tries to unite the orchestration of Jeffreys's
disintegration amid the foul mud, the gorged rats and the 'splattered
red mincemeat' which comprise the classical iconography of the
pacifist Great War book, with tempestuous Homeric scenes of avenging Diggers wielding, with 'no beg pardons', the ever-faithful bayonet.[28] It is an impossible marriage, one which grievously damages
the coherence of Mann's vision. Inconceivably, even the neurasthenic,
war-hating Jeffreys is himself occasionally transported by ecstatic
visions of glory. During a military parade . . .

> there arose in Corporal Jeffrey's [*sic*] breast a sort of exaltation. His throat
> for a minute constricted painfully and his eyes glinted. The Australians—
> the Australians. Ah, if the five divisions had been there, company on
> company. But they were scattered into different corps. They should all
> be one—one corps, one and indivisible in body as they were in spirit.
> Were the Tommies afraid of the new nations?
>   . . . Heads up, while the bands blared Tara—tara—They were the

Aussies—the Diggers, the Diggers—tara—tara— the Diggers—the Diggers—tara—tara.[29]

The gathering together of the Australian divisions into one homogenous 'Australian Corps', the consummation of national consciousness craved by Jeffreys above, was effected in late 1917. It provides the author with an opportunity to interpolate hubristic assertions of national prowess which sit most uneasily with the theme of protest Jeffreys apparently embodies. The unified A.I.F. impatiently awaiting battle during the summer lull of 1918 is described by means of an extended epic simile:

> There was thus ready for the former civilian, Monash, and Rawlinson, his leader, and Foch Generalissimo, a weapon of magnificent cold temper, hammered through the fires of many an engagement and battle, experienced and skilled in warfare more than any others, dangerous so that some of those who were to use it were almost afraid of it themselves. Frank Jeffreys, returned from blighty and became a particle of it, knew, in his own personal thrill, the spirit and morale of the whole . . . not without prescience of its high purpose . . . its flash and clang in the crisis of war would be like a thunderbolt and forked lightning through the storm.[30]

The startling destructiveness of the force when it is finally unleashed upon the Germans is celebrated in a series of chapters grouped together under the title 'The Path of the Thunderbolt'. To presage the swathe cut through the enemy lines by this corporate Achilles, Mann makes liberal use of historical documentation, repeating verbatim General Monash's hortatory message to the troops on the eve of the great Somme battle of 8 August, *Der Schwarze Tag* of Ludendorff's faltering army. Monash's communiqué highlights the fact that all five Australian divisions were to participate together in an important operation for the first time. He exhorts the men to 'rise to so great an occasion . . . for the sake of Australia', and wishes them 'a glorious and decisive victory, the story of which will re-echo throughout the world, and live for ever in the history of our homeland'. While the ever-sardonic Diggers undercut such pomposity with comments like, 'Anyone'd think . . . that no one was going to be stonkered', Mann then goes on to illustrate just how wonderfully the Diggers do indeed rise to the occasion. The potential for the bolstering of the anti-war theme invested in Frank Jeffreys is abandoned in favour of trite publicity. In the succession of battles which follow 8 August, the depleted Australian force—driven by its commander

Monash to the brink of its endurance—advances toward and then through the Hindenberg Line with a fatalism described as 'baleful and ferocious'.[31]

The storming of the key German position on the 'impregnable' Mont St Quentin, in which the A.I.F. was opposed by a division of the élite Prussian Guards, is given an unreservedly heroic treatment. But even the architect of the operation, Monash, must have been disappointed with Mann's fictional version of it. The great commander considered that the exploit provided the substance for 'a classic in military literature'.[32] But Mann muffs his chance, resorting to prosy acclamation and vulgar hyperbole. Such terms of praise as 'one of the greatest feats of arms of the whole war' and 'the venture was desperate almost to madness' more befit a work of popular history than one of serious fiction. The unrestrained use of the adjective 'magnificent' in relation to acts of Australian valour seems particularly tasteless in a novel whose main action revolves around an individual who is incapable of forceful action, except to end his own life.[33] The reader in confusion begins to wonder whether the author's real purpose is to show Jeffreys up, to disgrace him.

The story of Frank Jeffreys's private reaction against war is thus consumed by an affirmation of Australian military *savoir-faire*. Narrow pride in specifically Australian attributes and performance also subverts the philosophical theme Mann introduces into the narrative and then virtually disregards altogether. In the central metaphor of the novel, he had striven to make a Christian statement about the universality of the Great War tragedy by meditating upon the sanctity of each individual soul:

> Where, then, was Christ? Not in the nations, their groups, their parties, or their armies, but, if anywhere, in the hearts of these men . . . Nationality, politics, religion were superimposed on each human being like an outer covering, making them seem, for the purposes of the world, in spite of the inner individual man, something which they were not . . . if Christ should exist anywhere, He must exist in that flesh and soul within . . . There, Christ must be in each; not in nations and sects, parties and armies, but in the breasts of the soldiers, in the flesh within the armour . . .[34]

But far from ecumenically insisting upon the preciousness of every individual's 'flesh within the armour', whatever the nationality, Mann typically flaunts the superiority of the Australian 'cut' over all others. *Flesh in Armour* is a long celebration of Australianness. Like Baylebridge before him, Mann sought to give Australians an image of themselves. But his presentation of what he constantly terms 'distinctive nationality' differs greatly from that chosen by Baylebridge. The artificial eloquence of *An Anzac Muster* may be 'wretched and even repulsive', Brian Elliott has observed, but 'at least . . . we are not reminded at every turn that this is the land of the Kangaroo, the Koala and the Kookaburra'.[35] Mann, on the other hand, works into his fiction national symbols and motifs of the most plainly popular kind. Jeffreys takes Mary Hatton to see the Australian actor Oscar Asche in a West End production of 'Chu Chin Chow'; later, they gaze at the kangaroos at London Zoo. An athletics meeting in a French town (a debased version of the Homeric games) is turned into a toast to Australian sporting abilities and gambling habits. And then there is the Australian idiom, rendered indulgently by Mann. Whereas the speech of Baylebridge's soldiers is often absurdly inflated, Mann goes to the other extreme, exploiting the vernacular to such a degree that whole passages of *Flesh in Armour* become virtually incoherent. Here two soldiers grippingly discuss the news of impending battle:

"Dinkum?"
"My oath."
"Christ!"[36]

Tedious vindications of Australian battle discipline and commendations of the classless nature of the A.I.F., after the manner of the *Official History*, further corrupt Mann's fiction. And just as Charl Bentley's 'distinctive Australian nationality' is 'nurtured by his resentment towards this cold alien England' when on London leave, so Mann is at his most stridently chauvinistic when dealing with the Diggers in the Motherland. On occasion, as in his account of the social visit of a group of Australians to the ancestral home of an English noblewoman, the clash of national attitudes and conventions provides the source of much good-humoured comedy, adeptly handled. More often, however, Mann disseminates through his characters diatribes against the British High Command and acid references to the incapability of the Tommies. The Australian military uprising of September 1918 against the threatened amalgamation of battle-weakened A.I.F. battalions provides an attractive context for the expression of anti-English feeling; it also occasions a celebration of the spirit of men who are 'disruptive of the whole hierarchical spirit in which authority was presumed to flow'.[37] Mann's labours to highlight the raffishness and the sense of humour of the Australians also confounds his attempt to philosophize about war. The exposed skeleton of a human hand sticking out of a trench wall – a standard image of the Western Front horror – is duly described as 'Neither Fritz, nor Tommy, nor Poilu, nor Digger, nothing but a string of bones'. But then along the trench comes the effervescent Ted Marshall, jauntily claiming the booty that is every hero's privilege:

> Ted Marshall squeezed his way past the others. "Wish us luck, mate," he said, and he laughed as he gave the thing a hearty grip. It came to pieces in his fist, and, putting the thumb into his pocket for a souvenir, he squeezed back again to his position in the queue.[38]

In the concluding chapter of the novel the fissure that had gradually developed in the fiction becomes a gaping crack. While recognizing, through the meditations of Harry Mullane as he leaves the battlefield for the last time, that the war had shown that Australians were 'a people', Mann appears to wash his hands of the notion of warlike activity as the apogee of national endeavour, proposing instead the quieter pursuits of art and science:

> The A.I.F. – was it not . . . the first manifestation that a spirit had begun to work in the material mass? How long before there was some other sign, some manifestations of a small creative ferment? Once he had read some speech of Pasteur's. Only by science, letters, art, can a people become great. . . .[39]

Yet, in the very next paragraph, Mann inexplicably brings the narrative to a close with a prolix recapitulation of Australia's role in the 1918 Offensive, and furnishes a list of glowing statistics which point to the disproportionate percentage of territory, prisoners and weapons taken by the all-conquering A.I.F. divisions. This boastful peroration occurs a mere two pages after the pathos of Frank Jeffreys's self-destruction. Such a final reliance on the incorporation of the coarsest of historical strands into his fictional fabric indicates not merely Mann's uncertain control over his material, but a curious lack of faith in the quality of his own perceptions. *Flesh in Armour* goes from being an incisive critique of the Australian heroic ethos to a mathematical vindication of the same. Mann tried to be a literary nonconformist; but in the end, his heart just was not in it. Mann was too much of a nationalist for his own good as a writer. His novel has a certain integrity, however; its very earnestness, its insights, values and enthusiasms put the screaming opportunism of the wartime propagandists to shame.

THE EQUESTRIAN EPIC: *THE WELLS OF BEERSHEBA*

The audacious charge of Australian Light Horsemen on the heavily defended Palestinian village Beersheba on 31 October 1917 affords fit material for the publicist. For a serious writer with Frank Dalby Davison's naturally nationalistic inclinations, it is even dangerously seductive subject-matter. Yet his novella *The Wells of Beersheba* is enduring publicity of the very best kind. Davison picked up one small seed of the national war effort, transplanted it into a meticulously crafted fictional structure encompassing a mere nine thousand words, and produced a credible model of human striving. The story is affirmative and even celebratory, but only rarely does it lapse into an outmoded rhetoric liable, these days, to estrange rather than engage the sympathies of all but the most jingoistic readers.

Frank Dalby Davison did not fight at Beersheba; he was not even a member of the A.I.F. He was the son of Fred Davison, a former editor of *The Advance Australia* (the voice of the Australian Natives' Association), who had taken his family to live in the United States in 1908. When war broke out, the twenty-one-year-old Davison was engaged as a ship's printer aboard a British vessel plying the tourist and trade route from New York to the Caribbean. Excited English expatriates from all over the Americas had congregated in New York to offer their services to the homeland, and upon his return to that city Davison was caught up in the tide of sentimental feeling for the Old Country.[40] Unable to enlist in the United States, he was sent up to Halifax, Nova Scotia, by British officials, from where he acted as an escort for a load of several hundred prospective cavalry horses being transported to England. Once in Liverpool, he joined the British cavalry (the Queen's Bays), and saw action on the Somme and at Arras in 1915, before fighting in the trenches as an infantryman. Not given to post-war boasting about his prowess, Davison was to claim that he was awarded his Corporal's stripes for 'saluting under shell-fire'.[41] Like deracinated Australians in war novels such as Mary Grant Bruce's *Captain Jim* and Frederic Manning's *Her Privates We*, Davison repined at his displacement in the British Army. Fighting with foreigners, he later claimed, made him 'homesick' for the Australian forces, and *The Wells of Beersheba* was 'in the last resort an expression of that nostalgia, notwithstanding that it did not appear until years afterward'. A possible reason for the book's belated appearance was its author's self-consciousness that, not having served in the A.I.F., he did not really belong to the local military tradition and hence was ill-equipped, even unfit, to write about it. As it was, he tackled the Beersheba story only because no actual participant seemed willing or able to do so. No grand literary enterprise like the *Official History*, *The Wells of Beersheba* saw the light of day as an Angus & Robertson half-crown Christmas gift suggestion, 'something less than a book, but something more than a Christmas card'.[42]

That the Light Horse charge at Beersheba had not been pounced on earlier by either a memoirist or a non-combatant with ambitions in the legend-making line is surprising. As a military feat, it possesses all the mythopoeic potential of Gallipoli, with the bonus that it was in fact a glittering victory. The scenario seems irresistible: sunset falling fast—the dire necessity to capture the town and its water-wells or have a huge desert army perish through thirst—the strategic imperative of winning Beersheba, the fortunes of the British infantry at Gaza back down the coast hinging upon it—the dogged, day-long resistance of the fortified Turkish troops—and, at the last moment, the outrageously reckless headlong gallop of the Australians, their bayonets extended in their hands . . . the Turks' astonishment and panic . . . the brief bloody battle at their trenches . . . the swift Australian triumph . . . an army is saved . . . a town is captured . . . a vital victory is achieved against all expectations. It is little wonder that the director Charles Chauvel, nephew of the Australian commander at Beersheba, made the charge pivotal in his tribute to the Light Horse, *Forty Thousand Horsemen* (1940), the film which did much to boost the national morale during the Second World War.

Before Davison, Ion Idriess was the only writer of note to deal with Beersheba, and his account in *The Desert Column* is extremely brief. Idriess was a Light Horseman who had participated in the operations around the town, but he was not involved in the final blitz. He apportions the incident a meagre six pages out of his book's total of some three hundred and eighty, and his rendering of the charge itself encompasses little more than a single page. Not surprisingly, H. S. Gullett gives the Battle of Beersheba the full heroic treatment in his volume of the *Official History*. Gullett sees the equestrian assault in sporting terms. 'These Australian countrymen had never in all their riding at home ridden in a race like this', he declares. (In *Seven Pillars of Wisdom* T. E. Lawrence uses a similar metaphor to illustrate the relentless attacking qualities of the Light Horsemen, saying they 'saw the campaign as a point-to-point, with Damascus the post'.)[43] Like Bean, Gullett employs the Homeric epithet 'great-hearted' to define the Australians' courage, and to corroborate his adulatory account of the charge he refers to the ironic praise of an unnamed German officer: 'They are not soldiers at all; they are madmen'.[44]

Though he had not personally participated in it, Davison was well qualified to write about the mounted desert war. He had ridden on the battlefields of France, and, importantly, he had an intimate knowledge of dry-country conditions. Upon his return to Australia at the end of the war, he had taken possession of a soldier settlement block in southern Queensland, a venture which after four years of hard labour was aborted by drought. A great deal of historical research into the Beersheba battle provided depth to his own related experiences. He later admitted that he had read enough on the campaign to write a 'treatise' on it. The meticulousness of his research is confirmed by the fact that veterans of the charge who read *The Wells of Beersheba* thought that its author must have been a comrade.[45] In fact Davison does his homework a little too well, leading him to commit acts of literary petty larceny. His description of Beersheba village, for example, bears an uncomfortably striking resemblance to that of the official historian. As Davison pictures Beersheba:

> Its houses sprawled widely apart; except for white mosque and high minaret, it might have been a township in the Australian bush.

A decade earlier, Gullett had written:

> As the Anzacs first saw it . . . it had, except for its new mosque built by the Germans, the appearance of a struggling township in the pastoral country in Australia.[46]

But *The Wells of Beersheba* is not mere potted history. Davison achieves his major aesthetic aim, which was 'to clothe literal fact with those imaginative truths of which historians do not speak'. His success in bringing the Beersheba episode to literary life depends on his ability to lend the story a fictional vitality of its own rather than on a simple restructuring of 'the facts' in accordance with established national myth. That Davison was well aware that he was dealing with more than a mundane desert scrap is indicated by his choice of 'A Light Horse Legend' as a subtitle. Perhaps out of deference to the kind of book he had written as well as to the battle itself, he changed this subtitle to 'An Epic of the Australian Light Horse' when he revised the text for its republication in 1947. Davison maintained that *The Wells of Beersheba*, despite its brevity, is 'not really a short story', but 'a short prose epic'.[47]

'Epic' is indeed the correct generic term for *The Wells of Beersheba*, since it reveals most of the attributes and preoccupations of the form. The work 'includes history', as Ezra Pound would say; it contains that kernel of historical truth which is intrinsic to the genre. Secondly, *The Wells of Beersheba* is an admitted 'memorial' to a chivalric mode of warfare which had been superseded, and therefore it commemorates a closed chapter of Australia's military achievement.[48] As such, it has the epical intention to enshrine national tradition. Thirdly, its characters are men who in the true manner of epic heroes exhibit exceptional qualities of courage and communal faith and identity. But while the book is written in nationalistic praise of a certain race at a specific point in time, it manages to avoid temporal parochial concerns. As the epic should, it universalizes the experiences of individuals in a period of extreme personal testing. Finally and perhaps most relevantly, the narrative is related in an elevated ceremonial style meant to dignify past events. As Harry Heseltine has said in discussing the 'loftiness' of Davison's utterance, 'The eloquence of *The Wells of Beersheba* seeks its sanction through an appeal to one of the great formal traditions of literature'.[49] These three attributes help to inflate the book's diminutiveness—it is, after all, hardly larger than some of Bean's footnotes—and to raise it to the status of an epic. Its long historical perspective combined with a certain visionary immediacy add the necessary comprehensiveness. 'Epic proportions' are in any case 'not a matter of length or size, but of weight'.[50] In all Australian war literature, only the *Official History* manages to blend 'weight', or a kind of epic grandeur, with an imposing dimensional massiveness.

Within the book's narrow confines, Frank Dalby Davison develops a narrative which is tightly structured in four sections, but which also is expansive and even panoramic in effect. He prefaces the story with a succinct 'Historical Note' placing the events to follow in the context of the brilliantly successful war waged by Lieutenant-General Sir Harry Chauvel, Australian commander of all Allied mounted troops in the Middle East. Davison sensibly uses this introduction to get the boasting out of his fiction's system; it is regrettable that Leonard Mann did not use a similar device in dealing in *Flesh in Armour* with the A.I.F. Offensive on the Western Front in 1918. Sadly, Davison made the mistake of incorporating the 'Historical Note' into the main text of the revised version, as an opening section called 'Parade'. This unbalances the narrative and weakens the impact of its real beginning, in which the Australian troop horses—'the veterans'—are introduced virtually one by one. The wonderfully lyrical invocation of the chargers' origins in the distant Australian bush, culminating in the final tribute, establishes a tone which is both profoundly nationalistic and unromantically sober in its appraisal of the struggle in which they are involved. It is worth quoting at some length:

> They all are Australian bred—bone of her bone. They are the troop horses.
> The grey with the neat forehand was foaled where Illawarra's hillsides tumble down to the sea. The bay mare with the white off hind ran beside her dam where Jimbour Plains sweep unbroken from sky to sky. She was five-off before she felt a girth around her.
> The bay gelding is from the Flinders grass country, out Barcaldine way. The other bay mare—the one with the white fleck on her muzzle—was accustomed to drink from a stream chilled by Kosciusko's snows. Those round, high-walled hoofs and short pasterns were shaped for running on steep and rocky pasture.
> The brown horse with the balley face was with a drover's outfit, once. He was foaled in the far Kimberleys, beside a lost lagoon, peopled with wildfowl. The bay with a white star on his forehead knows the marches of the painted inland. He was got when a blood stallion covered a brumby mare. His home lies fenceless below the Flinders Range. [etc.]
> . . . Victory is by endurance; and through the hard-won advance across Sinai's dry and wrinkled waste, the burden of it was laid upon these. The fight was from bir to bir—from water to water. Did racial tradition live again in that? They drank from desert springs and were ridden out to seek the enemy where he lay embattled before the water, farther on. They drank again when he had been routed from his stronghold. Failing, they were ridden back when their tortured bodies could endure no more.
> . . . These are the old campaigners, whom Fate has spared and Time has tried . . . These are the great-hearted ones.[51]

As H. M. Green observed, this opening catalogue of the Australian troop horses recalls Homer's enumeration of the Greek heroes and their ships early in the *Iliad*.[52] It is only appropriate that Davison should give the horses a heroic rank virtually equal with that of their riders. In the Light Horse, as in any branch of mounted infantry, man and horse formed a strong single unit. Certainly, the Australians regarded their mounts as compeers rather than mere conveyances, and Homer's epithet 'horse-loving' is as applicable to them as to the Greeks. Davison, of course, is famous for his sympathetic insights into animal life, notably in his tale of a renegade red heifer, *Man-*

Shy (1931), and in his 'biography' of the part-dingo *Dusty* (1946). In these charming but unsentimental and even tragic novels, animals and mankind are essentially antipathetic, the latter encroaching upon the former's impulses to freedom. But in *The Wells of Beersheba* they are the consummate comrades, compatriots a long way from home, holding out together against enemies which are both military and environmental.

The second section, 'Bivouac', shifts the perspective to the soldiers. In suitably languorous prose, 'Bivouac' pictures a rest-camp on the stifling Palestinian plain, with man and beast eating in the hot midday sun. They are between engagements, storing strength for 'the big show', and the atmosphere is subdued, almost torpid. The noontide having passed, and the troops having crawled into their shelters for a 'sticky, fly-tormented doze', the focus is then narrowed and intensified. Davison directs his attention to one trooper left to guard the horse-lines. The trooper is the epitome of vigorous and self-assured manhood:

> His face and arms were burnt nearer black than brown; and were lean with the leanness of strenuous living. Though young, his face was seamed. Hardship, short food, and insufficient sleep were his portion. Yet he did not look harried! Squatting there, in repose, his hearing directed toward the horses behind him, and his eyes alertly watching the scene in front, his bearing of himself was easy. It suggested a man who had found his body and spirit able to meet the demands made of them.
>
> He was what he looked—a man of the desert and the plains.[53]

The final nomenclature, 'a man of the desert and the plains', is clearly ambiguous. Frequent reiterations of the term 'a man', in the above objective description and when the narrative withdraws into the trooper's consciousness, suggest an all-inclusiveness, leading us to think that Davison is portraying *all* men engaged in the desert war, whatever their nationality. Specifically, however, Davison has in mind the stereotypical Australian bushman of literary convention. The 'desert' and the 'plains' refer as much to Australia as to the Middle East. Not only does the trooper look like a bushman, he thinks and sounds like one. In describing his attitude to the simple matter of headgear, for instance, Davison captures the stereotype with a Henry Lawson-like lexical accuracy: 'A hat was a hat to a man who lived beneath a blistering sun, not a piece of flash millinery'.[54] Davison's connection of the lot of the stoical desert warrior with that of the bushman without actually proclaiming the correspondence is an example both of the economy of his story-telling and the relatively subtle nature of his nationalism in *The Wells of Beersheba.* At this point in the narrative, character is related to event. The trooper's wandering senses and observations are underscored by 'the throb of distant guns . . . a prelude to battle'. These sounds of war from distant Gaza recall him from his reverie and stir his pulse. Buoyed by his faith in his commander, Chauvel, and by a 'quiet and sustaining fatalism', he sharpens his thoughts toward the military task at hand:

> A big fight! A man felt it in his bones . . . A tremor passed through the nerves just under his skin. Was it fear? A man didn't call it that! Rather it was the elation that comes to the brave and the near brave on the eve of battle.[55]

Maintaining his disciplined orchestration of the rhythm of the narrative, Davison allows this early peak of excitement to lapse into lassitude, with the trooper withdrawing from the scene to join his comrades in sleep. The activity and movement of the next section, 'Night March', in which the horsemen move up to the battlefield, sees an increase in the story's tempo. Dialogue breaks up the narration, serving the dramatic function of illustrating the confidence of men who are soon to go into battle confirmed in their sense of self-identity. 'Who are you? Who are you?', asks a lost soldier who is in search of his own unit. The horsemen's ironical and evasive retorts conceal a deep contentment:

> They were the Such-and-Such of the A.L.H. . . . The tradition that the southern breed were warrior horsemen rested with them, and they were proud in sustaining it. There was not one of them who would that night have changed his saddle for a throne.[56]

'Night March' concludes with the dawning of the day of battle and the arrival of the troop at the theatre of war. The climactic 'Battle' section traces the day's events from the hasty early-morning breakfast to the triumphant feasting that night at Beersheba's wells. Men with their nervously battle-wise horses move off toward their objectives, the village is within view, and the earth is already heaving with the impact of the enemy artillery. The sounds of the guns, which had swollen throughout the night march, have risen now to a continuous roar. Davison is careful, at this crucial stage, not to lose the Australian flavour of his narrative. An officer's revolver 'dispensing mercy' to badly injured horses is said to have 'recalled to memory the cracking of a stockwhip'.[57] The Turks proving hard to shift from their defences and nightfall being close at hand, the urgency of the situation is stressed. The life-blood of the desert army, water, is desperately needed, and the efforts of the British infantry in storming Gaza would come to nothing if the enemy flank was not turned at Beersheba. At last Davison ushers on to centre-stage the great man Chauvel, the very name phonetically suggestive of nationalistic ardour and chivalric accomplishment. To carry out his 'unprecedented' order for cavalry to attack well-entrenched and armed infantry, Chauvel selects the tried and true 4th and 12th Light Horse regiments for the charge in preference to the willing British Yeomanry, who are 'eager for renown among the desert men'. The General's trust in his troops is reflected by their own sublime self-confidence:

> In such a moment the minds and hearts of men rise to a condition in which mean things cannot touch them . . . Circumstance has dedicated them to grand adventure. They are buoyed up by a heroism in which all share. Consequences no longer matter. Death is an incident. Fear falls from them, and they become more than men.[58]

A kind of lyricism is introduced to add intensity to the moment of epic crisis. With the Homeric sun's 'coppery glow . . . diffused through the dry mist of the battlefield', the troop wheels 'prettily' toward battle, 'like men and horses at drill'. As the charge gathers speed and the enemy fire intensifies, the prose quickens in rhythm, keeping pace with the *accelerando* beating of the hooves:

> Nostrils reddened, eyes widened, jaws gaped, and tossing heads sent the spume flying. They shook the ground as they thundered across it.[59]

Davison's search for an appropriate style to commemorate the charge is now illustrated by his revision of the original version of the battle. Once more he turned to the *Iliad* for inspiration. In the original, the Australians sweep through the murderous Turkish fire 'resolute and unheeding'. Davison changes this to 'they swept on; line after line, unheeding as a shore-bound comber'. We are reminded of the early attack on Troy by the Greeks in the days before Achilles restored himself to the fray: '. . . battalion after battalion of Danaans swept relentlessly into battle, like the great waves that come hurtling onto an echoing beach'. To describe the terrific impact of the charge, Davison makes use of another Homeric simile. Compare his, 'They poured across the plain like a living flood, leaving a wide track littered with their fallen', with the *aristeia* of Diomedes, who 'stormed across the plain like a winter torrent' in pursuit of the Trojans and further glory.[60]

The audacity, resolution and prowess of the Light Horsemen quickly settle the issue. From a nearby vantage point (a Palestinian Mount Ida) the commanders watch the events, which are now bathed in 'empurpled twilight', with a godlike satisfaction and keen interest. 'Jove' himself, General Chauvel, puts down his own field-glasses in silent contentment. With typical economy, Davison then telescopes the action, drawing future historical circumstance into the narrow orbit of his own fiction. In 'prophetic vision' Chauvel foresees 'the battles to come and the entry of his cavalry into the cities of Palestine'. Consistent with what Hume Dow has described as the story's 'classical unity of action', a brief coda concludes the book where it began, with the horses. No final burst of chauvinistic trumpets is sounded, just the murmuring of the steeds enjoying the simple spoils of victory, drinking 'with slackened girths and bitless mouths at the wells of Beersheba'.[61]

The Wells of Beersheba, Davison once remarked, is a young man's book, 'written by a happy warrior'. He had gone to war as a 'Kiplingesque romantic', and though his idealism was soon shown to have been misconceived, 'to have pulled a poor mouth would have been squealing'. This attribution of Australian reticence on war terrors to a code of manly forbearance Davison implicitly gives as the reason why Australians 'did not contribute . . . to that terrific flood of bitter anti-war fiction that broke out . . . from about 1927 on'.[62] The fundamentally affirmatory view of war contained in *The Wells of Beersheba* was renounced in a story he wrote in 1939, 'Fathers and Sons'. The story opens with the narrator watching the first bunch of Second World War recruits marching through Sydney streets, after which he visits the Shrine of Remembrance in Hyde Park. Contemplation of Rayner Hoff's statue of 'Young Manhood sacrificed on the Sword' stirs angry thoughts about the futility of 1914–18, leading to a sustained vilification of the war as 'the bloody consummation of competitive nationalism', and of the shoddy part played by an amoral press in promoting it: 'If we were not enjoying the war there must be something wrong with us, the newspapers implied'. Davison himself is not absolved; 'Fathers and Sons' becomes a confession of personal guilt:

> . . . the blame was on us all; our common selfishness and stupidity. Hadn't

I, who might have known, and had the power to speak, gone unmoved
for half a lifetime?[63]

Davison is being too hard on himself. If he felt ashamed of *The Wells
of Beersheba* when he made this confession, then his contrition was
misguided. Certainly, the book exudes a boundless nationalism, and
yes, Davison asserts the superiority of the Australian soldier by trans-
lating the bush mythology to martial terms. The exploitation of bush
metaphors and stereotypes makes that intention perfectly plain. It
has been noted that the narrative action itself, that of an army fighting for water in the desert, 'echoes the pattern of life in the outback,
where the thought of water is always in an Australian's mind'.[64] But
therein lies the integrity of Davison's account. He celebrates a struggle
for survival rather than conquest, an endeavour that is elemental rather
than purely militarist. Davison hit the right note when he defined
the novella as 'a working model of communal effort'.[65] While its mood
is unequivocally patriotic, Davison's commitment throughout is to
narrative balance and tonal control, to the satisfaction of aesthetic
standards first, and the ravenous popular appetite for heroic
propaganda second. *The Wells of Beersheba* is an unusual, and superior,
work of Australian war prose.

IV

The Art of Self-advertisement

OLD DIGGERS NEVER DIE

Leonard Mann's unsatisfactory attempt to synthesize fiction and history in *Flesh in Armour* exemplifies an unavoidable technical problem confronting the novelist whose subject is war. As the New Zealander Dan Davin remarks in the Foreword to his *For the Rest of Our Lives* (1947), a novel set in North Africa during 1939–45, 'it is easier to introduce fiction into fact than fact into fiction'.[1] The war memoir – a genre which, fed by conflicts involving highly literate armies, has flourished in the twentieth century – confirms Davin's point. More than any other single branch of prose writing, the war memoir exhibits an effortless facility to move from documentary personal and public history to flagrant fiction. Commenting on its close kinship to the first-person novel, Paul Fussell suggests that the memoir resides 'on the knife-edge' between modes.[2] In connection with Oliver Hogue's wartime 'faction', I referred earlier to Fussell's remarks about the difficulty of trying to 'sex' autobiographical narratives. With the Australian soldier-books that appeared in the 1930s, the problem of accurate definition is just as acute as with the wartime propaganda. Here is the befuddled reviewer from the returned servicemen's journal, *Reveille*, trying to come to grips with Joseph Maxwell's *Hell's Bells and Mademoiselles* (1932):

> The book is, in fact, a curious mixture. At first glance it looks something like an autobiography, but, though it is told in the first person, it is hardly that. Then again, it looks something like a novel, but although it has a couple of love stories and others [*sic*] bits of romance running through it, it is not a novel either. And it is certainly not a war history.

To be sure, it records many incidents which are undoubtedly authentic, but which no historian would care to include in his work.[3]

To complicate these matters even further, E. Morris Miller's standard bibliography of Australian literature classifies memoirs such as G. D. Mitchell's *Backs to the Wall* (1937) and E. J. Rule's *Jacka's Mob* (1933), both of which Bean mined for documentary material for the *Official History*, as 'fiction'. John Laird, in a more recent extensive checklist of Australian war literature, finds a separate category for autobiographical records, placing them under the innocuous term 'Personal Narratives'—thus following the example of T. E. Lawrence, who defined the 'self-regardant' *Seven Pillars of Wisdom* as 'a personal narrative pieced out of memory'.[4]

The feeling that the classification of war reminiscences ultimately depends upon the personal judgement (or whim) of the individual is confirmed in Denis Winter's study of British responses to the First World War, *Death's Men* (1978). Under the major section, 'published *memoirs* cited in the text', Winter's bibliography lists, along with the old reliable *Goodbye to All That*, the arrantly fictional *Death of a Hero*, *Her Privates We* and *Under Fire*.[5] The nature of these narratives has been misrepresented; though to some extent created out of personal military memories, they contain far too many 'lies'—patent fictions, even myths—to be considered factual records. Yet does even *Goodbye to All That*, the most famous of all Great War memoirs, qualify? Paul Fussell's startling exposé of its fictional character in *The Great War and Modern Memory* suggests not.[6] Memoirs are almost inevitably composed of falsehoods and deceptions simply because they are the re-creations of dead experience. The 'truth', writes Frank Hardy in the epigraph to his novel *Who Shot George Kirkland?* (1981), 'resides in memory and the memory is clouded with repression and a desire to embellish . . . To recall an event is to interpret it, so the truth is altered by the very act of remembering'.[7] The heightened nature of the battle experience makes the 'act of remembering' it an especially fictive process. According to Robert Graves, the war memoir should actually tell a few lies if it is to have real veracity:

> The memoirs of a man who went through some of the worst experiences of trench warfare are not truthful if they do not contain a high proportion of falsities. High-explosive barrages will make a temporary liar or visionary of anyone.[8]

Michael Herr, who covered the war in Vietnam for American journals and newspapers, is rather more blunt on this question. War is so disorienting and unfathomable an involvement, he remarks in *Dispatches* (1977), that one afterwards is perfectly free to 'make up any kind of bullshit' one cares to about it.[9] In a way, the problem of historical truth is irrelevant: what has ensured the survival of *Goodbye to All That* as a valuable record of the Great War is its author's dedication to the standards of the literary craftsman rather than to those of the historian. A 'tongue-in-cheek neurasthenic farceur whose material is "facts" ', Robert Graves does not try merely to recapture the past.[10] The past is re-created, emerging as a new, fresh, distinctly 'literary' experience. He dramatizes and ironizes his time in battle, vitalizing its multitude of absurd, terrifying and bizarre moments. His aloof tone is a contrived medium for the painless unburdening of four dreadful years. Hence the cool aesthetic distance from which he recalls battlefield carnage:

> The colour of the dead faces changed from white to yellow-gray, to red, to purple, to green, to black, to slimy.[11]

A different kind of dissimulation is at work in the reminiscences of Australian servicemen. As in Britain, the inter-war years, especially the late 1920s and early 1930s, saw the publication of a large number of war memoirs in this country. Given the lapse of time and the rather cooler climate of nationalism in which they were written, a modulation of the loudly self-promotional tone of the wartime soldier-books might have been expected. This, with very few exceptions, is not the case. Obviously there are many ex-Diggers who left the war, in the words of Geoff Page's poem about Bill Harney, 'decently unwritten'; men who like Harney were either so appalled or so ashamed by their experience that all they wanted to do was to forget, and try to get on with the rest of their lives.[12] Nevertheless, one can justly argue that the literary testimony of the A.I.F., as set down in the 1930s memoirs, reads like a revival of egotism and chauvinism of the war years. Memory and imagination acting upon raw experiential material formed a fiction which, if anything, vindicated the excesses of such cheerful wartime liars as Oliver Hogue and R. Hugh Knyvett. The general formulation embraces a retrospective recognition of the excellence and uniqueness of the A.I.F., a military myth in which the individual Australian soldier-writer happily luxuriates.

The veterans were determined to perpetuate and consolidate the Anzac legend. Perhaps the more altruistic among them were moved to write by a perception that in the troubled economic and political times of the 1930s, a harking back to the years of heroic achievement would have a beneficial effect on the nation in terms of morale and the reinforcement of old values. The March 1936 issue of *Reveille* applauds the reminiscences of G. D. Mitchell for their 'inspiration' during a period when 'pitiful poodle-fakers have top control in all our high points of public morale', when 'our defence scheme is languishing', and when 'our public self-conceit is paralysed by the cuttle-fish grip of foreign exploitation; and our national action urge is bound fast by boot-licking subservience to so-called leaders who idolise foreign gods'.[13] It seems more likely, however, that the Great War memoirists were motivated by the same impulse to self-advertise as their wartime predecessors. The Australian soldier's obsession with his image extended to well after 1918. In March 1930 *Reveille* angrily denounced the 'nauseating muck' spread by 'scurrilous' war writers— specifically, it was responding to *Goodbye to All That*, in which Graves recorded a boastful Australian admission of atrocities committed against German prisoners. *Reveille* went on to comment that the Federal Executive of the R.S.L. had discussed 'setting up a censorship against authors of war books who defame Australian soldiers', and indicated that representations to that effect would be made to the Government.[14] Such a draconian measure was never implemented, though given the earlier governmental enforcement of the inviolacy of the 'Anzac' name, the publicists of the R.S.L. might well have contended that this new step was merely a logical progression.

It is not difficult to feel sympathetic towards the ex-servicemen. They (or some of them) were troubled by the dreary obscurity of peacetime existence and looked back fondly to those days when life offered a challenge and they were made to feel important. As Les Murray writes in his verse novel *The Boys Who Stole the Funeral* (1980), the war was for many old Diggers 'their only proud employment ever'.[15] In the *Iliad*, Achilles is faced with the choice between a long life of relative inactivity and a short career of battlefield fame and glory. Knowing that the second course of action would result in his death, he nonetheless made the heroic commitment. Many of the Australian memoirists seem to indicate that, put in the same position, they would have made the same fatal choice. The frankness of Joe Maxwell, a notably devil-may-care soldier, as he begins *Hell's Bells and Mademoiselles*, is revealing:

In 1932 one sees the futility of 1914–18; the insane folly that cost millions of lives and disorganized the whole world. Yet behind the sense of uselessness lurks that peculiar fascination of war. Back through the years of disillusion flashes some cameo of heroism, some epic of self-sacrifice, and the constant expression of good-fellowship that illumined those red pages. When Digger meets Digger the memory goes jogging back to the Peninsula or to the mud and blood and mad ruin of northern France. We talk war, we live war once again. Time has mellowed sorrows and dimmed the horror. But even now, after more than a decade, the prosaic life of a city palls at odd moments, the dull struggling routine of tram, train, office, and rule of thumb.[16]

Maxwell was a boilermaker's apprentice when, as a 'horribly green' eighteen-year-old, he enlisted in the A.I.F.[17] Fêted and famous as a winner of the Victoria Cross, he worked as a journalist upon his return to civilian life. Mundane post-war life must have been at least as hard to bear for H. R. Williams, who on the evidence of *The Gallant Company: An Australian Soldier's Story of 1915–18* (1933), was the happiest and proudest of warriors. A warehouseman before the war, he laboured as a 'soft-goods agent' after it.[18] In *The Gallant Company*'s sequel, *Comrades of the Great Adventure* (1935), Williams's peacetime frustrations emerge in a fond remembrance of the war which reveals much about the character of the literary product churned out by the memoirists:

> Civilian life has failed to furnish many returned men with all they deserve; peace has not been enriched with the comradeship they knew in the army; baser ideals are preferred to their old unselfish spirit . . . Most have found the post-war years slipping by drab and uneventful. Therefore the very monotony of present-day life has caused many soldiers to recall their war-time experiences as momentous happenings in an otherwise dull existence. Strangely enough, too, in looking back to those days, hardships, dangers and awfulness have become obscured by pleasanter memories.[19]

Writing about the Anzacs in his *Gallipoli Diary*, General Sir Ian Hamilton prophetically, if unwittingly, suggested why the war continued to act as such a powerful emotional magnet: 'Men live through more in five minutes on that crest', he wrote, 'than they do in five years of Bendigo or Ballarat'.[20] But perhaps D. H. Lawrence's observation in *Kangaroo*, that 'the war was the only time they ever felt properly alive', is the more telling.[21] Whatever the psychological source of their nostalgia, many Diggers, like Clarrie, the deceased hero of *The Boys Who Stole the Funeral*, spent the rest of their lives 'looking for [their] platoon'.[22] In the end, the Australian soldiers were the post-war victims of their own wartime publicity. They had been promoted so heavily during the years of combat that anything less than adulation must have seemed tantamount to downright rejection. The war reminiscences of the 1930s can be seen as the manifestation of a hankering for the sense of mission and self-worth that once inspired and elated so many.

The war sparked literary activity in men who had otherwise shown no propensity to write. As John Carroll has noted of the profundity of combat to those who have experienced it, most old soldiers 'spend the best moments of the twilight life that follows, until they die, reminiscing, as if their imagination had been captured by one brilliant moment, and then went blind'.[23] The artistic limitations of those ex-Diggers who set their experience down on paper is proclaimed by the fact that they usually published little or nothing else for the rest of their lives. The majority of the authors included in Angus & Robertson's 'Gallant Legion' series, for instance, wrote only about the war and their involvement in it. All other areas of human experience, apparently, could not so move them. Since they are usually the products of an essentially non-literary sensibility, the war memoirs tend not to display a high standard of accomplishment or sophistication. Men like Joe Maxwell and H. R. Williams, in contrast to British war memoirists such as Robert Graves and Edmund Blunden, were soldiers first and writers second. From the point of view of the Allied war effort, it was fortunate that they fought better than they were to write. There is something almost *anti*-literary about the A.I.F. reminiscences: something suggestive of the Quixotic view which maintains that the labours of the 'sword' are superior to those of the 'pen'.[24] This is not to say that the memoirs are without interest, charm, or even the occasional burst of stylistic panache; it is also wrong to imply that worthwhile literature cannot be made by people with no real literary proclivities or record of performance. Nevertheless, John Hayward's opinion of British military reminiscences of the Second World War is applicable to the general run of Australian personal narratives of the 1914–18 conflict:

> Too many of these personal records, it must be frankly admitted, are little more than collections of inconsequent anecdotes, dashed down on paper by men who had almost every qualification except the essential one of knowing how to write about them.[25]

Deference to artistic values, in the personal narratives of the First A.I.F., is often overlooked in the push to regain lost and longed-for kudos. Advocacy, rather than artistry or even in some cases articulateness, is their common characteristic.

FIDDLING WITH 'THE FACTS'

Thankfully some A.I.F. memoirists managed to combine the inclination to big-note with the ability to write well. Ion Idriess was one. Idriess was no rank literary amateur. Dubbed 'the best-selling bushman', he was the popular and prolific author of many descriptive works of life and travel in the remoter parts of Australia and the South Pacific. *The Desert Column*, which appeared in 1932, emerged out of his most creative period, the years in which he wrote *Lasseter's Last Ride* (1931), *Flynn of the Inland* (1932) and *The Cattle King* (1936). Idriess, who in his time tried his hand at most up-country occupations, from horse-breaking to opal-gouging, wrote his books from personal experiences enjoyed and endured, from sights seen, and yarns heard. From about 1931 on, however, he was virtually a full-time professional writer.

At the outbreak of war in 1914, Idriess was up in the Cape York Peninsula. He managed to stow away as far south as Townsville, where he enlisted in the Light Horse. During his service at Gallipoli, in the Sinai and in Palestine, he was wounded three times. Based upon the war diaries he kept assiduously during the conflict so that in future days he would have 'a private picture show' to 'refresh his memory', *The Desert Column* remains the most compelling of the A.I.F. personal narratives. Having gone through no less than six editions within two-and-a-half years of its initial publication, the book has retained its popularity and appeal—as its 1982 inclusion in Angus & Robertson's 'Australian Classics' series attests. Adherence to 'fact', of course, has little to do with *The Desert Column*'s enduring success, even though the facts of the desert fighting are exotic and exhilarating enough. Idriess's major descriptive talent, the brilliant clarity of his observation, was supplemented by what H. M. Green calls an 'inventive imagination'.[26] As a result *The Desert Column* is something more than a mere personal record. Frederick T. Macartney's comments about Idriess in E. Morris Miller's revised bibliography are instructive here. His books, says Macartney, are 'factually, however freely, based on phases of experience or observation indicated by their titles, but heightened in such a manner which led to their being previously classified in the bibliography as fiction'.[27]

In the case of *The Desert Column*, the vexing question of to what degree the individual memoirist's artistic licence refines or 'heightens' raw factuality is easily answered. Subtitled 'Leaves From the Diary of an Australian Trooper', the book purports to record the quotidian eyewitness impressions of nearly three years' active service, and indeed it does follow the diary format. The only change to the diary notebooks he is prepared to admit is the excision of 'fully twenty thousand words' so that the 'diary' could appear 'at a reasonable price to the public'.[28] But, as I indicated in the opening chapter, the text of *The Desert Column* differs from the original document held by the Australian War Memorial. Much more interesting than the editing of his wordy primary source are the *additions* which Idriess saw fit to make. Indeed, if the re-reading of his diary after some years re-awakened memories in Idriess, then it also activated a creative process which was directed more toward the maintenance of myth than to the faithful reproduction of actuality. 'The further personal written materials move from the form of the daily diary, the closer they approach to the figurative and the fictional', Fussell asserts.[29] Ion Idriess in *The Desert Column*, however, manages to have it both ways. He makes fiction of the war from the emotional and temporal perspective of nearly fifteen years while giving the impression that his book is still the 'real thing' so to speak, an immediate literary response to the heat of the moment, jotted down whenever 'anything exciting . . . was happening'.[30] And just so as to ensure his readers are aware that they are dealing with a genuine process of record, observation and thought, Idriess takes the precaution of introducing into the narrative a few self-conscious references to the act of diary-keeping itself, which lend it a strong air of circumstantial realism. Feverishly ill aboard a hospital ship off the Gallipoli coast in early June 1915, he writes in *The Desert Column*: 'My safety-valve is in this diary. It keeps my mind strangely occupied. And besides, if I really live through this war, I want to read through the old diary in after years, and remember what war was really like . . .'. These words are not to be found in the actual diary.[31]

Idriess's emendations to his source add colour and dramatic flavour to otherwise flat and drab passages of expository prose. Compare the diary entry for 30 May 1915 . . .

> Things are quiet now . . . A man was just shot stone dead in front of me. We were going for water. Sudden death is a horrible thing . . .

with the description of the same incident as it appears in *The Desert Column*:

Things are quiet now . . . A man was just shot dead in front of me. He was a little infantry lad, quite a boy, with snowy hair that looked comical above his clean white singlet. I was going for water. He stepped out of a dugout and walked down the path ahead, whistling. I was puffing the old pipe, while carrying a dozen water-bottles. Just as we were crossing Shrapnel Gully he suddenly flung up his water-bottles, wheeled around, and stared for one startled second, even as he crumpled to my feet. In seconds his hair was scarlet, his clean white singlet all crimson.[32]

The brutal colour-transformation of the soldier's 'snowy hair' and 'clean white singlet' in the blood-soaked aftermath of his shooting, the changing of 'a man' to 'a lad, quite a boy', and the cruel irony of his whistling as he strolls to his premature death – all these additions dramatize powerfully the diary's bland statement, 'Sudden death is a horrible thing'. The youngster's poignant end comes immediately after a vignette (transcribed virtually word-for-word from the diary) of a hare running across the Anzac battleground to the cheers and riotous laughter of the troops. Such an opportunity to juxtapose the comic and the tragic, the picturesque and the hideous, obviously proved irresistible to the memoirist's cultivated literary instincts. Most of the additions, however, spring from an authorial desire to magnify the heroism of the Australians. For example, the references to the high spirits of the Light Horsemen in *The Desert Column* are seemingly endless (a rough count reveals at least eighty) – but this levity was rarely recorded at the time, in the diary. In the book, Australian laughter is sometimes directed derisively at the enemy, is sometimes manufactured bravado to conceal fear, is sometimes callous or even bloodthirsty, and often, especially when riding to battle, is the product of pure warrior *joie de vivre*. The following description of the troopers as they set off to take part in the operations around Beersheba is a wholesale insertion into Idriess's diary narrative:

It was a grand sight, the thrill, the comradeship, the knowledge that soon hell would open out, filled us all, I know, with the terrible intoxication of war when the movement is rapid. I was scared for I understood what was coming, though most of us laughed when the first shells screamed towards us . . . I think all men get scared at times like these; but there comes a sort of laughing courage from deep within the heart of each, or from some source he never knew existed; and when he feels like that he will gallop into the most blinding death with an utterly unexplainable, don't care, shrieking laugh upon his lips.[33]

Like any writer who is trying to maintain an epic theme, Idriess has

a strong sense of history. In the conversion of his wartime record
to *The Desert Column* he exploits historical hindsight, which sometimes gives a distinctly artificial ring to the supposedly spontaneous
responses of the 'diarist'—as in his excitement on the eve of Beersheba:
'Here goes for the great fight and the grandest charge of mounted
men in history'.[34] In his diary Idriess had often mused on the antiquity of the battlefields upon which he had been fighting, and on the
great armies that had contested military honours in the desert theatre.
One such observation concludes with, '. . . and now the Australian
rides over their old dust, a conqueror'. The same passage, as it appears
in *The Desert Column*, elaborates on the heroic and historical context of the Australian endeavour, and tries to define the special character of this potent modern force:

> What strange scenes these oases must have witnessed throughout the
> centuries . . . The Pharoahs trod the place, the Babylonians and the
> Saracens and hosts of others, and now the army of the youngest nation
> in the world is fighting and riding across it, laughing and singing, joking
> and swearing and growling . . .[35]

To do justice to Idriess's manipulation of documentary material, it
should be added that he balances his book with an apprehension of
war's ugly side. The description of the snowy-haired young Anzac's
violent death testifies to that. In the chapters dealing with the claustrophobic trench life on Gallipoli—trench warfare was anathematic
to most Light Horsemen—Idriess extensively revises the diary in order
to launch a bitterly ironic assault on the 'Glories of War'. He extends his diary's terse reference to 'maggots crawling down the walls
of the trench' into a gruesome catalogue of war horrors. We could
almost be reading *Under Fire*:

> . . . Maggots are falling into the trench now. They are not the squashy
> yellow ones; they are big brown hairy ones. They tumble out of the sun-
> dried cracks in the possy walls. The sun warms them I suppose . . .
> We have just had "dinner". My new mate was sick and couldn't eat.
> I tried to, and would have but for the flies. I had biscuits and a tin of
> jam. But immediately I opened the tin the flies rushed the jam. They
> buzzed like swarming bees . . . I wrapped my overcoat over the tin and
> gouged out the flies, then spread the biscuit, held my hand over it, and
> drew the biscuit out of the coat. But a lot of the flies flew into my mouth
> and beat about inside. Finally I threw the tin over the parapet. I nearly
> howled with rage. I feel so sulky I could chew everything to pieces. Of
> all the bastards of places this is the greatest bastard in the world. And

a dead man's boot in the firing-possy has been dripping grease on my overcoat and the coat will stink for ever.[36]

A degree of perspective and proportion, as well as that intimate detail curiously missing from the original, are what Idriess seems to have sought when preparing his old notebooks for publication. The 'cold facts' as they stood on the now-alien pages did not properly convey the truth about the war as Idriess remembered it. In any case Idriess is too practised a literary artist not to be aware that, even in unadulterated form, the personal diary is an artificial structure. Expressing relief, at one point in *The Desert Column*, that he had finally brought his record up to date, he appears somewhat dissatisfied that he had not been able to say everything about the intense experiences he had just lived through:

> And so the diary is up to date again. It seemed an awful long time writing it up. Just a few of one man's experiences in a scrap. If every man of both armies wrote his experiences of one day's fighting only, it would take a great library to house the books.[37]

Selectivity, then, is the key to the writing up of personal experience — as of course it is with all artistic creation. Idriess may well have striven to forge a balanced account out of the brute creation of his war diary, one which retains and builds on qualities that are both whimsical ('The rifle-bullets . . . chirped among the bushes like busy canaries')[38] and unromantic ('we did not seem to know what was happening: we were hurrying somewhere to kill men and be killed');[39] but by the weight of his additions and emendations he makes it clear that he is as much in the business of myth-reinforcement as the cruder postwar publicists. Idriess lacked confidence in the ability of his original work to communicate a heroic message; his revisions ensured that any such deficiency was rectified. What most remains with us after having read *The Desert Column* is the excited anticipation of combat and the pride that comes from proving oneself and one's race in it.

THE SUPERIORITY COMPLEX OF THE A.I.F.

So earnestly do the Australian war memoirists swear to the accuracy of their reminiscences that one can hardly fail to be sceptical. Their defensiveness — or that of their publishers — is exposed by the practice of including at the head of the text a collaboration of the story to follow, usually penned by some respected military figure. Men like Generals Birdwood and Hobbs must have spent half their precious post-war days writing testimonials. Some of these should be taken with a grain of salt. Lieutenant-Colonel E. Hilmer Smith's Foreword to Gertrude Moberly's *Experiences of a "Dinki Di" R.R.C. Nurse* (1933) asserts that the events related therein 'are not those drawn from the imagination, but are really a collection of letters written at a time when impressions and incidents were fresh in the mind'. This is fundamentally untrue. Though Moberly genuinely was a Red Cross nurse, *Experiences* is not at all a 'dinki di' personal war record. Moberly's private papers reveal that she converted her war diary into the form of love letters to her husband some years after the war as 'the easiest way' to write what was her first book.[40] (She had not met the recipient of the love letters at the time they were purportedly written.) Some war memoirists even consider veracity to be of more importance than the quality of the writing. E. J. Rule, stressing that he had tried to tell 'the truth' in *Jacka's Mob*, says that his pen is 'unskilled'[41] – as if to imply that he is not stylistically clever enough to pull the wool over the reader's eyes. May Tilton, a nursing sister attached to the A.I.F., is more direct in her Author's Note to *The Grey Battalion* (1933): 'I have made no attempt to produce a work of any literary value. My aim has been to give a true, and I hope interesting account of my "trail with the warriors" '.[42]

But the fact is that most Australian eyewitnesses are more concerned with the reputation of the fighting prowess of the First A.I.F. than with historical exactitude. As C. E. W. Bean well understood, the safest method of illustrating combat effectiveness is to pile incident upon heroic incident. Any war, and any army, provides a multitude of examples of daring and strength. There are also, of course, the numerous instances of cowardice, of desperation, and of despair. It is all, as always, a matter of selection. By concentrating their attention on the uncomplicated description of battle movements and by playing down the darker side of war, the memoirists could hide their chauvinistic bias behind an authorial mask of 'objectivity'.

One of the more graphic accounts of the Western Front, G. D. Mitchell's *Backs to the Wall*, provides an excellent example of this strategy. As against the more subjective and introspective treatment one generally finds in British war memoirs, which tend more to offer a view of war as it affected the author personally, *Backs to the Wall* relies on the 'realistic' portrayal of memorable battlefield events. Even when conditions are at their most oppressive, the action is influenced by (to reiterate Mitchell's wry phrase) 'the superiority complex of the A.I.F.'. Other than a fleeting dark desire to do away with certain infuriating English officers, the only moment of really intense personal feeling he registers occurs when he describes the enemy penetration of the Australian line at Dernancourt in 1918:

> The world had fallen. The Australian line had been broken. Not even pride was left. Tears of grief ran down my face.[43]

G. D. Mitchell, no doubt, had a lot to feel 'superior' about. For his own efforts in the crisis at Dernancourt he was awarded the Military Cross, while earlier, at First Bullecourt, he had won the Distinguished Conduct Medal and his commission in recognition of his outstanding bravery. Mitchell was fortunate as well as capable and courageous. He went right through the war, from the first Anzac Landing through some of the bloodiest actions in France, without receiving the proverbial scratch. But 'luck', in the world of Australian warriordom, does not possess the inevitably lethal force it has in anti-war books like *All Quiet on the Western Front*. According to A.I.F. ideology, the soldier does not face his fate passively, but continually exerts himself, heedless of the outcome. This attitude, of course, is in line with the ancient heroic code. As Beowulf says of his narrow escape from death in his encounter with the sea-monsters, 'fortune is apt to favour the man who keeps his nerve'.[44] Writing in admiration of Mitchell in *Reveille*, his old battalion commander R. L. Leane says: 'He always appeared to live a charmed life, in the thick of every fight, yet he always appeared to come up smiling, sometimes with prisoners, but always with souvenirs—a typical Digger who knew not the word "defeat". It was such as he that made the A.I.F. the finest force the world has ever seen'.[45] As is customary in the small world of A.I.F. literature, which often reads like the product of a mutual admiration society, Mitchell returns Leane's compliment in *Backs to the Wall*, paying homage to him as 'the complete and classic warrior', a 'beau-ideal' who would have been at home 'armoured and with short sword at the head of a Roman Legion'.[46]

Unusually for a military man, Mitchell's personal reputation amongst his comrades grew after the war in which they were all engaged. His fame was at its height in the 1930s. During this period he contributed several autobiographical war narratives to *Reveille* which proved to be enormously popular with the journal's predominantly ex-A.I.F. readership. He became something of a cult hero; *Reveille* proudly proclaimed him to be its own 'discovery' and regaled him with accolades such as 'Captain Mitchell *is* the spirit of the A.I.F.', and—even more flattering for a war memoirist—'a Great Soldier and a Great Writer'.[47] When *Backs to the Wall*, which is based

largely on the *Reveille* pieces and his war diary, finally appeared in
1937, the acclaim was almost absurdly generous. 'The book we have
all been waiting for', gushed *Reveille*. Bean's commendation was even
more fulsome: 'Captain Mitchell is the most powerful and impressive soldier-writer that I know of . . . His description of the winter
spent on the Somme . . . is possibly the best that will ever be written
in any language.'[48]

What so transported many of Mitchell's admirers, though, was not
so much his literary ability, but a general perception that his 'epic
of Australian valour' had restored the great days of the war to the
limelight they deserved. Mitchell's writings were in retaliatory reaction against the twin evils of 1930s cynicism and apathy, thought
by returned servicemen's circles to be destroying the good name of
the Digger. Noting how Mitchell had 're-vitalised . . . the spirit of
the A.I.F.', one of *Reveille*'s commentators calls Mitchell's pen 'a defensive gun for the A.I.F.' which is directed 'upon points of common
attack'.[49] There was also the feeling that in *Backs to the Wall* Mitchell had delivered the appropriate response to those war books, mostly
from overseas, which had given front-line soldiering a poor image.
His muscular presentation of combat as a hard, but 'healthy', masculine activity was an antidote to the insidious excesses of the morbid
writers of the Remarque school, most of whom were seen as being
motivated, through a perceived indulgence in sensationalism, by pure
greed. *Reveille* had no doubt as to which approach was the more real:

> Truth, as the saying goes, is stranger than fiction and Capt. Mitchell,
> as a front-line soldier from the Landing until the Armistice, has in actual
> fact experiences enough to chronicle without resorting to imagination
> and distortion, as many war writers have done in the belief that dilation
> of the horrible is a cute move in book sales.[50]

This is humbuggery. Pride in and admiration for the A.I.F. trigger
Mitchell's imagination as frequently as the loathing of battle provokes the anti-war writers. For example, literalness has little to do
with his assessment of the heroic posture assumed by those Australians
under his command on the grim French battlefields of 1918:

> Death only, in this unending war, was all to which they could look for-
> ward. But the reaper would be met with the stoic fortitude and pride
> that they knew so well . . . If, from Valhalla, chosen ones are called
> to storm the gates of hell, these will be in the forefront, laughing as
> they go.[51]

Confirmed in their 'sense of personal superiority', the Diggers in *Backs to the Wall* form a closed warrior-society in which deference to the pagan ideal of the heroic life takes precedence. Mitchell remembers:

> We Diggers were a race apart. Long separation from Australia had seemed to cut us completely away from the land of our birth. The longer a man served, the fewer letters he got, the more he was forgotten. Our only home was our unit . . . Pride in ourselves, in face of a world of friends and enemies, was our sustaining force. For a parallel, one would need to go back to some Roman Legion, serving many years in a foreign country, cut off from Rome, alien to the new land and the old, sure only of themselves.[52]

Just as the serving soldiers during the war saw themselves as forming 'a race apart', so the returned men felt isolated by their experience. Bill Gammage has written of Anzac as being in the end 'a dividing rather than a unifying experience. It separated those who had fought in the war from those who had not, and one generation of Australians from all those that went before or came after'.[53] The feeling of isolation and separateness borne by the veterans in the years following the war gives a sharp edge to their reminiscences. It explains their incestuousness, and the arrogant assumption of Digger pre-eminence. The Australian war memoirist is thus caught in a bind. He is trying to promote the heroism of the First A.I.F. to 'outsiders' while at the same time pandering to the exclusivist nature of his primary and most fervent readers, the old Diggers themselves.

Not all of *Backs to the Wall* is concerned with highlighting the acts and attitudes of Australian heroism. The physical, and to a lesser extent emotional, trials of combat are given some attention, though Mitchell is usually content to shrink behind the excuse that the horrors of Western Front warfare were 'indescribable'.[54] The work also contains some rather eccentric moments. There is an Edmund Blunden-like delicacy in Mitchell's description of the troops' responses to the beauties of the countryside as they move up the line to the metallic and chemical brutalities of the front; by contrast, his admiration for 'the beauty of shells as they thudded into farms and copses' reminds us of the mischievous Wyndham Lewis's aesthetic admiration of battle in his memoir, *Blasting and Bombardiering* (1937).[55] Generally, however, *Backs to the Wall* lacks that measure of flinty cynicism that can lend perspective to the war memoir, saving it from turning into a self-regarding recitation of past glories. It is sad that Mitchell chose not to integrate the sharp wit that is often evident in his war diary into his memoir. On the day of his departure for war, Mitchell as a young recruit in the Tenth Battalion (and free as yet from the compulsion to mythologize) saw fit to write:

> We are going to the biggest thing that has hit civilization of nineteen centuries, and a bit.[*sic*] Civilization means being able to kill and wound a lot of men in a short time, from a long distance. The Tenth Infantry is highly civilized.[56]

Backs to the Wall is staunchly and unapologetically affirmative of the war effort, and Mitchell has no regrets about his own involvement. At the end of the war his dominant feeling was not one of relief, but of 'indefinable sadness'. The battalion-family had broken up; mateships were 'sundered'. The 'wonderful times' were over. All that was to be looked forward to was 'the stress and fierce demands of civilian life'—as if the previous four years had been a halcyon period of boundless ease and careless joy. He writes, quite movingly, of the 'endless gallery' of 'well-remembered faces' who had died 'that our peoples might live'. The survivors, says Mitchell, 'must fight on'.[57] Mitchell himself set the example. In the 1930s he wrote articles which declared the imminent dangers threatening an ill-prepared and poorly-defended Australia, and argued for a massive reinforcement of the national military force.[58] His novel, *The Awakening*, published in the same year as *Backs to the Wall*, deals presciently with the invasion of an unready Australia by an Oriental power, which is met only by a bush commando formed and led by an ex-major of the A.I.F. The Second World War saw (Major) Mitchell involved in guerrilla warfare training in Western Australia, and then in charge of landing-craft in New Guinea. He was a truly indefatigable warrior.

The proselytism of H. R. Williams's *The Gallant Company* is even more overt than in *Backs to the Wall*. In the final seven or eight paragraphs of the book Williams embarks on a forceful defence of the Australian war effort. Against the 'doctrines of selfishness' being 'preached' in the post-war period, the 'noble spirit' of self-sacrifice and patriotic duty stands as a salutary lesson to the nation's youth.[59] As well as a conventional analysis of the reasons for the A.I.F.'s fighting prowess (an amalgam of 'sport, camaraderie and vanity'), Williams lambasts the 'revulsion of feeling' for the Great War that had taken place in the ensuing years. He argues that to depict war 'solely as ghastly, sordid, even unnecessary' is as 'unfair' a distortion as a picture of peacetime life which only takes into account poverty and urban degradation.[60] There is, perhaps, a simple logic in this connection. But it is impossible to imagine that a sophisticated modern war writer would even contemplate a defence of war in terms of the limitations or faults of peace.

There can be few soldiers who threw themselves with more gusto into the new life the war opened up for young men than H. R. Williams. His response to the masculine world of the army is one of unalloyed enthusiasm:

> The open-air life, plain food, regular exercise, and camaraderie in the ranks made us all strong, healthy, laughing, young animals. The army was beginning to teach us how much good there is in the companionship of our fellow-men, and to know one another with an intimacy impossible in civilian life.[61]

After extended service on the Western Front, Williams like G. D. Mitchell came to look upon his unit as his real home, populated by his 'truest and most trusted friends'. By contrast, his actual home back in Australia and his 'civilian associates' were but 'misty memories'. Consequently, the embarkation for Australia at the war's end was not a time for celebration but for 'sorrow at the passing of the army life'.[62] France stood for danger and hardship, but it also signified mateship and 'a great adventurous freedom', a freedom unobtainable and unimaginable in pre-war civilian life, and then coveted and glamorized after the war. Williams remembers the soldiers' yarns told in the London hospital where he convalesced after having been wounded near Péronne in September 1918 – tales of 'battles, sprees, women, race-horses and remote places' to make 'the Arabian Nights seem tame'.[63]

Precise description of the various combats in which Williams was engaged often gives way to boasting, especially in the chapters on the important engagements of 1918. Williams, in this connection, suffers from the same problem that plagued Leonard Mann: he is unable to decide whether to commit his aesthetic allegiance to realism or to propaganda. As in *Flesh in Armour*, it is propaganda which finally wins out. Williams's consuming admiration for the Diggers, in whom 'seemed to burn a military fervour akin to a religious fanaticism', often degenerates into the most puerile sort of adolescent idolatry. For instance Fred Fanning, his company commander, is imagined 'to have been in some other life a pirate chief' – all because he wore his hat turned down and 'cocked at a rakish angle'.[64] While Williams, pedantic in all matters to do with visual detail, confronts war's more grisly aspects more often and more directly than many of his reminiscing comrades ('My face, arms and head were smothered with the poor wretch's minced flesh and warm blood'), he too is apt to proclaim a linguistic inability to tackle war horrors. At least he is, being honest, though it would appear that, writing in 1933, a whole body of modern war literature had passed him by:

> As for the mud – a Dickens, a Zola, or a Victor Hugo might be able to describe it. Around our bivouac it was knee-deep. The whole terrain was a sea of mud.[65]

This reference to such traditional, nineteenth-century figures reveals not only the conservative literary leanings of most Australian First World War writers, it also highlights once more their disregard for the revolution in the literary presentation of war that had taken place during and since 1914–18. Owen and Rosenberg, Ford and Barbusse and Remarque might as well have never written a word. The problem of striking the right balance between heroism and horror is given little systematic attention by the Australian memoirists. Not that it could be solved simply by throwing in a few mangled bodies and several gallons of blood amongst all the shining bayonets and laughing Diggers. In *Jacka's Mob* E. J. Rule shows that he had given some considered thought to the question of aesthetic balance and historical veracity:

> Despite the common phraseology of war literature, the ground was not red with blood, nor did I ever see streams run red. One would imagine, to read some histories, that soldiers were human blood-tanks.[66]

A memoir drawn on extensively by Bean, who considered it to be, 'from the historical point of view, easily the best memoir that exists of the life of our infantry in France',[67] *Jacka's Mob* contains a breadth and depth of candid reportage that is rare in the Australian war memoir. The haunted looks on the faces of men as they came out of battle; the excesses of some soldiers, including the looting of dead bodies; the false heroics of wartime newspaper reports; the absurdly bloodthirsty speeches, intended to be 'invigorating', given by General Birdwood in a 'futile' attempt 'to arouse blood-lust'; the matter-of-fact cataloguing of young Australians 'blown to pieces' by shell-fire and the pathetic sight of defenceless Diggers gunned down 'like rabbits'; and introspective moments of personal despair, the private neuroses and nightmares – these are not standard elements of the typical personal narrative of the First A.I.F.[68] Rule's preparedness to recognize the spectrum of aspects to the war is revealed by his broaching the subject of Albert Jacka's nervous breakdown during an

English convalescence. It was all very well to portray, as Mann did with Frank Jeffreys, the psychological collapse of confirmed 'cowards', but Albert Jacka V.C. – the hero of Gallipoli *and* Pozières *and* Bullecourt *and* Ypres – was probably the most famous of all Diggers, idolized by his comrades, decorated by the authorities, and mythologized by the popular press. But Rule does not expend too much narrative energy analysing the reasons for the breakdown. Like the great soldier he was, Jacka overcomes his trauma and returns to the fray to set 'a standard of behaviour' to the men. Whatever his psychological torments out of the line, he displays nerves of steel while in it. From that heroic personage flowed a well-spring of courage that sustained those around him. The men of Jacka's company 'felt a thrill of self-esteem' at belonging to his unit; the men of his battalion were 'thrilled' to be called 'Jacka's Mob', and basked in 'the reflected glory' of his achievements.[69]

One of the most disappointing features of the Australian war memoirs is the lack of humour to redeem the overwhelming self-assertiveness. While the sardonicism of the Diggers is strongly accentuated, it is often used in a cliquish manner. For example, the rodomontade of a certain Sergeant Jack Garcia in relating his encounter with a 'big Hun' in *Jacka's Mob* is offered by Rule not in reproof but in delighted recognition of the A.I.F. talent for spinning yarns. The German, trapped in his own dugout by Garcia, implores him to spare his life, whimpering 'Me father of fourteen children'. Garcia responds with a curt, 'Well it's time you were b – – well dead', and then promptly shoots him.[70] (Can there be any wonder that Robert Graves made his supposedly scurrilous accusation in *Goodbye to All That*?) Some comedy is derived from the clash of Australian and English habits, as in *Flesh in Armour*. The general objective is to illustrate the superiority of the Australian Way. During a visit to the underground mess of British officers, G. D. Mitchell toys furtively with 'the idea of making a good, healthy *faux pas*', having the sneaking suspicion that his hosts thought that his hair was 'fuzzy' and his 'loincloth somewhat frayed'. Mitchell uses the occasion to make some pertinent remarks (later cited by Bean in Volume VI of the *Official History*) about the contrast of the boisterous egalitarianism of the A.I.F. with the formalism of the British Army:

> *Journey's End*, with its five company commanders sitting together in a front-line dug-out, could never have been written of an Australian company. Rather would you have seen each platoon officer glumly feeding

from his mess tin among his men, the company commander sitting in solitary glory. I have often had my rum issue swiped by some dissolute private when my back was turned. And cigarettes — blazes! While I had one left, the platoon considered they had an option on it.[71]

H. R. Williams becomes positively peevish in trying to make light of English hauteur. Responding to the protests of the citizens of Cambridge, who were dismayed that Australian and New Zealand troops were staying in the university colleges while attending Officers' Training School, Williams retorts:

> many Anzacs passed through Cambridge without any citizen having been garroted, murdered, or served up for a cannibal feast by Anzacs in the market-square. The dear, smug provincials of England loved to be frightened with the bogey of wild Colonial troops, held to be socially no-class, but "hellish stout fellahs, what?" when there was a strong point to be stormed or a line that wanted holding against massed German attack.[72]

In a paradox similar to that which afflicted wartime writers like Oliver Hogue, the A.I.F. memoirists exhibit a starchy conservatism at the same time as they press the rebellious individuality of the Diggers. G. D. Mitchell, for example, was a notably wayward soldier whose promotions, as Bill Gammage has indicated, tended to be matched by his demotions. Yet *Backs to the Wall* gives little sense of this 'unrelenting independence'.[73] The book's action is controlled by an emphasis on the military task at hand. In *The Gallant Company* H. R. Williams exhibits all the obsessions and biases that characterized the wartime propagandists. Among them a puritanical narcissicism: 'I was young, proud of my strength, had led for years an athletic life without drinking or smoking, and was in a state of perfect physical fitness'; disagreeable racism: 'The smell of unwashed Gyppo hung about heavily'; and obsequious imperialism: 'I was fully aware that the time was close at hand for me to prove my claim to be called a member of the British Empire'. Finally and perhaps most peculiarly, there is the preparedness to sacrifice not only his life but his very individuality in the name of patriotism: Williams praises the 'sacred' selflessness of the men who 'fought for their country, died for their country, taking only what consolation there is in the submerging of self in country'.[74]

As regards the Australians' often erratic behaviour behind the lines, the memoirists are somewhat coy, not to say confused. While E. J. Rule allows his Diggers to get drunk and 'as wild as dingoes' (arguing that it is this 'harum-scarum attitude that counts in battle'), he

Trooper Bluegum at the Dardanelles: Lieutenant Oliver Hogue posing inside and outside his dugout on Gallipoli, 1915

Promoting the heroic legends: publicity for Australian First World War memoirs, *Reveille*, 1 April 1936

The Anzac Book staff leaving Imbros, off Gallipoli,
29 December 1915: C. E. W. Bean fourth from left

The band of the 18th Battalion, A.I.F., at Abbeville in France,
May 1918: Joseph Maxwell, author of *Hell's Bells and
Mademoiselles*, is seated second from left, front row.

registers a Bean-like objection to the portrayal of the A.I.F. as a collection of unruly larrikins. According to Rule, those 'intimate memoirs' in which the Australian soldier figures as 'a sort of cave-man, uncouth and ruthless, undisciplined by law of man or God', came from the pen of those who did not know him.[75] A chief source of moral discomfiture was the reputed concupiscence of the Australians. Owing, perhaps, to tact and a degree of mature embarrassment at recalling the excesses of youth, the stance adopted by most memoirists toward sex is one of cool reticence, tinged often by a contempt for women. Leonard Mann's presentation of the conflict between Jeffreys and Bentley over Mary Hatton in *Flesh in Armour* upholds a fundamental tenet of military ideology, that women are a threat to the preservation of strong male comradeship within the self-contained fighting unit. G. D. Mitchell enunciates the 'official' A.I.F. position on the female sex in his *Soldier in Battle* (1941), an 'Australian Military Handbook' published by Angus & Robertson to guide the second generation of Anzacs in World War Two:

> In a fighting unit a man's relations with others are simplified by the almost complete absence of women . . . Men, *en masse*, removed from feminine influence, are amicable and easy-going, generally trusting and trustworthy.[76]

The sowing of wild oats is nonetheless seen as almost as important a part of the warrior's education and existence as the drawing of blood on the battlefield. Justifying the sexual propositions put to two harassed 'buxom wenches' in a popular *estaminet*, H. R. Williams comments:

> . . . these people had been used to soldiers for many months, and they knew that it was as natural for a soldier to ask an attractive ma'mselle for permission to sleep with her as it is in civilian life to talk about the weather. I really believe that if an attractive French girl working to quench the thirst of soldiers in war-time did not have the proposition put to her with every fresh drink that she served, she would hurry upstairs and critically examine herself in the looking-glass to learn what was wrong with her appearance.[77]

These are forthright opinions indeed; but Williams is himself strangely loath to detail his *own* participation in such a 'natural' activity. He is prepared to inform us that he is corresponding with a girl in London; but no further information is forthcoming. She is obviously one memory he would prefer to keep to himself.

Amid all the innuendo, selective memory and stuffy circumspection, Joseph Maxwell's *Hell's Bells and Mademoiselles* – for all the vulgar pot-boiling elements that put it on the bestseller listings[78] – comes as something of a revelation. This is a personal narrative without inhibitions; it rejects the rehashing of diatribes about patriotism and tries to recall the passions of the wartime days whether or not, in retrospect, they seem suitably right and proper. The literary genealogy of *Hell's Bells and Mademoiselles* includes the riotous and irreverent humour of *Saints and Soldiers* and even the semipornographic *jeux d'esprit* of *An Anzac Muster*. Its author was a brilliant soldier. D.C.M., M.C., M.C. with Bar, and V.C. – as *Reveille's* reviewer of his memoir remarks, Joe Maxwell ended the war with 'a considerable section of the alphabet after the name'.[79] But he was tight-lipped about his military achievements. In *Hell's Bells and Mademoiselles* he so doctors his account of the exploit which won him the Victoria Cross that it appears to be nothing exceptional in the general run of battlefield events, a mere 'scrimmage', as he calls it.[80] So modest is Maxwell that it is only by returning to the Foreword written by his old commanding officer, which details his deeds, that we glean any real sense that the memoirist performed any notable actions at all. Fear seems to have been his constant battlefield companion; disenchantment with the war is one of his major themes. He had enlisted with as many illusions about war 'as perhaps ever fluttered in the minds of adventurers in fiction'; but he does not pretend that the reality lived up to his adolescent dreams. He recalls his thoughts upon his arrival at Gallipoli:

> Boyish fancies came back to me, fancies of deeds of derring-do, of emulating Wellington, heroic notions of dying like Wolfe. But now, face to face with the chance of "passing out," not in the role of a Wellington or a Wolfe, but somewhere in those lonely brown gullies, obscure and unseen, the prospect lacked much of its old glamour . . . Let those who prate of heroically facing fire for the first time console themselves with such delusions. I am not one of them. With every yard of that slow sheering in towards those hills my brain seemed to whirl faster and faster. The gentle seething of the vessel's wash past her grey plates sounded to me as the surge and crash of a waterfall. Let psychologists analyse the feeling as they choose. I want to be brutally candid in this narrative. What did I think? What did I say to myself?
>
> "God! what a damn fool I was to get into this."[81]

And these are his reactions to his first engagement on the peninsula:

> So here, in this dismal forbidding gully . . . lay glory! It was not the heroic, theatrical war of the history books. Those black bundles out there,

dim and shadowy under the pale starlight, had not even struck a blow at their enemies. In fact they had not seen a Turk . . . To me it seemed murder, nothing short of cold-blooded murder. I felt sick with the horror of it all.[82]

Early in the book, Maxwell promises to deliver the 'hard, brutal, devastating facts' about the war. From the Diggers' derision in recalling Andrew Fisher's pledge that Australia would stand by Britain to the 'last man and last shilling' as they toil in the ooze of the Western Front, to the detailed description of what he terms 'the whole grisly paraphernalia of war', Maxwell's approach is both all-inclusive and uncensored.[83] Stylistically, Maxwell is not always up to the task of giving anything more than a superficial account of what he has seen and encountered. Dreadful clichés ('this insane vortex') reveal the acknowledged literary 'assistance' of the well-known journalist, Hugh Buggy. But this attempt at 'polish' serves only to dull the natural charm and verve of Maxwell's narrative. Maxwell also revels in showing the unsavoury side of his wartime career. A fracas with the military police in a sleazy Piccadilly cabaret, which earned him an appearance at Bow Street and a hefty fine, is given more prominence than anything he achieved in combat. He displays hard-nosed larrikin logic in examining the balance sheet of his activities in and out of battle:

> To a village near Poperinghe was the next move. It was here that I was notified that I had been awarded the D.C.M., and a few days later received a commission. Of my fine for the disastrous London exploit £15 was refunded, and as the D.C.M. carries with it a grant of £20 I came out on the right side of the ledger.[84]

Maxwell's many brushes with the military authorities are documented, thus are verifiable. His memoir is not completely reliable, however: just as the majority of his colleagues embellish acts of heroism, he tends to magnify his acts of insubordination. Indeed, he invents a couple of them. He gives, for example, a rollicking account of his (albeit peripheral) involvement in Cairo's 'Wasser' brawl, calling it his first glimpse of 'active service'. But, as his own Foreword tells us, he did not leave Australia until June 1915, and the street-fight had in fact taken place the previous Easter.[85] This apocryphal story signifies Maxwell's tendency to promote the cult of individualism in opposition to the conservative corporate dogma preached by Bean and others. Clearly, he too is a mythologizer; but it is a very different version of the national war myth that he relates. Maxwell's seem-

ingly exhaustive romantic involvement with the women he encounters in his forays behind the line illustrates his relative radicalism.
Admittedly, his expansiveness on his many 'conquests' is as tiresome
as the boasting of military triumphs that ruins the reminiscences of
old soldiers like H. R. Williams, and in this sense he is just as conceited as the most insufferable military big-noter. In the literature
of the First A.I.F., however, almost any relief from the constant battlefield bravado is an 'aberration' to be accepted gratefully.

The national type championed by Maxwell is obviously not the
bush-bred patriot but the beer-swilling larrikin 'dag' patronized by
Harley Matthews. His most outstanding larrikin is the exuberantly
comic (and, one guesses, largely invented) Shamos Doherty:

> A rackety, full-throated, hairy-chested zest of life was Doherty's. Wor
> ries, reflections, introspection, he scorned. Yesterday was gone: to
> morrow may never come. To-day was here, pulsing, throbbing under
> the flare of the sun or glowing amid the wrack of storm. It mattered
> not to Doherty. It was there to be seized, to be lived through intensely
> with the vitality of a great flame. Life, each minute a crowded atom
> of life, triumphant and arrogant . . . A lumbering, carefree Irish-
> Australian, with a heart of gold, whose very presence was a vitalizing
> force. He had to the full that racial capacity for striking trouble, glory
> ing in it, and emerging triumphant and arrogant as ever.[86]

Three major things distinguish Doherty. Firstly, his courage. He is
as brave as any bronzed bushman – at Gallipoli, he 'faced the storm
as cool as a college professor playing chess'.[87] Secondly, his outrageously excessive behaviour out of battle, whether it be hunting military police with a rifle and fixed bayonet (an exploit which earns him
a court-martial), or unfurling the Australian flag on the stage of the
Folies Bergère in Paris. In battle, Doherty's truculence is manifested
in blood-curdling invocations of the name of the legendary Ned Kelly:
battle cries it is impossible to imagine coming from loyal subjects
of the King like G. D. Mitchell or H. R. Williams. Thirdly, and
perhaps most importantly, there is his irrepressible humour. Doherty's
comedy is that mix of the perverse, the mordant, the macabre, and
the forthright which is occasionally evident in *The Anzac Book* and
which is highlighted in *Saints and Soldiers*. Here is how he breaks
the news of a comrade's death to the dead man's fiancée back in
Australia:

> DEAR MISS,
>   Last night we raided the Germans. They were a pretty lively mob
> and didn't like being killed or taken prisoners. Your "finance" was a pretty

decent bloke and was puttin' the boot into a couple of Germans when he got shot in the leg. We was crawlin' into our own lines, when strike me handsome if another flamin' shell didn't land and blows his head clean off.

Hopin' this finds you in the pink as it does me.

I remain,

Yours truly,

SHAMOS DOHERTY

P.S. I souvenired them last pair of socks you sent him. They are a bit small, but hope you won't mind.[88]

A dynamic character himself, Doherty reserved little patience for those who do not meet his own heroic standards—especially if they happened to be British. His rejoinder to two Fifth Army Tommies as he escorts a barefoot German prisoner at the time of the enemy offensive in 1918 has about it that familiar ring of Australian contempt for English military abilities:

"Hi, choom, where's yon prisoner's boots?" they inquired. "He wore 'em out chasing you blokes," observed Doherty.[89]

The arrogance of this response is revealing, as it suggests that Maxwell is unwilling (or unable) to let go totally the entrenched idea of Digger superiority. He is unprepared, in analysing the halting of the German advance to Amiens in 1918, to give the A.I.F. all the credit for turning the tide of the war, but, like Bean, he implies that it was lucky for the Allies that the Australians were available in the crisis to rectify the English *sauve qui peut*: 'It so happened that a band of daredevils were in the critical place at just the right minute when iron resolution was needed and when faltering for an hour would have been fatal'. Furthermore, while *Hell's Bells* offers an adventurous, unorthodox Australian retrospection of the Great War, Maxwell finally agrees with such conventional 'daredevils' as Mitchell and Williams that the war spelt the beginning of a 'humdrum' civilian life. His distaste for war seems curiously mitigated by his depressed recognition that the Armistice meant the end of 'a carefree, colourful, and reckless existence'.[90]

The ambivalence towards war that is detectable in the memoirs of common soldiers like Idriess, Rule and Maxwell is even more marked in the writings of that most exalted of Diggers, General Sir John Monash. To command a force so 'magnificent' (his habitual term to illustrate the quality of the A.I.F.) was considered by Monash in his wartime correspondence as 'something to have lived for', and he wrote effusively about 'the dynamic splendour of a modern battle'. But he was also at some pains to point out his hatred of war, his disgust at its 'horror' and its 'destruction'.[91] Monash's apparent wartime uncertainty about war is even more pronounced in his major account of the conflict, *The Australian Victories in France in 1918* (1920). This is a strictly historical work (though Bean carped about it containing an abundance of factual errors), but since its author was so intimately involved in the great events he describes, it may be counted as a personal memoir. As such, it was included, along with *The Desert Column, The Gallant Company, Hell's Bells and Mademoiselles* and the like, in Angus & Robertson's 'The Gallant Legion' series. Dedicated to 'The Australian Soldier', who 'by his Military Virtues, and by his Deeds in Battle, has earned for Himself a Place in History which none can Challenge', *The Australian Victories in France in 1918* is written in a sustained spirit of praise for the courage, initiative, and adventurousness of those in his charge. All that stops the book from being an unqualified exercise in hero-worship are Monash's occasional suggestions that such individualistic heroes were in fact mere puppets being controlled by his own guiding military genius. Yet, at the end of the narrative, he provides a shock by proclaiming his lack of enthusiasm for war, it being a 'waste of human effort'.[92]

Donald Black's *Red Dust: An Australian Trooper in Palestine*, one of the first A.I.F. narratives to appear (1931) in the 1930s boom in Australian war literature, is torn even more strongly by internal contradictions. 'Donald Black' is the *nom-de-plume* of John Lyons Gray, who served with the Light Horse in the desert campaign and who, on the evidence of *Red Dust*, hated every minute of it. His sustained use of the present tense, an unusual device for a memoirist, brings home to the reader his disgust at his involvement in an enterprise which he sees as both lacking in moral credibility and disastrous in its effects upon its participants. There is no glamour in this cavalryman's war; none of the Light Horseman's usual pride and elation as recorded by Ion Idriess in *The Desert Column*. Black would rather talk about the sweaty and smelly feet, the lacerated backside and the piles, that come from excessive riding.[93]   The literary and intellectual influences that seem to have most affected Black when writing *Red Dust* are not Australian but European, which may explain why the work was published in London by Jonathan Cape, and not by Angus & Robertson or some other local publisher. For example, his continual declarations to the effect that 'there is no glory in war, only sorrow, suffering and illusion', and that battle is actually 'licensed murder', bring to mind Henri Barbusse's protesting *poilus*, and, going further back, Tolstoy's penetrating appraisal of the morality of war in *War and Peace*. And Black's theme of a 'lost generation' of young men thrown to the 'wolves' by their selfish elders is strongly reminiscent of one of Remarque's major obsessions in *All Quiet on the Western Front*, just as is his assertion that combat brutalizes rather than ennobles. In a lengthy passage in which Black analyses the reasons for the habitual gravitation towards brothels by soldiers when they are out of battle, he finds that such sexual immorality is in keeping with the combatant's 'war coarsened mind', that is, part of a more general debasement. Proclaiming no personal pleasure in outlining the soldier's 'carnal associations', Black states that he writes of them so as 'to build up the case against war' – and so recalls the admitted didacticism of the narrator of *Under Fire*. Again, when we read of his meditations upon 'the pity of it all, the infinite pity' as he watches the slow death of a boy-warrior whose stomach had been shredded by gunfire, we think, automatically, of Wilfred Owen's famous phrases in 'Strange Meeting'.[94]

The war entailed for Black the breakdown of personal patriotic and religious belief. When, fairly early in the narrative, he rebels against his soldierly lot, he enunciates his disaffection in a classic statement of Great War disillusion such as might have been written by Siegfried Sassoon:

> . . . I feel an imbued bitterness that hitherto has not penetrated, despite many weary months of campaigning . . . I feel entirely changed, filled with a spirit of sad rebellion, whereas I had hitherto accepted everything as it came, it was the war, what could one? I had my faiths and beliefs, these helped me along; but now, I can no longer lean to my creed, I feel it is a sham. An unutterable loneliness, a desperateness seems to envelope me . . . To go through life with fixed and asserted principles and beliefs teaches one to lean to them for support. To find a doubt of them, a suggestion that the solace they should offer is a mockery, that the faith they profess is an hypocrisy, makes me very bitter, bitter with a bitterness that I cannot shake off.[95]

'Bitterness', 'sad rebellion', 'sham', 'loneliness', 'desperateness', 'mockery', 'hypocrisy' – these are the catchwords of an epoch, at least of that experienced by an articulate generation of young Europeans. They rarely intrude upon the lexicon of most Australian Great War writers. Indicative of Black's maverick treatment of the Light Horse effort is his astonishingly perfunctory handling of the celebrated

Beersheba operation, in which he took part. He gives the exploit barely two short paragraphs, and in fact only identifies the town by placing its name in parenthesis. And in contrast with Ion Idriess's eager references to the classical military associations of the desert battlefield, Black employs the terrain's characteristic 'red dust' as a metaphor for the accumulated bloodshed and death of centuries of futile combat.[96]

Yet there are several occasions when Black relaxes his rigid anti-war stance and engages in passages of derivative myth-making. He invokes the familiar hereditary, historical and environmental factors used by Bean in the *Official History* to explain the distinction of the First A.I.F. Pioneering 'bloodlines' and way-of-life, a fluid egalitarian society removed from insidious European 'intrigue and ambition', and the special nature of a land 'too scarcely populated for us to have become sluggish and citified', make the Australian 'freer and happier' than his effete cousin from an England suffering from a 'growing senility'. Compared with the sedate and automaton-like Tommy, the Digger is 'mentally as well as physically . . . a husky'.[97] In weighing up the efficacy of both armies, British and the A.I.F., Black displays what C. E. Montague called 'the old Australian sneer'. Indeed, for someone who professes to detest war, Black is loud in his championship of those—Australians, naturally—who happen to be good at it. War may be 'licensed murder', but Black is flexible enough to admire a proficient killer. He defends Australian military big-noting thus:

> He [the Australian soldier] is sincere in what he does, whether it be killing Turks or getting drunk and he does one equally as well as the other. When he fights he fights and everyone knows about it; if they don't, he tells them, so that he has in some degree earned the reputation of a boaster, but whether this be true or not he has acquitted himself sufficiently well to be able to boast.[98]

And in a final act of narrative harakiri, Black ruptures the thematic credibility of his memoir by his enthusiasm for the racial 'spirit of adventure' which sends all good young men of British stock off to battle. One starts to wonder if the pseudonymous 'Donald Black' is not really a resurrected R. Hugh Knyvett in some post-war guise:

> To breed men who will rove, who will dare, who will carry the British flag to all corners of the earth, requires courage and unquenchable grit and determination. Granted we possess these attributes, then what is the power that propels these forces, makes them function and bring to fruition what otherwise may only be dreams? The force that sent men

forth to find and populate new countries, and propagate in them the same breed that urged their habitation, and in turn supply other races to grow up and emulate the example. The only thing that could supply the vital spark to set burning the flame of conquest, whether over a foe or the elements . . . is the inherent love of adventure, in seeking which we never count the cost.[99]

The position of the prisoner-of-war memoirist in the ebullient climate of First A.I.F. literature was problematic. Isolated by the stigma of his capture from the elevated military endeavour, the POW was confronted with the difficulty of knowing just what to say – and how to say it. The confident tone and the self-assertiveness of memoirists like Williams and Maxwell is missing; in its stead we find a blend of humility and querulousness.

Naturally capture must have been a great disappointment to the ambitious warrior. As R. F. Lushington expresses it in an early memoir, *A Prisoner of the Turks* (1923), it was 'an ignoble ending to all our brilliant aspirations'.[1] But capture was more than a mere anticlimax. John Halpin's *Blood in the Mists* (1934) typifies the defensive, almost cringing, posture assumed by the ex-prisoner under the cultural dictatorship of a national war ethos so aggressively supportive of a heroic view of battle. Surrender to the enemy entailed more than personal entrapment; it meant the renunciation of one's claims to manhood. What is the calibre of a man, Halpin implies, who allows himself to be taken? If he cannot stay in the fight, what value is he as a man and as a soldier? Somewhat self-pityingly, Halpin chooses to describe himself as a dishonourable 'reprobate', as one 'unwanted' and 'damned' to 'the dung-hill of captivity'. Divorced from the manly elect of the combatant A.I.F., he bears a burden of loss and of shame which is 'more devastating than any bodily affliction'.[2]

A schoolteacher before 1914, Halpin had at first been rejected for war service because of his poor physique, and had promptly been mailed a white feather for his trouble. Finally sent to Egypt in 1917 as one of the 'happy, carefree volunteers' constituting Light Horse Reinforcements, he was seized after a skirmish in Palestine. *Blood in the Mists* is the tracing of what Halpin calls 'the Via Dolorosa of Turkish prisondom', the sacrificial marches through Palestine, Syria and Turkey forced on those taken by the Turks in the Middle East war theatres. Subjected to a level of starvation, disease and cruelty equal to that endured by the prisoners of the Japanese in the Second World War – he worked on the construction of the Berlin–Baghdad

Railway in Anatolia, a horrific equivalent of the Burma–Siam – Halpin fought a very private war, concentrating solely on the lonely business of staying alive. It was a war of unremitting mental effort, of wild fluctuations between hope and despair rather than of overtly 'heroic' exploits. When the will to live capitulated, the body soon followed. Paradoxically, a sense of humiliation acted as a spur to self-preservation in these circumstances. The tradition of heroic battle action Australianized by the Great War, though largely responsible for the POW's woeful self-image, serves Halpin well when he comes to weigh the pros and cons of a prisoner's death:

> There is no glamour in a captive's death. It is sinister, without hope, unidealistic, actionless, a wilting . . . a filthy process . . . 'Killed in action.' There is beauty in the utterance, an heroic halo round the memory of a mangled mass or stiffened limbs; but, 'Died a prisoner . . .', that sounds a condemnation of dishonour, an aimless and unnecessary sacrifice.[3]

Bitterness, internecine wrangling over food and favours from the guards, and the abject philosophy of 'every man for himself' were the staples of Halpin's existence. Deprived even of the redeeming bonds of mateship, Halpin nevertheless is able to think positively about his contribution to the war effort. In one final burst of self-apology he proclaims that it had all been worth it. He had played a part, however minor and off-stage, in the world drama, and in so doing had helped save Australia from dreaded German expansionism.[4] It all sounds rather hollow after the lugubrious tones of the preceding pages: as if he is trying to convince himself as much as the reader.

Frustrated by his former impotence to hit back militarily, the POW writer commonly resorts to compensatory racist attacks on his captors. Listen to R. F. Lushington:

> For all pure thick-headedness give me the Turk; he reigns supreme and will always remain so, an uneducated, unreasonable human being, with a born heritage of innate cruelty . . .[5]

Similarly, the thrust of another memoir by a prisoner of the Turk, T. W. White's *Guests of the Unspeakable* (1928), is not hard to guess. The desire for some sort of belated revenge is understandable, and perhaps even justified by the mass of historical data which points to the ill-treatment Turkey dished out to its prisoners. In the particular case of *Guests of the Unspeakable*, however, the work of documentation is a pretext for xenophobic propaganda. Certainly, *Blood in the Mists* is not free of racial slander, either – Halpin mocks just about every nationality other than his own, including the 'weedy' and incessantly 'chattering' English. But White's memoir is a cranky compendium of nineteenth-century imperialist prejudices and parochialism. Taking the reader on a Cook's tour of the 'classic ground' (the memoir is subtitled 'The Odyssey of an Australian Airman') he traversed after his capture in Mesopotamia in 1915, White intersperses elaborate commentary on the places of interest he visited with attacks on the 'unspeakable' Turk. Promising references to 'the aeons of ennui which make the life of a prisoner so unendurable' and to the 'spectre of hopelessness' stalking the POW camp are left undeveloped, White quickly resuming his exposé of the more depraved aspects of Middle and Near Eastern civilization in comparison with 'the manifold advantages of being British'.[6] White, who was a Federal politician after the war, eventually snared the plum job of Australian High Commissioner in London. *Guests of the Unspeakable* must have provided a perfect 'personal reference' for this appointment. Then again, just about all Australian memoirs of the Great War are fixed somewhere in the self-advertising mode.

V

Dissenting Voices

'PEACEFUL PENETRATION' OF THE HEROIC IDEAL

Not all Australian First World War novelists and memoirists participated in the feast of self-congratulatory chauvinism I have been
describing. During the war years and after, a minority of writers
showed a preparedness to challenge some of the nation's most treasured assumptions about the nature and substance of heroism.

In Australia, no less than in Britain, it was the poets who first wrote
in emotional reaction against the war and the cult it created. Two
non-combatants, John Le Gay Brereton and Frank Wilmot ('Furn-
ley Maurice') were among the first literary voices to depart from the
propagandist line. In his contempt for warfare's 'vast vulgarity' and
his attack on mindless patriotism in poems collected in *The Burning
Marl* (1919), Brereton repudiated the prevailing belligerence of Australian war literature – as did, in a different register, Wilmot in *To
God: From the Weary Nations* (1917), a quietistic appeal for peace
which remains one of the most highly-regarded Australian war poems.[1]
The fact that it was mostly left to non-participant intellectuals like
Brereton and Wilmot to condemn the conflict confirms the vindica-
tory nature and intent of Australian writing about the Great War.
In Britain it was the soldiers themselves – committed anti-war poets
like Owen and Sassoon – who set out to change cultural attitudes to
martial endeavour. While some poetical head-scratching can be discerned in *Songs of a Campaign* (1917), by the original Anzac and
superior A.I.F. poet Leon Gellert, 'no literary outcry' against war
emanated from the Australian trenches.[2]

That the prose writers lagged behind the poets in registering their
protest is explained, at least in part, by the nature of their art. Unlike

146

the war lyric, which is immediately and emotionally responsive to the event, the autobiographical prose narrative emerges only after a period of meditative gestation. Thus it took some years before the prose works of many intensely anti-war sensibilities came to fruition. This hiatus is illustrated by the careers of two of the most notable British First World War writers, Robert Graves and Siegfried Sassoon. Graves, a prolific war poet, did not produce his first war prose, *Goodbye to All That*, until 1929; and it took a decade and more of peacetime reappraisal before the attitudes informing the vitriolic wartime verse of Siegfried Sassoon were processed into the fictionalized memoirs which constitute his 'George Sherston' trilogy. A similar pattern is evident in Australian First World War literature. It was not until the late 1920s and early 1930s that the isolated wartime utterances of poets like Wilmot were supplemented and supported by a number of prose assaults on the literary fortress enshrining the national war effort.

Considered together, these renegade works form a kind of literary 'peaceful penetration' of the Australian heroic ideal. 'Peaceful Penetration', the ironically-named practice of the A.I.F. infantry on the Western Front during the lull in the fighting in the spring and summer of 1918, was a tactic of constant though small-scale harassment of German outposts, of what C. E. W. Bean called a 'nibbling' at the enemy line.[3] By this method of unobtrusive infiltration, chunks of German ground were captured without a full-scale attack having to be launched. It cannot be said that Australian anti-heroic prose constituted a literary movement as such; nor did it have as destructive an impact on the philosophical 'enemy' as did the military tactic on the German front line. Comprising authors and personalities as varied as Vance Palmer and Martin Boyd, the anti-heroic writers are a disparate group, linked by their common concern to question, to impugn, or even merely to ignore, the assumptions and attitudes of the popular myth. And, for all their efforts, the elevated status of the Digger remained sturdily intact, in good shape to be further magnified by another horde of publicists after the myth-reinforcing military events of 1939–45. Nevertheless, 'Peaceful Penetration' is a useful description of the character and function of the anti-war narratives. At their most insipid, in a romance like Leslie Meller's *A Leaf of Laurel* (1933), the view of the Australian soldier as a strong-willed swashbuckler is qualified; at their most penetrating, such as in Angela Thirkell's satirical exposure of the tawdry reality lying behind the Digger's self-image in *Trooper to the Southern Cross* (1934), the shaky ground upon which many of the 1914–18 legends are built is significantly undermined. The encroachment of iconoclasts like Thirkell into literary territory formerly occupied virtually exclusively by mythologizers occurred at a point in time when the art of Australian military self-advertisement, in the shape of 1930s memoirs like *The Gallant Company*, was at its zenith. It was a welcome development, since it brought some fresh ideas and new modes of expression into a stuffy literary climate. In a genre noted for its indulgent partisanship – a kind of literary backslapping – it was about time for the appearance of a few writers independent enough to snub the hallowed ideal.

'ART' OVER 'ACTION'

It says something revealing about the culture reflected by the national war literature that the anti-heroic 'message' has usually been invested in or propagated by men of a conspicuously sensitive, imaginative and artistic temperament. The idea that men of refined sensibility are likely to be incompetent on the battlefield is repudiated by the example of the venturesome T. E. Lawrence, and also by 'Mad Jack' Sassoon, who combined his hatred of war as expressed in his poetry with a penchant for making reckless excursions into No Man's Land. But, for their part, many Australian Great War writers seem to hold that it is impossible to be brave as well as 'bookish': C. E. W. Bean, for example, doubts Monash's courage at least partly on the grounds that the famous commander was an intellectual. Again, they would have us believe that only introverts or effeminate aesthetes are severely debilitated by fear. That roisterous man-of-action, Joe Maxwell, was one of the few memoirists of the 1930s bold enough to confess his fear of combat, and indeed it took until 1981, and Bert Facey's *A Fortunate Life*, for a soldier-writer of the First A.I.F. to admit unequivocally to being 'scared stiff'.[4] In fiction, in a novel like *Flesh in Armour* for example, it is implied that disaffection, trepidation and ineptitude are the properties of inward-looking 'outsiders' only.   It was left to a non-combatant, Vance Palmer, to show that the model soldier could also buckle under the intense strain of battle. Palmer's short story 'The Line', which appears in his 1931 collection, *Separate Lives*, deals with the 'baptism of fire' in France of two young recruits. One, Snowy Fraser – 'tense, finely-strung, moved by the impulses of romantic boyhood' – spends the pre-battle period in the grip of 'the most subtle of all fears, the fear of being afraid'. He is convinced that he will 'snap at the first strain'. His mate, the good-natured Melbourne larrikin Chook Delaney, is 'unimaginative, gross, thoughtless to the point of imbecility'. The kind of soldier, in other words, generals love to command. Fraser emerges from the ordeal physically and mentally unscathed. In fact, he feels happy and fulfilled by the experience, newly 'poised and sure'. The irony of Palmer's story lies in what becomes of Delaney. He survives, to be sure, but is reduced by battle to a gibbering, weeping shell of a man, suffering torments drawn 'from the deep abysses of his mind – a mind that never looked ahead and rarely behind'.[5]

Arthur Wheen's thematic juxtaposition of 'active' and 'passive' temperaments in his short story, 'Two Masters' (1923),[6] similarly tends to confound the conventional Australian wisdom about warfare. Wheen, the original translator of *All Quiet on the Western Front*, was especially well qualified to dramatize the special dilemma of the soldier-intellectual. A teenage student at Sydney University when war broke out, he returned there upon his arrival back in Australia after his military service (which was sufficiently distinguished for *Reveille* to include him in its 'Celebrities of the A.I.F.' series);[7] in 1919 he won a Rhodes Scholarship to Oxford, and later became a librarian at the Victoria and Albert Museum in London.

The narrator of 'Two Masters' is an untried recruit named Carter. He begins the story in December 1915, at Tel-el-Kebir in Egypt, where he and other novices had been sent to reinforce the remnants of the force which had campaigned on Gallipoli. Carter, who frankly admits his 'enthusiasm for heroics', refers to the tall stories which the Anzac veterans told to young recruits such as himself in order to foster *esprit de corps* and 'to hand on . . . the tradition of Gallipoli'.[8] He is impressed by both the reminiscences and the raconteurs themselves. Naive and ardent, Carter is in the fictional mould of hero-worshippers like Crane's Henry Fleming and Stendhal's Fabrizio; but unlike them he is not forced to reappraise his unreal vision of soldiering, and he undergoes no process of disillusionment. This is no accident of omission on Wheen's part, whose tacit purpose is to reveal the inadequacy of the Australian fixation with aggressive heroism.

Among the 'Peninsula men' in Carter's unit is Ralston, a placid man who strives to live in 'the world of art and imagination' rather than in the world of action. 'Sensitive' and of an unprepossessing, unsoldierly appearance, Ralston prefers to spend his time sketching while his comrades resurrect and embellish past exploits. His cynicism about their reminiscences extends to a denial of the value of

warlike effort itself: as he warns Carter at one point, '*Virtus* is out
of date and place these days'. Carter, stung by Ralston's view of him
as being 'more credulous than Quixote', despises the veteran for his
diffidence and his scepticism, and dismisses him as 'a fatuous dreamer'
who is meanly envious of 'success in the field of action . . . which,
in a world of deeds, effectually eclipsed the pale successes of a dilettante'.[9] But what Carter really finds hard to accept about Ralston
is the latter's undeniable personal bravery. The mere fact that he had
served on Gallipoli had at first seemed incongruous, 'the height of
comedy'. But when Carter witnesses Ralston's military virtuosity first-
hand, in battle in France, his bewilderment turns to 'unmixed
astonishment':

> I had come to think of him as a man too rich in imagination, too sensi-
> tive to conscience, too gifted in understanding, and too deficient in
> vigorous character, to face the reality of war without an access of fear
> which would paralyse him for action. I was prepared to excuse him,
> in circumstances which must in their nature unman him. I say I was
> amazed at his conduct . . . When I had marked him out as a man of
> broken purpose and trembling faith, he would suddenly overthrow my
> judgment by some act of intrepid devotion, of sustained and matchless
> coolness, which belied all my suspicions of desperation and infirmity.[10]

The real reason for Ralston's detached indifference to the robust *bon-
homie* of his comrades is a moral one. Unlike the typical Digger, who
(albeit often ruefully) accepts his role as a hired gun in the service
of his country, Ralston is divided by a sense of conflicting allegiance. He must serve the public, patriotic cause and also adhere to
the principles and practices of his strong religious faith. Inspired by
Christian virtue rather than by heroic *virtus*, Ralston is distressed
that he has pawned his soul to the national interest, and his morale
is finally shattered when, on assignment impersonating a German
officer behind enemy lines, his duty forces him to murder in cold
blood a German to whom he had formed a deep attachment. Dis-
traught, he eventually walks out alone into No Man's Land, and is
killed. Carter's reaction to the news of Ralston's self-destruction is
the key to Wheen's ironic exposure of the misconceived preconcep-
tions, biases and prejudices of the Australian heroic ethos. Having
acquired some battle-wisdom, Carter had seemed to have revised his
initial false assessment of his comrade. But the shocking manner of
Ralston's death revived the old animosity. Ralston's wretched surrender of his life showed that 'there was cowardice in his woman's

heart after all'.[11] Carter's inability to empathize with Ralston's predicament suggests that he had learnt little from his own war experience. He remains a sadly immature figure, tied to an invalidated military philosophy which insists that all the trials of the battlefield are physical, and that mental or emotional trauma are the product of personal weakness, or signs of effeminacy.

Few Australian writers highlight the plight of the 'thinking' soldier as movingly as Arthur Wheen. Suffice to say, however, it is that kind of individual who struggles the hardest and most unsuccessfully to meet the heroic ideal. Frank Jeffreys in *Flesh in Armour* remains the outstanding case study, but there are others of interest, such as John Fairbairn, the protagonist of J. P. McKinney's novel *Crucible* (1935). As morosely circumspect as the men of the *Official History* are extroverted achievers and those of *Saints and Soldiers* are irrepressible ratbags, Fairbairn bears little resemblance to the much-beloved hero of the typical Australian war book. An accountant by profession, he had gone into battle as 'a rather proper, rather stiff, unyielding sort of chap', protected by a carapace of 'ready-made standards and conventions'.[12] This early delineation of character is close to that of the intractable pre-war personality of Christopher Tietjens in *Some Do Not*, the opening volume of the Ford Madox Ford's *Parade's End* tetralogy. As happens to Tietjens (an employee of the 'Imperial Department of Statistics'), the crucible of war remodels Fairbairn by modifying the rigidity of his former self. After the Armistice, he congratulates himself for being 'a better and a bigger man for these exacting years of war – more of a man than ever he would have been in peace days'.[13] We should not be misled by the terms of Fairbairn's self-praise. He does not see himself as 'more of a man' in the chest-beating sense; he is approving his new gentleness and flexibility, not the belief that combat had augmented his physical strength and hardened his will. We will have to take his word for it: whereas Tietjens's inner transformation is plotted convincingly in meticulous psychological detail by Ford, Fairbairn by the end of *Crucible* is only marginally less self-absorbed and stiff-necked than he was at the outset. Kudos should be afforded McKinney, however, for his ambitious, if limited, use of the interior monologue to dramatize the impact of war on Fairbairn's isolated consciousness. This is a flirtation with modernism all too rare in a national genre bedevilled by banal naturalistic exposition.

For all his unredeemed priggishness, Fairbairn is somewhat

eccentric for the hero of an Australian war novel. No compliant and contented warrior like H. R. Williams's persona in *The Gallant Company*, he is unimpressed by romantic military stereotypes. Conscious of the army's ability to 'crush inspiration out of a man', he concentrates his energies on warding off its 'all-pervading, depressing, damned demoralizing influence' rather than on the ostensible enemy.[14] Soldiers like Joe Maxwell, of course, had played the army for all it was worth, pitting their individuality against the institution in the constant quest for free-spirited self-expression. Fairbairn's hostility to the military world is more fundamental. While the Maxwells found many of the rituals of army life irksome, they would never have thought of the war itself, as McKinney's hero does, as

> merely an unpleasant interlude in a decent man's life, to be endured rather than lived, and forgotten as soon as possible after it was over.[15]

The problem of fear complicates Fairbairn's abhorrence of soldiering and turns him into a decidedly unhappy warrior. In *Flesh in Armour*, Frank Jeffreys resolves his struggle with his 'cowardice' through suicide; Fairbairn comes to terms with his dread of battle through dispassionate analysis of the malady. Specifically, it is the fear of fear, the fear of being afraid when the time comes to perform on the battlefield, that perturbs him. Like many thousands of his comrades, he had enlisted with naïve ideas about war, and was shocked by the reality of it. Imbued with a 'soldierly *élan*' while marching to Pozières for his first real taste of combat, he recalls the exhortation of his cockney bayonet instructor: '*Yer jabs it in, yer screws it rahnd!*' But there was little opportunity for the virtuoso use of the bayonet at Pozières. There, as elsewhere on the Western Front, it was the indifferent, brute force of the big guns that prevailed. Uncommonly for an Australian war writer, McKinney recognizes what Europeans had been saying since 1915 or 1916 – that the dominance of impersonal artillery in the modern arena signalled the demise of the individualistic hero. Mechanized weaponry reduced its operators to automata, 'slaves of their metal masters', thereby debasing the concept of heroic action and perverting combat into a deadly game of chance, 'a toss of the dice' in which willing, skilled soldiers would get blown to bits while the timorous and ineffectual survived.[17] Burdened – or relieved – by the knowledge that the pursuit of glory is doomed to failure in this military context, Fairbairn dispenses with martial ambition and secures for himself a 'cushy' job as an assistant Area Commandant well behind the lines. The commonplace tasks attached to this sinecure are 'not exactly what he had enlisted for', as he admits. But 'his patriotic fervour was a corpse long since', and his commitment is redirected to the preservation and development of his own individuality in opposition to an unthinking participation in 'a damned, rotten, degrading business'.[18]

McKinney is no indiscriminate iconoclast, however. The magnetic chauvinistic appeal of the Australian role in reversing the German Offensive of 1918 induces him to toy with the legend of A.I.F. pre-eminence. The almost mandatory attack on the alleged ineptitude of the British is boosted by references to the 'elation' which the war-hating Fairbairn, newly returned to his old unit, feels at being involved in a great enterprise. McKinney even recycles clichés from the wartime propaganda machine, including an allusion to 'the old swinging stride' of the Diggers – a feeble mystification of the kind lampooned by Harley Matthews as early as 1919.[19] Fairbairn surprises us by performing with credit in the 'exploit' at Villers-Bretonneux, earns promotion and commands his own company. But McKinney manages to check this temptation to lapse into the familiar myth-making manner by his controlling insistence on the ignobility of the actions of soldiers, which are likened to those of 'navvies on the spree'.[20] Fairbairn's reflections at the time of the Armistice indict the very ethical foundations upon which the Allied war effort was launched. His attack on the vacuity of the old war rhetoric reminds us strongly of Hemingway's Frederic Henry and his famous denunciation of war in *A Farewell to Arms*:

> Over! . . . The thing they had fought for – victory, peace, civilization, decency, a safer world, a world purged of Prussianism, and so on and so on – well, they had it, whichever and whatever it was. And what did it amount to? All phrases.
>
> Life was bound up in words which, after all, never really seemed to give a clue as to what men actually wanted. Why had the sordid struggle dragged on through all these years? . . . That was what civilization had come to – words, either meaning on analysis nothing, or not meaning what they pretended to mean . . . "Fighting for civilization!" – while civilization, like the jungle-man's cub panther, had grown up and turned from a pet to a beast of prey. The world had suffered all this misery "for civilization!" . . .[21]

There is one final indicator of the dissenting earnestness of McKinney's handling of the war theme in *Crucible*. Fairbairn, engaged to be married to a woman back in Australia, leaves a baby behind in France, the legacy of an affair with a local girl. In *Hell's Bells and*

Mademoiselles Joe Maxwell had summarily killed off his mistresses with the abandon that is characteristic of him, while in *Flesh in Armour* Leonard Mann allowed Frank Jeffreys the 'luxury' of resolving his problems with Mary Hatton by blowing himself up. McKinney offers his hero no such conclusive solutions. At the end of the war Fairbairn returns to his homeland, and his waiting fiancée, to face what is called his 'own private "hop-over" '.[22] The illegitimate child he leaves behind signifies, as Humphrey McQueen has intimated, a loss of innocence and a burden of responsibility for both Fairbairn as an individual and for Australia itself as a nation.[23] What is implied is that the real time of testing for man and country came not on the battlefield during the 'sordid' conflict, but in learning to cope with the challenges of the ensuing peace. Of all the fictions to appear in the renaissance of Australian battle literature that took place between the wars, *Crucible* is among the most convincing in its coherent expression of a distaste for bellicose patriotism, and among the most persuasive in its renunciation of the whole heroic machinery.

While there is something refreshing in the refusal of a character like John Fairbairn to be seduced by the mystique of the martial life, a common attribute of the nonconforming soldier is an intellectually-based arrogance similar in effect if not in nature to that often embodied by the more conventionally heroic Digger. Fairbairn's contemptuous dismissal of the apparently casual acceptance with which most men submitted to the rigours of soldiering provides an example. According to him, they obviously just 'didn't think'.[24] But at least Fairbairn is a man of some substance and conviction – unlike Anthony Hyde, the disagreeable hero of Leslie Meller's *A Leaf of Laurel*. From a wealthy South Australian pioneering family, Hyde possesses a 'lyrical' temperament and a preference for ideas and abstractions over the attractions of unthinking action. Having enthusiastically enlisted in the first South Australian infantry battalion to leave the home shores, he finds the warfare around Anzac Cove to be a harrowing test of his nerves, which he compounds by his own dread of appearing afraid to his stolid, earthy comrades. Hyde's manner of differentiating his own responses to combat from those of his brother soldiers has about it an air of precious condescension. He makes it clear that he regards his own sensibility as being more refined than that of his comrades: 'He would never be able to accustom himself to the spectacle of violence and death as all these others had done'.[25] Wounded for the second time on Gallipoli, he assures himself that he is not of 'the stuff from which fighting men are made', and spends most of the rest of the war convalescing in Cairo as a 'willing non-participant' in the military struggle, engaging in a series of fantastic adventures in both brothel and bazaar.[26] Hyde's intellectual interests, in particular his love of literature, are made to explain his aloofness from his comrades and therefore from the heroic spirit. He, in turn, is scorned by the others, who derisively call him 'a bit of a professor':

> Book-learning might be a fine quality in other circumstances, but it was something to be hidden away, ridiculed, flatly denied if necessary in such days as these.[27]

Hyde, in fact, is unworthy of the men's ridicule, on intellectual grounds at least. They need not have bothered – he is really no more than a shallow dilettante, an aspiring writer whose indiscriminate 'passion for beauty' is unable to be channelled into creative effort. Like his literary pretensions, his wartime suffering is, one suspects, something of a sham.

One is perhaps more inclined to be sympathetic to the discomfort of Eric Partridge, who published two heavily autobiographical and highly similar war narratives, 'A Mere Private' (1928) and 'Frank Honywood, Private' (1929).[28] Partridge could not be called a typical soldier-writer of the First A.I.F. Born in New Zealand, he went to live in Queensland in his youth, and in 1914 was studying at the University of Queensland. Like Arthur Wheen, he interrupted his studies to serve in the Australian Army. Upon his return to Queensland after the war he completed his degree, graduating in English and French, and in 1929 secured a travelling scholarship which took him to Oxford, where he was granted his B. Litt. for a published work, *Eighteenth Century English Romantic Poetry* (1924). He went on to win an enduring reputation as a critic and lexicographer.[29] Unlike many Australian soldier-writers, Partridge placed literary endeavour above fighting in his list of priorities, and was acutely affected by the frustrations of soldiering. Nevertheless, it is difficult to accept his assertion that he, as an artist, suffered more during the war than 'ordinary' men. There is a superciliousness about his attitude to the common soldier which verges on the distasteful. 'Military dispensation', he claims, was 'rightly' directed at the

> prosaic, or to put it otherwise, at some ninety-five per cent. of the men. The remainder consisted of the imaginative, the highly strung, the sensitive, from whom spring the majority of the world's thinkers, artists,

writers, but who, as soldiers pure and simple, are not superior to their more humdrum fellows. When intelligence was required, this minority came into its own; but apparently intelligence was seldom required, and when it was it was usually brushed aside. Such scouting and flouting of intelligence did not make it any easier for those possessing it, for they already suffered keenly; their courage was sheer will overcoming those sickening fears which a lively imagination evokes, whipping horrified minds to action, riding rough-shod over nerves lacerated and hypersensitised. Morally, the courage of such men is superior to that of the prosaic, sturdy, and dull . . . but let no high-brow belittle the work of the dull, honest fellows who comprise the greater part of every army, for though the latter suffered less intimately, much less agonisingly and maddeningly than the sensitive and intelligent, yet suffer they did . . .[30]

Whatever the sharpness of Partridge's intelligence, he had gone off to war with as many false ideas about combat as the most 'humdrum' raw recruit. 'Glamour', 'ardour' and 'elation' are the terms used to reflect his feelings at the time of his embarkation. His romantic disposition is indicated by his chosen reading for the long voyage – he takes along a volume of Hugo's lyrics and another of Chateaubriand's romances. Not getting enough fighting to make him 'fear war or even to dislike it', he finds Gallipoli tolerable, even, at times, 'very pleasant'. But later, on the Somme, one particularly bitter night of fighting is enough to turn the happy young warrior into a prematurely-aged, embittered dissenter who sees the war as 'a witches' sabbath [in which] all were victims'. By the time of the Battle of Pozières in 1916 he is a self-confessed coward; possessed by fear and with his nerve gone, he considers deserting and even contemplates suicide.[31] Yet Partridge, loathing war, decides to do what he calls 'the right thing'. He endures. Battle was 'evil', 'ghastly' and 'indescribably terrible', but he had enlisted to defend his nation's existence, and 'if fight one must, it was difficult to justify any decision other than that to fight bravely and intelligently'.[32] We are reminded here of the stoicism of Robert Graves, who in *Goodbye to All That* maintained that, despite the intensity of his distaste for what he observed around him, it was his duty as a professional soldier 'to fight whomever the King ordered to fight'.[33] It is surely ironical that soldiers such as Partridge and Graves, those men most intellectually aware of the futility of the activity in which they were engaged, made such willing cannon-fodder.

One of the more piquant aspects of the wartime lives of these dissenters from the heroic creed is that their friendships with their fellow soldiers tend to take on an exclusivity and an intensity quite unlike the more general matiness which suffused the A.I.F. In an autobiography, *A Single Flame* (1939), Martin Boyd defensively asserts that a kind of love between two soldiers has 'nothing to do with effeminacy', though he does recognize that it might have a Freudian basis.[34] Such a suggestion would have appalled self-consciously masculine soldiers like H. R. Williams, who might have been consoled by the fact that, as Boyd goes on to point out, a mutual 'vow of love till death' was the 'same emotion that inspired the Greek heroes'.[35] One thinks particularly of the almost mystical bond between Achilles and Patroclus in the *Iliad*. (In 'Two Masters' Ralston says he loved the German he is duty-bound to liquidate 'as Jonathan loved David, as Achilles loved Patroclus'.)[36] Nevertheless, by virtue of their emphasis on shared *emotion* rather than shared *action*, on a delicacy of fine feeling divorced from the exaltation derived from actually *fighting* together, the romantic enthusiasms embraced by Boyd are inimical to the robust corporate heroic identity characteristic of the A.I.F. Boyd's ideal of comradeship involves the meeting of like minds who together try to escape an environment which produces only horror and death. Here is his description of one of the few such deep attachments he formed during his service with the British forces:

> There was a subaltern named Hazelrigg with whom I enjoyed a brief friendship. One summer evening we were walking together across a harvest field near our billets. Some suggestion of home in the harvest field, our youthful unfocussed desire for beauty, stimulated by the loveliness of the evening, and our awareness of a mutual fate gave us a sense of romantic identity.[37]

Eric Partridge's search for a kindred tender spirit among the horde of dull creatures with whom he serves leads him to Jim Hicks. This young man Partridge nicknames 'Felipé': their intimate circle would allow no matey 'Snowy', 'Bluey', or 'Smithy'. Yet not even the 'golden hours' they spend apart from the philistines can alleviate the deadening misery of involvement in a kind of warfare which left the 'almost inevitable impression that a man had not a dog's chance' of survival.[38] In *Iron in the Fire* (1934) Edgar Morrow similarly describes how he teamed up with a special friend in a vain attempt to escape the 'degenerate and unnatural' life at the front. As these two would-be sophisticates read through Palgrave's *Golden Treasury* together, they decide that they are 'wasted in such a thing as war'.[39]

MARTIN BOYD, THE OUTSIDER

More than a posturing aestheticism set Martin Boyd apart from the Australian heroic tradition. The divided cultural loyalties of this member of the famous Anglo-Australian artistic family are well known, and constitute a major shaping force of his fiction. Boyd could just as easily have been analysing himself when he has one of his key characters, Guy Langton, remark that he suffered from a form of 'geographical schizophrenia which has made it impossible for me to regard any country as wholly my own'.[40] But too literal an interpretation of this diagnosis underestimates and even distorts Boyd's feeling of displacement. When he writes, in *A Single Flame*, of his 'lifelong fate of never quite belonging to my environment',[41] he hints at a deeper source of isolation, one which is a problem of sensibility and philosophical belief as much as a matter of mere geography.

Early in his account of his war involvement in *A Single Flame*, Boyd gives us a signifier of his separateness from the other young Australians questing after military glory. On the troopship to Europe, he loses himself in the whimsical world of Max Beerbohm's *Zuleika Dobson* while the others – clearly the 'prosaic' nonentities patronized by Eric Partridge – dutifully pore over the military manual, *Infantry Training*.[42] Boyd was *en route* to England to be commissioned into the British Army. In consideration of Martin's delicate constitution and somewhat morbid temperament, an uncle had succeeded in convincing his family that he would not survive the apparently barbarous life of an Australian private. More importantly, however, the uncle thought it proper for a member of a landed family with distinguished Irish, English and European ancestry to fight alongside men of his own class and culture. Boyd was later to acknowledge his relative's insistence as doing him a 'good turn'.[43] The family's cultural roots and sympathies lay far to the north of the Great South Land – an inheritance reinforced by Martin's education at Trinity Grammar in Melbourne. As he wrote in *A Single Flame*:

> All the images awakened by my education were English and European. There was something called Australian history but it seemed to me so uncultivated and flat . . . .[44]

Boyd's arrival in England is an epiphany of 'homecoming'; it provides him with a feeling of reintegration (confirmed by a visit to the family tombs in Wiltshire) which he thinks most Australians would regard as 'shameful and renegade'.[45] He is overstating the point a little, as not a few antipodeans, during and indeed well beyond the

Great War, still regarded Britain as 'home'. Yet it is true that most Diggers thought of themselves as foreigners when visiting the Mother Country. The case of Charl Bentley in *Flesh in Armour*, who sees himself a 'little proudly' as an 'alien' in wartime London even though his father had been born within five miles of Trafalgar Square, is representative.[46] Whether dining with Bertrand Russell at the studio of Roger Fry, calling on aristocratic relatives, or partying with wealthy friends, the ease with which Boyd took to cultured life in England stands in marked contrast to the loneliness which awaited most visiting Australians. The discontent felt by many Diggers in England was compensated by a magnified sense of their own national identity. Charl Bentley's 'resentment towards this cold alien England', for instance, encourages an awareness of his 'distinctive Australian nationality'.[47] Boyd's homecoming, on the other hand, was both illusory and shortlived. The war experience forces him to accept that he was not fully committed to either world, British or Australian. For all the 'emotional love' he feels for England and despite his professional affiliations with the British services, he still talks in *A Single Flame* of Australians as 'my countrymen'. Conversely, the unfriendliness of Australians aboard the ship 'home' at the war's end (who dismiss him as a 'Pommy') restores his former feeling of dissociation from the people of his own land. A brief taste of life back in Melbourne convinces him that he is in a 'foreign country'. We can gauge his lack of sympathy with the local scene by the fact that he is angered by a correspondence in the Melbourne *Argus* which canvasses that cherished theme of Australian military enthusiasts, the alleged cowardice of the British Army.[48]

Boyd must therefore have been one of the few Australians who returned home from the Great War with a sense of national self-awareness that was, if anything, reduced rather than increased. As Brenda Niall has posited: 'Being a Boyd was more important than being an Australian: it gave him a sense of identity strong enough to bypass nationalism for civilization'.[49] This indifference to patriotism was compounded, from the time of his youth as recorded in *A Single Flame*, by a temperamental incapacity to respond to the ethos instilled into the boys at Trinity Grammar. (The same school, it is worth remembering, that produced Neville Ussher, the hero from Roy Bridges's *The Immortal Dawn*; Boyd, indeed, was a contemporary of Ussher, co-editing the school magazine with him.) The outbreak of war left Boyd 'immeasurably depressed' rather than panting with expectation. His incipient pacifism, so at odds with the belligerence

of his fellow students, who 'seemed to think some glorious picnic
had begun', manifested his innate isolation:

> In an argument with my father about the war he told me that I was
> 'curiously constituted' because I did not enjoy the prospect of fighting,
> and again I had the sense of being a misfit.[50]

Yet Boyd was only too aware of what was expected of him. From
his days in the Trinity cadets, he had accepted that should his
country – England, in this case – go to war, then it was ordained that
he should fight to protect her. An atavistic commitment to the ideal
of patriotic duty overcame his distaste for war, and by the time of
his arrival at the front he was among the most eager of warriors.
During the period of military training he had lost his 'sense of being
a misfit', experiencing a 'release from intellectual responsibility' by
zestfully entering into the life of his unit.[51]

In *Disenchantment* C. E. Montague writes with some eloquence
of such British Army recruits as Boyd, 'men of handsome and boundless illusions' who renounced their own individuality for the greater
good of the corporate effort and in order to discharge an obligation
of honour. He terms their selflessness a 'willing self-enslavement',
an 'acquiescence in some mystic will outside their own'.[52] To the
intensely romantic Boyd, who during his adolescence had been
attracted to Catholicism as part of a longing for 'ecstatic spiritual
union with something outside [him]self', the army seemed to offer
a commitment which bordered on the religious. But, as with the military acolytes Montague describes, this initial idealistic engrossment
soon lapsed into cynicism. This of course is a paradigm of the classical European Great War experience. The encounter with actual
combat taught Boyd the great lesson of modern warfare, that 'noble
gestures . . . are anachronisms'.[53] Perhaps more than any other soldier-
writer, Boyd personifies a point made felicitously by Eric Leed in
his study of combat and identity in the Great War, *No Man's Land*
(1974) – that it was 'a war in which Don Quixote assumed the features of a Sancho Panza'.[54]

Boyd did not allow his disaffection to sour into an outraged pacifism.
Like Graves and Partridge, he continued during the conflict to go
through the proper military motions of a serving soldier, maintaining a stiff upper lip and seeing the thing out to its bitter end.
Moreover, in literary terms his rebellion against war is modestly and
even at times offhandedly outlined. Apart from rancorous references
to the 'old men' who 'butchered' a generation, there is little of the

vitriol used by other disaffected soldiers of privilege (Sassoon, Aldington) in pouring out their disenchantment. Boyd's recognition that his enlistment in the so-called 'war for civilization' was a monumental self-deception is revealed through the controlled use of an urbane and bittersweet irony:

> We were ordered to lecture our platoons on bayonet fighting and the spirit of the offensive, to try and stir them to a vicious hatred of the Germans. I thought: 'There is no escape from this filthy thing, so I will go the whole hog.' In an old barn, built of thatch and clay and smelling of cows, I gave them a lurid and savage harangue on the delights of murder, on kicked genitals, and jabbed guts. Unless they cultivated these pleasures, the war for civilization could not be brought to a successful conclusion.[55]

The Great War was a pivotal event in Boyd's life, one which challenged and helped transform his early beliefs about the patriotic responsibilities incumbent upon an inherited social position. The sad awareness that the ethos he was brought up to champion may not in fact be defendable is given a gloomy epilogue in the final part of *A Single Flame*—written as it was in the shadow of the Second World War—by an analysis of the moral sickness of a moribund civilization. By confronting the gulf between expectation and actuality in such quietly intimate terms, Boyd made a major contribution to the steady stream of Australian soldier-books published in the 1930s. Despite its lack of interest in the national martial mythology and its avoidance of the vacuous and vainglorious 'reminiscing' that is the common expedient of the Australian military memoirist, *A Single Flame* is not an anti-Australian war book. It is the product of a sensibility contemptuous of a culture in which, as he observed of post-Second World War Melbourne, 'one's respectability depended upon one's enthusiasm for war and all military activities'.[56]

The autobiographical material contained in *A Single Flame* underwent a fictional reincarnation in *When Blackbirds Sing* (1962), the final novel in the Langton tetralogy, Boyd's expansive story of an Anglo-Australian family upon which, along with *Lucinda Brayford* (1946), his reputation as an Australian writer of the first rank largely rests. *When Blackbirds Sing* has had a chequered history, one marked by indifferent publishers, then by commercial failure and, in the short term at least, by critical apathy. In his memoir, *Day of My Delight* (1965), Boyd argued that the novel was rejected by publishers on the grounds that its uncompromising anti-war theme was not considered commercially viable, even in England.[57] (He remembers a critic telling him that 'No one could go to war again after reading that book'.) And there was certainly little in the novel to provide hope that it would be popular in an Australia then being deluged by a wave of fiction proclaiming the heroism of the Second A.I.F.

While the autobiographical basis of *When Blackbirds Sing*, like that of the entire 'Langton' series, is undeniable, it should not be exaggerated. As has been noted,[58] the war experience of Dominic Langton, upon whom the focus of Boyd's omniscient narrator is concentrated, corresponds closely with that described in *A Single Flame*, right down to the ironical harangue on the 'pleasures' of slaughtering Germans. But Dominic has a genuine fictional life of his own, one introduced to us in detail in the second novel of the series, *A Difficult Young Man* (1955). Boyd admits in *Day of My Delight* that he put 'most' of his wartime life into *When Blackbirds Sing*, but insists that the novel's hero 'bears no resemblance' to himself.[59] Of more interest than mere autobiographical fidelity is the novel's reapplication of the constellated themes of alienation, fractured allegiances and the withdrawal from patriotism that are so central to *A Single Flame*. The Anglo-Australian motif is there in the very first line of the novel: 'All the way home on the ship Dominic thought of Helena'.[60] This is a classical Boydian ambiguity. Dominic is not, as literally seems obvious, returning to his wife Helena; he is leaving her and their family behind on their Australian farm as he voyages to his ancestral homeland, England, to enlist in the British Army. Darkly intense, with a 'sombre Spanish appearance' reminiscent of an El Greco pietà, Dominic is not quite the familiar sunny-natured, freckle-faced Digger. But Boyd, who strove to draw his characters 'as people, not as nationals', was an artist indifferent to stereotypes.[61] Dominic's family, concerned to find a unit congenial to a man of such a brittle and passionate temperament, had thought a commission in an English regiment rather more suitable than the crude, egalitarian A.I.F. This homecoming offers Dominic, who is described variously as a 'queer fish' and a 'black sheep' unable 'to make any real contact with his fellows', the promise of belated integration. Initially 'isolated and alien' in England, he soon becomes 'reacclimatized', especially after a return to the family estate he had visited before the war and a pilgrimage to the tombs of his forebears.[62]

Following the pattern of Boyd himself, Dominic throws himself whole-heartedly into army life, enjoying the intricacies of drill and feeling 'for the first time' that he was 'no longer an outsider': 'At last he was doing the same kind of thing as other young men'.[63] Dominic is not merely playing at being a soldier. Like another romantic warrior driven by an ideal of honour, Guy Crouchback in Evelyn Waugh's Second World War trilogy, *Sword of Honour* (1965), his enthusiasm has about it the nature of a chivalric quest. 'He had left his home to fight for his country and for the values of civilization . . .'. Such a commitment demanded 'a form of knightly dedication'. Prior to his departure for the front in France, he visits a church in London and takes Holy Communion so as to bid 'farewell to all the associations of his life hitherto, offering them in defence of the freedom without which life is worthless'. Guy Crouchback, to whom the military calling is also an alternative to alienation, similarly ritualizes his war by petitioning before the tomb of an English knight in an Italian church before setting off to enlist.[64] The brutal and disillusioning encounter with the realities of warfare forces a redefinition and redirection of the crusades of both these dedicated warriors. Langton, like Crouchback, withdraws from the defence of public, 'civilized' values in the search for a more private, spiritual, fulfilment. Indeed the whole movement of the action of *When Blackbirds Sing*, of which the hero's confrontation with the battlefield is critical, is directed towards Dominic's repudiation of the ancestral-patriotic ethos as 'part of the panoply of battle and murder and sudden death'.[65]

Upon arrival at the front, Dominic feels 'noble and important'; after all, he is 'fighting evil'. But battle progressively awakens him to the fact that it was the evil 'inherited violence' in himself that was being consummated. A humanitarian who craves reconciliation more than conflict, he learns that the idea that 'civilization' can and should be defended by organized murder is a grotesque absurdity. In a tunnelling party beneath a German dugout, he lingers to listen to the sounds of the enemy's voice, the voice of a 'common humanity' he was about to annihilate.[66] A feeling of brotherhood with the enemy is clearly undesirable for the fighting soldier if he is to be at his most callously effective; it rarely seems to have impinged upon the destructive Diggers. In Dominic's case, it makes it impossible to continue in combat. On a raiding party, he comes face to face with a young German: the two soldiers exchange a look of 'mutual human recognition' before Dominic, armed with a revolver, shoots him dead. Their exchanged glance had been a 'recognition of kind' which had 'wiped out all the material obligation of their opposed circumstances', making the killing a pointless act of destruction.[67]

After a crisis of conscience not dissimilar to that suffered by Ralston in 'Two Masters', Dominic arrives at the intransigent moral position fundamental to modern anti-war literature as advocated in novels from *All Quiet on the Western Front* to Joseph Heller's *Catch-22* (1961)—the belief that it is unnatural if not plain silly to kill people one does not know merely to appease the political powers of one's own country. For a soldier as self-consciously chivalric as Dominic, the cold-blooded murder of his human brother with an impersonal bullet had rendered his romantic crusade all the more fatuous. More shaming still, the deed earned him a Military Cross for bravery. Disgusted with himself, he opts out of 'the cult of death and violence'.[68] Invalided out of the army after his Sassoon-like rebellion against the war is diagnosed as severe shell-shock, he returns to Australia, and 'home'.

That Dominic's fluctuating geographical sympathies seem finally to have stabilized in Australia's favour does not imply some sort of authorial imprimatur confirming the superiority of one nation over the other. Dominic's peregrinations, like those of Henry Handel Richardson's unstable Richard Mahony, are not simply the result of conflicting national allegiances. His is a restless soul which is pursuing adjustment to life itself, not merely integration into a particular social world. Wanting to redeem his 'black inherited streak', he seeks the place where he can develop the positive aspects of his character, in particular his innate 'longing for complete human fellowship' and his 'deep feeling for the natural world'.[69] These had been frustrated and even perverted by his participation in the European war. On the ship back to Australia, he

> entered that strange dream-like existence between two worlds . . . He had sweated Europe out of his system, and had done so with his blood. He had left the traditional room. His place was out in the open, in the natural world where Helena was waiting for him. That was the only place where he had come to terms with life.[70]

The final chapter of *When Blackbirds Sing* strongly suggests that Dominic will not achieve his dream of absolute harmony. His wife Helena, who was to 'restore him to life and innocence' after his ordeal, cannot comprehend his pacifism. This becomes an 'unresolved difference' between them, threatening their chance for future happiness. At the end of the novel Dominic is as isolated as ever. His act of throwing his military medals into a pond is a symbolic gesture which antagonizes his wife, who, believing the war to be 'the noblest experience of mankind in their century', feels that he had insulted the sacrifice of a generation.[71] But Helena's faith in the virtue of warlike achievement belongs to a creed to which her husband had never really adhered.

Dominic Langton's rejection of the martial role places him beyond the pale of Australian heroism, just as *When Blackbirds Sing* is in itself a singular Australian war book. The novel owes far more to the memory of *Under Fire* and *All Quiet on the Western Front* than it does to the tradition of C. E. W. Bean and Leonard Mann. If it inherits some of the characteristic faults of the violently anti-war novel pioneered by Barbusse—the reliance on melodramatic situations and the occasional use of lurid over-statement, for example—then it at least spares us the nationalistic rhetoric of the local literary convention.

A FOREIGN VIEW: THE DIGGER DEBUNKED

Given the parochial tendency of Australian war literature in the years following 1918, it is not surprising that those writers who were least influenced by the heroic myth were expatriates. Arthur Wheen, Eric Partridge and Martin Boyd all spent their post-war lives outside their homeland. Conversely, it was perhaps inevitable that the most convincing fictional celebration of the English Tommy, Frederic Manning's *Her Privates We*, was produced by an expatriate Australian who fought in the British Army.

Though the subject-matter of *Her Privates We*, based as it is on activities of a group of English infantrymen on the Somme and Ancre fronts in 1916, places the novel outside the specific focus of this book, it warrants attention for exemplifying the general view that a detached cultural perspective can be critical in determining the nature of the literary response to war. Manning, who left Australia for London in his early teenage years, lived for the rest of his life in England, and during the war fought in France as a private in the King's Shropshire Light Infantry. Returning to the land of his birth on a brief visit in 1934, he remarked that he could leave it 'with very few regrets', acidly commenting that 'it has nothing to recommend it except its climate, and its skies, which are an effect of its climate'.[72] Both the poetry and the prose of this classically-oriented writer—described by his friend and publisher, Peter Davies, as 'an intellectual of intellectuals . . . delicate in health and fastidious to the point of foppishness'—bespeak this indifference. There is little in his writing to suggest that Australia exercised an imaginative hold over him.[73]

Yet, while Manning does not glorify warlike striving in the uncritical manner of many Australian writers, it has been argued that a certain vestigial Australianness colours *Her Privates We*, making it a different war book in some respects from other novels dealing with the English in combat.[74] Certainly, the Australian influence, which is principally if vaguely invested in the autobiographical central character Private Bourne, helps shape a picture of the battlefield which allows equally for self-assertion and even nobility as well as the more familiar (in an English war novel) passivity and base animality. The book's avoidance of anti-war sentiment, its egalitarianism and its enthusiastic championship of comradely endeavour seem especially to be of Australian origin. Most British war novels and narratives concentrate on the isolated, oppressed young officer; the point of view of *Her Privates We*, by contrast, is that of the courageous, fatalistic Other Rankers, men who, if hardly demigods in military performance, draw inspiration and energy from each other with an intensity that reminds us of Homer's warriors.[75] Given the sustained battering the British military self-image had taken, it is not surprising that the novel, when it first appeared (in unexpurgated form) as a limited edition under the title *The Middle Parts of Fortune* in 1929, was greeted with relief by many English critics. The remarks of the historian Cyril Falls, writing in his seminal guide to Great War literature, are typical: 'Other books cause one to be astonished that we won the War; this helps one to understand that we could not have lost it'.[76] Falls, in the process of grossly simplifying the novel, praises *Her Privates We* in terms which unwittingly point to its Australian authorship. Applauding it in the language habitually favoured by the *Reveille* reviewers of Digger memoirs, he describes the novel as 'a man's book, written from a man's outlook and appealing to men's sympathies'. In this it contrasts starkly with the 'hysterical' anti-war fiction that appeals so successfully to the tastes and temperament of women.[77]

If the 'masculine' vigour of *Her Privates We* can be attributed to the thematic 'backbone' Manning's Australianness afforded the portrayal of the Tommy, then it almost logically follows that the most comprehensive debunking of the Digger during the inter-war period, Angela Thirkell's story of a nightmarish repatriation voyage, *Trooper to the Southern Cross*, should have been written by an expatriate Englishwoman.

In retrospect, Angela Thirkell was a supremely unlikely candidate for the role of Australian war writer. From an accomplished family which included, on her mother's side, the Pre-Raphaelite painter Edward Burne-Jones (her grandfather), Thirkell was a poor woman's

Jane Austen, a writer of what her biographer describes as 'middle-class novels for middle-class tastes' about genteel English rural society.[78] She would scarcely have contemplated a book like *Trooper to the Southern Cross* had it not been for falling in love with a 'romantic Australian soldier' while 'on the rebound' from a failed marriage.[79] That glamorous Digger, George Lancelot Allnut Thirkell, was an affable Tasmanian engineer who had served on Gallipoli with some distinction. For his prominent part in the hazardous exploit of 3 May 1915, in which a party of Anzacs attempted to reconnoitre the heavily fortified Turkish position atop Gaba Tepe, he gained an honourable mention in Bean's *Official History*.[80] Thirkell was eventually posted to a training depot on the Salisbury Plain, where he met Angela, who was staying in a nearby manor house. They married in London in December 1918 after a brief courtship.

The union began inauspiciously. Despite Angela's tearful remonstrances, George elected to take her and her two young sons from the previous marriage back to Australia in early 1920 on a troopship crowded with Australian soldiers returning home after the war. She would have preferred a berth on a liner; George argued against this, consoling his wife that a troopship would be 'more fun'. The journey, aboard a dilapidated German vessel called the *Friedrichsruh* (which, handed over to the British as part of the war reparations, had been sabotaged by the Germans so that its cold water pipes dispensed sewage), was certainly eventful. The anarchic behaviour of the Diggers, who were bored and infuriated that the ship was 'dry' of alcohol, was bad enough to horrify the most stoical of passengers, let alone the petulant Angela. The Australians roamed the decks muttering expletives which soon became an integral part of her sons' vocabulary; they rioted when the *Friedrichsruh* pulled into Colombo; they rioted aboard the vessel itself. The ship contained in its bowels a number of prisoners, mostly Australian deserters from the war. When these desperate men broke out of their cells, armed themselves with belts and bottles, and raided the crew's quarters, the Diggers took the opportunity to relieve their stifled energy in their accustomed manner. The fighting went on for hours. When all the lights on the ship failed, it continued on in darkness. As if this unpleasantness was not enough, the *Friedrichsruh* travelled at an incredibly slow pace, was poorly ventilated and hellishly hot, and finally developed a form of engine trouble which made it go round in circles. There was a chronic shortage of fresh food and water, and measles broke out among the children. After nine horrendous weeks the ship arrived in Melbourne, where customs officials suspiciously examined the prized Dürer prints Angela had brought from England, just stopping short of confiscating them as obscene objects.[81] Here was a wealth of documentary material to be transmuted into the fiction of *Trooper to the Southern Cross*.

Determinedly 'cultural', Angela Thirkell during her ten years' residence in Melbourne established a salon of sorts while her husband buried himself in his small engineering firm or spent his leisure hours drinking with old comrades at the Naval and Military Club. Among visitors to her home were Monash, Melba, and the historian, Ernest Scott. But she never really acclimatized. Unable to lose her High Tory distaste for the easy egalitarianism of Australian society, and contemptuous of its philistinism as personified by her husband (the model for the narrator of *Trooper to the Southern Cross*), she pined for the rarefied world of art, music and literature she had left behind. An extended trip home to England in 1928 was followed by her return for good, without George, in late 1929.

Trooper to the Southern Cross was written some four years later,[82] appearing under the pseudonym 'Leslie Parker', chiefly because of Thirkell's fear that the novel, so fundamentally unflattering in its picture of Australia's national heroes, might provoke a controversy. Yet years later she sent a copy of the novel to the National Library in Canberra as a 'token' of her 'regard' for Australia and 'its people'.[83] One suspects an element of mischief in this gift. Perhaps Angela considered that Australians would no longer be offended by whatever insults the novel contained; it is just as likely, though, that she thought that the satire as diffused by the attitudes of the narrator, Tom Bowen, was subtle enough to be missed by many parochial Australian readers. Indeed, for a long time *Trooper to the Southern Cross* was assumed to have been written by a medical major in the A.I.F., like Bowen himself.[84] Certainly her recent biographer appears to have misread the novel. She sees Bowen as an 'affectionate, even loyal' portrait of George Thirkell.[85] She cannot be serious. A complacent vulgarian who embodies the lack of sophistication that Angela discerned in Australian society, Bowen/Thirkell is hardly presented 'affectionately', still less 'loyally'. As her son, Graham McInnes, wrote in his autobiography, *The Road to Gundagai* (1965), Angela Thirkell had 'an invincible contempt for things Australian and made no bones about it'.[86] *Trooper to the Southern Cross* is therefore more correctly read as a rather venomous, if amusing, parting shot at a country (and her husband as a typically Australian 'thing') she never felt comfortable with, grew to despise, and finally gladly rejected.

Major Tom Bowen, in his role as a supposedly objective recorder of events aboard the ill-fated troopship, the *Rudolstadt*, likes to think of himself as a social and intellectual cut above the common Digger, whose excesses he feigns to abhor. He boasts about his landed Western District family, his successful Sydney medical practice and his incomparable North Shore home, and he sees himself as a man of culture, possessing, among other refinements, a certain depth of literary learning and appreciation. But the fact is, as Adrian Mitchell asserts in his incisive analysis of this otherwise neglected novel, Bowen 'completely and uncritically identifies himself with his countrymen, and submerges his individual self in the commonplace of the collective identity'.[87] Not that Bowen is entirely negative in his treatment of the Australian soldiers anyway. He describes them, by turns, as 'warmhearted', 'wonderfully independent', a 'cheery lot' with a 'wonderful' sense of humour, 'wonderful' judges of character, 'wonderfully generous', and 'wonderfully decent' to their sick comrades. They are even kind to children. He finally exonerates them by blaming their barbaric behaviour on their unsuitable accommodation on an overcrowded ship, making the apologetic, Bean-like remark that, in the long run, 'the digger isn't a bad chap if decently handled'.[88]

When Mitchell refers to Bowen's 'unshakeable belief in the superiority of the species',[89] he touches on what we have seen to be the dominant shaping force of Australian war writing. A major paradox of the Australian involvement in the Great War was that though it thrust isolated Australians on to the world's stage, the effect of this broadening of the national experience was to confirm the culture's essential insularity. Thus, in *Saints and Soldiers*, we see Harley Matthews's caricatural 'Dinkum Australian', hospitalized in England, telling all who would listen of the transcendent virtues of his homeland. On furlough in London some time later, he decries the 'historic piles' of that city, though he admits that the Houses of Parliament are 'not bad', adding that 'they might look well if they were at the new Federal capital in Australia'.[90] In C. Hampton Thorp's *A Handful of Ausseys*, the Diggers' 'deep-rooted' love of country is 'solidified' by overseas travel: '. . . the more our boys saw of the world . . . [the more they] . . . realized by comparison the great value of Australia to them'.[91] Likewise Tom Bowen is inclined to view all foreign things in a derogatory light. Paris, for example, he considers 'all right', but it suffers by comparison with Sydney ('or even Melbourne') because it 'doesn't have the same homey feeling'.[92] Bowen sees the war as a great adventure, to be sure, but it was one which reinforced his satisfaction with Australia. Europe, he seems to say, was a fine place to visit and to fight in, but he wouldn't like to live there. Here are his remembered thoughts as he sailed home:

> Away behind us was the old Europe where I had seen so much. Gallipoli, Sed-el-Bahr, Gaba Tepe . . . France, Pozières, Bullecourt, Villers Bret, St. Quentin, Salisbury Plain, London, Leeds, all gone into yesterday. I'm glad I saw them, but I don't want to see them again. Good old Aussie will do me every time.[93]

The Australian superiority complex is so ingrained in Bowen that he advertises not merely the pre-eminence of the national character but the fine details of its culture as well. Many of his remarks, delivered as they are in extemporaneous monotone, are absurdly provincial. Describing his English wife's ignorance of the necessity for the permanent presence of a bottle of tomato sauce on the dinner table, he notes in wonderment, 'They don't seem to understand etiquette so much in England'. Bowen's account of his first meeting with this unfortunate woman, Celia, reveals something of Thirkell's satirical purpose and method. The two had met in England after the war. Celia, whom he discovers to be his cousin, lived at the time in Hampstead with his aunt. To the Australian this apparently remote place was in 'the back-blocks'. When the girl expressed her ignorance of this colloquialism, Bowen attempted to explain by asking if she had ever read *On Our Selection*. When he learnt that she had not even read *We of the Never Never*, nor *While the Billy Boils*, he knew at once that 'she wasn't literary'.[94] Ever the victim of his unconscious irony, Bowen continually exposes the narrowness of Australian attitudes and becomes the medium through which the literary culture that encourages such provincialism is lampooned. Bowen's anecdotal style and unemphatic laconicism in itself mimics the yarning narratives of such influential Australian writers as Steele Rudd and Henry Lawson.

Though Bowen's self-portrait teeters on the brink of caricature, he is in fact an index of recognizably Australian religious bigotry, racial prejudice (he pays the plucky Ghurkas the ultimate compliment of calling them 'real white men and as clean as you and me'), and, most of all, assumptions about manliness. Disdainful of the man 'that can't keep his feelings to himself', he regards himself as the strong silent type, even if he does possess a womanish 'feeling for the poetical side of life'. He is one of the kind who thinks that wearing a fresh white shirt to dinner is 'cissy', and whose respect for his wife is based mainly on her ability to polish his boots 'as good as a batman'. Lost in admiration at such industry, he applauds her for being 'a great little worker'. The small-mindedness of Bowen's attitudes towards women is a fertile source of satire for Thirkell, who was herself no champion of the housewifely virtues, being highly irritated by her husband's expectations in this area during their marriage. As usual she allows Bowen to hang himself. 'I always have a very protective feeling about women', he tells us, 'They are different from men somehow'.[95]

The limitations of Bowen's thinking are compounded by his comically inept use of language. Laughable *non sequiturs* abound. This is how he remembers his grandfather's death in a horse-riding accident:

> He wasn't tight that time; no, he was just riding after some sheep quite peacefully, when his horse stumbled . . . and Grandad got his neck broken. It was a pity, because she was a good little mare, and after she'd broken her knees she wasn't ever quite the same.[96]

Leaving the war itself to the correspondents – 'real writers' – Bowen spends little time recounting his experiences at Gallipoli, or even his 'happy days' on the Western Front, where it seems the most harrowing thing that happened to him was a breakfast of *pâté de foie gras* and Benedictine looted from a ruined village near Pozières: 'I hope I never go through an experience like that again as long as I live'.[97] On the few occasions he does look back to the battlefield, his unintentional black humour emerges in all its grim glory. The death of one of his men is described thus:

> . . . he wasn't a bad chap when he had learnt to toe the line. I was quite sorry to see the last of him. Not that there was much to see, because the shell-hole was about ten feet deep, but you get a kind of feeling for the chaps that you have under you.[98]

That Major Tom Bowen should be at his most woefully inarticulate when dealing with his personal reactions to violence and death is symptomatic of the literary malaise that afflicts actual Australian soldier-writers in general. Linguistically and stylistically unable to come to grips with an experience inadequately understood, they all too often seek refuge in the crude boast or the bald assertion. We should be grateful to Angela Thirkell for bringing to attention, and in such an entertaining way, the cultural shortcomings that fostered the Digger cult. One wonders whether a satire such as *Trooper to the Southern Cross* could *only* have been produced by an outsider – a writer, indeed, both female and English – during the conformist literary climate of the 1930s.

VI

Sons of Anzacs

ENCORE

Any cracks in the revered image of the Australian war hero made by the few iconoclasts of the 1930s were cemented by the feats of the national soldiery during 1939–1945. The Second A.I.F. proved that its legendary predecessor was no mere fluke of history. To a new crop of publicists, the force showed by its achievements on the battlefield that the heroic capability was so ingrained in the race that it would automatically manifest itself to meet fresh challenges on fresh arenas of combat. The original legends created by 'The Old and the Bold' were thereby authenticated and perpetuated. Indeed, the Second A.I.F. was held to demonstrate that Anzac was no pejorative 'myth' at all.

The two divergent streams of modern western battle literature – Australian and Euro-American – do at least meet in this one area: in both literatures the myths bred during the Great War endured to shape the responses to succeeding conflicts. If the Second World War regenerated the Australian heroic tradition born in April 1915, then in Britain, for example, the war provoked a revival óf the bitterly ironic and reactionary writing of a generation earlier. Disillusionment with grand military gestures had so neutralized the rosy hues that had once coloured British views of warfare that even the temperamentally romantic and belligerently chauvinistic Evelyn Waugh contemplated the struggle to follow with an icy realism. In his diary in late 1939 he asks, 'how is victory possible except by wholesale slaughters?'[1] In *The Great War and Modern Memory* Paul Fussell confirms the dominating influence of the First World War on the Second. His searching study of the persistence of the images and motifs

172

of 1914–18 reveals that such internationally famous Second World War fictions as Joseph Heller's *Catch-22*, Norman Mailer's *The Naked and the Dead* (1948), Evelyn Waugh's *Brideshead Revisited* (1945) and *Sword of Honour* trilogy, and Thomas Pynchon's *Gravity's Rainbow* (1973) are saturated with the tragic myths and gruesome memories of the Great War. Its grip on the imagination of Second World War poets is illustrated by the wry admission of Keith Douglas (in the poem 'Desert Flowers') that his evocation of the Libyan battlefield is only a 'repeat' of what Isaac Rosenberg had said of war nearly thirty years before. Further confirmation comes in the memorable lines of the British poet Vernon Scannell, himself a participant in the later conflict:

> Whenever war is spoken of
> I find
> The war that was called Great
> invades the mind . . .[2]

The events of 1914–18 also impinged upon the Australian imaginative and emotional reaction to the Second World War. And what a painless 'penetration' it was. The almost slavish receptivity of novelists and memoirists to what one of them, Eric Lambert, termed 'the legends of the terrible, laughing men in the slouch hats',[3] indicates that the earlier war not only influenced, but actually inspired, literary endeavour. As a fighting force, the Second A.I.F. was correspondingly stimulated. Observing the Australian troops in New Guinea in 1942, the war correspondent David Meredith in *My Brother Jack* detected an 'almost pathetic desire . . . for the right sort of publicity'.[4] While the Second A.I.F. never earned the same exalted place in Australian society achieved by its fêted forerunner, all but the most hungry for kudos must have had their craving for recognition satisfied. The new generation of Diggers had its praises sung in a chorus of promotional support which was a reprise of that which greeted the actions of the First A.I.F.

There was a huge audience to applaud this revival of Australian military genius. David Walker has written of the 'extraordinary vogue' of Second World War fiction in this country, a popularity which cannot be simply explained by the fact that aggressive competition among publishers for a share of the burgeoning post-war Australian literary market guaranteed decent sales for anything half-way readable.[5] The spectacular success of Eric Lambert's prodigiously reprinted *The Twenty Thousand Thieves* (1951), a novel both indignantly anti-war and stubbornly chauvinistic, far eclipsed the commercial coups of C. J. Dennis during the Great War.[6] Qualitatively, the pressure to cater to the insatiable Australian appetite for a military myth at once anachronistic in its literary application and possibly unique in the general cultural context, proved ruinous. The degeneration of Lambert's career after his powerful first novel is an example. The exploitation of his premature fame as a war writer resulted in a sequence of decreasingly effective war novels, culminating in the trashy *Diggers Die Hard* (1963). If, as the old saying goes, money is 'the sinews of war', then war is the 'sinews' of popular literature. Nowhere more so than in Australia.

The 'legends of the terrible, laughing men in the slouch hats' were not revived without some revision. As Harry Heseltine has remarked while alluding to the 'deflating jokes' about 'bronzed Anzacs' that are rife in Second World War fiction, national pride is worn in these novels 'with a shrug as often as with bravado'.[7] Importantly, however, the Anzac ideal is rarely repudiated. Ironic references to the Gallipoli demigods should not be interpreted as a deliberate debunking of the mythology itself, but as a sign of the acute sense of heroic tradition functioning within both the Second A.I.F. and the vision of its propagandists. What they especially connote is the depressing awareness that the men of the new force could never hope to emulate the glories of the old. This eroded self-confidence paradoxically produced writing which in its way is as immoderately boastful as that of the Great War. A feeling of inferiority to those who started the legend complicated and aggravated the innate 'superiority complex' of the Australian soldier. Hence the bluster of both soldier-writers and publicists has a touch of desperation about it. One is reminded of the words of Achilles, preening himself over the stricken Lycaon in the *Iliad*: '. . . look at me. Am I not big and beautiful, the son of a great man . . .?'[8]

Compared with the volatile haste of the self-assured men of the father force, the first military steps taken by many sons of Anzacs were tentative, even timid. Australia's response to the Second World War in general lacked the 'nobility' and the 'grand passion' of 1914, observes Michael McKernan in *All In! Australia during the Second World War*. As was the case in Britain, 'the dominant passion was not bellicose excitement but rather regret tinged with disappointment that war must come again'. The reaction was 'leisurely, almost languid', recruitment for the newly-raised army in no way resembling the deluge of volunteers in 1914.[9] Soldier boys were unloved in the Australia of 1939. The lure of relatively well-paid (if not exactly secure) employment in harsh economic times, along with the curious practice of judges and magistrates of offering suspended sentences to petty criminals if they undertook to join up, gave rise to the not wholly unreasonable belief that those who did quickly volunteer were no more than down-and-out economic conscripts, or, more harshly and unfairly, 'five-bob-a-day murderers': 'It became a popular myth that Australian recruits were irresponsible adventurers or misfits, usually with the stigma of unemployment attached'.[10] The resentment engendered by this sort of vilification emerges in the war diary of Eric Lambert. On the occasion of the visit of the Australian Prime Minister to camps in Palestine in 1941, Lambert scribbled in his notebook:

> Bob Menzies due to-day. No one will turn out for him as the rumour is he called us "5/- a day killers".[11]

Civilian disparagement not only annoyed the young tyros of the Second A.I.F., it also affected their image of themselves. Even in a 'late' personal war narrative like Ken Clift's *The Saga of a Sig* (1972), the account of the act of enlistment is so defensive that it seems as if the author feels he has some sort of case to answer. Clift assures us that he, like his comrades, was certainly *not* an economic conscript. Rather, he had just returned from a working trip to Fiji and New Zealand when the war broke out, and he felt that 'further adventures wouldn't go astray' – 'a tremendous sense of excitement' raced through him.[12] But all this jaunty exuberance rings a little false.

In order to stimulate recruitment and to win over a sceptical public, the propagandists were from the outset diligent in stressing the intimate relationship of the new force to its glorious military heritage. The decision to call the army the Second A.I.F., as well as the implementation of the old battalion numbering of the original force, tended (writes McKernan) 'to encourage pride . . . it was hoped that the new force would acquire reflected glory by association with the old'.[13] The indefatigable C. E. W. Bean, in his pamphlet *The Old A.I.F. and the New* (1940), asserted that the two armies were 'as like as father and son – which to a considerable extent is their actual relationship'. The account of the deeds of the Great War Diggers at the end of the sixth volume of the *Official History* (published in 1942) pointedly concludes with the observation that the Second A.I.F. was 'in every sense the child of the first'.[14]

In choosing a sobriquet for the new generation of warriors the professional wartime publicists opted for a tag which blurred the distinctions between the two forces even further. The heroes of the Second A.I.F. naturally were to be called 'Anzacs'. The despatches of the Australian Official War Correspondent, Kenneth Slessor, consistently invoke the magical name. Describing the activities of the Australians on Crete in 1941, for example, Slessor writes that they engaged in 'a hand-to-hand fight of the sort the Anzacs longed for in Greece itself but which they were never able to obtain'. Like the originals, the new breed were old-fashioned warriors who were frustrated by the futility of 'trying to match their bayonets against bombs'.[15] Crete, of course, proved to be an even greater débâcle than Greece, but the use of the illustrious appellation reassured the nation that the Australian soldier was as brave and as bold as ever.

A similar determination to unite the Second A.I.F. to the myth is evident in George Johnston's *Australia at War* (1942), the result of a tour of the Australian defence areas (carried out at the invitation of Army Headquarters) while Johnston was working for the *Argus*. In response to the Japanese bogey, then at its most threatening, Johnston adopts a tone which is blatantly propagandist. In attempting at the same time to encourage recruiting and to steel the nation for the dark days ahead, he falls back on the old faithful – Anzac. 'The story of a young nation's manhood, that begun at Gallipoli, has gone into a second volume', he declares. The latest Diggers, in other words, were chips off the old heroic block. Johnston advises his readers to

> Go to the local war memorial. Read the names of the men who fought in the last war. Then look at the enlistment rolls of that town for this war. You find the same names that were graven in stone on the war memorial . . . Another generation has put to one side the ploughshares and picked up the swords.[16]

Australia at War illustrates just how powerful a debaser of literary integrity the role of the hired publicist can be. George Johnston possessed a cultivated talent, but in trying to maximize the enduring glamour of the Anzac legends for popular consumption his writing takes on the crudely racist and boastful character of Great War propaganda.[17] Labelling Australians 'the best fighting soldiers in the world', he grandiloquently asserts the right of the new 'Anzacs' to take their place in some imagined military Hall of Fame beside the most legendary of all warriors. The Australian involvement in the abortive campaign in Greece and Crete inspires this response:

> There is material for a new Iliad and a new Odyssey in the tales of Greece

and Crete, in the adventures of these twentieth century soldiers among the islands where gods and men once fought.[18]

Extravagant publicity like this, however fatuous, proved effective. Certainly the soldiers of the Second A.I.F. soon began to see themselves as both literal and metaphorical legatees of the heroic inheritance. In one of their most popular songs they big-note themselves as 'Sons of Anzacs who/Won deathless fame', and as 'The sons of the breed/And the true Anzac creed'.[19] And a slim volume of humorous Digger tales prepared by returned servicemen capitalized on the real and imagined link between the two armies by being called *The Diggers' Annual: Sons of Anzacs*. By the war's end, the initially deprecated soldier of the Second A.I.F. had been transformed into a sort of comic-strip hero, a son of the antipodean superman.

The Anzac legacy, so freely bestowed by the publicists, was paid for by the combatant in the form of the onus it placed on him to excel in battle. From the time of his enlistment, through the training period to the actual martial arena, he bore, like the proverbial son of the sporting hero, the transferred fame of his father. The overwrought language used by Ken Clift in the portentous 'Prologue' to his collection of anecdotes, *The Soldier Who Never Grew Up* (1976), can be seen as a direct result of the coercive pressure exerted by the Great War legends:

> Youthful volunteers poise on 'the brink' – the very brink of a promise, a promise of proven lusty mature manhood. Yet there is an awareness deep, deep down of a trial yet to come; a gnawing doubt, a nagging fear . . . Shall he thus be able to proclaim to his true inner self that he ranks as an Australian – bravely, proudly displaying the plumes of long dead pioneer ancestors and bearing a flaming torch thrown from the hands of those who assailed the grim shores and ragged slopes of Gallipoli, or climbed unafraid and restlessly from the muddy bloody trenches in Flanders Fields . . . ONLY TIME WOULD TELL.[20]

It was up to the men of the Second A.I.F. to illustrate once more the greatness of Australian soldiery, and also to reveal to themselves and particularly to their elders that they were 'true' Australians. By their performance on the battlefield they had to ensure that the breed was not seen to have become enfeebled, effete, in a single generation. Time and time again, in novels and personal narratives, they appear to be conscious of their tenuous 'Son of Anzac' standing and mindful to uphold their fathers' hard-earned prestige. Some, like Mick Reynolds in *We Were the Rats*, actually pit themselves against the historical stereotype. Reynolds, originally cynical about the Anzac tradition, decides to enlist partly out of a mixture of youthful restlessness and 'save the world' idealism. But generation-gap rivalry is the primary spur to action. Reynolds senior had been killed in France in 1917, inspiring his son to bluster that, 'What was good enough for my father was good enough for me. If he could take it so could I . . . If the last generation could take it surely this one could'.[21] Logically, Mick opts to join his father's old battalion. By the time of his arrival in Palestine, and prior to his first engagement, he realizes that the task of emulation might well be more demanding than he had at first envisaged. It was a problem of high, and possibly unreal, expectations. As he ruefully remarks to one of his mates:

"The trouble is the world expects so much of Australians . . . They think we all swear like troopers, drink like fish, and fight like wildcats, and that we don't know the meaning of the word 'fear'. We can blame our fathers. It makes it hard for us . . . All our lives we've read about the Diggers being the best troops in the world . . . I hope to hell that when our turn comes we don't let everybody down."[22]

Military honours, when inevitably they did come the way of the Second A.I.F., were greeted with great jubilation. The victorious North African advance through Libya to beyond Benghazi in early 1941 was seen by the participating members of the Sixth Division (the first new division raised in 1939, and entirely volunteer in composition) as a revelation of the new force's equality with the old. Reminiscing about the triumph of the outnumbered Australians over the Italians at Bardia in his memoir, *Not As A Duty Only: An Infantryman's War* (1976), Henry ('Jo') Gullett remembers his elation that his platoon had not disgraced their fathers. (His own father, Sir Henry Gullett, was the Great War historian and wartime Cabinet Minister killed along with the famous Anzac Brudenell White in an air crash in 1940.) Gullett also recalls his personal satisfaction that he had earned his spurs and could finally be considered to be a 'proper soldier'.[23] These fond memories of Bardia are verified by the observations of John Hetherington, who covered the battle as a war correspondent. The mood of the Australians after the fight was one of 'intoxication', Hetherington noted: 'The Australians had tasted battle and they liked its harsh flavour'. Yet it was primarily their relief that they had emerged from under the shadow of their fathers' reputation and had begun to build one of their own that made them so flushed with their success:

More than one man came to me that night in Bardia and said: "Correspondent, eh? Well, when you write to the papers tell them we're as good as the First A.I.F."[24]

Uplifting as it may have been in the general military sense, the sustained cultural influence of the Anzac mythology proved destructive in some individual cases. Like their Great War predecessors, most Second World War soldier-writers were unwilling to canvass their private battle traumas, and ignored the humiliation that came with not living up to the perceived heroic model. It was principally left to non-participant, Alan Seymour, in his novel *The One Day of the Year* (1967), to probe the murky side of the shining national ideal. Adapted from the controversial 1960 play that still does the rounds of the suburban repertories every 25 April, *The One Day of the Year* dramatizes the tribal potency of the Australian war myth. Its plot, it will be remembered, revolves around a series of heated arguments between an ex-serviceman of the 1939–45 conflict and his rebellious son about the merits and meaning of Anzac Day, 'the one day of the year'. The father, Alf Cook, is a cantankerous veteran of Tobruk who considers the returned soldier to be the one true repository of Australian values and traditions; Anzac Day is both his day of celebration and the day he is celebrated. The son, Hugh, is a university student filled with his generation's distaste for the 'sacred' rituals (the marches and the bibulous reunions) and holy houses (the local R.S.L.) of old and decaying warriors. Acting as a kind of buffer between these two antagonistic forces is 'Wacka', an old family friend who, with Alf's own father, had actually participated in the April invasion. It is testimony to the success of the promulgation of the Gallipoli legend that, while Wacka is himself indifferent to the Anzac Day ballyhoo, Alf patronizes the event with a reverence which borders on the mystical—as is evidenced by his deeply respectful attendance at the annual Dawn Service which heralds the celebration. After all, his father had died a hero's death on the famous peninsula.

Yet Alf Cook's own experience of war had fallen far short of the heroic. The paralysing fear that gripped him on the battlefield was irreconcilable with 'the standards that seemed to have been set for him'. The shocking discovery that he was no swashbuckler led to a self-loathing which he sublimates through an aggressive chauvinism based on the idea that war service is proof-positive of individual worth. But in fact his reverence for the war experience comes vicariously through an imaginative engrossment in the Great War rather than in the one in which he himself fought. The wartime trauma of this disagreeable and tormented man can only assume its due poignancy if the cultural power of the myth of 1915 is recognized:

> The Second World War was something Alf later thumbed out of his mind. It should have been the greatest time in a man's life, he would sometimes tell himself, greatest time in a man's life. Instead – Cyrenaica, Libya, the names confused him, half the time he wasn't sure what damn country he was in, then it started . . . Noise, a yowling of fear and excitement, confusion . . . no idea what he was doing or what he was supposed to do but doing it, and shaking all the time, and wet, a thick coat of sweat all over him . . . and fear, fear through to his bowels.[25]

THE ANZAC UPDATED

An important development in the Anzac literary tradition, from at least the time of the publication of the controversial *We Were the Rats* in 1944, was the revamping of the original heroic figure to meet the more 'sophisticated' tastes and tolerances of a readership which had altered to a degree since the time of the Great War. If the national response to the conflict, initially at least, was relatively subdued, then the fiction it produced was the reverse. The Second World War novel, often brazenly packaged and toughly, vehemently written, appealed to a market which had shed some of its inhibitions, and which liked its wars fought by strong men with passions to match. Digger Mark Two is a vastly different model from the 1915 prototype – more sceptical and more narrowly egocentric, given to violent language and to antisocial behaviour and attitudes, and vastly more indulgent in the gratification of his sexual longings. He displays his virility flamboyantly, exhibiting a less constrained brand of antipodean machismo than the Digger of the Great War.

The second generation of publicists was more committed to naturalistic representation than its predecessor. The easing of censorship regulations meant that the Diggers' speech, for instance, could be reported far more accurately than before. This, of course, was a gradual process. In April 1946 *We Were the Rats* was banned as obscene and Angus & Robertson, its publisher, fined on the evidence of the New South Wales Vice Squad, which claimed that a few pages (some of which contained the word 'bloody') were 'offensive to delicacy and chastity'. The *Bulletin* sarcastically reported this absurd prosecution under the headline, 'We Are the Mice'.[26] Sumner Locke Elliott's play *Rusty Bugles* (1948), set in a Northern Territory Ordnance Depot in 1944, met a similar fate two years later. The 'bad language' of the bored non-combatant soldiers, faithfully rendered by Locke Elliott, caused the play to be briefly banned by the Chief Secretary of New South Wales.[27] Just how greatly the passing of time has liberated the reproduction of the language of soldiers is obvious from this assessment of the Battle of Crete by the hero of Richard Beilby's novel *Gunner*, published in 1977:

> Nine months the 'Bines have been on this lousy island and what have they got? Fuckall! No planes, buggerall transport, not even decent maps![28]

The once heavily bowdlerized and stilted, 'folksy' speech of the Australians has thus been transformed into an argot both colloquial and determinedly indelicate, into a welter of idiomatic expressions like 'shit a brick!' and 'she'd had more bangs than Guy Fawkes night'.[29]

A somewhat excessive commitment to physical or pictorial realism also marks the Second World War novel. In the prose of the 1914–18 war, such instances of bloodthirstiness as Oliver Hogue's vignette of an Anzac pitchforking a Turk over his shoulder have a make-believe quality about them. The victims, like cartoon characters, shed no real blood: it's all good clean boyish fun and games. Here, by contrast, the violence seems crueller, more lurid and sensationalist in intended impact. The nadir is reached in Jon Cleary's *A Very Private War* (1980), which contains a vividly described episode of a wandering nun being gobbled up by a crocodile in the jungles of New Britain. Eric Lambert also overreaches in straining for dramatic effect in his handling of the sensitive subject of Japanese cannibalism in the New Guinea novel, *The Veterans* (1954).[30]

It is in their treatment of the Australians' sexual activities, however, that the Second World War writers most radically sought to modify the heroic prototype. With a couple of exceptions, William Baylebridge and Joseph Maxwell, Great War novelists and memoirists treated the fleshly indulgences of the Diggers with coy implication. The more 'modern' writers of the later conflict, encouraged by the liberalization of the censorship laws and pandering to an enthusiastic public, saw fit to impose fewer constraints. They brought the sexuality of the soldiers out into the open and indeed magnified it, making sex itself a theme to rival and counterpoint the cut and thrust of the battlefield. But there is no attempt, as in Ford's *Parade's End*, to correlate 'love' and 'war' in the cause of Freudian inquiry into the fundamental impulses of human behaviour. Rather, the generous insertion of lust into the battle zone is designed to flavour the narrative, all in the name of a 'good read'—some carnal sweat to season all that blood and bile as it were. The gaudy cover of Eric Lambert's *Glory Thrown In*, published by Frederick Muller in 1959, eloquently illustrates this. Amid the post-combat disarray of the Alamein battlefield stands an exhausted (but handsomely blond and blue-eyed) soldier frozen in a posture which disconcertingly suggests that he is doing up his fly buttons.

To be fair, American novels such as Mailer's *The Naked and the Dead* and James Jones's *From Here to Eternity* (1951) prove that not only Australian Second World War novelists spiced their battle narratives with erotica. Writing in the early 1960s about the difficulty of obtaining an English publisher for *When Blackbirds Sing*, Martin Boyd complained that he wrote the book 'to appeal to the minds and not to the glands of the reader, which is expected in war fiction today'.[31] But there is something particularly contrived about the sudden 'sexiness' of the Digger. It is as if the novelists recognized the futility of promoting the Second A.I.F. as militarily superior to its forerunner, and compensated by portraying it as a force of sexual athletes, partaking of pleasures denied their more strait-laced fathers. They would have us believe Wycherley's tired old dictum that women do indeed 'adore a martial man'—especially if he happens to be in an Australian uniform.

Philandering Australians either fighting a rearguard action in enemy territory or else engaged in espionage or intelligence work also have their war-related adventures complicated by encounters with alluring local women. The emphasis is on the physicality of the relationship, by way of titillating references to the visual charms of the women and their effect on the red-blooded soldiers. Here is Richard Beilby's picture of the eponymous Greek heroine of *No Medals for Aphrodite* (1970), as she rouses the manhood of one Digger caught up in the German advance through Greece:

> It was then that he saw Aphro return, stepping purposefully, her splendid breasts riding jauntily . . .[32]

Such whimsies are lent some substance by the women being portrayed as having hearts—if not brains—as ample as their bodies. Though their affairs usually prove disastrous for them, their intimate experience with the demigods from down under is implied to be well worth the risk. Thus the local Greek girl in John Hetherington's *The Winds Are Still* (1948) who helps protect a fugitive Australian is reduced to such a state of emotional turmoil that she asks of her beloved Digger: 'Hugh, there've been other girls? Haven't there?'[33] She hardly has time enough to hear his answer as she is soon killed in a hail of German gunfire as they try to escape together to Egypt. Hugh, of course, lives to fight another day . . .

Taking the sensible view that love and war are serious subjects, most Australian Second World War novelists try not to trivialize and debase the broad theme by indulging in the purely pornographic. But there are some pitfalls in this approach, as is clear from the woefully 'romantic' prose of Jon Cleary as he struggles to convey in *A Very Private War* the sexual tensions between Ruth, a half-caste medical practitioner who is 'not interested in one-night flings', and Mullane, a New Britain coastwatcher:

> She gazed at his back as he walked ahead of her; he was well-made, every inch of him. She was a physical woman who responded to the physical side of men; had she been totally white she might have been promiscuous.[34]

It is almost (but not quite) with some relief that one turns to Richard Beilby's *Gunner*, which goes beyond the usual puerile breast-fixations of most Australian novelists of the war, describing in graphic detail the seamy Alexandrian couplings of Gunner Lewis, a deserter from the Sixth Division, and his voluptuous French-Egyptian mistress Ondine. Lewis, who is a cultural as well as military outcast, has no time for the handed-down images of Australian larrikinism. Observing a group of vomiting, soliciting Australians in the streets of Alexandria, where he is in hiding from the authorities, he growls:

> "Big bronzed Anzacs, eh. Because their fathers burned the brothels down in nineteen fifteen they think they've got to do the same."[35]

Gunner Lewis is in many respects an unusually complex character for the hero of an Australian war novel, but Beilby mishandles his portrayal. He is at once the cynical renegade on the run from the hegemonical legend, and the conventional Dionysian Australian warrior of Second World War fiction. Indeed, Beilby pictures him as not only 'big' and 'bronzed', but as something of an embodiment of the male life-force itself. Avoiding the provosts in Alexandria, Gunner finds refuge in a brothel, in which he happily chances upon a prostitute who

> received him easily, capaciously, taking him down into the warm moist earth-mother eternal darkness where all life began, all maleness returned.[36]

The repeated fulfilment of Gunner's 'maleness' in the above manner virtually provides the plot of the novel. Lewis—and Beilby, it would seem—reveals his addiction to all those weary ideas about male striving (as well as a corresponding contempt for women) when he analyses 'that fear of fear which drove young men to risk their lives to prove their manhood'. The imagery is awesomely unsubtle:

> In the past he had done it with horses, choosing some raving mad-eyed buck, his backbone rattling like castanets, his eyeballs almost jolted out of his head . . . just to prove to watching men that he was tough. That he wasn't afraid. It wasn't riding the buck to a standstill that mattered. It was having a go, controlling your fear, tucking it right down into your coldly sweating balls and throwing a leg over that insanely heaving horse. And war was the most terrible test of all. But that was another thing Ondine wouldn't understand: no woman would really understand it.[37]

Robust sexuality in alliance with combat experience, then, is seen as the trademark of true manhood. But when the time comes to decide which activity to promote the most—they cannot, after all, be performed in unison—the Australian war novelist tends to lose his nerve. For instance, Eric Lambert in *The Twenty Thousand Thieves* views sex as a vital stage in the making of a man, but only in so far as it makes him more capable of fulfilling his patriotic duty on the battlefield. You cannot be a great fighter without being a great lover first, he seems to say, but it is still the fighting which is the more important. Lambert's hero, Dick Brett, is a moody, university-educated young soldier motivated by a vague socialistic hatred for Fascism and a determination not to disgrace the Australian martial traditions. He is no embittered and dissipated Gunner Lewis. Encamped in Palestine and preparing for his first taste of battle, Brett meets a young Jewish woman who is living and working in a kibbutz near by. The woman, Naomi, is a sophisticated individual who possesses a wisdom that is eagerly tapped by the Australian, though Lambert does heavily rely on references to her 'swelling golden breasts' to convey her rich maturity. The two develop a firm, but non-sexual, friendship, Brett playing the unformed youth to Naomi's Earth Mother. Battle, at Tobruk, changes the nature and the balance of the relationship. The boy has become a man. But not quite—the consummation of his manhood depends upon the delayed consummation of their association. The sexual encounter will emerge naturally out of his passing the test of combat:

> In Tobruk Dick had almost forgotten Naomi, but now he began to think

of her again. A lot of what had formerly passed between them now seemed remote and contemptible. He recalled a feeling of security, of being half-mothered in her presence because he had told her about the tragedies of his boyhood and she had understood; a sense of friendship; a kiss. Now, these meant nothing. His thoughts and feelings about her now were reckless and direct.

He looked forward to seeing Naomi again because she was a woman, a very desirable one. He laughed at himself because he had not already taken her body. She was older than he, more mature. She would have expected it. She must have laughed at him secretly for respecting her![38]

If there is a note of irony in Lambert's presentation of Brett's coarse new assertiveness, this is thoroughly muted by the once-independent Naomi's willingness to accept the brash young titan on his own terms when they re-meet:

> Naomi lay watching him through half-closed eyes. He had changed, she thought . . . This time he had come to her confident and possessive, showing her at once that she must change her attitude. Now, if she comforted him, it must be as his mistress, and if she dared ridicule him, it must be as an equal. . . . She watched him tenderly and proudly. The fierceness of his love-making had left her elated as never before. His body, vibrant with a long-stored hunger, had seemed to draw on untapped wells of passion in her own . . . All day she had been conscious of her body as something tender and passionate, something belonging wholly to him.[39]

Lambert leaves this intense relationship unresolved. Like a host of other women in Australian war fiction (such as Mary Hatton in *Flesh in Armour* and Joe Maxwell's luckless girlfriends), Naomi plays her part in the grand narrative of the warrior's march to manhood, and then is promptly disposed of. Dick's manliness assured, he can now turn his attention to the serious business of winning a war:

> Dick did not want to think very deeply about Naomi or to remind himself that the future would demand a choice of them. Such decisions were at the whim of war. And the war was now something he believed in, something in which he had to play a part – and something which might destroy him.[40]

In *We Were the Rats* Lawson Glassop takes the linked theme of Australian sexual proficiency and contribution to the war effort a step further. From the beginning of the novel the narrator, Mick Reynolds, goes to extraordinary lengths to impress upon the reader his urbanity, his literariness, his political awareness, his sporting talents, and, not least, his enviable success with women. This, it is clear, is a man amongst men. All he had lacked, before the war, was direction. He was 'restless'; he needed to channel his talents into some great endeavour. As a necessary part of his single-minded dedication to the national cause Reynolds makes the ultimate sacrifice of concentrating all his sexual energy on one female, a chorus girl. He proves that his moral revivification is complete by going to the extent of making an honest woman out of her by marrying her while on leave from the Middle East – though he shows no compunction in truncating their blissful honeymoon when he hears the patriotic call once more:

> "Oh, Mick," cried Margaret, "why do you have to go? Haven't you done enough? Seven months in Tobruk should be enough sacrifice for any man to make . . . Why do you have to go?"
> " 'Man was born free'," I said, " 'but is everywhere in chains'."
> "Who said that, Mick?"
> "I think it was Rousseau. It doesn't matter."[41]

Reynolds's attitudes on sexual matters are patently hypocritical. As if to magnify the intensity of his romantic predicament, this self-styled Byronic figure abrogates his policy of 'knockin' back the sheilas' (in itself a source of amazement to his earthy comrades) when he meets a temptress in a Sydney bar just before his first campaign overseas. His magnetic appeal to women and his healthy male appetite are obviously forces too powerful to overcome. But it is the woman who is to blame for his inconstancy. Accepting the stranger's invitation to go home with her, he ruefully comments, 'You women . . . you make a tiger trailing a bleeding deer through the jungle look like a benevolent old lady'.[42] Once abroad with his unit, Reynolds affects aesthetic disdain and moral outrage at the indiscriminate fornication of his brothel-haunting mates. Yet, for all his virtuous abstinence and his professed repugnance at sleazy sexuality, Reynolds retains his manly appreciation of the opposite sex. How greatly he must have suffered for his self-denial is meant to be revealed by his comments on the so-called 'Perv Gallery' of photographed nudes kept by his closest mate:

> "Most of 'em have a pretty decent sort of upper deck," I said. "It's a woman's most valuable visible asset. It's the tangible manifestation of femininity."[43]

The two-faced prudishness of many heroes of Australian Second

World War fiction arises in great part from their inability to accept that the dislocation of civil life brought about by the war opened up social and economic avenues for women which were previously considered the domain of men only. Greater sexual freedom for women seems particularly to trouble the Digger. Promiscuity is perfectly reasonable for the serving soldier; indeed, his combatant status is assumed to include a *carte blanche* in that area. But the same in women is plain moral turpitude and vile treachery. Bill Farr, the angry young narrator of Lambert's *The Veterans*, muses upon his return from the Middle East that 'drink', 'mates', and 'the casual woman' are all that is left the serving soldier, betrayed as he is by an unfeeling, selfish civilian world. But Farr is irritated by evidence of similar alienation and rashness in the women of wartime Sydney, who had the audacity to be 'obsessed by some desire to prove themselves as reckless as soldiers'. Farr's sexism (which may be held to be typical) is inadvertently illustrated later in the novel, when he describes his distaste for the New Guinea jungle by talking in terms of 'a poisonous, material thing, heavy with foul scents; a huge infested womb, swallowing us, mingling us in its corruption'.[44]

In Dymphna Cusack and Florence James's *Come in Spinner* (1951), one of the heroines argues that women were as much casualties of the war as the men who actually fought it. While the men went off to play their military games, their wives, sweethearts and female relatives had to cope with transformed domestic circumstances, and then were vilified if they did not correspond with the ideal of the Penelope waiting chastely for the wandering warrior to return:

"When men get into the Services they just shelve all their personal responsibilities and women have to take them on. We've got to manage on less money, bring our kids up without any help, and we're expected to put up with the loneliness and having no social life and all the rest of it. You complain about me going out with other men, but I'd take a bet on it that if I ever discovered that Jack had been out with other women, you'd advise me to overlook it – even if he'd been unfaithful – because he's a soldier."[45]

Come in Spinner is an unsentimental social realist novel which recognizes that women also ranked amongst the economic and sexual parasites that were common in wartime Australia. Cusack and James, however, do at least make an attempt to deal sympathetically with their plight. Male writers of Australian Second World War fiction, by contrast, tend misogynously to portray women as malevolent opportunists, both sexually pliable and exploitative, and traitors to the real war effort being conducted by the men in the deserts of North Africa and the jungles of the South West Pacific. While it is probably unfair to condemn a book on the excesses of the advertising on its jacket, the back-cover blurb to the Panther paperback edition of his novel *Soldiers' Women* (1963) indicates the tone of Xavier Herbert's attack on female decadence during the war:

> These are the Women—
>
> IDA—
> the unprincipled Dresden-china coquette . . .
> SELINA—
> the loving young mother . . .
> FAY—
> the child harlot . . .
> ROSA—
> the rebellious young wife . . .
> PATRICIA—
> the schoolgirl who will stop at nothing . . .[46]

In some battle narratives, Diggers are shattered to learn that while they are away risking their lives, their wives and girlfriends are 'playing up' back home. One soldier, 'Smiler' in Glassop's belated sequel to *We Were the Rats*, *The Rats in New Guinea* (1963), commits suicide when he hears of his wife's adultery with an American stationed in Australia. The 'Yank' presence in wartime Australia is a real bugbear. The soldier home on leave felt aggrieved that a horde of big-spending foreigners had integrated themselves so well into the comfortable world he had gone off to protect from alien invasion. 'A bloke feels like a bloody foreigner in his own country', complains an Australian on leave in *Come in Spinner* as he waits to be served in a bar crowded with Americans.[47] But what most angers the Diggers is the G.I.s' popularity with the female community (though their monopoly of taxis runs a close second). With some sarcasm, Jon Cleary in *The Climate of Courage* (1954) implies that the sexual success of the visitors was due to their belief that 'women meant more to a man than beer and racehorses, something that had so far escaped a good many Australian men'.[48] Cleary may have a point. Given the fairly primitive nature of most of the men who pass for heroes in Australian war fiction, the women could hardly be blamed for turning their attentions elsewhere.

It is not surprising to discover that homosexuality within the Second A.I.F. was not a favourite subject of the war writers. As David Walker has pointed out, its avoidance is clear evidence of 'the pervasiveness of the code of heterosexual manliness in the Australian war novel'.[49] One suspected homosexual, John Hemilton in *The Rats in New Guinea*, is an overweight alcoholic with a 'flabby' pink face, 'weak and shifty eyes', chubby chin and a worryingly 'flaccid' handshake — hardly the usual heroic type. His section leader, Mick Reynolds, is concerned that the presence of 'a queen' would upset the sturdy camaraderie of his fighting unit. But, to the relief of all, Hemilton proves that he is no queen at all, in a series of wildly brave exploits in battle. He even loses weight, fining down to something resembling the becomingly lean, hard, 'Anzac' look.[50] In Geoffrey Dutton's comic novel about the wartime adventures of a young R.A.A.F. pilot, *Andy* (1968), the obsessive belief that homosexuality disrupts the smooth functioning of a male community is hilariously parodied. The warden of the Detention Camp in which the anarchic Andy is periodically incarcerated enunciates the standard anti-homosexual line:

> "Mind you . . . out of prison I've got nothing against poofters. Decent quiet fellows, many of them artistic too. As long as they keep themselves to themselves . . . But the trouble is that in gaol . . . you got to watch this sex thing. You can't stop the poor devils banging away at themselves. But you get real bad poofters inside, and if you let 'em rip they'd bugger the place up completely."[51]

The nonconformity of Andy himself runs only to his chronic inability to behave in a manner acceptable to the military authorities. He is an exuberantly heterosexual creature, 'a free, irregular man' who embraces sex, along with friendship, courage, and skill, as 'one of the few things left that we can test and find true'. Andy wants to display his flying prowess in fighting action in the war. When his indiscipline leads to his spending virtually the entire war in Australia, he does the next best thing, testing his manhood in a string of sexual adventures. In one bizarre episode, he attempts intercourse with a nurse on a mortuary slab. This uncongenial setting, reeking of formalin and disinfectant, causes his 'manhood' to fight with his 'turning stomach', with the nausea emerging triumphant.[52] With incidents such as this in mind, the healthy revelry of the original Anzacs seems not only distant and quaintly old-fashioned, but as belonging to another century altogether.

In respects other than their freely described sexual proclivities, the men of the Second A.I.F. differ from their rather more ingenuous and upright fathers. A strong strain of cynicism, or worldly wisdom, has wormed its way into the old idealistic framework of Australian war literature. Even those characters who most earnestly profess their patriotic and political motives for volunteering, freedom-fighters like Dick Brett and Mick Reynolds, admit that their enlistment was also based on selfish and ignoble grounds. An immature wanderlust and a desire to escape domestic turmoil propel Brett toward the battlefield, while Reynolds has the ambition to emulate the 'old man' as well as the need to alleviate the crushing boredom of his pre-war life. The war would provide an antidote to ennui: 'I was going into a new world. Great events and experiences lay ahead, and if death was there, too, at least it would not be dull'.[53]

The memoirs of men like H. R. Williams and Joseph Maxwell reveal that many of the patriots of the First A.I.F. also exposed themselves to the dangers of battle because it offered an alternative to the dull regularity of civilian life. But a cynical, if misguided, self-interest appears to have governed the choice made by many of the next generation. To Tommy Collins in *The Twenty Thousand Thieves*, the army 'meant freedom', and the war 'seemed to have licensed drunkenness and the pursuit of women'. Young Oscar White, wondering 'how the hell' he got involved in the jungle warfare depicted in T. A. G. Hungerford's *The Ridge and the River* (1952), admits that the reason was not patriotism, 'for he didn't know the feeling and hardly recognised the word'. Rather, he joined up because it was 'the thing to do': 'Why not leave the drudgery of nine to five and get a uniform to dazzle the sheilas?' The incorrigible deserter 'Horrible John' in Lambert's *Glory Thrown In* sounds even more pragmatic: 'I joined the army 'cause I wanted a trip abroad . . .'.[54] But for an unromantic approach to soldiering, the *realpolitik* of Vince, one of Geoffrey Dutton's collection of recidivists in *Andy*, is hard to beat. Asked to give a short speech on his interpretation of Australia's war aims at one of the Detention Camp's 'rehabilitation classes', he responds:

> "My war aims is what's best for Number One. Volunteers, conscripts, I couldn't care a stuff where they come from. I don't care who we're fighting, and it doesn't matter a frogskin to a poofter who they are because in a few years after she's over we'll be trading with them again and probably joining up with the Krauts and the Nips to fight the bloody Bolshies.
>
> . . . when Hitler turned up, I was pleased, real pleased. It was one up for the old Number One. I joined the Sixth Divvy because I wanted a job, and there's freedom to look after yourself in the Army. In the

Army you can go through the world like a packet of salts."⁵⁵

Dutton's purpose here is satiric—he wants to lampoon the portrait of the idealistic defender-of-his-country habitually sanctioned by Australian popular culture. Despite the disavowals of men like Ken Clift, however, the economic circumstances of the time did in fact encourage the creed of 'looking out for Number One', an attitude for which the army seemed to provide some sort of outlet. In *My Brother Jack* Jack Meredith tells his brother that soldiering was 'a real bloody picnic' for many men after the long rigours of the Depression.⁵⁶ These were not the complacent innocents of 1914. They were tough, sceptical and usually embittered men who were unenthusiastic about defending a way of life which had offered them little but hardship. 'Horrible John', for instance, sees Australian society as his own personal 'enemy'.⁵⁷ Gunner Lewis had had 'a gutsful' of his itinerant life by the outbreak of war. His enlistment 'wasn't for King and Country', he says, and then explains:

"The king meant bugger-all to me and I don't think the country would have given a stuff if I starved. Australia will be there! That's bullshit! Blokes might have felt like that in the last war, back in 1914, but not this time. I've heard it said that the war was started to stop the Depression, give the unemployed a job. I know that sounds crazy but at times it seems like it."⁵⁸

Another of the Depression's victims, a soldier called Blain in Hetherington's *The Winds are Still*, develops his distrust of the society he was supposed to defend into an indifference to the outcome of the war itself. Blain, who had been 'pushed round since [he] was a kid', looks at the conflict in terms of what it will achieve for his own sorry situation in life. 'Australia don't seem so good to me', he tells a more contented comrade—'What in hell difference will it make to me whether we win the bloody war or lose it?'⁵⁹ These disaffected Diggers are contemptuous of patriotic slogans; on occasions their perverse pragmatism hardens into a sneering anti-nationalism which would have been regarded as actively treacherous a generation before. In Peter Pinney's novel about an Australian Independent Company in Bougainville, *Road in the Wilderness* (1952), another rootless and resentful child of the 1930s puts patriotism into perspective:

"You think I love that rabble of tin-roofed shanties I was born in, way out in the Mallee? . . . Feller, I couldn't tell you what the first line of the anthem is, though I believe I heard it once in a bar. You think the accident of birth leaves me in a sweat, all hepped up and singing 'On, on, Australia'? Does it, bulldust! Anyone does that, he's the biggest sucker of the lot."[60]

For all their solitary rebelliousness, most of these delinquent Anzacs eventually come to the patriotic party in a crisis, managing to subdue their individuality for the good of the collective cause, and so achieving a kind of redemption. Anthony Harding, a loner engaged in intelligence work in Malaya in Eric Lambert's *The Dark Backward* (1958), complains about living in 'an age made for heroism, but not for heroes . . . these days it was the collective, the team . . . it was the loyalty to everything but yourself'.[61] Most Australian promoters of the heroic ideal would argue, on the other hand, that it is through collective achievement that the so-called rugged individualist most constructively realizes his own potential. Thus Gunner Lewis, the reprobate who had 'welched on his mates' by deserting them, is reclaimed at the end of Beilby's novel by returning to his unit; thus the obstreperous misfits of *Road in the Wilderness* are bonded into an 'independent' lethal fighting force through their mutual dislike of the mainstream military organization; and thus Blain, the perpetual loser of *The Winds are Still*, comes to terms with his bitterness by acting upon his belated realization that 'there ought to be somethin' better, an' maybe I can lend a hand to get it'.[62]

While the theme of personal completion through communal warlike striving was not new to Australian war literature (think of Ginger Mick), the Second World War novelists gave the old idea a new impetus by embodying it in men who are both disenchanted and unendearing. The blurb of a penny dreadful about a collection of incorrigibles serving in Malaya, Roger Hunt's *The Drongoes Who Dared* (1960), succinctly defines the pattern of rehabilitation – and the literary strategy which promoted it:

> They were a bunch of no-hopers – admitting it themselves – and when they were cut off from their companions in the depths of the Malayan jungle, it seemed no power on earth could save them from annihilation.
>   But since they didn't want to die, they had to stick together and fight . . . and by the time they won through, they weren't drongoes any more. They were hard, expert soldiers . . . they were heroes who had won a lasting fame . . .[63]

An even better insight into this philosophy of war as a life-enhancing activity emerges from the portrayal of soldiers who, though cynical, are not recalcitrant 'drongoes' of the Gunner Lewis mould. One such example is Jack Savanna, in Cleary's *The Climate of Courage*. Savanna, a sophisticated and reserved former radio announcer with the Australian Broadcasting Commission, is no rough-and-ready Digger, though he does possess a familiar 'stubborn streak of rebellion'. In a literary forum in which even minor deviations from the rules of Anzac etiquette are not to be dismissed lightly, Savanna's use of the appellation 'chum' in greeting his comrades rather than the usual 'mate', for instance, indicates his highbrow singularity. But combat integrates the aloof Savanna into both the army and the culture he affects to scorn. The battle experience and the sharing of hardships with his countrymen teaches him to replace his selfish egotism with the 'Australian religion of mateship', a 'spirit of fraternalism' he had once derided. This achieved, Savanna's evolution into a warrior of Anzac status is assured. In the beginning, the war had merely been 'an adventure' to him, 'a chance to rebel' against convention and monotony, 'perhaps even against the human race, so many members of which he had once despised'. His acquired dedication to his military calling and his marriage to one of the superb beauties who seem to gravitate towards the heroes of Australian Second World War novels signify that 'his life would at last have taken on some meaning'.[64] As if to offer the world some outward sign of his inner transformation, Savanna even shaves off his patrician moustache. Genuine Australian war heroes, it seems, do not feel the need to present themselves as being a cut above their mates.

'ACTION' OVER 'ART'

Warfare reforms Jack Savanna because he becomes a man who acts rather than thinks. Such a transformation is common among the more intellectual characters in Australian Second World War fiction. As we have seen, the gulf dividing the representative men-of-action from the passive and sensitive outsiders in the A.I.F. was of interest to several important First World War writers. That gulf is usually bridged in the Second World War novel. And, more often than not, it is the thinker who makes the compromise, a compromise based not on a stoical acceptance of the soldier's lot, but on a conversion to the philosophy of action. Mick Reynolds in *We Were the Rats* provides the most striking example of the dilettante turned daredevil. Just as Bill Farr in *The Veterans* checks his tendency to ruminative excess by befriending the semi-literate malefactor, 'Lasher' Daniels, Reynolds's 'noble friendship' with a larrikin, Eddie Wilson, signals that he had climbed down from his ivory tower and joined the mass of common, active man. This unlikely alliance begins in classical fashion. To prove his toughness to the rugged Wilson, who considers him 'a bit of a queen', Reynolds engages him in a fist-fight. He knocks Wilson down, bloodies his face . . . and they become instant 'cobbers'. Living with men he had formerly thought to be his inferiors forces a change in Reynolds's outlook. Whereas Edgar Morrow, a self-conscious intellectual from the 1914–18 conflict, was inclined to insist that he was 'wasted in such a thing as war', Reynolds confesses that his pre-war self was essentially counterfeit. He had over-rated the value of 'culture'. As he tells an old friend from his home town:

"You know, back in Nerridale I must have been an insufferable snob. Always prided myself on knowing taxi-drivers and boxers and racecourse urgers and fellows who worked on pie carts, too. But inside I despised them because they'd think Cavour was a racehorse, *Sartor Resartus* a fellow in C. Company, and William Makepeace Thackeray a delegate to an armistice conference . . . I used to think that a man who couldn't speak the King's English didn't deserve to be a subject of the King. They've made me ashamed. Here in Tobruk you don't worry about such things. Here you find the real man revealed, and the man whose ignorance I've sneered at is twice the man I'll ever be."[65]

Not all soldiers find the transition from the 'intellectual' to the 'man of action' as smooth. Philip Masters, in Norman Bartlett's novel about the air war in the Pacific, *Island Victory* (1955), is a man of some intellectual substance, unlike the pretentious Reynolds. A university lecturer in modern English literature, he had enlisted only after an intense personal debate in which he had been forced to choose between his philosophically anti-war, and politically anti-fascist, sympathies. He decides he must serve, though his reasons for selecting the R.A.A.F. and not the A.I.F. show that his sensibility is more influenced by European literary memories of the Great War than by Australian:

He had chosen the air force because his mind, burdened with the stinks and frustrations of *Goodbye to All That*, *All Quiet on the Western Front*, and other post-war disillusionments, could not face the prospect of foot-slogging.[66]

Regarding himself as 'a constitutional non-combatant', Masters serves as an intelligence officer. He finds himself moving in 'a world where literature and philosophy were vague, useless values compared with technical ability and heroic motive'. He quickly recognizes that he had neither of these two requirements. His involvement, however peripheral, in a fighting organization makes him reconsider his scepticism about the value of the life of action. He comes to see himself as a 'prig' whose hatred of warlike endeavour had been unreasonably narrow—'smug in his book-lined room, he had explained away courage and purpose'. He even finds that he can learn things from the fighting men. Sounding just a little like Glassop's patronizing hero, he admits that the cheerful, life-risking pilots 'could teach him more real wisdom than he'd ever gathered from the box of intellectual tricks that represented the result of his education'. But despite this revelation, and though he strikes a bond with a fighting ace, a man who is 'bored' by talk and 'vaguely uneasy' about ideas, Masters remains unmoved by the warrior ethos. He understands and even sympathizes with the 'team spirit' that moves the fighting force, appreciates its 'natural gregariousness' and its 'combativeness toward anything or anyone outside the pack'—'but he could not feel it'.[67] The war modifies some of his attitudes, but it does not change the man.

At least Masters acknowledges the attraction of the creed of action. In George Turner's opposition of the thinker with the doer in *Young Man of Talent* (1959), conflict rather than compromise results. The novel, a psychological study rather than strictly a 'war novel', centres on the ennui of an Australian soldier, Peter Scobie, a self-described 'thinking introvert' who adopts a refractory private as a kind of pet project to while away the war in a transit camp in New Guinea. A writer before the war, Scobie had begun his martial career as a fire-eater, but he had long since lost his stomach for soldiering. This diminution of military will is paralleled by his increasing preoccupation with philosophical issues, 'always the ruin of the artist as a man of action'. In Private Andy Payne, Scobie discerns a 'good soldier' whom he wants to turn into 'a good man'. Payne is a man of exceptional physical strength but, like Gunner Lewis, he has a chip on his shoulder. Seemingly 'born' for action and nothing else, he is savagely anti-intellectual, and is especially contemptuous of book-learning. Scobie's literariness—he numbers *Hamlet, Eminent Victorians,* and *The Psychopathology of Everyday Life* among a catholic reading collection—marks him out as 'effeminate' to Payne. Conversely Scobie sees Payne as 'the nexus of an heroic frieze'.[68] This is a classic dichotomy of Australian male character types, anticipating George Johnston's more subtle investigation of the myth of Australian maleness in *My Brother Jack*.

After the initial period of animosity the two men form a fragile friendship, until – in a brief encounter with the Japanese in which Scobie performs to far less than Payne's exacting standards – the final and inevitable split. Revealing himself to Payne as a 'gutless bastard', Scobie deserts the scene of battle at a critical moment, for which he faces a certain court martial for cowardice. This prospect he regards as 'cleansing' rather than 'shameful'. Rebirth, in his case, does not mean participation in the epic venture, but an abandonment of it. Payne, meanwhile, has become more of a lost soul than ever, humiliated by his former mate's timidity, and having almost certainly lost faith in what he had earlier seen as 'the one worthwhile product of war, the peculiar and induplicable oneness of a group'. What had been an attempt at communion between opposites ends with Payne wildly weeping 'for the friend who, in truth, had never existed'.[69]

George Turner's uncompromising handling of the problem of aggressive action and intellectual retreat is not common in Australian Second World War fiction. Usually the relatively cultivated figures, like Mick Reynolds, learn to accommodate the ways and manners of the instinctive active types, apparently the dominant psychological caste among the men who comprised the Second A.I.F. The case of 'Turk' Bennet in Beilby's *No Medals for Aphrodite* is instructive here. Sensitive and meditative by nature, Bennet is said to be a reader of Zola, Wells, Steinbeck and Upton Sinclair. This, we can be assured, is a sign of excessive intellectuality. His comrade, Harry Cole, with whom he is trapped in Greece during the Nazi invasion of 1941, is representative of what Beilby blithely calls 'rugged Australian maleness', that breed which is 'so sanely unimaginative'. Cole, Bennet suspects, had never read 'anything more imaginative than a race-book'. Bennet despairs of the inarticulateness of his comrades, whom he derisively calls 'the Mob'. He also despises their flaunting of a 'proudly proletarian mediocrity':

> A man could drink and whore and scrounge and the Mob admired him, but let him so much as speak of the Imponderable and he was eyed askance.[70]

But Turk Bennet, who is a discerning fellow, has to acknowledge that his comrades have their appealing qualities. Indeed, so much does he come to admire these coarse but doughty men that he abandons his old standards and scruples, adopting their profane vocabulary and trying to emulate them in bars, brothels and detention-cells. Bennet wants to fit in; he also fears the Mob's disrespect. To ap-

pease that fear, he had performed 'deliberate audacities' on the battlefields of North Africa. These feats had 'proved himself to himself' and, more importantly, his acceptance by the Mob had given
him the 'sense of integration' that he had vainly sought in his hungry, wandering years in pre-war Australia.[71] (Certainly, Bennet and
Harry Cole never become really close, but the major source of dis-
sension between them—the affection of the enticing Aphrodite, for
which both men strive—is after all a bone of contention of the most
justifiable kind.) Though the price of integration is the sacrifice of
his once-treasured individuality, this is assessed to be less costly than
isolation from the group identity. For an army which prided itself
on the individualistic talents and traits of its members, the Second
A.I.F., like its father force, seems to have fostered a curiously conformist spirit.

In *My Brother Jack* the issues of conflicting allegiances to the group
and the private imagination, and of integration and nonconformity,
are given a complex and moving treatment by being directly related
to the national ideal of the 'Anzac' man-of-action. Like *The One Day
of the Year*, *My Brother Jack* registers the Great War's reverberating
impact on Australian culture by reviving much of the mythology of
Gallipoli and applying it to the generation who went to the next war.
Though the vulgar proselytizing of *Australia at War* suggests otherwise, George Johnston was not an uncritical promoter of the myth.
Writing in the magazine *Walkabout* the year after *My Brother Jack*
was published, he remarks that the ebullience of the Australians in
New Guinea and in the Western Desert during the 1939–45 war 'was
never any "inheritance of the Anzac spirit"—as if the myth was something to be handed on like a used coat or a family heirloom'. Johnston considered the story of Anzac to have an application outside
its historical sequence or national significance, as the manifestation
of a *universal* human willingness to face adversity and even death
with adventurousness, cheerfulness and fraternal sympathy and solidarity. In this sense the 'Anzac spirit' becomes synonymous with a
heroic attitude to life itself. Nevertheless Johnston, like C. E. W.
Bean and a host of war writers before him, also believed that Anzac
'derived from something special in Australian character and instinctively seems to transmit itself to Australian character'.[72] Here Johnston comes close to defining one of his major themes of *My Brother
Jack*, in which he implies that the dominant species of the Australian
male, as epitomized by Jack Meredith, thrives in the martial role.

Observing his brother training at Puckapunyal army camp in late 1939, David Meredith, as the novel's narrator and Johnston's *alter ego*, was

> intrigued, and impressed, at the change in him. He was so darkly sun-burnt that his hair seemed almost white, and he looked tough, hard, and very fit . . . there was a look of absolute *rightness* about him . . . What had changed about him, I began to realize, was both subtle and profound: it was almost as if he had been fined down to the "essential Jack," as if this was what my brother really *should* look like . . . Even more than this, for I saw that this was not only that he looked as *Jack* should look, but that he looked as a proper *man* should look.[73]

By thus preparing himself for the battlefield, this quintessential Australian – this quintessential *man* – attains 'the realisation of his true self'.[74] Jack is the Anzac redivivus, drawn like his father before him by the primal pull to distant warlike adventure which, Johnston theorizes, is the Australian's natural shuddering reaction against the invincible native wilderness he inhabits:

> Jack's almost passionate response [to the war] was typical enough of many Australian young men at that time – he was roused very probably by the same pull which a quarter of a century earlier had taken Dad away . . . the pull, I am inclined to think, was almost mythic, and dic-tated by the land in which he lived.
> . . . The vast dry heart of the land is dead, and it is on this intractable central wilderness that the teeth of adventure have long since been blunted . . . It is the one challenge from which the adventurous Aus-tralian has always had to retreat . . . So he has been obliged to look else-where for the great adventures, the necessary challenges to the flesh and spirit . . . He is, because the merciless quality of his own land dictates it to him, the soldier of far fortune. This is why his armies which are sent to these faraway places are always of volunteers . . . I have been with the armies of many races, but I have known no other soldier with such pure and passionate regard for the adventure in itself.[75]

Like Andy Payne in *Young Man of Talent*, Jack had arrived at the threshold of the experience for which his entire life had been built.[76] From his childhood he was the happy, if naïve, recipient of the Anzac legacy, a heritage which almost tangibly permeated the Meredith household after his parents' return from the Great War. His heroic lineage is manifested early, in his adolescent appearance as remem-bered by his brother:

> Jack was fairly tall and rangy, with blue eyes, a beaky nose, and disord-erly cornsilk hair . . . His mouth was wide and full, but it could set in

a hard, tight line when he was angry, like the jaws of a trap. He had ears which, in his own words, "stuck out like jug handles." There was a gawky, awkward look about his bodily movements, but it was dangerous to bank on this for I never knew anybody as fast on his feet or as quick with his hands in a boxing ring or a street brawl. He was wiry rather than strong and there was a savage, whipping sting to his punches.[77]

As he appears here, Jack is strongly reminiscent of the soldiers depicted in *The Anzac Book*, the pages of which David had pored over in his childhood – perhaps David's memory of his elder brother was subconsciously formed by that juvenile fascination with Bean's prototypical Digger. Temperamentally as well as physically, Jack seems to have been created by Johnston with the legendary Anzac in mind. 'Undisciplined' and 'pugnacious', the youthful Jack is 'a hater of authority', though he is quick to defend the rights of the innocent citizens (the metaphorical outraged women and children of Belgium and France) who were then being terrorized by the Hunnish hooligans roaming the streets of Melbourne. Both linguistically and sexually precocious, he also exhibits early signs of that panache exuded by the revamped Anzacs of Second World War battle fiction. Colourful colloquialisms like 'as dreary as bat-shit' flow from his lips, while the adolescent sexual encounter was merely 'another part of the adventure and hazard of living'. It was his irrepressible audacity which most captivated the opposite sex: 'Anything he tackled was tackled with immense gusto, almost as if he had to eat life in huge gulps . . . while his appetite was strong . . . or before they cleared away the table'.[78]

Above all, Jack possesses the gusto that Johnston thought to be typical of the famous men of Gallipoli. He lives by the principle of 'having a go', even when circumstances conspire against him and he is, as he tells David, 'pissin' into the wind'. His response to the Depression reveals his never-say-die spirit. During the Depression the old greatcoats of the First World War Diggers ('that brave khaki of 1914–18') were taken out of Defence Department warehouses, dyed a dull black and issued to the workless poor to keep them warm in the Melbourne winter. Johnston uses the dyed greatcoat as a symbol of the debasement of the Australian spirit; significantly, Jack refuses to wear one. Instead, he fights the economic-cultural crisis 'on his own terms and in his own way'. Repudiating the dole, he goes on rabbiting expeditions, and, later, on gold fossicking jaunts into the bush. Both enterprises, which David describes as 'quests', fail dismally. But Jack is unbowed, claiming that it was 'still worth givin' it a go!'[79] Better to go down fighting than not to fight at all.

In the Second World War as in the Depression, Jack, the mythic urge for adventure 'lodged and burning deep inside him', meets failure. Ill-luck and injury together thwart his martial ambition, and the aspiring 'soldier of far fortune' is to his shame forced to look on passively while his countrymen fight and die all over the world. This strangely noble figure, who could have enacted 'some passionate Conradian drama', finishes up as a travesty of his former dynamic self. He gives up and admits defeat, pathetically compensating for his personal disappointment by investing his 'brave pride and passion and purpose' in his younger brother, who had shot to prominence as a war correspondent during the conflict.[80] Nevertheless, the vanquishing of Jack's spirit, while it can be seen as Johnston's sharp social comment on a race whose cockiness is apt to degenerate into meek torpidity,[81] is not intended to represent a broadside at the heroic myth itself. In its idealized form at least, Johnston/David Meredith worships the Digger as passionately as C. E. W. Bean himself. Indeed, the tension in *My Brother Jack* is produced by David's inability to unite his admiration for men who like Jack embody the myth, with his alienation from the culture which breeds and nurtures them.

David Meredith is the antithesis of the outgoing heroic adventurer. At many points in his recollection of their childhood life together, David self-effacingly notes how fundamentally he differed from his brother. Jack was tall, wiry, and intrepid – David was 'chubby, soft, pink and fearful'; Jack was a good boxer and a destructive street-fighter – David was 'hopeless' as a pugilist; Jack attracted droves of girls – David shrank from them and they from him; Jack was the active extrovert – David was the introvert who spent all his time in his room reading and writing stories . . . and so on. Young David's appalled response to the Great War as it corrosively persisted among the physical and emotional war-wreckage who populated the Meredith home is an early sign that he will develop outside the mainstream culture that nurtures the 'Jacks'. His separateness gives him a feeling of being 'shut out', and he endures the pain that goes with 'an incapacity to reach standards imposed not by oneself but from outside'.[82] Jack deplores David's 'sonky' shrinking manner and his 'poofter' arty friends; more wounding still is the abuse his hostile father hurls at him for engaging in such an unmanly pursuit as literature. As one of the celebrated

Diggers of the Great War, Meredith senior is a champion of the value of physical exertion, and equally certain of the enervating effect of the intellect. As he berates his son:

"You and your blasted books! . . . All you're doing, my lad, is muddling your mind and ruining your eyesight! Why the devil don't you get out and *do* something."[83]

For all the destructive sense of personal inferiority it had given him in his early years, David's maladjustment eventually provides him with a source of escape from a society in which he had felt increasingly isolated. His adolescent literary labours secure him a position with a Melbourne newspaper, leading to his role as an overseas war correspondent. It is while he is abroad on assignment during the war that he begins the 'proceedings of divorcement' from Australia and its people that end in a long period of post-war expatriation, first in Britain and then on a Greek island. (This expatriation is ironically described in *Clean Straw for Nothing*, the 1969 sequel to *My Brother Jack*, as a 'doughty battle, if you want to impart a certain spurious flavour of the heroic, to uphold the principles of individuality'.)[84] Yet David remains disturbed by his inability to match the heroic spirit that functioned so purely in his brother. The assertion of his own identity was achieved to the detriment of that mythic truth which is the privilege of Australians. The price he had paid for his individuality was base cynicism. Studying his reflection in an Italian hotel during the war, he sees a face that is

a little world-weary, and a shade too cynical around the deep-set eyes, and then I looked closer and I realised that it was not at all the same face as those other faces under the broad-brimmed hats . . . not the same, for instance, as my brother Jack's face. A difference had grown into it, or developed out of it . . . I realised that there was a sort of calculation in it, that this was a face watching for opportunities, that what was lacking in it was the truth those other faces had for the passionate regard for the adventure in itself . . .[85]

The Australian myth as it functioned within Jack and others like him is regarded by Johnston as a romantic, if ultimately tragic, attempt to transcend the circumscribed limits of their existence. At Puckapunyal, Jack had appeared to David as 'a kind of sunburnt Icarus, a free man, buoyant and soaring in his own air'.[86] David too had tried to rise above what he rejected as an inhibiting family background anchored in 'shabby suburban squalor'. But his escape, and the worldly success which came with it, resulted only in a sense of loss and a confirmed self-image as ignoble and unworthy. David, whose journalistic career soars during the war in inverse and ironical proportion to the collapsing of his brother's ambitions, castigates himself as an impostor who had snared a measure of false fame (in reality he had spent the war in far more bars than battles), when it was Jack who had 'earned the right to it'. At least Jack was a 'trier'; David, by pitiful contrast, was an opportunist.[87]

The shame and the sadness David Meredith struggles to express towards the end of *My Brother Jack* is a touching revelation of the inveteracy of the Anzac ideology within the Australian sensibility. The former champion of artistic over active achievement realizes that his personal 'victory' over Jack is Pyrrhic; deference to the heroic ideal wins the moral case over noncomformity. The final message of *My Brother Jack* may well be that it is more worthy to *fight* than to write.

VII

The Second A.I.F. in The War

TROUPERS OF THE SOUTHERN CROSS

At the beginning of *The Soldier's Art* (1966), one of Anthony Powell's trilogy of novels set during the Second World War, the narrator Nicholas Jenkins recalls his purchase in 1939 of an army greatcoat at a Shaftesbury Avenue store which specialized in theatrical costume as well as military attire. The elderly shop assistant, a devotee of the theatre, mistakenly assumes that Jenkins will wear the greatcoat in a stage production:

> "What's this one for?" he asked.
> "Which one?"
> "The overcoat – if I might make bold to enquire?"
> "Just the war."
> "Ah," he said attentively. "*The War* . . . I'll bear the show in mind," . . .
> "Do, please."[1]

The argot of warfare is of course laced with the language of the stage, and euphemisms such as 'theatre of war' and 'the big show' have long appeared in battle literature, especially since the Great War. R. Hugh Knyvett, for example, embarked for Gallipoli armed with 'front seats for the biggest show on earth'. If Knyvett was inclined to view war as some sort of popular circus spectacular, Evelyn Waugh in *Sword of Honour* characteristically turned to a more exclusive form of dramaturgy in describing the dying posture of a soldier: 'A car approached . . . Sprawled in the back, upheld by a kneeling orderly, as though in a gruesome parody of a death scene from grand opera, lay a dusty and bloody New Zealand officer'. At a more general level, one is reminded of Wyndham Lewis's caustic assessment of the Great

War as a 'squalid serio-comedy'. But the theatrical metaphor functions in more than a purely descriptive way in *The Soldier's Art*. The unhistrionic Jenkins—himself only scripted for a 'walk-on part' in *The War*—employs it as a qualitative yardstick to measure the response of conscripted and inexperienced 'actors' to the roles thrust on them by the forces of history. His interest is in how these rank amateurs, mere non-combatant 'bit' players in the grand international spectacle, discharge their tedious duties behind the scenes while the heroes enact the drama itself.[2]

The 'theatre of war' metaphor was applied by Australian Second World War writers at the most basic level: military history provided the raw material for a blood-and-thunder play in which the A.I.F. could be cheered, or on very rare occasions booed, for its performance in the starring role. Consequently their fictions tend to resemble modes of extended dramatic criticism. When the Australian performance rivals the composed virtuosity of the most illustrious of all campaigners, the Anzacs (admittedly a hard act to follow), as was the case at Tobruk in 1941, the notices are glowing; when it is listless or indifferent, as in the enervating jungles of the Pacific, they are correspondingly lukewarm; and where there is no 'performance' at all, as with the prisoners-of-war, they border on the hostile. In the case of the POW memoirist, ruefully reviewing his own wartime disappearing act as it were, it looks as if he wished he had never entered the theatre in the first place.

George Eliot once contended that armies might not exist 'if there were not pacific people at home who like to fancy themselves soldiers. War, like other dramatic spectacles, might possibly cease for want of a "public" '.[3] Warfare's magnetic power is illustrated by the Second World War prose penned by non-combatants. While soldier-writers often 'play to the crowd', the starstruck non-combatants get involved in the drama by re-enacting the excitement, the pain, and the glory of it all. Lawson Glassop's *We Were the Rats* is an example. Glassop, a professional journalist who served with the Army Press Unit attached to a Divisional Headquarters in the Middle East, working on the staff of the *A.I.F. News* in Cairo, was never at Tobruk, the famous theatre which provides the setting for his novel. Yet *We Were the Rats*, as narrated by Glassop's fictional surrogate Mick Reynolds, is almost unremittingly exhibitionistic in its spotlighting of Australian martial brilliance. David Walker has asserted that Australians generally are under 'great cultural pressure to bow approvingly before the memory of those who fought'.[4] Glassop's vicarious heroism also stems from an embarrassed sense of inferiority. His intensely deferential dedication of *We Were the Rats* to the A.I.F. infantry (cited by Walker) belies a sad admission of personal inadequacy:

TO
THE INFANTRY OF THE A.I.F.

The men who, as long as I live, will have my
admiration, my respect, my gratitude. I did
so little; they did so much.

Both soldier-writer and non-combatant used the same criterion when assessing the Australian martial performance. Just 'being there' was not enough, it was the *quality* of the endeavour they were interested in honouring. The mythologized feats of the old troupers of the First A.I.F. had spoiled Australians when it came to war, and had instilled in them an extraordinary passion for prowess. The tradition dictated to writers that it was the national force's execution of its military role, rather than *The War* itself, which was important. As the publicists of 1915 well knew, battle virtuosity is the *sine qua non* of the epic war narrative. To this essential element of their trade, the promoters of Second World War heroism were equally receptive.

BATTLE PERFORMANCE AND LITERARY STRATEGY

The premium placed on prowess was such that the form and quality of the combat being described usually dictated the shape and texture of its fictional representation.

Indeed, the mode of warfare could also determine whether it was deemed worthy of depiction at all. One of the oddities of Australian prose of the Second World War, for instance, is the curious lack of attention given the war in the air, the particular theatre for which the overall conflict will be historically remembered. As Robert Hewison's study of literary life in London during 1939–45 reveals, the English market at the time of the Battle of Britain was inundated with heroic fictions whose enormous popularity balanced a contrary craving for works, such as those of Austen and Trollope, from happier, more secure periods of the national history. Skilfully and assiduously promoted by the R.A.F. Public Relations Branch, which commissioned such things as H. E. Bates's hyperbolically-titled story of a Bomber Station, *The Greatest People in the World* (1942), the airmen became World War II's answer to the 'fine flowers' who blithely entered the ranks of the British Army in 1914. Richard Hillary, the Spitfire pilot whose *The Last Enemy* (1942) is in fact a harrowing and anti-idealistic account of his war experiences (among which he was horribly burned), was mythologized into a cult figure of Rupert Brookean dimensions, a process consummated by his accidental death in 1943 during a practice flight.[5]

For the British, of course, the Battle of Britain was an everyday reality, a matter of national (and personal) life and death. The Japanese raids on remote Darwin and Broome aside, Australians had less occasion to be impressed, either positively or adversely, by air warfare. Emotionally tied to the legends of Anzac virtuosity, they still believed that 'real' combat was conducted with the feet squarely planted on terra firma, man facing man. Certainly, courage was still a factor up among the clouds, and a major one at that. Two personal accounts of Australians involved in the hazardous night bombing missions over Europe, Don Charlwood's *No Moon Tonight* (1956) and John Beede's *They Hosed Them Out* (1965), make almost unbearably tense reading; one wonders whether the participants must have had some sort of death wish. Yet the prevailing notion – an untenable one, given the sophistication of the weaponry available to modern armies – was that air warfare was 'cold-blooded, scientific butchery' to a degree that landed combat was not. That, at least, was how L. W. Sutherland, an Australian veteran of the Royal Flying Corps, described even the primitive air combat of the Great War.[6] The poet David Campbell, who served as a wing-commander in the R.A.A.F, touches on this attitude in his story 'Zero Over Rabaul', in which an Australian Hudson on reconnaissance over the islands of the South-West Pacific in 1942 encounters a Japanese fighter:

> . . . I was just straightening from the turn, headed for cloud, when I felt a sudden hammer blow on my left wrist and pins and needles in my hand. At the same time the instrument panel began to fall to pieces. I looked at my wrist in surprise. Where my watch had been there was a round blue hole. The palm of my hand was ripped open and the end of my little finger was missing . . .
>
> And I was surprised; completely surprised. I am convinced that a man, until he sees bullets flying around him, does not basically realise that war is serious, that the enemy is out to kill him. Height detaches the bomber pilot from actual violence. He runs over a ship; four small darts slide from the belly of his aircraft and disappear below. Looking down he sees a plume of smoke start from the stricken ship and he congratulates himself on his good bombing. He knows little of the panic and destruction where his small darts have struck. He has lived a normal peaceful life and he is immune from this until his instrument panel be-

gins to fall apart and he sees his hand flapping suddenly like a dying fish.[7]
The bravura performance of the footsloggers of the First World War
also conditioned Australian literary reactons to 'normal' combat. For
example, while the despair and defeat of Crete produced one notable heroic, albeit elegaic, poem, John Manifold's 'The Tomb of Lt.
John Learmonth A.I.F.' (1944), the novels set in that theatre are few
in number and rancorous in tone. To borrow a couple of Manifold's
phrases, there is little 'courage chemically pure' and few 'old heroic
virtues' in evidence in a novel like *Gunner*, whose author, Richard
Beilby, had himself served on the island.[8] While most of the blame
for the débâcle is reserved for incompetent military strategists, Beilby
does not spare the soldiers themselves. Of Gunner himself the most
that could be said is that his 'panache . . . sparkles' (to plunder
Manifold's fine poem again) rather more often and more brightly in
the bedroom than on the battlefield. Not that the belligerent Gunner cannot fight. In fact he likes to fight, and the atrocious muddle
he endured as one of the 'ragged-arsed mob' on Crete had been a
major source of disillusionment with the military life. In a manner
strangely akin to Evelyn Waugh's Guy Crouchback in *Sword of
Honour*, who viewed Crete as an 'island of disillusion' which
represented the degradation of his knightly idealism, Gunner had
been 'shocked and ashamed' by what he had witnessed on the island.
The inglorious *sauve qui peut* of the routed Allies, enacted to Lord
Haw Haw's taunt 'Run, Rabbit, run', is to Gunner an unbearable
'humiliation'. To add insult to this injury to the Anzac tradition of
never-say-die, Beilby reveals among the Australians on Crete internecine friction and a shattered *esprit de corps* unimaginable in the
idealized men of Galliploi.[9]

If the failure of the Australian troops in the Greek theatre invited
the kind of sneering bitterness embodied by Gunner, then the successful desert campaign in North Africa told a vastly different story.
In North Africa the Second A.I.F. pulled off three great combat
achievements. The first, involving the Sixth Division (soon to be
sacrificed in Greece), was the rapid advance through Libya of January and February 1941, which pushed the much larger Italian Army
from the Egyptian border to Benghazi, more than eight hundred
kilometres to the west. The second was the defence of the Libyan
port Tobruk in the same year, which gave birth to the legend of the
indomitable 'Rats'. The third was the battle at El Alamein in late
1942, in which the soldiers of the Ninth Division played a vital role
in Montgomery's crucial victory over Rommel.

It was the thrust to Benghazi which first entrenched in the collective heart and mind of both the A.I.F. and the Australian people the continuity of the home-grown heroic tradition. Consider its galvanizing effect on Dick Brett in *The Twenty Thousand Thieves*, who has just arrived in Palestine as a member of the 'Second X Infantry Battalion'. As a garrulous veteran of the campaign relates how the triumph was achieved, the uninitiated young Brett, his eyes alight, entertains a Boy's Own vision of the Australian juggernaut:

> One after another, the coastal towns of Mussolini's brand-new empire fell to the handful of men in the big hats with their long bayonets and their lumbering tanks, cheerfully overwhelming the powerfully-armed enemy who outnumbered them fantastically. It was a savage, exultant vision.
>   . . . [Dick] was fiercely aware of being an Australian soldier and for the first time believed whole-heartedly in the legends of the terrible, laughing men in the slouch hats.[10]

The siege of Tobruk, which like that celebrated confrontation of a generation earlier took place between the months of April and December, appeared to the publicists to be bursting with heroic associations. Barely a single year after the event, George Johnston linked Tobruk with Gallipoli. In describing the personal qualities of the 'Rats' he listed almost precisely those attributes he was wont to apportion the Anzacs, those of 'courage and resource and wild adventure'.[11] His fellow war correspondent, Chester Wilmot, in his descriptive history *Tobruk – 1941* (1944), also commemorated the parallels between the two struggles:

> There was much in common between these men and the original Anzacs. Although the one was a successful defence and the other an offensive which failed, the same spirit was engendered in Tobruk and on Gallipoli. In both, the constant threat of an enemy who hemmed them in with their backs to the sea bound men together in unbreakable comradeship. Because of this, Tobruk and the spirit it typified became woven into the pattern of the Australian heritage, just as surely as Gallipoli was twenty-six years before.[12]

Yet another of the huge crop of internationally respected Australian correspondents, Alan Moorehead, noted that Tobruk had 'hardened and trained' General Morshead's Ninth Division soldiers, and had given them 'a pride in fighting'. Writing in his *African Trilogy* (1944), Moorehead asserts that the successful siege had given the Australians self-confidence. The men he saw going 'so willingly' into the Alamein Line for the historic 1942 confrontation were suffering no stage fright. They were 'much more sure of themselves' than formerly, and they 'no longer attempted to impress themselves on a stranger—they knew what they were and who they were'.[13] El Alamein itself was a boon to the reputation of the Second A.I.F. This was one occasion when the subdued Barton Maugham, who under Gavin Long's editorship wrote the official account of the battle, allowed himself a little of the grandstanding often indulged in by C. E. W. Bean in his history of the earlier war. Maugham talks of the 'homeric fighting' performed by the Diggers, and copies Bean's tactic of presenting non-Australian documents that are highly complimentary to the A.I.F. effort.[14]

In North Africa the Australians fought across a landscape almost naturally intended for the performance of war, and over which armies had immemorially campaigned. It was a theatre made for barnstorming displays of tactical brilliance and virtuoso acts of valour: the perfect arena for an exhibition of the virility of Australian manhood. Alan Moorehead, usually a temperate observer, swoons like the enraptured Compton Mackenzie on Gallipoli at the sight of sun-bronzed and athletic Australians 'swarming everywhere' along the Alamein Line:

> . . . they looked magnificent . . . Their bare backs and shoulders fascinated me. They were burnt brownish-black by the sun. Under the shining skin the muscles bulged like tennis balls.[15]

The final sporting simile is of particular interest, not merely for its general 'Australianness' but also because it comes within a literary tradition of romantic physiognomical representation. Specifically, it recalls the self-description of a seminal Australian fictional male, Rolf Boldrewood's Dick Marston, who in the opening paragraph of *Robbery Under Arms* (1881) boasts that he can feel his arm muscle swell 'like a cricket ball'.[16]

Given the kind of free-wheeling warfare that occurred in Libya (and even, in its way, within and around the confines of the Tobruk Perimeter), it is hardly surprising that the two most consciously 'epic' Australian novels of the Second World War, *The Twenty Thousand Thieves* and *We Were the Rats*, should be set there. Eric Lambert and Lawson Glassop complemented and expanded upon the rave reviews given the desert campaigners by the wartime propagandists. Having said that, it should not be overlooked that both novels contain their fair share of anti-war polemic. But this paradox is nothing new to Australian war literature. As evidence of the analogy between the typical Australian war writer and the theatre critic who lambasts the play but extols the acting, we have already seen how such Great War books as *Flesh in Armour* and the *Official History* contrive an anti-war theme while indulgently applauding the lethal combat capability of the A.I.F. In an extraordinary accommodation of these antipathetic positions, the war writers rationalize their inconsistency by implying that if war were not so atrocious, then the proclaimed magnificence of the national battle performance would somehow be downgraded. Only in an Australian war book could a novel like *The Twenty Thousand Thieves* fuse an attack on war comparable in ferocity with Mailer's *The Naked and the Dead* with a series of spectacularly heroic infantry skirmishes which assert the grandeur of the A.I.F. fighting machine.

In a review of Hungerford's *The Ridge and the River* and Pinney's *Road in the Wilderness* in *Meanjin*, Eric Lambert argues that the basis on which a war novel should be judged is the strength of its 'war-hating standpoint'. What made *Under Fire* and *All Quiet on the Western Front* such classics, he believes, was their authors' 'anger and hatred against war' as the 'supreme crime against humanity'.[17] In *The Twenty Thousand Thieves* Lambert is as good as his word. He savages *The War*. The thoughts of Dick Brett in the approaching Zero-hour desolation at Alamein constitute as strident a pacifist statement as is available in the entire canon of Australian war literature, and show why Lambert was dubbed 'a new Remarque':

> How many were there like himself? . . . The betrayed, the lost, the unhappy, and the deceived. The fearing, the noble, the mean, the loved, and the detested. This night they would have in common fear and agony . . . This was war. *Curse and damn to the ends of the world all those who had made it necessary.*[18]

To prove his point, Lambert then concludes the novel with a post-battle vista of the Alamein battleground. From massed heaps of corpses to scattered viscera, he details the horrors with a verve which matches Remarque at his most lurid.

War is just one of two targets in *The Twenty Thousand Thieves*. Like many Australian war books written from the viewpoint of the Other Ranker, the novel pillories the officer caste within the A.I.F. At the time of the writing and publication of the novel Lambert was a committed member of the Australian Communist Party, energetic in left-wing literary circles and a comrade and confidant of Frank

Hardy, then besieged by the litigation and controversy over his novel *Power Without Glory* (1950). With one exception – Captain Gilbertson, a romantic figure who dreams of a world crusade against fascism – Lambert's officers are censoriously portrayed. They are caricatures, literary counterparts of the evil creatures lampooned by political cartoonists in journals such as the official organ of the Victorian branch of the A.C.P., *The Guardian*, for which Lambert was a feature writer. There is the haughty and autocratic Colonel Fitzroy, the commander of the 'Second X'; his right-hand military man, fellow pastoralist and implied business partner, the power-mongering parvenu, Major Pomfret; and also the egomaniacal Lieutenant Crane, a psychotic dedicated to the winning of kudos through a private cult of violence. Crane is part antipodean Julian Grenfell, part Nietzschean 'overman', and wholly deplorable. These men are hardly the generously egalitarian, altruistic officers Bean portrayed as populating the A.I.F.

The contempt Lambert's rogues' gallery of 'Establishment' figures reserves for the riff-raff it commands is returned in kind. In Dick Brett's opinion the only role played by battalion leader Fitzroy was the 'driving' of his hapless charges 'to the slaughter'. (Since Fitzroy was a grazier before the war, at least he was eminently well qualified for it.) More hostile still is the perception of one extreme hater of officers, Dooley Franks, who snarls: 'Let the Nazis win the war. They couldn't be any worse than Crane and Pomfret and Fitzroy'. Lest this be regarded as the perverse belief of one whose dislike of authority is intense even among men who are defined as natural enemies of the rich and the powerful, both Fitzroy and Pomfret proclaim their admiration for Hitler, while Crane clearly feels some affinity with Nazism, a movement which Lambert was later to describe as the historical 'child of capitalism'.[19]

Predictably, *The Twenty Thousand Thieves* caused a furore in conservative circles. In August 1952 it was reviled in the national parliament by Jo Gullett, the Liberal Government Whip, as 'a disgraceful attack on the Australian Army', a charge which the truculent Lambert – always keen to take on the ruling class – challenged him to repeat outside parliamentary privilege. The conservatives' anger was coupled with embarrassment when, in that unhappy era of communist witch-hunt, it was publicly canvassed that Prime Minister Menzies himself had as Opposition Leader been a member of the judging committee that had awarded Lambert a 1949 Commonwealth Literary Fund fellowship to write the novel. Suggestions that the scholarly Menzies even made a few stylistic suggestions on Lambert's manuscript (gratefully accepted, of course, by the author) were strenuously denied.[20] Lambert had just cause to be aggrieved at Gullett's charge. Far from trying to besmirch the reputation of the A.I.F., to which he claimed to have been 'proud' to belong for more than five years,[21] Lambert merely repainted it in his own political colours. He did not reject the Anzac myth. Far from it – the novel abounds with men who think, act, and even look like the heroic stereotype, as in the following cameo of an Australian soldier at Tobruk:

> There was something urchin-like, defiant and humorous about him as he stood there and spat. The sort of man who would enjoy himself somehow, anywhere.[22]

What Lambert did was to revise the myth along class lines. His are working-class heroes, with a recognizably proletarian and political, as well as national, identity. Behold Dooley Franks, for instance, as seen through the eyes of Dick Brett:

> A rebel. An adventurer. Worked at everything. In the bush. In the factories. A boss-hater. Believes in the Unions . . . The typical Australian? Tall, burnt, lanky, eagle-beaked . . . What would you call Dooley? Larrikin? Militant? Anarchist? Hard, generous, comical. Good mate . . . Unconquerable.[23]

Renegades from the totalitarian restrictions of military propriety, Lambert's Diggers are Ned Kellys in khaki, armoured by their steely anti-fascist resolve. Lambert's obsession with the anti-authoritarian and egalitarian strains in the Australian character, to which he returned in two fictional treatments of the Eureka uprising, *The Five Bright Stars* (1954) and *Ballarat* (1962), and in the novel *Kelly* (1964), is here embodied by a laconic ex-union organizer called Slim Sullivan. The battalion's prime mover in the confrontation with Colonel Fitzroy over the fundamental issue of Christmas beer rations, Sullivan equates Alamein with Stalingrad, seeing both as victories against the forces of fascism by a committed proletariat. But the novel is not all ideology. For good measure Lambert throws into the fray a conventional, apolitical Australian warrior, the awesome Chips Prentice, a champion footballer before the war and now a champion soldier. Chips of the 'great lithe body', the 'idol of the platoon', who makes venereal disease instantly 'glamorous' when he catches a dose; 'Chips the beautiful gay animal. Tender as a child, terrible as a panther';

Chips, a man of instinctive heroism, whose all-round puissance extends to an ability to deliver inspirational pre-battle pep-talks on the value of freedom. The only problem with Chips is that he is simply too good to be true—as A. A. Phillips complained to Lambert in an otherwise generously laudatory letter, he 'seems to be seen through a hero-worshipper's eyes and therefore impersonalised'.[24] Slim, Chips, and other irrepressible Diggers are sacrificed to the hateful war god; but the very vibrancy of their characterization illustrates that Lambert felt compelled to promote his belief that, in the Second World War, 'Australians and the way they went on were still a little legendary'.[25]

There was enough in *The Twenty Thousand Thieves* to please pacifist, chauvinist and communist alike. 'The spirit of Lawson is abroad in the land', enthused the *Guardian* in a review headlined 'A Great Australian Anti-War Novel', before going on to recommend the book as a celebration of 'the true Australian tradition of humanity, radicalism, and courage', and as 'a "must" for all true Australians [*sic*]'.[26] Unlike C. J. Dennis in *The Moods of Ginger Mick*, Lambert exalted 'Pride o' Class' and 'Pride o' Race' simultaneously without weakening the claims of either. And while his sense of the moral and physical horror of war is sincerely and powerfully communicated, it should be remembered that the anti-war propagandist's depiction of brutality depends on pictorial devices very similar to those favoured by the heroic battle writer. Battlefield gore is easily converted to battlefield glory. In any case, Lambert's scenes of 'whooping' Australians scampering across the desert after their routed enemy leave their mark on the reader as much as any maudlin anti-war or malcontented anti-authoritarian sentiments. Divided into four sections with Homeric titles like 'The Plain' and 'The Fortress', which patently correlate the siege of Tobruk with that of Troy, *The Twenty Thousand Thieves* reverberates with a descriptive energy and a tonal resonance straight out of the heroic tradition. The tragic but Homerically sublime death of Chips Prentice as he leads his Myrmidons forward at El Alamein exemplifies Lambert's celebratory intention:

Swift and terrible, Chips led B Company out in a charge to retake the position.

Beside him Hamilton fell. But still his company saw Chips on his feet. They did not know he was riddled. He tried to throw a grenade. The life was leaving him but he found new strength to hurl the grenade. The blood gushed down him. Fearsome and splendid, he leaped among the Nazis. His great voice rose above the clamour of gun-fire; feet apart, he wielded a rifle like a club and the Nazis fell about him. He went to his knees with a roar of rage and another Nazi shot him through the head. He turned his bloody face round and cried to his company. Then he sank to the ground. They fell on the Nazis like maddened beasts.[27]

No doubt Lambert would have claimed an element of realism in this vivid cameo of desperate heroism. To those cynics who believed that by having as his most valorous Digger a renowned Australian Rules footballer Lambert indulged in the worst kind of parochial myth-reinforcement, he could have rejoined that the Ninth Division in North Africa apparently used as its battle-cry a popular term – 'Up there Cazaly!' – which commemorated a noted Victorian footballer.[28] Then again, Lambert was an expert, if careless, mythologizer, particularly where sporting prowess was concerned. His false claim that he opened the bowling for the Victorian cricket team (presumably in partnership with his famous cricketing contemporary *Harry* Lambert) so took root that it was mentioned in his obituaries, as was the blatant untruth that he was educated at Charterhouse and at Oxford. Zoe O'Leary, his biographer, remarks that Lambert both identified with his fictional heroes and was 'prone to great exaggeration'.[29] There is nothing especially reprehensible about this; the problem is that his habitual improvement on the truth in *The Twenty Thousand Thieves* somewhat compromises its 'war-hating standpoint'.

Lawson Glassop's attitude to war, as it filters through to us via Mick Reynolds, is similarly double-edged. Never one for understatement, Reynolds calls war 'murder' and 'insane slaughter', and he registers the various degradations that are the routine attendants of combat, especially of the siege warfare practised at Tobruk. But Reynolds himself is the primary source of some of the novel's more unacceptable contradictions. Any sense of reality in the novel is undermined by the fatuous romanticism of its narrator.

Like Lambert, Glassop affects the manner of the epic novelist, assembling a collection of vigorous, humorous, defiant Australian warriors: men no doubt derived, as is Reynolds himself, from good Anzac stock. Together they join Reynolds on his quest 'to stem the red tide of an outrageous tyranny', in fighting 'for civilization, for all that decent men hold dear'.[30] They are miners, businessmen, taxi-drivers, jockeys, schoolteachers, and wool-classers. Rather curiously, the charismatic Reynolds himself had been a furniture salesman: a wasted talent, we are doubtless meant to think. The only type missing from this broad cross-section is a champion footballer, like Chips

WHITE COOLIES
BETTY JEFFREY
TELLS THE HARROWING STORY OF
THIRTY AUSTRALIAN NURSES WHO
SURVIVED THE TERRORS OF A
JAPANESE PRISON CAMP

Panther

Merchandizing war: popular
Australian books of the Second
World War

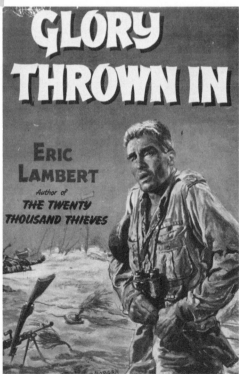

**GLORY
THROWN IN**
ERIC
LAMBERT
Author of
THE TWENTY
THOUSAND THIEVES

Diggers on the prowl: an illustration in *Active Service:
With Australia in the Middle East*, published in 1941

Prentice – a gap which Glassop happily filled when he revived the 'Rats' for *The Rats in New Guinea*. (But never mind – Reynolds, the warrior-poet, is also a cricketer of apparently Bradman-like batting prowess and the toast of his home town, as he constantly reminds us while at the same time swearing that he had lost interest in the game and was bored and embarrassed by all the adulation.) Through a series of incidents great and small, Glassop portrays how these 'ordinary' Australians were able under intense pressure to summon those heroic qualities which he advertises as being innate to the national character. The novel's loose episodic structure supports his purpose, though the antagonism his narrator creates in the reader works against the theme's credibility. If his catalogue of illustrative battle exploits fails to convince us of the superiority of the A.I.F., then there is also ample self-flattering dialogue such as could have been concocted by C. E. W. Bean himself. Here Reynolds discusses the brilliance of the Australian soldiery with a comrade:

"Why do you think Australians are such good soldiers? I've often wondered."

"I have too. It's hard to explain. I think it's because . . . we play so much sport and get so much sunshine we're always fit, and because we've still got the initiative and spirit that helped the pioneers to fight drought, fire and flood."

"I suppose that's it," I said, "plus an adventurous spirit and, among many of us, an unawareness of what lies ahead. You can't, for instance, imagine fellows like Eddie and Jim knowing what danger means. They just don't give a damn. Australians, like Americans, have still got the virility of a young nation. We haven't had time to go to seed. And we don't have to depend, as the Tommies and Germans do, implicitly on our officers . . . An Australian's used to fending for himself . . ."[31]

At least Glassop's admiration for the A.I.F. is tempered by a knowledge of the grimness of battle. He had witnessed it first-hand as an army pressman. Yet, because of his lack of combat experience, his anti-war rhetoric seems rather vacuous; it lacks the rugged conviction of Lambert's. Having to kill people acts as a wonderful check on mindless idolatry. It also instils in the soldier an acute sense of irony, as is revealed in *Sojourn in Tobruk* (1944), a collection of stories by the veteran 'Rat', G. H. Fearnside. In a story called 'Dug-Out in Tobruk', Fearnside relates an Australian soldier's relationship with a genuine rather than metaphorical rodent, a rat which boldly moves in to share his rocky shelter. Reminiscent of the 'queer sardonic' rat of Isaac Rosenberg's Great War poem, 'Break of Day in the Trenches', Fearnside's rodent is attributed cultivated human characteristics. Indeed, the soldier regards it with the respect and admiration one expects from a lesser creature towards a greater. And the soldier's name for the rat? What else but 'Homer'?[32]

The fictions of civilian publicists are sadly devoid of a chastening ironic perspective. For example, Molly Skinner, chiefly known for her collaboration with D. H. Lawrence in *The Boy in the Bush* (1924), wrote of the Libyan campaign in such a naively enthusiastic way that she took her readers on a nostalgic journey back to the days of 1915. In her novel *WX – Corporal Smith* (1941) she tried to revive the rhetoric of the previous generation to assert the pre-eminence of the Digger as a roving representative of the Australian people. 'Australians', she announces, 'are of a new birth – of a new nation'; 'entirely different' to the 'decadent' Europeans, they are not enfeebled by 'medieval superstition and fear'.[33] Et cetera. It had all been said before. Answering what Skinner calls the 'ancient urge' to fight which is 'part of a man's make-up', the Diggers of the Second A.I.F. await action with a childlike excitement. 'Passive, yet volcanic', they are 'splendid kangaroos' who are 'sharp on the spring and swift in action, ready to fight to the death if cornered'. Such men are palpably the progeny of Anzacs. Skinner even has them riot among the brothels of Cairo to show they are as lusty and as fiery as the Diggers of old. Battle itself proves that 'the old traditions were not dead'. In combat at Tobruk, Skinner's principal hero becomes so transported that he experiences 'an ecstasy of communion with man, with nature and with God'. Even the combative Anzacs would have thought this was going a bit far. Skinner's lack of acquaintance with the fighting itself (though she had served with the nursing services in the Great War, an experience which formed the basis for her 1918 novel *Letters of a V.A.D.*) is further manifested by her insistence on how much pure pleasure was enjoyed by the Australians in battle. She observes swaggering Australians out of the line, 'laughing and full of defiant fun . . . leaping in their skins to join the fighting'. Of one particularly exuberant character, a soldier remarks: 'Gosh, it's fun with him along in battle! He's up and over singing and shouting like the devil himself'.[34] These are not the inventions of a novelist, but a clumsily sycophantic wartime propagandist.

The war fought in the jungles of the South-West Pacific, by marked contrast with North Africa, offered little scope for an epic literary

treatment. The perpetual green gloom and the tortuous tropical terrain were inimical to the kind of dazzling valour witnessed by the
Mediterranean. Perversities of country and climate entailed a
claustrophobic, fragmentary campaign of tense patrols and stunning
ambushes, of small-scale skirmishes conducted in a wet, tangled and
mountainous wilderness in temperatures which ranged from extremes
of damp, exhausting heat to bone-shaking cold. As the historian John
Robertson has simply stated, New Guinea 'was not a good place to
fight a war'.[35]   The attacking skills of the A.I.F. were severely inhibited by the nature of the battlefield in the Pacific theatre. The
jungle 'absorbed and dissipated an attack like a sponge absorbs water',
writes David Forrest in his award-winning New Guinea novel, *The
Last Blue Sea* (1959).[36] The incredulous reaction of Tom Hungerford's beleaguered commandoes in *The Ridge and the River* to the
news of the cataclysmic effects of the dropping of the atom bomb
on Hiroshima – an event which in itself put the endeavours of the
jungle fighters into a humbling perspective – aptly sums up how in-
conquerable the jungle seemed to its martial inhabitants: 'Suppose
they do drop one of them split atoms here, where d'you think it's
likely to get us? The flaming jungle'd swallow it up like a sponge'.[37]
The jungle confounded the notion that strength and courage are the
deciding factors in any military issue. Instead, deadly cunning, stealth
and opportunism were the prized attributes. Peter Ryan's memoir,
Fear Drive My Feet (1959), makes this clear. In describing the Australian response to the surprise Japanese infiltration of the New
Guinea township, Wau, Ryan deftly substitutes bathos for the customary bravado:

> Overcast weather had delayed the landing of planes from Moresby
> carrying reinforcements, and it seemed that the Japanese would capture
> Wau. Then, through slightly cleared skies, Douglas transport planes
> roared in to land right among enemy machine-gun fire. "Right! Where
> are the bastards? Let's at em!" shouted one massive infantryman as he
> jumped down from the plane waving his sub-machine gun. Crack! went
> a Jap sniper's rifle from the end of the drome. They picked up the sold-
> ier and took him back to Port Moresby in the same plane, a casualty
> in thirty seconds.[38]

Other factors than the intricacy of the terrain helped justify the title
of the American edition of George Johnston's *New Guinea Diary*
(1944), 'The Toughest Fighting in the World'. The jungle encouraged
physical debilitation and fostered mental malaise, both of which
proved as difficult to overcome as the feared Japanese. The Japanese,

to be sure, were a resourceful, fanatical and merciless opponent. Yet, as Jon Cleary says of the tortuous tug-of-war on the Kokoda Trail, they were 'no more destructive than the jungle'.[39]

In his analysis of the New Guinea war novel Nigel Krauth notes that the realities of the jungle war demolished 'the dangerously self-aggrandising myths [that] had made for the Australian soldier the self-image of a conqueror of towering fates, a tamer of torrid conditions, and a champion of prowess'. The myth's 'hyperbole', says Krauth, 'was stripped back to proper human proportions'.[40] As David Forrest insists in *The Last Blue Sea*, 'A man had no illusions among the leaves, or if he had, he quickly lost them'. New Guinea was removed from the mythopoeic battlefields of the Mediterranean in more than distance. To the veteran of the North African campaign who commands the militia battalion in *The Last Blue Sea*, it was the scene for a painful dissolution of long-cherished virtues:

> On the day that the Battle of Salamua began, there were no illusions left to him, for war had deprived him of the last and greatest illusion that a man can lose. He was far from Bardia Morning in the Western Desert, and he had lived long enough and survived enough battles to know that fortitude and courage wear out, like a gramophone needle or the sole of a shoe.[41]

Jungle warfare attacked not only the Australian soldier's illusions, then, but the physical prowess upon which they were primarily based. The adventurous heroism displayed in theatres from Gallipoli to Tobruk and El Alamein was supplanted by a vastly less majestic 'Job-like patience and resignation', which was 'the only defence against cracking up completely'.[42] The men of Hungerford's commando patrol in *The Ridge and the River* are transformed from jungle fighters to jungle slaves:

> . . . their bodies were wrung dry, like kippers, yellow with atebrin and wrinkled with the damp, in a perpetual nadir of fatigue and discomfort, moving automatically to the dictates of nerves that had almost forgotten the reaction to comfort . . . while that little patch of their brains stayed awake to spy and notice and to remember, the rest was sunk in a torper [*sic*] of resignation, and their bodies, like wound-up mechanical toys, went on, and on, and on.[43]

Pulsating like a living thing, the teeming matted landscape is in a sense itself the hero of the jungle war fiction, stealing much of the limelight usually reserved for the Diggers. In *The Last Blue Sea*, for example, the jungle dominates physically, as an irresistible, triffid-like vegetable force which devours all matter. And it invades psychologically, eating its way into the consciousness of the individual soldier, contracting his universe and engendering a sense of isolation which threatens his very self-identity.[44]

The novelist of the war in the Pacific is not interested in the grand strategic or even tactical struggle. Eric Lambert's choice of the intimate first-person narrative for *The Veterans* in place of the omniscient point of view he used to convey the sweeping battle vistas of *The Twenty Thousand Thieves* points to the limited specifications of the jungle war novel. The classic of the genre, *The Ridge and the River*, describes a single, insignificant patrol over a few days in a place (almost certainly Bougainville) which is not even named. Eschewing a panoramic historical perspective, Hungerford concentrates on the personal wars which each individual soldier fought with the elements and with himself. Along with *The Last Blue Sea*, whose taut, elliptical style and fragmentary structure simulate the private war, *The Ridge and the River* demonstrates how the mode of battle operative in the jungle decided the nature of its fictional portrayal. Hungerford's chosen compressed scope and the terse but pregnant economy of his writing ('at his waist clusters of grenades hung like huge, bloated blowflies')[45] transmit a sense of the toxic oppression of the tropical environment and the interior struggles it induced. The book exudes an atmosphere of suspense and lurking violence every bit as arresting as the epic warfare of Lambert's Middle East novel.

Norman Bartlett, in his novel *Island Victory*, implies that the jungle terrain was hostile to the artless, uncomplicated character of Australian men. Hating the jungle, in which 'everything was always damp, soft, effeminate', one of his servicemen 'longed for the bare earth and dry grass crackling under his boots. And the home smell, the good, dry, earthy, gummy Australian smell'.[46] In his wartime portrait of the A.I.F. in New Guinea, *Soldier Superb* (1943), Allan Dawes argues along similar lines. Though it suited the Japanese, jungle fighting 'did not come naturally to the Australian', with his 'adventurous background' and his love of 'the free and easy life of the open spaces'.[47] Both Bartlett and Dawes may have something. Certainly, the Australians seemed much more at home in the spacious North African theatre (so similar to the Outback, as Frank Dalby Davison indicates in *The Wells of Beersheba*) than in the tight, entombed world of the jungle. It sapped their self-confidence and it frustrated their fondness for space and movement. It encouraged, writes Jon Cleary in *The Climate of Courage*, 'a feeling of defeat'.[48] Raymond Paull's documentary account of the New Guinea campaign in 1942, *Retreat from Kokoda* (1958), describes the 'claustrophobic influence' of the terrain on the Diggers thus:

> Mentally conditioned to the honest contrasts of night and day, to the sparkle of sunshine, moonlight's pale beauty, clouds, the soft gleam of stars, men became uneasy, suspecting the perpetual twilight of the jungle day, the enveloping cloak of darkness which descended around them at night. The strange, small noises, magnified at night, took hold of the imagination, and were transformed into the stealth of some lurking beast or enemy at one's elbow.[49]

Many men broke under the strain. They could never acquire what Allan Dawes calls 'jungle genius'.[50] The different emphases of the New Guinea and the North Africa war novel become apparent when Chips Prentice's trailblazing death in *The Twenty Thousand Thieves* is compared with the ignominious collapse of Chilla Troedson in *The Last Blue Sea*:

> Chilla Troedson stared down through the fringe of the undergrowth at the track where he would presently have to lead the way. He stood there, staring, hating the leaves, feeling the terror of the unseen upon him. He stared in dread, and began to quiver. The leaves of the jungle and the last of his self-respect fought madly in his mind. They made a battlefield of him and he could stand no more. His mind began to crumple, not courageously as history would have it, but pitifully, as it befell in the world of leaves.[51]

Those who did survive 'the world of leaves' had to be careful that they were not converted into automata, mere machines obeying the simple imperative 'to kill and kill and kill' in an environment which brewed 'hate and savagery, contempt and retribution'. Such creatures abound in the New Guinea novel. There are the two 'coldly automatic' young killers, Howard and Wallace, in *The Ridge and the River*, whose relationship was 'cemented' by a mutual love for their bren-gun, with which they lovingly sleep, like children with a teddy bear; there is the sadistic, 'gimlet-eyed' sniper, 'The Mouse', in *The Road in the Wilderness*; and there is the spiritually bankrupt rifleman in *The Last Blue Sea*, Jack 'Nervous' Lincoln, who 'moved and hunted and hid and fought by the promptings of blind instinct'.[52] These are soldiers without any cause other than self-protection. Under the twin terrors of the jungle and the Japanese, once-proud Sons of Anzacs

> had lost their enthusiasm for the war and would fight now only for their own survival. Ideals and causes, patriotism and anti-fascism, were buried somewhere in the black slime . . .[53]

Eric Lambert and Lawson Glassop, for all their detestation of war
as a 'crime against humanity', never so denuded their characters of
all pretensions to a heroic cultural and politico-military role. The
opposite, in fact. While the heavy fighting at El Alamein had left
Lambert's infantrymen as 'men without souls', there is no doubt that
this was a temporary price worth paying in the name of liberty. The
heroes of *The Twenty Thousand Thieves* never descend to the hopeless nihilism embraced by Kevin Manetta in *The Ridge and the River*,
who, crawling Sisyphus-like up a greasy jungle slope, is 'overcome,
almost terrified, by the futility, the no-meaning of what they were
doing'.[54]

The related themes of degradation, futility and sabotaged ideals
also emerge from Peter Ryan's gripping New Guinea odyssey, *Fear
Drive My Feet*. Only nineteen and a recent arrival in that strange
land, Ryan was working for the Australian New Guinea Administrative Unit when he was charged with the responsibility of patrol-
ling the wild and Japanese-infiltrated Lae–Salamua area as an
intelligence scout in 1942. This solitary role, in which Ryan's task
was not to seek combat, but to see and not be seen, epitomizes the
isolation of the jungle war. As Ryan comments in his Introduction,
he treats war 'on the smallest possible scale', not aspiring 'to chronicle the clash of armies', but concentrating on 'what happened to one
man'.[55] And it is a powerful story. Subjected to sickness, appalling
privations and dangers, Ryan soon lost that 'thrill of adventure' which
had first sent him 'striding down the jungle trail, a pioneer', feeling
'exactly like your favourite hero from the *Boy's Own Paper*'. Driven
by fear and hounded by the 'shut-in sensation' exercised on the individual by the jungle, he undertakes a final 'nightmare journey' back
to his base in a frame of mind 'only one degree removed from despair'.
Staying alive was the sole object. After one last dreadful encounter
with the death that always lurked close at hand among the leaves
(which he survives by burying himself in pig-filth so as to avoid the
glare of searching Japanese), Ryan makes it back to safety—
traumatized:

> I had no sensation of joy or relief, though I knew in a remote and abstract
> way that I was now safe. I had no thoughts, no feelings whatsoever.
> I felt neither grief on account of Les nor anger at the Japanese . . . Nor
> did I feel any sense of warmth or companionship towards the soldiers
> who were now preparing water for me to wash, and giving me articles
> from their own scanty clothing to cover my nakedness. I was
> too spent, emotionally, to feel or think or care, and I know now that

such a state is the nearest one can come to death – an emptiness of spirit much more deadly than a grievous wound.[56]

For many writers of fiction about the war in the South-West Pacific, the rank fecundity of the jungle came to symbolize war itself. In this they took their literary lead from European novelists of 1914–1916, for whom the blasted tree-stumps and miasmic mud of the Western Front connoted the shattered illusions and damnable slaughter of that conflict. To Barbusse, Remarque and Frederic Manning the primal ooze of the French battlefield signified a gigantic devolutionary step taken by mankind. The soldiers in *Under Fire*, for example, regress to 'the state primeval' in the 'slime-beds' of 'liquid putrescence' in which they fight and die; and in *Her Privates We* the men – 'almost indistinguishable from the mud' – revert to 'a more primitive stage in their development', becoming 'nocturnal beasts of prey, hunting each other in packs'. Eric Lambert takes up the devolutionary idea in *The Veterans* by suggesting that the jungle fighters underwent a degenerative, dehumanizing process. The veterans of the glorious victory in North Africa are reduced to the 'necessity to kill in order to live', thereby changing into the 'monsters' who had similarly 'occupied slime . . . aeons ago, in the time before our kind of creature began'.[57]

Not all the literary news was unkind for the Australians who served in the Pacific, however. With the Yellow Peril at Australia's doorstep, they could no longer be considered participants in the 'mythic far adventure', writes George Johnston in *My Brother Jack*, but they could still reasonably see themselves 'as men almost of heroic stature, up against it, certainly, but steadfast and staunch, doughty defenders of their native land'. This was the line taken by the wartime publicists like Johnston himself, who played up the defence of Port Moresby, correctly asserting it to be at least as nationally important an undertaking as the siege of Tobruk, by then an already famous deed.[58] The New Guinea Diggers, furthermore, were replicas of the Australian heroes of yesteryear. Allan Dawes pictures them as tanned (jaundiced?), 'lean and hard and muscular' (emaciated?).[59] In an article issued to all Australian newspapers by the Department of Information in 1943, the official correspondent, Kenneth Slessor, while noting the 'fantastic' contrast of front-line jungle combat with that of the Middle East, made the most of the chance to magnify the opportunities for heroism in the theatre. In the jungle 'a special sort of soldier is required', Slessor said, implying that the A.I.F. had a ready supply to throw into the fray:

> He must be young, strong, lithe, resilient, battle-cunning and weather-grilled, with nerves half-steel and half-elastic; he must be cautious and reckless, disciplined but unorthodox, crafty and patient in ambush, audacious at the end of the bayonet.[60]

(It is imperative to stress here that Slessor valued his literary independence too much for an official correspondent, and he eventually tired of trotting out the government line. As Clement Semmler has described, disillusionment with military censorship and war heroics soured his initial, idealistic 'poet's view of the Anzac tradition', and he resigned his commission in early 1944. If he hadn't, he would have been disaccredited anyway.[61] Slessor's deliciously scathing hatchet job on the vainglorious General Sir Thomas Blamey in his poem, 'An Inscription for Dog River', is a fitting epitaph to his turbulent career as a paid propagandist.)

Osmar White, a non-officially affiliated war reporter, found it impossible to transform the jungle into a forcing house for traditional Australian martial virtuosity. But this is not to say that his account of the New Guinea war in *Green Armour* (1945) is at all denigratory. White concentrated on the qualities required merely to survive, let alone thrive, in the jungle. The simple 'dignity' and 'nobility' he observed among common Australian soldiers coping with 'the most merciless war of all' made White 'proud to be of their race', and led him to wonder 'if *all* men . . . were creatures of the spirit, eternal and indestructible as stars'.[62] Equally, the determination of the jungle war novelists to 'tell it like it was' did not involve any attempt to belittle the Australian effort. It was as if they wanted to pass on to future generations an idea of the adversities overcome by those who performed in the Pacific theatre. Tom Hungerford, who intended *The Ridge and the River* to be 'an essay in praise' of the Australian soldier, wrote the novel

> so that someone a thousand years from now could pick it up and know what that jungle fighting was like . . . I can read passages from *The Ridge and the River* now that were written straight from experience — and they can still make my hair curl.[63]

Novels such as *The Rats in New Guinea* and *The Climate of Courage*, which contain characters who served in both theatres, point out that the Pacific was vastly more testing than the Mediterranean. In Glassop's novel *Tobruk* is laconically dismissed as 'that holiday joint on the Mediterranean', while Cleary's rugged Vern Radcliffe refers to his first three weeks in the jungle as being 'worse than the whole accumulated time in the Middle East', and Jack Savanna nostalgically remembers 'what a lovely war' it had been in North Africa.[64]

The jungle, for all its spiritually corrosive and physically debilitating effects, could not totally stultify those constituents of the heroic myth that seemed to have resurfaced so unmistakably at Tobruk and El Alamein. Eric Lambert in *The Veterans*, as in *The Twenty Thousand Thieves*, dilutes his anti-war vitriol by investing in his soldiers a freedom-fighting flair that is defined in strongly romantic terms. His New Guinea Diggers are classically Australian. They are fetchingly irreverent and anarchically self-reliant; they move through the jungle with an *élan* which is only marginally less reckless than that displayed by the likes of Chips Prentice in the desert. 'Lasher' Daniel in particular, with his alternately smiling and snarling visage and his 'slouching' body resembling 'a piece of whipcord', appears to have stepped straight off the rocky ridges of Gallipoli. The brilliantly improvisatorial fiery spirits ('hardened products of the hard outback') who comprise the élite Independent Company of Pinney's *Road in the Wilderness* similarly seem to have sprung from a desire to try to perpetuate the legend of the bushman-warrior. And if the jungle instigated a degenerative process in some soldiers, then there were others who not only bloomed in the jungle habitat, but were revitalized by fighting in it. John Hemilton in *The Rats in New Guinea* and Vern Radcliffe and Jack Savanna in *The Climate of Courage* emerged from their service in New Guinea fulfilled and reinvigorated. Robert Nelson, a dissolute former schoolteacher in *The Last Blue Sea*, regains his lost manhood and his self-respect through the discovery of the fundamentally swashbuckling code of 'one for all, and all for one'. These 'lapsed' and reborn Anzacs aside, proven tough guys like Mick Reynolds just get tougher in the difficult tropical conditions. Finally, the pressures and circumstances of jungle warfare produced a revival of that cathartic, macabre brand of Digger wit originally memorialized in *The Anzac Book*.[65]

The reappearance in the South-West Pacific of the old virtues is no better illustrated than in *The Ridge and the River*. The novel, for all the sinister murk of its locale, positively glows with the sort of refulgent courage and warm humanity that is synonymous with Gallipoli. The excitement section-leader Shearwood feels at the end of the novel, when by taking a commission he accepts full personal responsibility for his mates in their shared ordeal, manifests that same 'radiant force of camaraderie' that General Hamilton detected among the fighting Anzacs in 1915:

> All around him in their holes they lay dreaming, awake and asleep, his men, the comrades of his heart . . .
> "My men, now," he said softly.
> The words filled him with a gladness that flowed from the pit of his stomach and enveloped his chest and filled his head with drumming cascades of emotion in which pride and ambition were strangely mixed with foreboding and resolution. In the tide of feeling that hammered at his temples, his consciousness soared to the stars . . .[66]

Such an epiphany of the original spirit of Anzac in a work otherwise notable for its avoidance of histrionics testifies to the enduring vitality of the Digger legend in the battle fiction of 1939–45.

HORS DE COMBAT

The heroic war myth has so permeated Australian popular culture that the non-combatant who wishes to set down his war experiences must overcome an acute problem of 'public relations'. As the sceptical Harry Cole comes to learn in *No Medals for Aphrodite*, 'what mattered' about the Anzac tradition was that it involved men who stood by their comrades and 'had a go'.[67] The Anzacs met eventual failure, all right, but they were triers who had performed valiantly against tremendous odds; the soldiers of the Second A.I.F. in the Pacific theatre might well have had their natural brilliance dimmed by the jungle gloom, but they also 'had a go'. We have already seen that fictional characters who are consigned to the 'back stalls' for the duration, disappointed heroes such as Jack Meredith and Geoffrey Dutton's Andy, endure frustration and even humiliation at being denied the martial role that is their birthright as Australians. A keen sense of shame similarly distinguishes the personal war narratives of the men who did not fight from those who did. This is particularly evident in the memoirs of the men of the Second A.I.F. who became prisoners-of-war. There is little loud boasting to be found here; more a sombre grappling with what was a confusing, humbling and profoundly shocking experience. At its best, in a work such as Ray Parkin's trilogy, the prisoner-of-war book makes a refreshingly reflective and impartial departure from most Australian battle narratives, concerned as they are with celebrating stirring achievements in combat; at its worst it is an embittered document, both recriminatory and self-vindicating.

A useful introductory insight into the cultural and literary plight of the prisoner-of-war writer is offered by Kenneth Seaforth Mackenzie's unusual novel, *Dead Men Rising* (1951), based on the suicidal mass-escape of Japanese prisoners from the prison camp at Cowra, New South Wales, in August 1944. Like *The Twenty Thousand Thieves*, it was written under a Commonwealth Literary Fund fellowship granted in 1949, and it is heavily autobiographical, being based on Mackenzie's own time as a guard at Cowra during the war. So closely does *Dead Men Rising* follow the sensational and tightly censored historical event, in which two hundred and thirty four Japanese POWs and four Australian guards died, that Angus & Robertson withdrew the work for fear of libel charges. Consequently, the novel was published first in England (by Jonathan Cape), although even copies of this foreign edition were withheld from Australian circulation.[68] In the light of the heartburn their choices caused, the literary establishment must have retrospectively rued their 1949 selections of Lambert and Mackenzie for financial assistance.

Dead Men Rising is interesting not so much for its picture of the actual prisoners, who remain remote and alien, if menacing, figures throughout the novel before their bid for freedom, but for its presentation of the deadly diurnal routine of the Australian garrison soldiery. Derided by an experienced campaigner as a 'Company of bloody f— — crocks and no-hoper c—s', the 'P.O.W. men' generally are not the charismatic types of *We Were the Rats* or *The Veterans*. They are 'human rejects', men either too old or too infirm to contribute to the national cause on the battlefield. Removed from the challenge and comradeship of the fighting unit, they are bored, resentful and embittered by the futility of their calling; men bogged down in red-tape pettiness. Instead of the healthy fear known by the active soldier, they experience the administrative *angst* of orderly-room duties (rather delightfully called 'ordeal by f— — returns' by one character) and the disgruntlement of demeaning prisoner surveillance.[69]

Mackenzie's central focus is on Corporal John Sergeant, a man who, despite having vision in only one eye, is in fact in the classical mould of the Australian soldier-hero. His intelligence, eloquence, and 'bronzed good looks' make him immensely 'popular with men and women'. He is a man of superior sensibility to the deeply flawed people with whom he serves, a sort of astigmatic Mick Reynolds. But within the grounds of the camp, all men—guards and POWs alike—are prisoners, Sergeant among them. Entrapped in the 'impersonal net' cast by 'second-rate army life', Sergeant undergoes a personal crisis caused by 'atrophy of the will, that sweet enemy of . . . natural self-respect'.[70] This is no exultant Digger. Sergeant is as metaphorically dead as the Japanese prisoners, to whom capture and incarceration meant a state of disgrace which could only be atoned by a physical death to purge the dishonoured soul. Like his fellow comrades in 'futile bondage', Sergeant had been relegated to a wartime limbo, somewhere between the hell of the battlefield and the heaven of the Home Front as represented by the prosperous rural security of the town of nearby Shotley, the fictional Cowra. 'This is a dead world, a lost world and these are lost men, lost each in his own separate limbo, banished from his own memories, exiled even from himself', wrote Uys Krige, a captured South African war correspondent, from a POW camp in Italy.[71] Sergeant's *accidie* closely approximates this abject sense of death-in-life. Particularly galling is that the prison camp wasteland offers none of the compensations available to the active soldier, not even pain and grief:

> There was no liberty, he saw, on either side of that exact octagon of tangled barbed-wire. An insane centripetal force held him and his fellows fast to its perimeter: they too were prisoners, more hopelessly imprisoned than the men they professed to guard, for all about them was home and their native land, and in it they were unspeakably lonely. For them none of the passion of action and movement, no swaggering thrills from foreign lands and foreign girls under other skies; no grief hid by curses and singing at the sight of their own shores drawing away closed in astern as though rid of them like a womb; no joy like that of those who did return at last. In a servile apathy they emerged from each night into day, lived grumbling and thoughtless through the hours of light, and from each day drifted again into another night. For them there was no war, only other men's nightmare reported from beyond the horizons of their circumscribed world . . .[72]

Prisoners-of-war suffered from the same emotional and spiritual afflictions that beset Mackenzie's garrison men. The blighted self-image, the feeling of damnation and the sense of segregation all contribute the rendering of military documentation vastly different in tone and substance from the combined testimony of the combatant soldiery. As noted earlier, the precarious position of the POW writer in a hero-worshipping literary culture is reflected by the defensive tone of memoirs by Great War prisoners, self-described 'reprobates' such as John Halpin. While the combatant had a licence to advertise the exploits in which he took part, the prisoner had to justify his inaction. Like his predecessor, the Second World War POW had to counter the suspicion that by having been captured he had effectively forfeited his manhood. Given the lusty milieu of 1939–45 heroism, the prisoner moreover had to answer the implied charge that he had relinquished his very sexuality as well as his manly courage and independence. In *Andy*, a woman with whom Dutton's licentious hero has a torrid sexual encounter brutally denigrates her husband—then a POW in Germany—for being incompetent as a sexual partner. As she says, 'The sort of man who would be taken prisoner'.[73]

A glaring example of the defensiveness of the POW is to be found in the narrative organization of the official in-service history of the 2/30th Australian Infantry Battalion, *Galleghan's Greyhounds* (1949). The 2/30th, under the command of 'Black Jack' Galleghan, fought in Malaya for a period of about two months before it, along with most of the Eighth Division, was engulfed by the Japanese military tidal wave which swept down Malaya to Singapore in early 1942. Remarkably, the history devotes virtually as much space to that one brief battlefield spree as it does to the three-and-a-half-year ordeal which followed capture. The historians rightly suggest that 'the treasured period of any unit's story must always be that which was spent in battle against the enemy'. But the book's structure, and the inclusion of sentiments proclaiming the 2/30th's 'pride in believing that it behaved and fought according to the highest traditions' of the A.I.F., reveal that the work's primary purpose is to vindicate the battalion.[74]

The fragility of the prisoners' self-esteem is given a fictional reference by Randolph Stow in his characterization of Rick Coram in *The Merry-Go-Round in the Sea*. Coram, who had endured almost unimaginable horrors as a POW of the Japanese, returns to his Western Australian home at the war's end tormented by recurring nightmares, resentful and restless. And most of all shamed. To his doting young cousin, who had asked why he had not brought back a trophy of the battlefield, he snaps: 'I wasn't a − −ing soldier, mate, I was a − −ing slave'. Like many returned prisoners, Coram is also sensitive to the unwanted pity commonly showered on the POW. At university at Perth, he is upset by the habit of his room-mate (who had been a commando in New Guinea) of sitting on his bed and commiserating with him 'on the humiliation of being a prisoner'.[75]

Though it is easily appreciated how a wartime career spent in servitude could result in a prolonged injury to his pride, it must be said that the returned POW's shame was misplaced. He could never have been lionized as a conquering hero, certainly, but there was no rejection of him by his countrymen, either during or after the war. The warmth of concern, respect and love evident in the collected letters of the Curlewis family to Captain Adrian Curlewis, a staff captain of the Eighth Division who was imprisoned in Changi and later worked on the Burma–Siam Railway, is proof enough of that.[76] The situation was very different for the Japanese prisoner, who was written off by both his family and his country. The honour of the Japanese soldier was related to the ideal of 'no surrender' and the determination to fight until death. Disgust with the idea of capture is enshrined in the Japanese Military Field Code, under the heading 'Regard for Reputation':

> Those who know shame are strong. Have regard for the honour of your family first and endeavour to satisfy the wishes of the family group. Never live to experience shame as a prisoner. Never die in disgrace.[77]

A divergence in cultural attitudes to the prisoner-of-war provides much of the horror of Joe Harmon's frightful crucifixion and whipping in Nevil Shute's *A Town Like Alice* (1950). To Western readers, who take for granted the Geneva Convention rules regarding the care and custody of prisoners, the attitude to Harmon of his captor, Captain Sugamo, is an incomprehensible mixture of sadistic barbarism and reverence. To prove the 'element of holiness' that dictated his treatment of the Australian, Sugamo gives him an opportunity to expiate his dishonour by suffering a lingering death. That Harmon's 'resurrection' is aborted by his survival of the ordeal in no way influences *our* estimation of his personal worth.[78]

Survival, indeed, is the key to our recognition of the character and the courage of the prisoner-of-war. By any standards of service and self-sacrifice, they could claim to have had their manhood verified by the test of war. This applies particularly to the prisoners of the Japanese. Nearly three times as many Australians died in Japanese captivity as in the campaigns of the Ninth Division in the Middle East and New Guinea, and many of the survivors made it (almost literally) by the skin of their teeth. As one officer, describing the discipline of one force which engaged in herculean labours in especially bad conditions along the Railway, put it, 'more decorations were earned during this episode than during any period of battle'.[79] Fighting a prisoner's war demanded a different, but not inferior, kind of valour from that associated with the active combatant. The retention of sanity and humanity in the quest for self-preservation was the thing. And in this, on the evidence of the writings of men like Stan Arneil, Adrian Curlewis, 'Weary' Dunlop and particularly Ray Parkin, many succeeded heroically.

As a prisoner-of-war memoirist, Ray Parkin is a unique talent. Chief Quartermaster aboard the cruiser *Perth* when it was sunk by the Japanese fleet in the Sunda Strait in March 1942, Parkin spent the following three years and more in Japanese bondage. His endurance of the ordeal, as it is described in *Out of the Smoke* (1960), *Into the Smother* (1963) and *The Sword and the Blossom* (1968), was based upon the forswearing of what he terms 'the egocentric point of view':

> . . . with death constantly imminent, to consider one's own death as the central tragedy of Time was to get so out of touch with reality as to suffer a thousand worse horrors.[80]

Parkin's tactic of objectivity as an essential part of his prisoner's self-survival kit is reflected by the narrative strategy of his memoirs. In both the first and third volumes of the trilogy he conveys his experience in the third person, substituting himself for the humble sailor 'John'. (*Into the Smother*, it should be noted, is written in the first person with no great diminution of detachment.) The combination of this extra-personal approach, which universalizes the POW's predicament, with an avoidance of sensationalism works to the trilogy's advantage, as it allows for a complexity of related experience not at all common in the POW narrative. Parkin is by turns dreamily mystical, whimsical and acutely observant of nature, laconic and earnest, and disarmingly humorous.

Most other Australian POW writers are unable to find the same balance between representation and tone. The problem is one peculiar to the genre itself. Unlike the writer of the conventional war narrative, who is able to leaven his tale with varieties of human experience on both battle and home fronts, the POW is reduced to the kind of special pleading of passive suffering that Yeats found so unacceptable in British poetry of the First World War.[81] Horror and oppression are the staples of the prisoner's existence, prison wall-to-wall. He is *hors de combat*: disabled, out of the fight, often forgotten by his military and civilian masters and associates. It is the role of the memoirist to redress that neglect and to place that misery on the public record. In a contemporary review of Russell Braddon's *The Naked Island* (1952), 'Ek Dum' of the returned servicemen's magazine, *Stand-To*, expressed his reservations about a genre which deviates from the characteristic aggressive tone of Australian war literature:

> The new type of P.O.W. book which has become so popular — and profitable — recently, and to the writing of which young Australians are becoming addicted can usually be summed up in the sentences: "I was

a P.O.W. Oh, how I suffered." And inferentially, there always seems to be a whisper somewhere in the background which says: "Pity me," though some of the authors concerned, no doubt, would be righteously indignant if told that it was there.[82]

'Ek Dum', whose opinions are reminiscent of the knee-jerk response of Australian military journals to foreign anti-war books of the 1914–18 war, certainly overstates his case. Nevertheless it is true that some POW authors exploit the horror and the hardship of it all. As often as not, the effect on the reader of this cataloguing of suffering is quite the opposite to what the author intended. The imperfections of John Romeril's play, *The Floating World* (1974), highlight the technical dilemma facing the prisoner-of-war memoirist. In dramatizing the psychological collapse of Les Harding, who had done his time under the flag of Nippon in the Second World War, Romeril selected some of the more gruesome incidents and aspects of life as a slave labourer on the Burma–Siam Railway from published accounts, notably those of Braddon and Parkin. In Harding's final strait-jacketed interior monologue, we hear of 'the sweet stench of gangrene', of 'blood and pus' and 'pus and bad air', or sick and starving men collapsing into latrines and drowning, of malaria, beriberi and cholera, and of Japanese atrocities in battle and in camp.[83] Romeril really piles on the misery; yet our response to Les's tirade is mixed. On one level, the long-term effects of that devastating time become readily comprehensible. Against this, the enumerated horrors tend to bludgeon the audience (or, for that matter, the reader of the text) into indifference, and the pathos inherent in Harding's trauma is dissipated.

Thus the POW, wanting, no doubt, to dispossess himself of his festering memories while eager to allow 'the rest' to participate in the fact of his private tragedy, invariably finds himself worrying whether people will believe and be sympathetic to what he has to say. Ian Sabey, an Australian captured and imprisoned by the Germans in 1941, refers in his *Stalag Scrapbook* (1947) to the artistic trap which lies in wait for the ex-prisoner when he settles down to write up his experiences. Defensively, Sabey declares that

> It is an acknowledged fact that few prisoners of war can resist 'telling the story', that is, piling on the agony. But there was little need for fabrication in their yarns . . .[84]

There is eminent support for this pessimistic view of the POW memoirist's craft. Arthur Koestler, who was interned in France as a political prisoner in 1939, concedes in his own testimony, *Scum of the Earth* (1941), that the difficulties facing the prisoner in his relationship to reader responses are insoluble:

> . . . most prison memoirs are unreadable. The difficulty of conveying to the reader in his armchair an idea of the nightmare world from which he has emerged makes the author depict the prisoner's state of mind as an uninterrupted continuity of despair. He fears to appear frivolous or to spoil his effect by admitting that even in the depths of misery cheerfulness keeps breaking in.[85]

One need look no further than Russell Braddon's *The Naked Island*, in tone and content one of the more uncompromising Australian war narratives, to discover the tensions inherent in both the composition and the comprehension of POW literature. Though written in a style untainted by excessive emotion and agonized posturing (whatever 'Ek Dum's' grumblings), *The Naked Island* is a powerful indictment of Japanese inhumanity towards their captives, a theme which impresses itself on the reader for the most part with a painful vividness. Two-thirds of the way through the work, however, there is an account of 'night life' at Changi which staggers us by its apparent incongruity. Braddon writes:

> . . . [on one particular night] in Changi I could have gone to lectures on ski-ing, contract law, communism or tiger hunting: I could have gone to any one of four plays or two musical shows: I could have heard Dennis East—peace-time violinist under Sir Thomas Beecham—give a recital. As it was, I went down to the Australian Concert Party, sat on the woodpile and talked . . . in the pleasant warmth of Singapore's evening.[86]

This vignette of a cultural idyll—even taking into account that Changi was 'heaven' compared with most Japanese camps[87]—is so beguiling that the cumulative thematic force of Braddon's entire narrative is threatened.

One area of Australian POW writing which is completely unambiguous is the authorial attitude to the captors. Invariably the memoirist, haunted by his wartime subservience, seeks vicarious vengeance through mercilessly attacking the old enemy in print. Memoirs and chronicles by Australians enslaved by the Japanese in the 1939–45 war are replete with racist imprecations. Wanting to flesh out that one dreadful, damning statistic—about 33 per cent of all Australian prisoners either died or were murdered in Japanese camps, as against 3 per cent of military internees of the Germans and Italians — writers such as Rohan Rivett (*Behind Bamboo,* 1946) and Eric Lambert (*MacDougal's Farm,* 1965) spread the gospel of Japanese barbarism with a passion.[88] Admittedly, the portrait of the Japanese in the battle fiction and the reminiscences of active soldiers is hardly favourable either. Henry Gullett in *Not As A Duty Only,* for example, calls them 'clever animals with certain human characteristics'.[89] But there is an especially bitter edge to the vituperation of the POW. Already dealing with historical material of a nightmarish, 'gothic' nature, few memoirists could resist the temptation to capitalize on the rich cast of oriental villains at their command. With some splendid exceptions, among them Ray Parkin, Stan Arneil (*One Man's War,* 1980) and Kenneth Harrison (*The Brave Japanese,* 1966), the Japanese guard is characterized as either a homicidal maniac or, lamentably, as a simian buffoon. Here is Russell Braddon's melodramatic picture, in the short story 'Song of War', of Japanese savagery toward a prisoner:

> At the sight of the blood the Japanese soldier's eyes had gleamed and he had licked his lips.[90]

With the passing of time Braddon revised and rationalized his enmity toward his captors — witness his book published six years after *The Naked Island, End of a Hate* (1958), the title of which is self-explanatory. But a consuming race-phobia has lingered on in many former prisoners, occasionally manifesting itself in such squalid ways as the following poem, called 'The Way I See The Jap', included in John McGregor's memoir, *Blood on the Rising Sun* (1980):

> The guy who put the 'ap' in Japan,
> Didn't even know his A.B.C.
> He didn't even know the little man,
> Or to 'ap' he MUST have added 'E'.[91]

Possibly because the Germans were generally regarded as equals or at least as white-racial cousins, works by prisoners of the Germans in the Second World War are less liable to be riddled with this sort of contempt. Relations between captor and captive appear to have been based upon a degree of mutual respect. For example, Paul Brickhill's bestselling *The Great Escape* (1951) concentrates on the exciting battle of wits and rival ingenuities between the German guard and the aspiring escapee. Brickhill takes considerable care to dissociate the ordinary, rather chivalrous *soldaten,* 'the real Germany', from the promulgators and enforcers of Nazism.[92] Such charitableness is rare in the Australian prisoner of the Japanese. Submission to the mercy of an enemy held to be racially inferior compounded the bitterness and dishonour he felt at being a part of the strategical shambles that led to the Allied capitulation at Singapore. Certainly, he was entitled to feel shocked and angered by the pitiless cruelty he encountered. But he had entered a war against an opponent of whom he was arrogantly ignorant, one whose fanaticism in and out of battle had been underestimated.

Norman Carter, a prisoner with a theatrical bent who helped produce stage entertainments for what the blurb to his personal account of the Burma–Siam Railway calls 'the grimmest circuit of all time', admits that before the war the Japanese were considered 'ideal material for musical comedies, operas and radio serials'; hardly contenders for the role of the war hero. Capture by them had been 'a frustrating and deflating experience':

> To be a prisoner-of-war was nothing to be proud of at the best of times, but it was especially galling to surrender to a race who . . . had been regarded as a simple-minded people, politely bowing their way through life amid a shower of cherry blossoms . . . a nation of geishas and houseboys. Now Honourable Houseboy had become dishonourable conqueror.[93]

Hatred of the enslaver, in books written by prisoners of the Japanese, is balanced by the desire to publicize the sheer guts of those enslaved. The refusal of the Australians to kowtow to their captors is an abiding theme of the memoirs—a theme supported by Douglas Valentine's *The Hotel Tacloban* (1984), the story of an American soldier imprisoned in a mixed POW camp in the Philippines. To enhance his status among 'the macho Australians', the American performed 'acts of defiance' as 'the best way to gain and hold their respect'.[94] Mateship is also a common concern of the memoirists. If it was impossible, given the nature of their situation, to proclaim their military supremacy, then they could always point to the Australian prisoners' *moral* superiority over the Japanese. In *Slaves of the Samurai* (1946), an epic poem about the POW experience in florid heroic verse, W. S. Kent-Hughes honours the 'close comradeships' that formed out of the mutual 'disgrace' at being held by the 'bestial claws' of Nippon. He invokes the Anzac legend to praise their cohesion. Life in Changi, he says,

> Was based on sacrifice, not selfish strife.
> The Anzac spirit in its finest form
> Repaired the damage of the early storm.[95]

Selflessness was not uniformly the case, however, in Changi or else-where. While such luminaries as C. E. W. Bean and Frederic Man-ning have ventured that self-interest, as a corollary of self-reliance, is integral rather than inimical to the ideal of good comradeship, the lack of a realizable collective goal within what Ray Parkin calls the 'small and mean' world of the POW compound often perverted the soldierly instinct for self-preservation into sheer venality.[96] The necessity for each individual to contrive the wherewithal to survive was acute. Though memoirists like Parkin, Arneil and Braddon stress the prisoner's capacity to enact the martial virtue of fraternal co-operation, they also indicate that a spirit of mercenary selfishness shared the human landscape of the camp. Some of the Australians with whom Adrian Curlewis 'served' are hardly more appealing than their cruel captors. As this normally most benevolent of men was moved to note in his war diary:

> My day is amongst foul-mouthed animals who have lost their self respect and decency, who rob their mates, who cry to me for help on all occa-sions and then let me down by lying.[97]

A society in microcosm, but differing from ordinary civilization in the nature and degree of its constraints and pressures, the prison camp tended to foster the best and the worst in its inhabitants, to breed tribes of saints and sinners. 'Men rose to splendid heights or sank to indescribable depths', states Eric Lambert in *MacDougal's Farm*.[98] For many the pursuit of personal survival entailed a total or partial renunciation of accepted standards of Australian military behaviour. *MacDougal's Farm* bears savage witness to this. The work pictures a Changi community which is fragmented by rampant backbiting, black marketeering and conspiratorial cliques, in which officer and N.C.O. collaboration with the enemy seems the rule rather than the exception. Sceptics would point out that *MacDougal's Farm*, which was purportedly drawn from the private notes and verbal communi-cations of a veteran of the prison, bears all the hallmarks of Lam-bert's ideological axe-grinding about the hedonism of the officer class, its incompetence and its abuse of privilege in breach of solidarity with the average soldiers. Nevertheless his portrait, though over-coloured, may well offer a rather more authentic impression of the POW experience than the official whitewash. Certainly, it brings the myth of the A.I.F. as a uniquely democratic and cohesive organization into question.

Out of all this wreckage of body and spirit, hopes and ideals, is there anything at all of positive value that the prisoner-of-war can salvage and pass on to the readers of his testament? A passage from Ray Parkin's *Into the Smother* springs to mind. At the end of a long anatomical description of an emaciated comrade who, racked by dysentery, is *en route* to the latrine, Parkin reminds us that 'This is a man', and then continues:

> A man who walks naked in the rain to the latrine. Side by side with other wretches, yet alone, he crouches like a dog without a kennel in a bitter wind. He is helpless and racked with violent spasms . . . In the rain he must crawl there and return to soiled blankets, to lie weak and helpless, without removing the mud of his beastly pilgrimage.
> This comes to us all in turn. Men watch each other in silent understanding. *What they see is ludicrous, but they don't laugh.*[99]

Nor do we. Grotesque and deeply disturbing, this fragment indicates to us that the true horror encountered by the POW is not communicated by a literary luxuriation in gore, but in the reader's realization that such an outrage was a by-product of mankind's endless recycling of that old favourite, *The War*. For this criminal commitment, of course, there are no words that really suffice. Yet, as if by definition, the prisoner-of-war book remains an urgent declaration of the absurd futility of warfare and of the tragedy of our blind dedication to its practice. From a strictly Australian viewpoint, a memoir like *Into the Smother* also proves that real nobility, or 'stage presence' if you like, has little to do with the ability to hand out a thrashing on the battlefield. If in that respect only, the POW author is capable of teaching a salutary lesson to most Australian writers on war.

VIII

Vietnam Survived

A CLIMATE OF REVISION?

Whatever the POW memoir's aesthetic value in providing the national war literature with some much-needed variety, the most encouraging aspect of its emergence as a leading branch of Australian war writing is that it has been received by such a large local readership. In a literature which has always promoted effective battle action while stifling virtually everything else about the experience, this indicates a relaxation of Australian attitudes and responses to war.

Before the Second World War, argued 'Ek Dum' in his review of *The Naked Island*, it was widely accepted that 'the less said about prisoners of war the better . . . the P.O.W. preferred not to advertise the fact'. 'Ek Dum' lamented the passing of such reticence and found it especially galling that this 'new type of war book' should have been 'pioneered' by, of all people, Australians.[1] Given his bias against the genre, his irritation is unsurprising—since 1945 the prisoner-of-war memoir has flourished remarkably in Australia, both in terms of the vast number of individual works produced, and in the number of copies they have sold.[2] In 1982 Stan Arneil's *One Man's War* even vied with Evelyn Waugh's resurrected *Brideshead Revisited* at the head of the bestseller listings. And this without the aid of an acclaimed and sumptuous television adaptation to help sell it.

Why has the POW book become such a commercial winner? A possibly uncharitable interpretation would be that its customary depiction of foreign barbarity appeals readily to a xenophobic audience which enjoys its war horrors uncomplicated by moral complexity. The POW narrative is the most crude kind of morality play, a story of 'good guys' who are very good, and 'bad guys' who are very nasty

237

indeed. The colourful titles of memoirs by prisoners of the Japanese — *Blood on the Rising Sun*, *White Coolies* (1954), *Slaves of the Son of Heaven* (1951), *Slaves of the Samurai*, even, titillatingly, *The Naked Island* and *G-String Jesters* (1966) — suggest a certain sensationalism, a trend confirmed by the recent retitling of memoirs first published in the 1950s and 1960s. The stodgily-named story of a captured Australian nurse, Jessie Simons's *While History Passed* (1954), reappeared in 1985 as the vastly more enticing *In Japanese Hands*, while Kenneth Harrison's 1966 memoir *The Brave Japanese* (an inauspicious title in post-war Australia) was republished in 1983 as the more 'significant' *Road to Hiroshima*.

But the more just conclusion to be drawn from the mutual readiness of ex-prisoners and the Australian public to share the POW experience is that, with time, the old cultural commitment to the heroic ethos has become somewhat emasculated. If Thomas R. Edwards's comment that national heroes start appearing in 'the adolescence or early maturity of cultures, or at least. . . find responsive audiences at such times' helps explain the initial impact of Gallipoli on the Australian imagination, then it follows that the recent accommodation of the POW's fundamentally unheroic perspective stems from a more assured cultural identity. It has become possible for Australians to write about war without indulging in the once mandatory boasts and without having to assume a forced jauntiness about the military life.

One of the latest in the current wave of POW narratives, Barney Roberts's *A Kind of Cattle* (1985), provides new evidence of the maturation of Australian war literature. Apart from the admirable adventurousness of Roberts's impressionistic style, the great virtue of *A Kind of Cattle* is the generous human sympathy it radiates. Generosity of spirit has not been a major characteristic of Australian war writers, most of whom are so intent on exaggerating the heroism of the Diggers that there is little goodwill left for anyone or anything else. After his capture by the Germans in April 1941, Roberts was herded and cattle-trucked from Greece through Yugoslavia and Austria, right to the heart of the Third Reich, then back to Austria, before fleeing captivity towards the advancing Russian Army in 1945. Hence the wry title of his memoir, which is clearly intended to contrast ironically with the aura surrounding the nominal national tradition of Anzac. His intimate encounter with the effects of the conflict in Western Europe — he laboured, for example, in an Austrian farming community, and witnessed the destruction of Berlin, avoiding the Allied bombs along with the 'enemy' population — provided him with a jarring insight into the wartime suffering of ordinary people. He remarks in his Introduction:

> I learned that in the chaos [of war] men lost their national identity and became just people. It was easy for me to accept Tolstoy's assertion that patriotism as a feeling was bad and harmful, and as a doctrine, stupid.[3]

What liberating sentiments these are. Roberts deflates the ideal of chauvinistic striving with a directness which would once have been inconceivable in an Australian war book. The almost euphoric reception afforded Bert Facey's *A Fortunate Life* since its appearance in 1981 is another indication that Australian attitudes to war have started to shed some of their old inhibitions. Facey, the man we remember as having admitted to being 'scared stiff' during the Anzac landing, is no nostalgic advocate of the triumphs of the battlefield. The bayonet, the unfettered use of which in so many Australian Great War books is meant to symbolize the nation's newly acquired nobility, comes in for special attention as both the instrument and the symbol of barbarism and inhumanity. Yet the heroic character of this unassuming man's journey through a 'fortunate' life of severe hardship (in which the war was just one of a series of personal trials) is in no way diminished by his evident hatred for war. For one who endured so much, Facey's aside that his four months on Gallipoli were 'the worst' of his life gives the modern reader as vivid an idea of how testing it was on the famous battleground as any amount of documentation Bean's voluminous *Official History* can provide.[4] Though in no way does *A Fortunate Life* court such kudos, Facey's personal standing is enhanced by his refusal to be intimidated by a mythology built up by soldier-writers over a period of more than sixty years.

Contemporary novelists and poets, many of whom have had no personal experience of battle, show a particular determination not to bow meekly before the Anzac deity. War—conflicts both as culturally relevant and remote as Vietnam and the Hundred Years' War—is the subject of many of the novels of Thomas Keneally, for example, yet the Anzac influence is conspicuous chiefly by its absence as a shaper of his fiction. Keneally's apparent indifference to the handed-down heroic tradition, which is most pointed in his political novel set in Australia during the Second World War, *The Cut-Rate Kingdom* (1980), is mirrored in much of the recent poetry written about the distant events of 1914–1918. In *Shadows from Wire* (1983), an anthology of modern responses to the conflict compiled by Geoff

Page, scepticism sometimes breaks out into open revolt. Rae Desmond Jones concludes his largely affectionate meditation on the fading photograph of a Digger with the savagely reactive injunction that it should be 'burnt' as 'sentimental junk'.[5] The heroic clichés by which the myth has long been codified are given especially cynical treatment. Roger McDonald's 'The Last Anzac Muster' (1976) contemptuously parodies the bloodlust of William Baylebridge's Gallipoli stories:

> My name was Neville Carver
> Though they called me Spike
> because I used the bayonet
> skilful, like.
>
> Easy the action was
> as spreading butter on bread:
> thrust, twist, pull, wipe,
> and the meal was – spread.[6]

David Malouf's novel about the Great War, *Fly Away Peter* (1982), is robustly independent of the influence of the traditional legends. In this story of a young Australian's migration from the idyllic southern Queensland coast, where he was a sort of naturalist in a swampy bird sanctuary, to the tumultuous Western Front, Malouf instead draws extensively on the grim iconography of the European 'horror school' of war fiction. Vomit, blood, bloated rats, eviscerations, the destruction of youth – he spares us nothing. For all this *Fly Away Peter* is not a modern Australian version of *All Quiet on the Western Front*. Malouf does not argue a case for one landscape, salubrious pastoral or hellish military, over the other, despite the obviously vast gulf in their appeal. In fact his hero, Jim Saddler, comes to recognize that he had been living in 'a state of dangerous innocence' before he volunteered to go to the war; the almost transcendental communion with nature he had enjoyed needed to be checked by an encounter with the realities of human violence. Saddler, like Australia, had luxuriated in languid isolation: he had needed a rude awakening. Vestiges of the 'baptism of fire' myth therefore remain. Malouf has remarked elsewhere that the ardent Australian reaction to the Great War was 'a claim to experience'. The volunteers were 'leaping beyond the limitations of mere geography into an experience that would amount to a remapping of their world', and because of their adventurousness Australians no longer thought of their country as an 'appendage of the real world or as a safe place out of it'.[7]

Fly Away Peter dramatizes this shift in national self-definition.

Nevertheless it should not be overlooked that Jim Saddler is killed by the war that promised to enhance him, and his 'senseless and brutal extinction' finally signifies 'waste'.[8] Ultimately the novel is unconcerned with national enrichment; its essential subject is the perennial human problem of exile and integration, something not simply 'solved' by historical events. The series of oppositions that provide the framework of *Fly Away Peter* spring from the same ironic understanding of the Great War that motivated the British war writers, but which is rare in Australian literature except in the work of expatriates like Martin Boyd. In *The Great War and Modern Memory* Paul Fussell shows that the important twentieth-century war themes of disenchantment and psychological disturbance originated in the schismatic contrast between expectation and actuality felt by those who fought in and wrote about the débâcle on the Western Front. The polarity of Jim Saddler's experience as formalized by Malouf's narrative juxtaposition of the pre-war pastoral and wartime battle landscapes implicitly reflects this crucial irony. The novel's structure echoes Sassoon's classic piece of Great War dichotomizing as sequentially organized in *Memoirs of a Fox-Hunting Man* (1928) and *Memoirs of an Infantry Officer* (1930). As Fussell observes, the 'symbolic status' of war itself (since it 'takes place outdoors and always within nature') is that of 'the ultimate anti-pastoral'.[9]

Malouf sharpens and intensifies the irony by presaging the 'hangover' of the war experience with a picture of the drunken anticipatory bravado exuded by the youths Jim meets in a Brisbane hotel upon the outbreak of the hostilities. He is not the only contemporary Australian novelist to illustrate the national disposition in August 1914 with hotel scenes of swaggering (and staggering) intoxication. In *1915* (1979), Roger McDonald describes a bar in a country pub, in which 'One nation stood, swayed, roared, shoulder to shoulder . . . The whole room was drunk'.[10] Both Malouf and McDonald seem to have in mind the scene in Patrick White's *The Tree of Man* (1956), when Stan Parker enters the Grand Railway Hotel at Bangalay on the momentous day of the news of war 'over the other side':

> . . . though many men were talking, few were listening to anyone but themselves. They had to tell all they knew, all that they had done, for fear that silence would discover nothing. So they talked, and some had come to blows, to show that they were brave, and one man could not keep his misery down, it rose up, and he vomited, and passed out. It

was all very impermanent and inebriating in the Grand Railway Hotel the day the news came, with a train coughing at the platform outside, and the smell of trains, which made men feel they were going somewhere, that they had been waiting to do so all their lives, and whether it was to be terrible and final, or an exhilarating muscular interlude to the tune of brass bands, would depend upon the nature of each man.[11]

The war experience of Stan Parker—no demigod, but eminently a 'common man'—is no less scarifying for his having embarked upon it with rather less enthusiasm than the exuberant drinkers in the pub at Bangalay. Stan sublimated 'the years of mud and metal' after the war, and would seldom talk about them. Unlike many veterans, he could not be wooed into telling 'interminable boys' adventure stories'.[12] Nor, for that matter, could Patrick White. His treatment of Stan's war is like Stan himself, terse, unemphatic, strangely diffident. But of course White's subject is the exploration of the buried vitality of 'ordinary' life; he is not interested in defining (let alone magnifying) the cultural significance of historical happenings.

Though Roger McDonald seeks, like White, to plumb the disturbances bubbling beneath the torpid surface of rural life in pre-war Australia, his major concern is to relate the Great War to aspects and nuances of Australian national life and identity. *1915*, indeed, is by far the most elaborate fictional foray into the mythological world of Gallipoli so far attempted by a contemporary writer. Bernard Bergonzi, writing in 1965 in *Heroes' Twilight*, referred to J. B. Priestley's view that the Great War provided a 'splendid challenge for an ambitious young novelist'. Making the point that the war was then as far removed in time as the Napoleonic campaigns were from Tolstoy when he began *War and Peace*, Bergonzi bemoaned the fact that there had not been 'any attempt at a Tolstoyan grandeur of re-enactment' of the event.[13] Albeit from a specifically Australian standpoint and with Australian cultural concerns in mind, Roger McDonald makes that sort of attempt in *1915*. Meticulously researched from the conversations, books, diaries and letters of Anzacs, *1915* succeeds as a historical reconstruction. McDonald re-creates a lost world and convinces us of its authenticity, while at the same time preserving his own authorial identity. His poet's feeling for rich symbolic language, his use of modernist devices such as the time-shift and the interior monologue, and his interweaving of domestic and military violence (Ford Madox Ford is a clear influence), combine to elevate the novel to a loftier artistic plane than most of the pedestrian battle narratives churned out by the Anzacs and their publicists since the famous year which provided McDonald with the title for his novel.

But if McDonald is an artist first and a historian second, there are occasions when the latter role impinges on the work of the novelist. There are times when, with historical hindsight, he force-feeds his characters with the platitudes we now associate with that distant age. Some of his writing has about it a sort of synthetic, apocalyptic portentousness: McDonald is writing a 'big' novel about an important subject, and he knows it. The description of Walter's responses to his home landscape upon his return to the family farm after the completion of his schooling in Sydney exemplifies McDonald's tendency to overload his prose with heavy symbolism. The time is just before the outbreak of the war that will send Walter and other young men to meet their various fates on the legendary Gallipoli battlefield – as the imagery makes all-too-obvious:

> . . . the familiar countryside looked strange, like somebody else's. He missed none of the landmarks he knew . . . but farther off the suddenly-revealed distant view was altogether new. Where had the red gash in the hills come from? The lone pine standing above the rest, he'd never before seen it.[14]

In striving to convey an impression of a nation's passage from a troubled adolescence to a kind of maimed adulthood, McDonald focuses on two boyhood friends for whom war offers the welcome prospect of escape from aimless boredom. The more intellectual Walter Gilchrist is a well-intentioned and well-educated youth with vague literary ambitions who sees himself as one sent on a knightly mission bearing the love of his countrymen and women, charged with the task of carrying a 'torch of passion hurled from the darkness of a million small lives'. A disarming mixture of 'roughness', 'ignorance' and 'self-confidence', his mate Billy Mackenzie more closely resembles the popular image of the coarse, but attractively devil-may-care Digger. Compared with the stiffly decent and shy Walter, Billy moves through the world of *1915* 'like a stray dog on the lookout for pleasure'. His instinctive impulses are toward action: 'Thinking about things might have helped someone else, but not Billy. If he acted, and the result went against him, he could only act again'.[15]

Only McDonald's probing excursions into Billy's turbulent mind prevent this pairing from conforming to the classic opposition of character types in Australian war fiction. McDonald has said that he saw Billy as being more 'spiritually gifted' than his friend.[16] But this gift comes at a price. Impelled by deeper and darker forces than the conventional romanticism embraced by Walter, Billy's aggression is psychopathic. His spectacular career as a solitary sniper (known as 'The Murderer') on Gallipoli is foreshadowed in the opening chapters set during the rural 'peace' of pre-war New South Wales. Billy had always suppressed his finer feelings. Kangaroo-shooting in his boyhood, he encounters a wounded animal whose 'lovely face' he 'wanted to nuzzle':

> Then a thought rattled through him; he wished to erase that lovely face for ever – this gaze of his, that gaze of hers, the trembling mirage of contact between them. The joining of thought to action was everything to Billy; finger on metal, thought thus cracking into life: a harsh word to bark out and settle something.[17]

McDonald subjects the stereotypical Digger to a more incisive character-analysis than George Johnston does in his creation of the Anzac redivivus in *My Brother Jack*. Jack Meredith is as benign and as altruistic as Billy Mackenzie is malignant and antisocial. Jack, like Billy, feels fulfilled by the martial role, but he is moved mainly by a spirit of adventure; Billy is moved by the spirit of death. Jack's belligerence is a product of a pugnacious engrossment in life; Billy's 'jaunty truculence' is liable to manifest itself in such ugly forms as the rape of a young Aboriginal girl. For all his superficially charismatic panache, he is essentially sinister and self-defensive. D. H. Lawrence's thoughts on the violent streak in Australian men, as personified in *Kangaroo* by Jack Callcott V.C., may well be relevant here. Lawrence detected

> an indifference with a deep flow of loose energy beneath it, ready to break out like a geyser. Ready to break into a kind of frenzy, a berserk frenzy, running amok in wild generosity, or still more wild smashing up. The wild joy in letting loose, in a smash-up.[18]

Appropriately for one who is so blankly drawn to acts of violence, Billy's reign as 'The Murderer' finishes abruptly when he is shot in the head. Repatriated to Australia, he ends the novel living his life in 'wintry clouds' of 'rage and bewilderment'. Meanwhile, Walter's dreams of chivalric achievement in a 'post-quaternary landscape, the soft heaven of a new epoch', end in a nightmare of fear, anger and broken ideals in 'the whirlpool of venemous geography' around Anzac Cove.[19] While Billy is committed to a kind of living death in an asylum in Australia, Walter (also wounded at Gallipoli) is captured by the Turks and endures a metaphorical 'death' as a prisoner-of-war.

Despite McDonald's penetration of the accepted public image of the Anzac, *1915* cannot be called a denunciatory work. One agrees with Veronica Brady's belief that though the novel 'revalues' the Gallipoli story, it falls short of 'outraging communal piety'.[20] Perhaps McDonald thought it was unnecessary and possibly even impertinent to remind modern readers of the terrible futility of the Gallipoli campaign. Nevertheless, there is very little in *1915* to please the sentimental 'convention-mongers' reviled by Baylebridge in *An Anzac Muster*. To McDonald's credit, he is even able to transcend the peculiar and specific concerns of the Australian Great War experience, formulating universal perceptions about organized violence that leave no room for comfortable notions of national achievement and sacrifice:

> It seemed they were all to be Christs at Gallipoli, devoting their lives to the enactment of a moral drama. But it didn't fit. Mankind was more a writhing garbage heap, dead or alive—feasting, competing, stealing one from the other. The rank discharges of the dead showed it last night, as did the living on the heights as they sought out the living of another race, and increased their self-esteem by killing them.[21]

McDonald is acknowledging a harsh, perhaps even unpalatable, truth about war which is usually overlooked by anti-war writers and promoters of heroism alike. War, he implies, is no mere aberration, but is intrinsic to the nature of man and crucial to the dreams of nations. People 'need' war, he writes near the end of *1915*. Like the 'sullen madman', Billy, they carry it within themselves and try 'to obey its simple imperative'.[22] As the wise Frederic Manning observes in his Author's Note to *Her Privates We*: 'War is waged by men; not by beasts, or by gods. It is a peculiarly human activity'.

GUNG-HO HUM

Though it was inevitable that the passing years would weaken Australia's emotional attachment to the Great War legends, the revisionary spirit that encouraged the writing of a novel like *1915* can be attributed to specific historical forces. Obviously, the nuclear-age revulsion with which warlike postures and practices are now generally greeted precludes the devotion to heroism felt by myth-makers like Bean and Baylebridge. In concrete historical terms, however, it was Australia's participation in the Vietnam War from 1962 to 1973 which was decisive in creating a climate in which the ideal could be questioned.

Roger McDonald, for example, was born in 1941; this places him in the so-called 'Vietnam Generation' which intensely debated a military involvement that offered little support for romantic ideals about war. While it is still too early to formulate any final judgements upon it, the Australian literary response to Vietnam so far confirms the impression that the war occasioned a critical period in the life of the national military myth.

Vietnam, as wars go, was an utterly unpleasant and unsatisfactory conflict which was brought to an unsatisfying conclusion. It was a traumatic time for the men who fought in it and for the nation which committed them to the fight. A messy guerrilla war in which the enemy targets often included women and children as well as the elusive Viet Cong, it ended in ignominious defeat. Compounding that blow to national pride, Australia lost the war while acting in a pathetically subsidiary capacity to its great American ally. This was not the starring role and triumphant curtain call to which the Australian soldier had become accustomed. In John Carroll's *Token Soldiers* (1983), a Digger bitterly broods . . .

> A sideshow, that's all the Australians are. A walk-on part in an expensive production. If we weren't here nobody would notice. . . Token soldiers, that's what we are. Token soldiers in a token army. Making mud pies while for the rest of the world it's business as usual.[23]

The domestic repercussions of the pragmatic political decision to enlist in the American crusade against South-East Asian Communism turned Vietnam into a divisive and destructive, rather than unifying and uplifting, national experience. While the conscription referenda of 1916 and 1917 also created deep scars in Australian society, the kudos won by the A.I.F. helped to heal differences. Vietnam afforded no such military panacea. The enforced conscription of young men into a morally ambiguous and increasingly unwinnable conflict set civilian against civilian, civilian against soldier, and—as Michael Frazer's novel *Nasho* (1984) dramatizes—the Regular Army soldier against the 'roped in' national serviceman. A cultural consequence of the general factiousness was a lapse in Australia's characteristic reverence for its fighting men. This is most strikingly apparent in the writings of the so-called 'protest poets', most of whom were non-combatants. In 'Epic Struggle', published in the 1971 'Anti-War Anthology' *We Took Their Orders and Are Dead*, Laurence Collinson plays the military killjoy with withering irony:

Lawson Glassop, then assistant editor of the *A.I.F. News*,
offers advice to a local printer, Cairo, December 1941

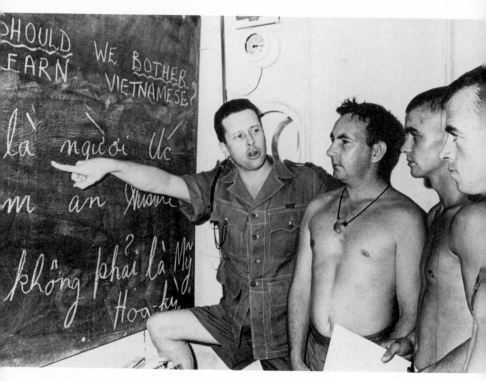

A disconcerting war: Vietnam recruits learn to say 'I am an Aussie' in Vietnamese, June 1965 (see 'Gung-Ho Hum', pp. 245-53).

> ho hum
>> nationality
> ho hum
>> brave and true and free
> ho hum
>> footie beer and bread
> ho hum
>> dead and dead and[24]

Most of the poems contained in a special *Overland* issue of non-combatant responses to the war, *Vietnam Voices* (1973), echo Collinson's cynicism. The clear apprehension was that this was a war in which, to quote Craig Powell's 'Wedding Feast', 'neither side' was 'worth cheering for'. Detachment and disinterestedness, however, are not abiding characteristics of the poets represented in the collection. In Roland Robinson's phrase, most of them 'knife in on the war', exploiting the controversial aspects of the conflict for pure political point-scoring, as in the attacks on the immorality of U.S. foreign policy (and Australia's subservience to it) and the glib expressions of sympathy for the Vietnamese peasants; or else they use the war as a medium for the airing of precious (to them) crises of personal conscience. All too often their rhetoric is windy enough to justify the stinging criticism of the conscript Rhys Pollard, who in his novel *The Cream Machine* (1972) turns on the 'bleeding hearts' of the 'protest band-wagon', whom he describes as 'tear jerking, psalm singing, eloquent intellectual[s], a million miles from the action, well fed and farting'.[25] Bruce Dawe's wise avoidance of pacifist polemic in 'Homecoming', his elegaic meditation on the human wastage of Vietnam, is perhaps a major reason for the poem's persuasive power as an anti-war statement.

Among the non-combatant novelists, John Carroll, a 'nasho' who did not make it to the theatre of war, debunks the Digger with a cavalier ruthlessness. The theme of *Token Soldiers* coalesces in the character of the aptly named Sergeant Neil Savage, a strong, resourceful and courageous Australian soldier of the old dispensation, a 'born warrior in the ancient mould'. He can even spin a spellbinding bush yarn or two. But Carroll turns this apparently typical Digger into a bloodthirsty psychopath who has more in common with Norman Mailer's notoriously sadistic Sergeant Croft than with the amiable hero memorialized by Bean. Mercifully, Savage is shot by one of his own men after ordering a My Lai-type massacre of defenceless Vietnamese villagers – and the two central motifs of the national war literature, the military mastery and mateship of Australians, thus go sailing down the drain. The low rating of the Vietnam veteran on the scale of antipodean heroism is revealed by the thoughts of the conscript Max Chatterton as he contemplates his comrades lying or standing about the sweltering jungle:

> . . . Chatterton thought briefly of those life sized bronze figures you see displayed outside museums: a still life composition in the tradition of Gallipoli and the Kokoda Trail. As a boy, Max had always been fascinated by such sculpted realism, the tortured lines of frenzy and despair cut into the haggard faces, old before their time, and timelessly heroic. He had looked at them: they were so marvellous it was as though some invisible hand could throw a secret switch and bring them back to life – it was a fantasy he held and lived many times in his imagination, so powerful and real and indestructible did they seem to him. And now here he was, lost in some obscure province in a most unheroic way. Looking at the others, he thought, how paltry, how unworthy.[26]

The iconoclasm of Kenneth Cook in *The Wine of God's Anger* (1968) is even more complete. The anonymous young narrator of the novel is a Roman Catholic who, like Waugh's Guy Crouchback, volunteers to fight 'to save the world from Communism'; but he lacks the confidence to match his early conviction. Bemused, then progressively confused, sickened and appalled by the war, he eventually deserts and sits out the war in a bar in Bangkok, feeling just a little deliciously guilty at his complicity in the catalogue of crimes that was Vietnam. His baffled reaction to his first patrol, the big moment in any soldier's career, forebodes his deviation from the heroic mould:

> The only feelings I'd had so far . . . was one [*sic*] of utter unreality. This was all so like every patrol we'd ever done in our jungle training. The only difference was the fact that we were actually looking for somebody to shoot – really shoot. I was holding an automatic rifle, loaded with live bullets, and I kept telling myself that I was at war. I was a soldier. A man at arms. Homer had written about men like me. I tried very hard to feel something, but all I could feel was hot.[27]

The one conventional 'good soldier' Cook puts into the book, the narrator's platoon leader, Lieutenant Roberts, is a caricature of the Hotspurian warrior after the manner of Eric Lambert's contemptible Lieutenant Crane in *The Twenty Thousand Thieves*. But whereas Lambert allows himself the moderate pleasure of making Crane have half his face destroyed during a typical display of 'mad courage', Cook makes Roberts (who had once idly boasted that he 'would give his balls for a good battle') pay a shocking price for his glory-seeking. Either Cook is being diabolically vindictive, or else he is attempting to symbolize the hollowness of Australian machismo . . .

> The dead and the wounded and the soldiers waiting to fight . . . but all over the plateau scraps of men. Bloody lumps of cloth and flesh and streams of entrails.
>   . . . And just at my feet a neatly amputated set of testicles, still half encased with a blood-soaked rag that had once been part of a man's underpants. Whose underpants?
>   Lieutenant Roberts was kneeling a couple of yards away from me looking out to the jungle. His thighs were a mess of blood. His trousers were half torn off. There was a patch of blood between his legs.
>   Those were Lieutenant Roberts's balls at my feet. What would that do to his career?[28]

The response of actual Vietnam veterans to the indifferent reception they have received from their countrymen has been a combination of anger, confusion and resentment. This remains especially true of the professional military men. On the tenth anniversary of the end of the war, the commander of Australian troops in Vietnam from 1962 to 1965, Ted Serong, caustically observed:

> Something has happened to our breed. We are not the people with the spirit and standards of 1914 and 1939. We are a people who send their soldiers to war, and spit on them when they come back.[29]

The writings of the lower-ranking Regular Army soldiers exude a similar rancour. During the war they had been showered with Agent Orange rather than adulation; they resented the lack of whole-hearted emotional support to which they felt entitled; and they thought that the difficulty of their martial task in the land they ironically dubbed 'The Funny Place' had been severely underestimated by the arm-chair critics at home. The latter accounts for the mind-boggling mix of napalm and nobility depicted by David Alexander in his documentary novel based on the endeavours of the First Australian Regiment, *When the Buffalo Fight* (1980). Alexander, the *nom de plume* of Lex McAulay, a career army man who did three tours of duty in Vietnam, struggles valiantly to portray truthfully the horrors faced by the men, the moral compromises they had to make, and the barbarism in which they had to participate. But in the final resort he falls back on some of the more inane sustaining clichés of Australian war heroism, shibboleths and hackneyed claims which derive ultimately from the happy knowledge that, as Alexander insists, 'the Australian is superior to the man of every other nation'.[30]

In William Nagle's *The Odd Angry Shot* (1975), the initial pride felt by the 'Regs' at being among 'the gutsy ones' who (unlike the 'long haired bastards' of the anti-war protest movement) were prepared to die for their country, is modified by an awareness that the Australian response to their military progress ranged from the lukewarm to the openly hostile. Nagle, who served as a commando in Vietnam from 1966 to 1967, places this perceived civilian ingratitude into a sharply ironical context. A soldier receives a letter re-addressed from Australia which demands payment of a small bill. This is his reply:

> Dear Sir,
>   I find it necessary to inform you that I am at present indisposed, and what's more I don't care a rat's arse about your $3.50.
>   Kind regards,
>   Son of Anzac.[31]

The frustrating nature of a war which did not allow for big decisive battles, and the bitter certainty that the communists would triumph in the end anyway, further eroded the self-image of the Australians. The 'professional gung-ho' of Nagle's élite regulars evaporates in the jungle. 'Tired, wet and sold out', they maintain their morale and solidarity through a mutual contempt for the people back in that 'wonderful nation' Australia, to whom, apparently, they had become an 'embarrassment'.[32] Distorted by involvement in a war devoid of heroic purpose or character, the legendary exuberance of the Australian soldier emerges in Vietnam as something uncomfortably perverse. But Nagle is no satirist. The larrikin intemperance of his Diggers—far more outrageous than anything previously drawn by Harley Matthews or Richard Beilby—is intended to be appealing. For all their animality, they remain Bloody Good Blokes. In Nagle's hands, the symbolic loss of a Digger's testicles in a mine explosion becomes an opportunity to denigrate the effete protesters back home. The unfortunate soldier may have been rendered 'half a man', but he's still 'so much more of a man than any one of the smug bastards safe at home who stand in the streets and scream to stop the war . . . At least he came'.[33] Unlike such exemplary American fictionalizations of Vietnam as Michael Herr's *Dispatches* and Stephen Wright's *Meditations in Green* (1983), which attempt to convey the craziness of the conflict, its phantasmagorical amalgam of sex, drugs, rock 'n roll and gut-wrenching violence, *The Odd Angry Shot* is a conservative novel in both the socio-political and literary senses. Ultimately the brutality of the Diggers is not intended to be seen as deriving from participation in a degrading war, but rather as the mere exaggeration of attractive racial attributes.[34] Nagle's 'tough', often almost flippant, realism is calculated and exploitative, designed to demonstrate such inherent Australian traits as stoicism and cynicism:

> A dirty, brown-coloured dog runs past us and stops next to the North Vietnamese corpse . . . Wagging its tail, it dips it [*sic*] head then races down the road and across the bridge, a length of grey intestine dangling from its mouth. No gun carriages here . . . and it's cheaper than Pal.[35]

Michael Frazer, in his fictionalized memoir *Nasho*, is less tolerant of the crude Ockerism of the Australians. His didactic purpose is fundamentally the same as that which motivated Erich Maria Remarque, who claimed that war accelerates the process by which man's 'inner forces' are exerted 'toward . . . degeneration'.[36] *Nasho* is a catalogue of bastardization, sadism, sexual degradation, paranoia, drunkenness and several varieties of bestial behaviour, such as gastronomic duels between soldiers involving the consumption of quantities of beetles, cockroaches, and lizards. Frazer was a conscript; perhaps he felt no compulsion to protect the reputation of the Australian Army. But his sternly anti-heroic stance is lent special credence by the fact that the semi-autobiographical central character of *Nasho*, Peter Turner, is no rabidly anti-war national serviceman bitter at being pushed into the conflict against his will. Indeed, when at the end of his training at Puckapunyal he examines his reasons for volunteering for the dreaded infantry, he reveals an atavistic sense of martial mission comparable to that felt a generation earlier by Mick Reynolds in *We Were the Rats*:

> Was it that his father and his grandfather had been infantrymen? Was it that this was possibly his one chance of a lifetime to discover if he too had that vague indeterminable "it" in him, that "it" which was needed to turn an ordinary civilian into a brave soldier?[37]

But Turner is denied his wish to follow in his father's footsteps. A journalist before being called up, he is allocated instead to the Army Information Corps in Canberra. This involvement provides Frazer with the perfect vehicle for a biting exposure of both the conduct of the war and its promotion among ordinary Australians. The AIC's function was to disseminate information on 'almost any Army activity which made the Army look good to the public', while the Service newspaper to which Turner is specifically assigned specializes in stories on 'battle honours' earned in 'long-gone conflicts'. Still anxious to discover if he is 'a real soldier', Turner volunteers to work for the AIC in Vietnam itself. It is there that he becomes enmeshed in the propaganda machine, publicizing successful Australian ambushes when in truth the victims had been women and children. When he becomes fully apprised of his role in the 'organised cover-up' of 'the facts' of the war, he is devastated. Depression and dissipation follow, ending in a nervous breakdown and the inevitable mental hospital.[38]

Frazer ends *Nasho* with a rueful defence of the misused and abused men who took part in the conflict. Gathered together in 1984 on Australia's day of martial remembrance, Anzac Day, a group of reminiscing Vietnam veterans search for 'a word' to describe their feelings about the war:

> Most of them had never mentioned it to their outside friends, unless it had come up by accident. Even then their talk of their experience was brief and fleeting. Eventually the word came out, a word they all agreed upon, to describe that they had been in Vietnam. That word, and they agreed on it, was embarrassed.[39]

That Australian soldiers should choose the word 'embarrassed' to describe their war service speaks eloquently about the demythologizing effect of Vietnam. It is also more than tangentially significant that a major Australian novel about the war, John Rowe's *Count Your Dead* (1968), barely glances at the Australian effort, focusing instead on the American execution of the war. And this 'treachery' from a graduate of Duntroon Military College, a professional soldier who served with the rank of major in Vietnam![40] When Australians do fleetingly appear in the narrative, they come across as, at best, drunken *ingénus*, or, at worst, as hopelessly gauche and parochial. Rowe's deviant literary behaviour, which must have had C. E. W. Bean (who died the year *Count Your Dead* was published) turning in his grave, is emulated by Hugh Lunn in *Vietnam: A Reporter's War* (1985). A Reuter's correspondent based in Saigon during 1967 and 1968, Lunn like Rowe is more concerned with the way the Americans conducted themselves than in the fringe part played by his countrymen. He is much too intent on interpreting what Michael Herr calls the 'psychotic vaudeville' of U.S. military propaganda—such euphemisms as 'pacification', 'kill-ratios', 'psywar' and 'whamo' ('winning the hearts and minds of')–to be bothered with creating propaganda of his own on the Australians' behalf. A remembered scene of inebriated Diggers singing 'Waltzing Matilda' in a Saigon bar and challenging nearby Americans with the taunt 'One Australian is worth ten Yanks' encapsulates the Australian experience in Vietnam.[41] Lunn relates the incident deadpan, without indulgence. The scene elicits pathos rather than pride. Like the tenacious Anzacs themselves, however, Australian military publicists are nothing if not persistent, and the indications are that Vietnam has not yet been given up as a lost cause. Most activity has centred on what happened in the Long Tan rubber plantation a few kilometres from the Task Force base at Nui Dat during the stormy afternoon and evening of 18 August 1966, when a company of just over a hundred Australians (mostly 'green' nashos under the leadership of a handful of Regulars) withstood the sustained assault of a battle-hardened Viet Cong force fifteen, perhaps even twenty, times larger. As the veteran war reporter, Pat Burgess, has noted, this startling achievement received smaller headlines at home than the infamous 'water torture' interrogation of a young Viet Cong woman–which in itself is a measure of the relentlessly negative bias of Vietnam media coverage and its relative freedom from official censorship.[42] Lex McAulay, shedding his fictional guise of 'David Alexander', seeks to redress this historical miscarriage in *The Battle of Long Tan* (1986), a painstaking reconstruction of the bloody engagement. With its use of rousing excerpts from Shakespeare's *Henry V* to preface each chapter, its abundance of intimate detail, its sense of drama, and its unabashed promotion of 'uniquely' Australian virtues, McAulay's book belongs happily in the tradition of Bean's *Official History*. The work's subtitle is the real give-away: 'The Legend of Anzac Upheld'. What could more vividly illustrate the determination to lift Vietnam out of the quagmire of historical controversy and condemnation? But one suspects that McAulay–and those who surely will follow him–are fighting a losing battle.

. . . BUT THE GALLANT LEGION LIVES ON

Vietnam tarnished the heroic tradition, but it did not destroy it. The fact that the imagery of Gallipoli and the Kokoda Trail still seems 'powerful and real and indestructible' to Max Chatterton, the otherwise cynical and disconsolate conscript in *Token Soldiers*, confirms that it has retained much of its old power to move Australians.

Recent sympathetic treatments of the Anzac legend suggest that the myth has even made something of a post-Vietnam comeback. This is not to argue some sort of concerted counter-movement against revisionism; rather (and more happily) it would seem that the gradual liberation of ideas about heroism has allowed the two 'schools' to co-exist. It is testimony of the enduring robustness of Australian nationalism that the past ten years have seen what Roger McDonald has called 'a massed re-entry into the Gallipoli experience by historians and imaginative writers', of which McDonald himself has been in the vanguard. If the word 'displayed' is substituted for 'born', says McDonald, then Bean's belief that a consciousness of Australian nationalism was born on Gallipoli is 'a sentiment that is attractive to present-day temperaments'.[43] Even *1915*, for all its probing beneath the surface of the Anzac story, nurtures a self-conscious nostalgia for a time when it was still possible for patriotism to propel men into an enterprise 'larger than oneself'. This contemporary enthusiasm might well be a peculiarly Australian phenomenon. It seems significant, for example, that the Canadian Timothy Findley, the author of a harrowing fictional re-enactment of 1914–1918, *The Wars* (1977), did not deem it important to tackle the grand national theme willingly shouldered by McDonald.

The longevity of the Anzac legend can be gauged by the flourishing audience that exists for works which either were important in the myth's development, or else which currently seek to maintain or embellish it. In the mischievous words of a commentator on Peter Weir's immensely popular motion picture *Gallipoli* (1981), 'recounting the story of the Anzacs has become something of a growth industry'.[44] The alert opportunism of publishers in pandering to public enthusiasm is illustrated by *Time-Life*'s glossy, fifteen-volume 'Australians at War' series coinciding with the 1988 Bicentennial (significantly, its first such incursion into an 'indigenous' market), and, more shamelessly, by Angus & Robertson's promotion of Jack Bennett's ersatz *Gallipoli* (1981), the fictional spin-off from Weir's myth-affirming film, as an 'Australian Classic'. Bennett, by the way, based his novel on a screenplay by David Williamson which pays such indiscriminate deference to the myth that it is hard to believe that it came from the same playwright who is so mordant in his dramatizations of contemporary Australia.

Above all, it has been the renaissance of C. E. W. Bean as a force in Australian culture that most reflects the resurgence of interest in the role of the Australian soldiery in the Great War. Bean's previously unpublished Gallipoli diaries appeared to some acclaim in 1983, while the University of Queensland's hard and paperback facsimile edition of the *Official History* has been one of the major Australian publishing events of recent times. Not only has Bean reached a new audience, it would appear that he has belatedly captured the admiration of literary critics. Its readability notwithstanding, the *Official History* had long been ignored by literary scholars, presumably because of its assumed generic nature as a 'non-imaginative' work. Only H. M. Green, Bean's friend from their days as young reporters for the *Sydney Morning Herald*, felt the epic worthy of discussion from an aesthetic point of view. This neglect has been reversed. In 1984 two of seven 'experts' listed the *Official History*, along with such accepted classics as *While the Billy Boils*, *The Fortunes of Richard Mahony* and *Voss*, among Australia's 'ten greatest-ever' books, which is quite an accolade for an official military record.[45]

The original 'Gallant Legion' of Australian soldier-writers of the Great War has passed on, of course; but the salvaging and publication of diaries, letters and manuscripts long mouldering in museums, libraries and attics suggests that their testimony is far from complete. *The Gallipoli Diary of Sergeant Lawrence of the Australian Engineers – 1st A.I.F., 1915* (1981) and its sequel, *Sergeant Lawrence Goes To France* (1987), are two of the worthier products of this burgeoning publishing pursuit – some of the recently unearthed war narratives should have been left to languish in obscurity. These 'new', if usually posthumous, literary offerings by men of the First A.I.F. have been supplemented by the overdue reappearance of seminal Australian war books other than the *Official History*, such as *Flesh in Armour*, republished in 1985 in paperback by George Allen & Unwin, and *The Wells of Beersheba*, republished by Angus & Robertson.

A number of civilian apologists have also surfaced to carry on the good promotive fight. Two of the more influential contemporary propagators of the myth are Bill Gammage, in *The Broken Years*, published in 1974, and Patsy Adam-Smith in *The Anzacs* (1978). Both these very popular historical investigations are based on the diaries, letters and verbal communications of the front-line First World War soldiers – scrupulously so in *The Broken Years*, in a rather more *laissez-faire* fashion in *The Anzacs*. The debt to Bean of Gammage (a historian happy to be cast in the anti-English, Australian nationalist's mould) is great, and one which he freely acknowledges in his absorbing book. No wonder the presence of Bean in the film *Gallipoli* is almost palpable: Gammage acted as a military adviser to director Weir and writer Williamson. In *The Broken Years*, Gammage recycles Bean's favourite epithet 'great-hearted' in dedicating the book to the Diggers, while his parting message that Gallipoli 'is with us yet' bespeaks his reverential regard for the mythopoeic nature of the event.[46] Adam-Smith's celebration of the Anzacs, men whom she has had 'the rare, and peerless, privilege of knowing', is rather more unctuous than Gammage's, though perhaps no less sincere.[47]

For those who like their legends served up in easily digestible chunks and unseasoned by the intellectual salt of historical research, coffee-table compilations of military anecdotes have proliferated in the last ten years. The blurb for one such work, which goes by the misnomer *True Australian War Tales* (1983), captures the tone of this outlet for myth-making. 'This is a book', it blusters, 'which will make every Australian throw out his chest and hold his head a little higher'; the book tells of 'various situations in which Australians have acquitted themselves magnificently in times of war – not those things that are taught in our history books, but the stuff of which history is made . . .'.[48] The rise of popular war histories, like those of the indefatigable John Laffin, whose *Digger: The Story of the Australian Soldier* (1959) reappeared in 1986 with the subtitle changed to 'The *Legend* of the Australian Soldier', has been matched by a surge in interest in the literature of war. To the growing list of anthologies, which includes John Laird's *Other Banners* (1971), Chris Wallace-Crabbe and Peter Pierce's *Clubbing of the Gunfire* (1984) and Carl Harrison-Ford's *Fighting Words* (1986), should of course be added interpretative works like this one. The specific genre of war journalism, an area in which Australians can claim to have consistently excelled, has received its due in Pat Burgess's *WARCO: Australian Reporters at War* (1986). Australia has produced a huge and diverse crop of distinguished war correspondents, men like W. J. Lambie (the *Sydney Morning Herald* reporter who, wounded in Sudan, later became the first Australian killed in action in the Boer War), Paterson, Bean, Moorehead, Johnston, John Pilger and the cameramen Damien Parer and Neil Davis. Burgess celebrates their intrepidity, independence and ingenuity in getting 'the story', getting it right, and getting it sent home. He thus praises them for possessing those qualities usually ascribed to the Diggers themselves. And the title of the chapter dealing with the peculiar proficiency of Australian war correspondents has a distinctly familiar ring – 'Aussies The Best'.[49]

At the root of Australia's remarkable cultural dependence on the war myth lies what George Johnston once called a 'slavery' to an 'obsolete image'. Johnston's description of his countryman in *The Australians* (1966) still holds true:

He can be a timid fellow and see himself a swashbuckler; the taciturnity of the old bushman he converts into a studied inarticulateness; long-ago heroisms provide him with a continuing spiritual comfort in the conviction of his own heroic qualities if put to the test; carried to the extreme of image-assertiveness he can be a city man born and bred who will travel to Europe wearing a "Digger" slouch hat turned up at the brim and with a kangaroo and the Southern Cross boldly painted on his baggage. The saddest thing about him is his inability to see that he does not have to flaunt or prove his unmistakable Aussie-ness, that the record of his people no longer calls for self-advertisement.[50]

Such a bondage to an obsolete image influenced the Second World War novelists to try to revive the glory of 1914–18 and to reapply it to the different military conditions of the new conflict; the same slavery induced the defensive boasting of David Alexander's Vietnam novel and pressured Michael Frazer's hapless nasho into volunteering for the infantry to see if he was made of the right Anzac stuff. Even the minuscule literary output produced by Australia's limited involvement in Korea abounds in anachronistic imagery. Lawson Glassop, who covered the war for the *Sydney Morning Herald*, wrote a story about an Australian soldier who could well have stepped from the yellowing pages of Oliver Hogue or R. Hugh Knyvett:

His cockiness was almost a swagger. He was a good soldier and he knew it, and his swinging gait and bright eyes told the wide, wide world. He scented a fight coming up, and he had to restrain his eager feet . . . but he was too good a soldier to allow his lust for killing the enemy to overcome his commonsense . . .[51]

Yet the hero promoted by Australian war writers was of course obsolete from the beginning. The indomitable Digger of Gallipoli and Villers-Bretonneux was as misplaced then in the context of modern mechanized combat as he would be now, in the era of the tactical nuclear missile. Australian war writers, critical of war but almost blindly impressed by warlike achievement, have never been able to combine successfully the conflicting responsibilities of the serious artist and the committed publicist. Their various excesses and inconsistencies reveal not only an understandable confusion about the battle experience itself, but the insecurity of a culture which has felt the need to promote itself in the most primal terms possible. It has been easier and less painful for them to big-note vacuously about war than to engage in a rigorous critique of it, an activity which just might have unearthed a more balanced portrait of the Australian warrior, if one not so superficially flattering to the national self-image. Ultimately, they have proved to be less intrepid than the men they have loved to lionize.

Notes

ABBREVIATIONS

A & R	Angus & Robertson
ALS	*Australian Literary Studies*
AWM	Australian War Memorial
MUP	Melbourne University Press
OUP	Oxford University Press
UQP	University of Queensland Press

The editions referred to below are those actually quoted. In some cases the year of publication may differ from the date of *first* publication as cited in the text. Full publication details are given in the first instance only.

I 1915 AND ALL THAT

[1] As advertised in *Reveille*, the New South Wales returned servicemen's monthly, 1 April 1936, pp. 32-3. Note that one of the volumes of *The Gallant Legion*, O. E. Burton's *The Silent Division*, is the memoir of a New Zealander who fought with the New Zealand Expeditionary Force. Note also that most of the works included in the series appeared prior to 1936, as independent publications.

[2] George Johnston, 'ANZAC . . . A Myth For All Mankind', *Walkabout*, 31, no. 4 (1965), pp. 15-16.

[3] Charles Rowan Beye, *The Iliad, the Odyssey, and the Epic Tradition* (Anchor Books, New York, 1966), p. 119.

[4] See C. E. W. Bean, *The Official History of Australia in the War of 1914–18*, vol. VI, *The A.I.F. in France During the Allied Offensive, 1918* (A & R, Sydney, 1942), pp. 876-7.

259

⁵ See Sidney J. Baker, *The Australian Language* (Currawong, Sydney, 1966 edn), p. 212. Also Eric Partridge, *A Dictionary of Slang and Unconventional English*, vol. II (Routledge & Kegan Paul, London, 5th edn, 1961), p. 997; and G. A. Wilkes, *A Dictionary of Australian Colloquialisms* (Sydney University Press, Sydney, 1978), p. 28.

⁶ Bean, *Official History*, vol. VI, p. 209; Geoffrey Serle, *John Monash, A Biography* (MUP, Melbourne, 1982), p. 401.

⁷ R. Hugh Knyvett, *'Over There' with the Australians* (Hodder & Stoughton, London, 1918), pp. 277, 225.

⁸ Robert Graves, *Goodbye to All That* (Jonathan Cape, London, 1929), p. 236.

⁹ Quoted in Bill Gammage, *The Broken Years: Australian Soldiers in the Great War* (Australian National University Press, Canberra, 1974), p. 259.

¹⁰ Gladys Hain, *The Coo-ee Contingent* (Cassell, Melbourne, 1917), p. 108.

¹¹ *'Over There' with the Australians*, p. 204.

¹² William Baylebridge, *An Anzac Muster*, Author's Revised Text, edited with a Preface by P. R. Stephensen, vol. II *The Collected Works of William Baylebridge* (A & R, Sydney, 1962), p. 33.

¹³ Ibid., p. 63.

¹⁴ I. F. Clarke, *Voices Prophesying War 1763–1984* (OUP, London, 1966), p. 131.

¹⁵ Samuel Hynes, *The Auden Generation: Literature and Politics in England in the 1930s* (The Bodley Head, London, 1976), p. 242.

¹⁶ Erich Maria Remarque, *All Quiet on the Western Front*, trans. A. W. Wheen (Putnam, London, 1929), pp. 89-90.

¹⁷ Quoted in Eric J. Leed, *No Man's Land: Combat and Identity in World War 1* (Cambridge University Press, Cambridge, 1979), pp. 156, 91. *The Storm of Steel* is the English title of Jünger's war novel, published in 1929.

¹⁸ John H. Johnston, *English Poetry of the First World War* (Princeton University Press, Princeton, 1964), p. 16.

¹⁹ Ibid., p. 9.

²⁰ Ernest Hemingway, 1942 Introduction to *Men at War* (Fontana Books, London, 1966), p. 10. According to Frank Field, *Three French Writers and the Great War* (Cambridge University Press, Cambridge, 1975), p. 39, *Under Fire* had sold nearly a quarter of a million copies by the war's end.

²¹ Siegfried Sassoon, *Sherston's Progress*, in *The Collected Memoirs of George Sherston* (Faber & Faber, London, 1972), p. 525.

²² See Johnston, *English Poetry*, pp. 12-13.

²³ Henri Barbusse, *Under Fire*, trans. W. Fitzwater Wray (J. M. Dent, London, 1926), p. 257.

²⁴ See Robert Folkenflik, *The English Hero 1660–1800* (University of Delaware Press, Newark, 1982), and Bernard Bergonzi, *Heroes' Twilight: A Study of the Literature of the Great War* (Constable, London, 1965). The quotation, from Samuel Richardson's *Sir Charles Grandison*, is cited in Ian Watt, *The Rise of the Novel* (Penguin, Harmondsworth, 1963), p. 254.

²⁵ Stephen Crane, *The Red Badge of Courage* (Collier Books, New York, 1962), pp. 17, 48.

²⁶ See Stendhal, *The Charterhouse of Parma*, trans. Margaret R. D. Shaw (Penguin, Harmondsworth, 1958), p. 52; and Leo Tolstoy, *War and Peace*, trans. Louise and Aylmer Maude (OUP, London, 1941), vol. III, p. 320.

²⁷ *War and Peace*, vol. II, p. 459.

²⁸ Cervantes, *Don Quixote* (J. M. Dent, London, 1906), vol. I, pp. 318-19.
²⁹ Ernest Hemingway, *A Farewell to Arms* (Jonathan Cape, London, 1957 edn), p. 161. The hero of another major American Great War novel, John Dos Passos's *Three Soldiers* (1921), is also a deserter.
³⁰ See *Under Fire*, pp. 287, 265; *All Quiet on the Western Front*, pp. 40, 117-18.
³¹ Douglas Jerrold, *The Lie About the War* (Faber & Faber, London, 1930), p. 21, *passim*.
³² 'War Books and their Effect', *Army Quarterly*, 20 (July 1930), pp. 373-4.
³³ Charles Carrington, *Soldier from the Wars Returning* (Hutchinson, London, 1965), p. 264. Carrington was no lover of what he called the 'self-pitying school' of war writing.
³⁴ George Orwell, *Collected Essays, Journalism and Letters*, ed. Sonia Orwell and Ian Angus (Secker & Warburg, London, 1968), vol. I, p. 523.
³⁵ Paul Fussell, *The Great War and Modern Memory* (OUP, London, 1975), pp. 147, 153.
³⁶ Ford Madox Ford, *Parade's End* (Knopf, New York, 1950), p. 752.
³⁷ *Under Fire*, pp. 167-8.
³⁸ Ion Idriess, *The Desert Column* (A & R, Sydney, 1932), Author's Note. The fictional nature of the work is discussed more fully in Chapter IV.
³⁹ *An Anzac Muster*, pp. 33-4, 251-2.
⁴⁰ *The Idler*, no. 30; in *The Yale Edition of the Works of Samuel Johnson*, vol. II (Yale University Press, New Haven, 1963), p. 95.
⁴¹ Robert Rhodes James, *Gallipoli* (A & R, Sydney, 1965), p. 154. Quoted in *The Broken Years*, p. 99.
⁴² *Argus*, 8 May 1915, p. 19.
⁴³ John Masefield, *Gallipoli* (Heinemann, London, 1916), p. 19.
⁴⁴ See C. E. Montague, *Disenchantment* (Chatto & Windus, London, 1922), pp. 158-9; Masefield, *Gallipoli*, p. 19; T. E. Lawrence, *Seven Pillars of Wisdom* (Jonathan Cape, London, 1973 edn), p. 352.
⁴⁵ Compton Mackenzie, *Gallipoli Memories* (Cassell, London, 1929), pp. 80-1.
⁴⁶ Frank Richards, *Old Soldiers Never Die* (A & R, Sydney, 1933), p. 226.
⁴⁷ Oliver Hogue, *The Cameliers* (Andrew Melrose, London, 1919), p. 55.
⁴⁸ Anthony Powell, *The Kindly Ones* (Heinemann, London, 1962), p. 70.
⁴⁹ D. H. Lawrence, *Letters*, ed. Harry T. Moore (Heinemann, London, 1962), vol. I, p. 378. From a letter dated 9 November 1915.
⁵⁰ *Official History*, vol. VI, p. 1095.
⁵¹ G. D. Mitchell, *Backs to the Wall* (A & R, Sydney, 1937), p. 255. In *'Over There' with the Australians*, p. 96, R. Hugh Knyvett talks about 'the adolescent nation of the South Seas' proving its 'fitness for manhood'.
⁵² Thomas R. Edwards, *Imagination and Power: A Study of Poetry on Public Themes* (Chatto & Windus, London, 1971), p. 17.
⁵³ 'The Star of Australasia', in *Henry Lawson: Collected Verse*, ed. Colin Roderick, vol. I 1885–1900 (A & R, Sydney, 1967), pp. 294-6.
⁵⁴ See L. L. Robson, *Australia and the Great War* (Macmillan, Melbourne, 1969), p. 1.
⁵⁵ C. E. W. Bean, *Anzac to Amiens* (AWM, Canberra, 5th edn, 1968), p. 9.
⁵⁶ Leonard Mann, *Flesh in Armour* (A & R paperback edn, Sydney, 1973), pp. 6-7.
⁵⁷ C. J. Dennis, *The Moods of Ginger Mick* (A & R, Sydney, 1976 edn), p. 39. *The*

Moods of Ginger Mick sold more than 40 000 copies in Australia and New Zealand in less than six months in 1916. *The Anzac Book* was at least as popular. In roughly its first six months, it sold over 100 000 copies. See K. S. Inglis, 'The Anzac Traditions, *Meanjin*, 24, no. 1 (1965), p. 36; and David Kent, '*The Anzac Book* and the Anzac Legend: C. E. W. Bean as Editor and Image-Maker', *Historical Studies*, 21, no. 84 (April 1985), p. 390.

58 Russel Ward, *The Australian Legend* (OUP, Melbourne, paperback edn, 1966), p. 223.

59 See Gammage's article 'Anzac' in John Carroll (ed.), *Intruders in the Bush: The Australian Quest for Identity* (OUP, Melbourne, 1982), esp. pp. 62-3.

60 Henry Lawson, *The Bush Undertaker and Other Stories* (A & R Classics, Sydney, 1975), p. 208.

61 *Poems of Bernard O'Dowd: Collected Edition* (Lothian Publishing, Melbourne, 3rd edn, 1944), pp. 187-8, 208.

62 E. Phillips, *Out in the Soudan* (George Robertson, Sydney, 1885), see pp. 29, 38-9.

63 L. M. Field, *The Forgotten War: Australian Involvement in the South African Conflict of 1899-1902* (MUP, Melbourne, 1979), p. 180.

64 Randolph Stow, *Tourmaline* (Macdonald, London, 1963), p. 8.

65 *The Forgotten War*, p. 129. Field gives examples of press adulation on p. 135.

66 Shirley Walker, 'The Boer War: Paterson, Abbott, Brennan, Miles Franklin and Morant', *ALS*, 12, no. 2 (October 1985), pp. 219, 209.

67 A. B. Paterson, *Happy Dispatches* (A & R, Sydney, 1934), p. 46.

68 J. H. M. Abbott, *Tommy Cornstalk* (Longman, Green, London, 1902), pp. 2-3, 9, 215, 5, 98, 264, 234.

69 H. M. Green, *A History of Australian Literature*, vol. I, 1789-1923 (A & R, Sydney, 1961), p. 738.

70 C. E. W. Bean, *Official History*, vol. I, *The Story of Anzac: From the Outbreak of War to the End of the First Phase of the Gallipoli Campaign, May 4 1915* (A & R, Sydney, 1921), p. 48. Graeme Davison's article 'Sydney and the Bush: An Urban Context for the Australian Legend', in *Intruders in the Bush*, pp. 109-30, argues that the bushman legend was created by city men—like Henry Lawson—who romanticized a world that was remote from their own experience. The term 'noble savage', it should be observed, was attached to the bushman by Russel Ward in *The Australian Legend*, p. 5.

71 See Bean, *Official History*, vol. I, p. 607; '*Over There*' *with the Australians*, p. 8; D. H. Lawrence, *Kangaroo* (The Phoenix Edition, Heinemann, London, 1955), p. 33.

72 John Halpin, *Blood in the Mists* (The Macquarie Head Press, Sydney, 1934), p. 122.

73 Randolph Stow, *The Merry-Go-Round in the Sea* (Macdonald, London, 1965), p. 112.

II SPREADING THE WORD

1 John Hayward, *Prose Literature Since 1939* (Longman, Green, London, 1947), p. 9.

² Holger Klein (ed.), *The First World War in Fiction: A Collection of Critical Essays* (Macmillan, London, 1976), p. 1.

³ See *Under Fire*, p. 341. 'Ian Hay' and 'Boyd Cable' were the pseudonyms of Ian Hay Beith and E. A. Ewart.

⁴ Ian Hay, *The First Hundred Thousand* (William Blackwood, Edinburgh, 1916), p. 202. The work first appeared, in parts, in *Blackwood's Magazine*.

⁵ Boyd Cable, *Action Front* (Smith, Elder, London, 1916), p. 80.

⁶ Arthur Machen, *The Bowmen and Other Legends of the War* (Simpkin, Marshall, Hamilton, Kent & Co., London, 1915), pp. 37, 35, 15.

⁷ Murdoch's letter to the Commander of Allied Operations in the Dardanelles, General Ian Hamilton, is quoted in full in Hamilton's *Gallipoli Diary*, vol. II (Edward Arnold, London, 1920), pp. 266-7. No doubt to his undying regret, Hamilton gave Murdoch (who was on his way to London to take up a senior position in the Australian news cable service) permission to visit the peninsula. Murdoch, in concert with Ellis Ashmead-Bartlett, formed a critical opinion of Hamilton's leadership, and issued a statement to the British Government to this effect. He thus played an important part in Hamilton's sacking and recall to England in October 1915.

⁸ Ernest Raymond, *The Story of My Days: An Autobiography 1888–1922* (Cassell, London, 1968), p. 127.

⁹ *Gallipoli Correspondent: The Frontline Diary of C. E. W. Bean*, ed. Kevin Fewster (George Allen & Unwin, 1983), p. 158.

¹⁰ Henry Lawson, *Song of the Dardanelles and Other Verses* (Harrap, London, 1916), p. 11.

¹¹ Kevin Fewster, Expression and Suppression: Aspects of Military Censorship in Australia during the Great War, Ph.D. thesis, University of New South Wales, 1980, p. 112.

¹² *Sydney Morning Herald*, 11 August 1915, p. 12. Quoted in Fewster, Expression and Suppression, p. 110.

¹³ See Expression and Suppression, p. 116.

¹⁴ Bean quoted in Dudley McCarthy, *Gallipoli to the Somme* (John Ferguson, Sydney, 1983), p. 128; Smith quoted in Kevin Fewster, 'Ellis Ashmead Bartlett and the Making of the Anzac Legend', *Journal of Australian Studies*, no. 10 (June 1982), p. 25. (Smith was writing in the *Argus*, 1 Nov. 1915, p. 8); *The Broken Years*, p. 13; *Gallipoli Correspondent*, p. 159.

¹⁵ *Age*, 17 May 1915, p. 10; see also *Gallipoli to the Somme*, p. 127.

¹⁶ *Australians in Action: The Story of Gallipoli* (W. A. Gullick, Government Printer, Sydney, 1915). Ashmead-Bartlett's despatch was also ordered to be read in all Victorian schools: see Brian Lewis, *Our War: Australia During World War I* (MUP, Melbourne, 1980), p. 139.

¹⁷ See Ernest Scott, *Australia During the Great War*, vol. XI, *Official History of Australia in the War of 1914–18* (A & R, Sydney, 1936), pp. 861-2.

¹⁸ E. C. Buley, *A Child's History of Anzac* (Hodder & Stoughton, London, 1916), p. 17.

¹⁹ *Argus*, 25 April 1916, p. 1.

²⁰ *Sydney Morning Herald*, 6 September 1916, p. 11.

²¹ Boyd Cable, *The Grapes of Wrath* (Smith, Elder, London, 1917), pp. 206-7.

²² *Aussie*, no. 5 (June 1918), p. 1; no. 13 (April 1919), p. 8.

[23] *Argus*, 24 July 1916, p. 7. Quoted in Expression and Suppression, p. 104; 'the tradition of Anzac Beach': *Anzac to Amiens*, p. 263.

[24] C. E. W. Bean, *Letters from France* (Cassell, London, 1917), p. 108; diary quoted in *Gallipoli to the Somme*, p. 247.

[25] See Fewster, 'Ellis Ashmead Bartlett and the Making of the Anzac Legend', p. 25; Expression and Suppression, p. 106.

[26] *Gallipoli Correspondent*, pp. 157, 161-2.

[27] For the *Bulletin's* contradictory stance on war reporting, see 15 March 1917, p.7, and 3 Dec. 1914, p. 7. The parody of over-optimistic war journalism appears (under the headline of 'The Fatal Habit of Pulling Your Own Leg'), in 26 August 1915, p. 7. Bean's criticism of Monash's style is quoted in *Gallipoli to the Somme*, pp. 282-3.

[28] C. E. W. Bean, *What to Know in Egypt: A Guide for Australian Soldiers* (The Société Orientale de Publicité, Cairo, 1915), pp. 11, 14-15.

[29] According to the figures supplied by David Walker in Spearritt and Walker (eds), *Australian Popular Culture* (George Allen & Unwin, Sydney, 1979), p. 143, the sales of Bean's volumes of the *Official History* ranged from 17 000 to 22 000 (approx.), compared with the 100 000-plus of *The Anzac Book*.

[30] *The Great War and Modern Memory*, p. 28.

[31] C. E. W. Bean (ed.), *The Anzac Book*, 'Written and Illustrated in Gallipoli by the Men of Anzac' (Cassell, London, 1916; Sun Books reprint, Melbourne, 1975), p. xiii; *Gallipoli to the Somme*, p. 194.

[32] See David Kent, '*The Anzac Book* and the Anzac Legend: C. E. W. Bean as Editor and Image-Maker', pp. 387-9, for Bean's efforts to secure the book's success.

[33] Ibid., pp. 376, 380, 387. Kent gives several examples of rejected contributions which deal with such 'unsavoury' matters. See pp. 381-5.

[34] Johnston, 'ANZAC . . . A Myth For All Mankind', p. 13.

[35] Kenneth T. Henderson, *Khaki and Cassock* (Melville & Mullen, Melbourne, 1919), p. 86.

[36] *The Anzac Book*, p. 44.

[37] Ibid., p. 109.

[38] Ibid., p. 165.

[39] Ibid.

[40] For examples of admiration for and identification with the Turk, see 'Abdul' (a poem by Bean himself), pp. 58-9; also 'Our Friend the Enemy', pp. 60-1. The one piece which really expresses soldierly depression is 'A Grey Day in Gallipoli', p. 106.

[41] See Kent, '*The Anzac Book* and the Anzac Legend', p. 386.

[42] *The Anzac Book*, pp. 1, 3, 4. See A. B. Facey, *A Fortunate Life* (Penguin, Harmondsworth, 1981), p. 256.

[43] *The Anzac Book*, p. 18.

[44] Ibid., p. 40.

[45] 'ANZAC . . . A Myth For All Mankind', p. 13. For a substantial lexicon of A.I.F. slang see W. H. Downing, *Digger Dialects* (Lothian, Melbourne, 1919).

[46] *The Anzac Book*, p. 100.

[47] K. S. Inglis, 'The Anzac Tradition', p. 36.

[48] H. M. Green, *A History of Australian Literature*, vol. I, p. 396.

[49] C. J. Dennis, *The Moods of Ginger Mick*, pp. 26, 32, 31, 45.

50 See Inglis, 'The Anzac Tradition', p. 36.

51 *The Moods of Ginger Mick*, p. 87.

52 Roy Bridges, *The Immortal Dawn* (Hodder & Stoughton, London, 1917), p. 9.

53 Ibid., pp. 20, 21.

54 Quoted in Alan Moorehead, *Gallipoli* (Macmillan, Melbourne, illustrated edn, 1975), p. 77.

55 *The Immortal Dawn*, pp. 41-2.

56 Ibid., p. 21; 'youth-heroic!': p. 43.

57 Bridges describes the Australian volunteers at the beginning of the war as 'brown men, strong body and soul; red-blooded, as though the southern sun had ripened the vintage for the wine-press, like the grapes in the southern vineyards'. Their 'red youth' he adds, would soon be 'poured like wine upon the Anzac sands'. See pp. 3, 6.

58 *The Immortal Dawn*, pp. 19, 2-3.

59 Gladys Hain, *The Coo-ee Contingent*, p. 11. Note that Hain has restructured and slightly amended the poem.

60 Ibid., p. 119.

61 Ibid., p. 122.

62 Ibid., p. 125.

63 Brenda Niall, *Seven Little Billabongs: The World of Ethel Turner and Mary Grant Bruce* (MUP, Melbourne, 1979), pp. 135-6.

64 Ethel Turner, *The Cub: Six Months in His Life* (Ward, Lock, London, 1915), p. 248.

65 Ethel Turner, *Captain Cub* (Ward, Lock, London, 1917), p. 249.

66 See Niall, *Seven Little Billabongs*, p. 150.

67 See Wyndham Lewis, *The Art of Being Ruled* (Chatto & Windus, London, 1926), pp. 111-12. Quoted in John R. Reed, *Old School Ties: The Public Schools in British Literature* (Syracuse University Press, Syracuse, 1964), p. 202.

68 *The Great War and Modern Memory*, p. 25.

69 Mary Grant Bruce, *Captain Jim* (Ward, Lock, London, 1919), p. 182.

70 Ibid., pp. 51, 16, 180.

71 *Seven Little Billabongs*, p. 86.

72 John Butler Cooper, *Coo-oo-ee! A Tale of Bushmen from Australia to Anzac* (Hodder & Stoughton, London, 1916), pp. 220-1, 162, 165. 'Weedy' is the adjective Paterson uses in 'Clancy' to describe the appearance of the city dweller.

73 Ibid., pp. 222, 24, 20-1, 252, 236, 117. In *The First Hundred Thousand*, Ian Hay cheerfully recalls that the Tommies became 'less individualistic' during the period of training. In battle, the Tommy is seen to be 'adjusting his perspectives. He is beginning to merge himself in the Regiment . . . He has developed . . . many of the characteristics of the regular soldier'. See pp. 17, 181-2.

74 The combined sales of the McGlusky novels topped the two million mark. See E. Morris Miller, *Australian Literature From Its Beginnings to 1935*, vol. I (Sydney University Press, Sydney, 1973), p. 452.

75 A. G. Hales, *McGlusky's Great Adventure* (Hodder & Stoughton, London, 1917), pp. 3, 6, 5.

76 Ibid., pp. 223, 211, 207; 196, 220, 207, 213, 205.

77 A. G. Hales, *Ginger and McGlusky* (Hodder & Stoughton, London, 1917), p. 245.

78 Steele Rudd, *Memoirs of Corporal Keeley* (UQP, St Lucia, 1971), p. 124.

79 See *The Anzac Book*, pp. 45-8. A third type, 'Bobbie of the New Army', briefly

describes the ruddy-faced, ever-cheerful Tommy – a simplification and idealization of similar magnitude.

[80] C. E. W. Bean, *Official History*, vol. II, *The Story of Anzac: From 4 May, 1915, to the Evacuation of the Gallipoli Peninsula* (A & R, Sydney, 1924), p. 294. Details of Hogue's life and career can be found in *The Kia Ora Coo-ee*, no. 3 (May 1918), p. 11.

[81] Sir Henry Gullett, *Official History*, vol. VII, *Sinai and Palestine* (A & R, Sydney, 1923), pp. 30, 33, 35-6.

[82] Oliver Hogue, *Love Letters of an Anzac* (Andrew Melrose, London, 1916), p. 21.

[83] See *Seven Pillars of Wisdom*, p. 663.

[84] *The Kia Ora Coo-ee*, no. 2 (April 1918), p. 1.

[85] See Homer, *The Iliad*, trans. E. V. Rieu (Penguin, Harmondsworth, 1950), p. 229:

> Ah, my friend, if after living through this war we could be sure of ageless immortality, I should neither take my place in the front line nor send you out to win honour in the field. But things are not like that. Death has a thousand pitfalls for our feet; and nobody can save himself and cheat him. So in we go, whether we yield the glory to some other man or win it for ourselves.

[86] *The Kia Ora Coo-ee*, no. 1 (March 1918), p. 5.

[87] *The Cameliers*, pp. 167, 163, 57-8.

[88] *The Great War and Modern Memory*, p. 310.

[89] Oliver Hogue, *Trooper Bluegum at the Dardanelles* (Andrew Melrose, London, 1916), Preface by the author's father, J. A. Hogue, p. 13.

[90] Ibid., pp. 20, 19, 102, 233, 66.

[91] Ibid., pp. 19, 33, 67, 70-1.

[92] Ibid., pp. 246-7, 104, 185, 97, 146, 167, 190-1, 153.

[93] *Love Letters of an Anzac*, pp. 47, 120, 146, 174, 9.

[94] Quoted in Carmel Shute, 'Heroines and Heroes: Sexual Mythology in Australia, 1914-1918', *Hecate*, 1, no. 1 (1975), p. 10.

[95] *Love Letters of an Anzac*, pp. 209, 219.

[96] *The Cameliers*, p. 32; in *Trooper Bluegum at the Dardanelles*, pp. 26-7, Hogue quotes the popular Light Horseman's song: 'We're rounding up the bushmen from the Darling to the sea/And we'll go marching through Germany!'

[97] *'Over There' with the Australians*, see Ch. 3, esp. pp. 24-5; p. 105.

[98] Ibid., p. 67; *Love Letters of an Anzac*, p. 57.

[99] *'Over There' with the Australians*, p. 271.

[1] W. J. Denny, *The Diggers* (Hodder & Stoughton, London, 1919), pp. 183-4.

[2] C. Hampton Thorp, *A Handful of Ausseys* (John Lane, The Bodley Head, London, 1919), pp. 101-6, 270. See also pp. 116-17. Thorp was a New Zealander by birth.

[3] Ibid., pp. 185-6.

[4] *The Coo-ee Contingent*, p. 94.

[5] *Under Fire*, p. 340.

[6] *The Broken Years*, p. 257.

[7] Suzanne Brugger, *Australians and Egypt 1914-1919* (MUP, Melbourne, 1980), see pp. 42-4, 62-4.

[8] In *The Straits Impregnable* (John Murray, London, 1917), p. 255, Sydney de Loghe

remarks upon the decline, and then the rise, of Bean in the troops' esteem. The phrase 'wowseristic whining' comes from a bitter poem about Bean's letter in the troopship paper *Euripides Ensign*, 2 June 1915. Quoted in K. S. Inglis, *C. E. W. Bean, Australian Historian* (UQP, St Lucia, 1970), p. 15. The letter itself appeared in (among other newspapers) the *Argus*, 20 January 1915.

⁹ *Goodbye to All That*, p. 236.

¹⁰ Michael McKernan, *The Australian People and the Great War* (Thomas Nelson, Melbourne, 1980), pp. 120, 123, 147.

¹¹ *The Cameliers*, p. 5; *The Diggers*, p. 38.

¹² *A Handful of Ausseys*, pp. 166, 169, 159-60.

¹³ See *Trooper Bluegum at the Dardanelles*, p. 85; *Love Letters of an Anzac*, pp. 10, 43, 82, 128, 132; *'Over There' with the Australians*, p. 36.

¹⁴ *'Over There' with the Australians*, p. 318; *Love Letters of an Anzac*, p. 9; *A Handful of Ausseys*, p. 13; *The Coo-ee Contingent*, p. 70.

¹⁵ Harley Matthews, *Saints and Soldiers* (W. H. Floessell, Sydney, 1918), p. 22.

¹⁶ Ibid., p. 75.

¹⁷ Ibid., pp. 69-70.

¹⁸ Ibid., p. 17.

¹⁹ Ibid., p. 19.

²⁰ Ibid., p. 71.

²¹ Ibid., p. 36.

²² Ibid., pp. 50-1.

²³ Ibid., p. 113.

²⁴ Ibid., p. 141.

²⁵ Herbert Scanlon, *Forgotten Men* (H. H. Watson, Sydney, 1927), p. 2.

²⁶ Scanlon, *Humoresque* (H. H. Watson, Sydney, 1922), p. 8.

²⁷ Two One-Legged Anzacs, *Dinkie Di Diggers* (Alpha Printing, Melbourne, 1927), p. 31.

²⁸ E. Wells, *Fragments From Gallipoli and France* (W. C. Penfold, Sydney, 1921), pp. 16-17.

III BOOKS OF THE TRIBE

¹ *Coo-oo-ee! A Tale of Bushmen from Australia to Anzac*, p. 237.

² Paul Merchant, *The Epic* (Methuen, London, 1971), p. 1.

³ Johnston, 'ANZAC . . . A Myth For All Mankind', p. 16.

/⁴ See Merchant, *The Epic*, pp. 4, 1.

⁵ See 'War History—An Epic Story For Future Generations', a report of Bean's speech at the New South Wales Institute of Journalists' Luncheon, *Sydney Morning Herald*, 4 April 1925, p. 16.

⁶ George Rawlinson, *The History of Herodotus* (John Murray, London, 1858), vol. I, p. 153; *Official History*, vol. II, p. 910.

⁷ See London *Observer*, quoted in Melbourne *Herald*, 13 February 1922, and London *Daily Telegraph*, 23 July 1929. both testimonials appear in K. S. Inglis, *C. E. W. Bean, Australian Historian*, pp. 20, 22. The *New Statesman* praise is quoted in *Reveille*, 1 April 1935, p. 33. The italics are mine.

[8] See, for example, Green, *A History of Australian Literature*, vol. I, p. 740; Inglis, 'The Anzac Tradition', p. 30; and Gavin Long, 'The Australian War History Tradition', *Stand-To* (March–April 1955), p. 17.

[9] C. F. Aspinall-Oglander, *History of the Great War*, vol. I, *Military Operations—Gallipoli* (Heinemann, London, 1929), p. 178; *Official History*, vol. I, pp. 254-6.

[10] Winston Churchill, *The World Crisis, 1915* (Australasian Publishing Co., Sydney, 1923), p. 316.

[11] See Bean, 'The Writing of the Australian Official History of the Great War', *Royal Australian Historical Society Journal and Proceedings*, 24, Part 2 (1938), p. 92; *Official History*, vol. III, *The Australian Imperial Force in France, 1916* (A & R, Sydney, 1929), pp. v-vi.

[12] Bean, *Official History*, vol. V, *The Australian Imperial Force in France During the Main German Offensive, 1918* (A & R, Sydney, 1937), p. 122.

[13] See McCarthy, *Gallipoli to the Somme*, p. 79; Bean was not actually appointed official historian until 1 July 1919.

[14] *The Straits Impregnable*, p. 255; de Loghe refers to Bean by the sobriquet 'Captain Carrot'.

[15] *Gallipoli to the Somme*, pp. 95, 154 (twice), 249.

[16] See Bean's comment in *Anzac to Amiens*, p. viii; K. S. Inglis, in 'The Anzac Tradition', p. 26, calls the *Official History* 'a monument to the men who fought—a literary equivalent to the National War Memorial . . .'.

[17] *Gallipoli to the Somme*, p. 106.

[18] *Official History*, vol. I, pp. 595-6.

[19] Rawlinson, *The History of Herodotus*, vol. I, p. 7.

[20] Beye, *The Iliad, the Odyssey, and the Epic Tradition*, p. 61. See also the view of General Sir Ian Hamilton, as expressed in the *Manchester Guardian*, 20 February 1922: the first volume of the *Official History*, he says, tells a story of 'minor tactics; of Homeric struggles of twenty men dwindled down to half a dozen'. (Quoted in Inglis, *C. E. W. Bean, Australian Historian*, p. 20.) Rule is quoted in *Official History*, vol. III, p. 720.

[21] See *Official History*, vol. III, pp. vi-vii.

[22] Ibid., vol. II, p. 540.

[23] Ibid., vol. I, p. 558; vol. IV, *The Australian Imperial Force in France, 1917* (A & R Sydney, 1933), p. 307.

[24] *Official History*, vol. V, pp. 522-3.

[25] Ibid., vol. VI, pp. 206-8; vol. I, p. 121.

[26] Ibid., vol. I, pp. 550-1.

[27] For details on the Bean/Murdoch anti-Monash intrigue see *Gallipoli to the Somme*, pp. 303, 334-6; description of White: *Official History*, vol. I, pp. 70-5; on likeness of Monash to Napoleon: *Official History*, vol. VI, pp. 196, 207-8. Monash's remorseless driving of his troops is discussed in the same volume, on pp. 795, 854, 876. His eagerness for military glory is alluded to on p. 209.

[28] *Official History*, vol. VI, pp. 208, 6, 1084-6; vol. I, pp. 45, 5, 550.

[29] Ibid., vol. VI, p. 22. The death rate of newly-commissioned second lieutenants is said to have given rise to the proverb, 'One star, one stunt'.

[30] Ibid., vol. I, see p. 80; vol. III, pp. 601-2.

[31] Ibid., vol. IV, pp. 481-4.

[32] Ibid., vol. I, p. 5; vol. VI, p. 1084.

[33] Ibid., vol. I, p. 126. Bean's diary offers a more explicit opinion on the reason for the decline of the British soldiery: 'The truth is that after 100 years of breeding in the slums, the British race is not the same . . . as in the days of Waterloo'. See *Gallipoli Correspondent*, p. 153.

[34] *The Great War and Modern Memory*, pp. 282-3.

[35] *Disenchantment*, p. 159.

[36] *Official History*, vol. V, p. 586.

[37] Ibid., vol. I, pp. 5, 126, 48; vol. VI, p. 6.

[38] Ibid., vol. VI, pp. 5, 1084-5; vol. I, pp. 48, 130.

[39] Lloyd Robson, 'C. E. W. Bean: a review article', *Journal of the Australian War Memorial*, no. 4 (April 1984), p. 57.

[40] *Gallipoli to the Somme*, p. 95.

[41] C. E. W. Bean, *On The Wool Track* (A & R, Sydney, 1963 edn), pp. 44, 53, 62, 104, 105, 106, 152 (references to 'the real Australia'); p. 74 (see also p. 64). *The Dreadnought of the Darling* (A & R, Sydney, 1956 edn), pp. 226, 228.

[42] *Official History*, vol. I, pp. 46-7.

[43] Ibid., vol. III, p. 601; vol. I, p. 553.

[44] *Aussie*, no. 7 (September 1918), p. 10.

[45] *Official History*, vol. VI, pp. 1078-9; see also vol. I, p. 46.

[46] Ibid., vol. I, p. 550; vol. II, p. 504; vol. VI, p. 30.

[47] David A. Kent, 'From the Sudan to Saigon: A Critical Review of Historical Works', *ALS*, 12, no. 2 (October 1985), p. 158; see *Death of a Hero*, p. 26.

[48] *Official History*, vol. I, p. 6; see also vol. VI, pp. 6, 1084.

[49] Ibid., v . I, p. 607.

[50] Ibid., vo.. V, pp. 175, 177.

[51] Ibid., p. 653.

[52] Ibid., vol. I, p. 254; vol. VI, p. 26; vol. IV, p. 308; vol. III, p. 858.

[53] Ibid., vol. V, p. 345. (Jacka's exploit is described in vol. II, p. 150.)

[54] Ibid., vol. IV, p. 948.

[55] *A History of Australian Literature*, vol. I, p. 751.

[56] *Official History*, vol. II, pp. 429, 502-4.

[57] Ibid., vol. VI, p. 546.

[58] *A History of Australian Literature*, vol. I, p. 745.

[59] Moorehead, *Gallipoli*, p. 184.

[60] See *The Great War and Modern Memory*, chapter 1, 'A Satire of Circumstance', esp. pp. 12-13.

[61] *Official History*, vol. II, pp. 617-18; see also pp. 615-16, 631-2.

[62] Ibid., p. 633.

[63] Ibid., vol. III, pp. 660-1.

[64] Ibid., pp. 957-8.

[65] Ibid., p. 419.

[66] Horace, *Odes* IV, 9, 25-8, *The Odes and Epodes*, trans. C. E. Bennett (Heinemann, London, 1960), p. 321. Quoted in Merchant, *The Epic*, p. 4.

[67] Baylebridge, *An Anzac Muster*, pp. 211-12.

[68] *Trooper Bluegum at the Dardanelles*, p. 240.

[69] *An Anzac Muster*, pp. 209-12.

[70] Ibid., p. 207.

[71] See P. R. Stephensen's Preface to *An Anzac Muster*, pp. 25-6.

[72] *The Great War and Modern Memory*, pp. 125-31, esp. p. 127.

[73] *An Anzac Muster*, p. 46.

[74] Quoted in Stephensen's Preface, p. 15.

[75] *An Anzac Muster*, p. 249; see also pp. 115, 170.

[76] John Kirtley, 'My Friend Baylebridge', *Southerly* (William Baylebridge Number), 16, no. 3 (1955), pp. 135, 137.

[77] *An Anzac Muster*, pp. 239-40.

[78] See Stephensen's Preface, pp. 10-12, for details of Baylebridge's life and career. Baylebridge was born William Blocksidge, the name under which his work between 1908 and 1921—including *An Anzac Muster*—appeared; see also *Australian Dictionary of Biography*, vol. VII, 1891–1939, ed. Bede Nairn and Geoffrey Serle (MUP, Melbourne, 1979), p. 219.

[79] Frederick T. Macartney, *Australian Literary Essays* (A & R, Sydney, 1957), p. 93.

[80] *An Anzac Muster*, pp. 31, 43, 261.

[81] Brian Elliott, *Singing to the Cattle* (Georgian House, Melbourne, 1947), p. 129.

[82] *An Anzac Muster*, p. 214.

[83] Ibid., p. 62.

[84] Ibid., p. 85.

[85] Stephensen's Preface, p. 22. It should be remembered that P. R. Stephensen, a long-time friend of Baylebridge, acted as an executor of his will upon his death in May 1942. In the will provision was made for a trust to 'publish and publicise' Baylebridge's writings. See p. 15.

[86] *An Anzac Muster*, p. 46.

[87] Ibid., pp. 260, 263, 33.

[88] Ibid., p. 40.

[89] Ibid., p. 188.

[90] Ibid., p. 69.

[91] Ibid., pp. 151-2.

[92] Ibid., p. 124.

[93] Ibid., p. 160.

[94] See Eugene M. Waith, *The Herculean Hero* (Chatto & Windus, London, 1962), pp. 38, 30. See also p. 54 for Waith's comments on the warrior's traditionally low regard for women.

[95] *An Anzac Muster*, p. 189.

[96] Miles Franklin, *Laughter, Not For A Cage* (A & R, Sydney, 1956), p. 142.

[97] *An Anzac Muster*, p. 145.

[98] Patsy Adam-Smith, *The Anzacs* (Nelson, Melbourne, 1978), p. 53.

[99] *An Anzac Muster*, pp. 40, 261.

[1] Ibid., p. 187.

[2] Ibid., p. 63.

[3] Moore, *Six Australian Poets* (Robertson & Mullens, Melbourne, 1942), p. 138. See also Judith Wright, 'William Baylebridge and the Modern Problem', *Southerly*, 16, no. 3 (1955), p. 144, and James McAuley, *A Map of Australian Verse* (OUP, Melbourne, 1975), p. 81.

[4] William Baylebridge, *National Notes*, in *This Vital Flesh*, vol. I *Collected Works* (A & R, Sydney, 1961), p. 148; *An Anzac Muster*, pp. 223, 181; 'hot-necked natural men': Baylebridge quoted in Macartney, *Australian Literary Essays*, p. 96.

[5] *An Anzac Muster*, pp. 254, 250.

[6] David Daiches (ed.), *British and Commonwealth Literature* (Penguin, Harmondsworth, 1971), p. 38.

[7] *An Anzac Muster,* p. 256.

[8] Friedrich W. Nietzsche, *Thus Spake Zarathustra,* trans. A. Tille (J. M. Dent, London, 1960), p. 39. For Stephensen's (and Harley Matthews's) embroilment in the Australia First controversy, see Bruce Muirden, *The Puzzled Patriots* (MUP, Melbourne, 1968).

[9] *The Great War and Modern Memory,* p. 206.

[10] *The Anzac Muster,* p. 258.

[11] E. Morris Miller, *Australian Literature,* vol. 1, p. 183.

[12] For example: J. T. Laird, 'Australian Prose Literature of the First World War: A Survey', *ALS,* no. 2 (October 1971), p. 153; Harry Heseltine, 'Australian Fiction Since 1920', in Geoffrey Dutton (ed.), *The Literature of Australia* (Penguin, Harmondsworth, revised edn, 1976), p. 198.

[13] See Harry Heseltine, *Vance Palmer* (UQP, St Lucia, 1970), pp. 14-15.

[14] Leonard Mann, 'A Double Life', *Southerly,* 29, no. 3 (1969), p. 167.

[15] See Humphrey McQueen, 'Emu into Ostrich: Australian Literary Responses to the Great War', *Meanjin,* 35, no. 1 (April 1976), p. 84. (McQueen is quoting a letter from Nettie Palmer to Frank Dalby Davison, 31 October 1933); *All About Books,* 5, no. 1 (January 1933), p. 10.

[16] 'A Double Life', p. 168.

[17] From Barnard's 1972 Introduction to *Flesh in Armour* (A & R, Sydney, 1973), no page number.

[18] See Barnard's Introduction; Cecil Hadgraft, *Australian Literature* (Heinemann, London, 1960), p. 250; Green, *A History of Australian Literature,* vol. II, p. 1131; Laird, 'Australian Prose Literature', p. 154; Laird, *Other Banners: An Anthology of Australian Literature of the First World War* (AWM, Canberra, 1971), p. 5; Franklin, *Laughter, Not For a Cage,* p. 170; *All About Books,* 5, no. 4 (April 1933), pp. 50-1.

[19] *Flesh in Armour,* p. 16.

[20] See *Flesh in Armour,* pp. 81, 92; *Death of a Hero,* pp. 256, 376, 428; *Parade's End,* pp. 492-3.

[21] *Flesh in Armour,* p. 113; *Parade's End,* p. 668.

[22] *Flesh in Armour,* pp. 228, 49-50, 230-1, 248.

[23] Ibid., pp. 250-1.

[24] *Death of a Hero,* p. 257.

[25] *Flesh in Armour,* pp. 172, 239.

[26] See the catalogue on pp. 38-9; also pp. 218, 214, 92-3.

[27] *Flesh in Armour,* pp. 92, 243, 35.

[28] Ibid., pp. 67-8. See also p. 246, for the description of the 'ruthless ferocity' of the Australians, and their 'battle ecstasy'.

[29] Ibid., pp. 95-6.

[30] Ibid., p. 161.

[31] Ibid., pp. 199, 215.

[32] See *War Letters of General Monash,* ed. F. M. Cutlack (A & R, Sydney, 1935), p. 266.

[33] *Flesh in Armour,* pp. 218, 219, 222-3.

[34] Ibid., p. 43.

[35] Elliott, *Singing to the Cattle,* p. 141.

[36] *Flesh in Armour,* p. 34.

[37] Ibid., pp. 234-5; see also pp. 175, 7, 140-7, 63, 65, 91, 107, 160, 237.

[38] Ibid., pp. 121-2.

[39] Ibid., p. 253.
[40] See Owen Webster, *The Outward Journey* (Australian National University Press, Canberra, 1978), pp. 93-4, 102. Davison was born Frederick Douglas Davison, Junior.
[41] 1969 interview with Owen Webster, Australian Broadcasting Commission Archival Transcript, Tape Two, p. 9. (Davison ended the war a lieutenant.)
[42] Ibid., Tape Four, p. 3. See also Louise E. Rorabacher, *Frank Dalby Davison* (Twayne Publishers, Boston, 1979), pp. 63, 68.
[43] *Seven Pillars of Wisdom*, p. 664.
[44] *Sinai and Palestine*, pp. 395-6, 404.
[45] Quoted in Rorabacher, *Frank Dalby Davison*, p. 63.
[46] Frank Dalby Davison, *The Wells of Beersheba* (A & R, Sydney, 1933), p. 56; *Sinai and Palestine*, p. 385.
[47] See Author's Notes to *The Wells of Beersheba* (1933 edn), and *The Road to Yesterday: Collected Stories* (A & R, Sydney, 1964), which contains the revised version.
[48] *The Road to Yesterday*, p. 3.
[49] H. P. Heseltine, 'The Fellowship of All Flesh: The Fiction of Frank Dalby Davison', *Meanjin*, 27, no. 3 (1968), p. 277.
[50] See Merchant, *The Epic*, p. 94.
[51] *The Wells of Beersheba*, pp. 13-14, 18-19, 20.
[52] *A History of Australian Literature*, vol. II, p. 1037.
[53] *The Wells of Beersheba*, pp. 28-9.
[54] Ibid., p. 28.
[55] Ibid., p. 33.
[56] Ibid., pp. 43-4.
[57] Ibid., p. 61.
[58] Ibid., p. 67.
[59] Ibid., p. 71; see also p. 68.
[60] See *The Wells of Beersheba*, p. 69, *The Road to Yesterday*, p. 24, *The Iliad*, p. 88; *The Road to Yesterday*, p. 24, *The Iliad*, p. 94.
[61] Hume Dow, *Frank Dalby Davison* (OUP, Melbourne, 1971), p. 13; *The Wells of Beersheba*, pp. 76-7.
[62] See ABC interview with Owen Webster, Tape Two, pp. 7-8; also Author's Note to *The Road to Yesterday*.
[63] In *The Road to Yesterday*, p. 227; see also pp. 222, 226.
[64] Dow, *Frank Dalby Davison*, p. 14.
[65] Quoted in Dow, p. 14.

IV THE ART OF SELF-ADVERTISEMENT

[1] Dan Davin, *For the Rest of Our Lives* (Michael Joseph, London, 1965), p. 8.
[2] *The Great War and Modern Memory*, p. 312.
[3] W. L. Paterson, 'Joe Maxwell—Author', *Reveille*, 1 November 1932, p. 5.
[4] *Seven Pillars of Wisdom*, p. 9. See J. T. Laird, 'A Checklist of Australian Literature of World War I', *ALS*, 4 (October 1969), p. 159.

⁵ Denis Winter, *Death's Men: Soldiers of the Great War* (Allen Lane, London, 1978), pp. 269-72.

⁶ See *The Great War and Modern Memory*, pp. 203-20.

⁷ *Who Shot George Kirkland?* (Pan, Sydney, 1981), no page number.

⁸ Robert Graves, *But It Still Goes On* (Jonathan Cape, London, 1930), pp. 32-3.

⁹ Michael Herr, *Dispatches* (Pan, London, 1978), p. 25.

¹⁰ *The Great War and Modern Memory*, p. 206.

¹¹ *Goodbye to All That*, p. 211.

¹² See Geoff Page, 'Harney' (1980), in Page (ed.), *Shadows from Wire* (Penguin, Ringwood, 1983), p. 64. See also 'Harney's War', *Overland*, no. 13 (October 1958), pp. 8, 12.

¹³ *Reveille*, 1 March 1936, p. 9.

¹⁴ Ibid., 1 March 1930, p. 48. The offending remarks are to be found in *Goodbye to All That*, pp. 236-7.

¹⁵ Les Murray, *The Boys Who Stole the Funeral* (A & R, Sydney, 1980), S 128.

¹⁶ Joseph Maxwell, *Hell's Bells and Mademoiselles* (A & R, Sydney, 1932), p. 1.

¹⁷ Ibid., p. 4.

¹⁸ See H. M. Green, *A History of Australian Literature*, vol. II, p. 1323.

¹⁹ H. R. Williams, *Comrades of the Great Adventure* (A & R, Sydney, 1935), p. 305.

²⁰ Quoted in Alan Moorehead, *Gallipoli*, p. 132.

²¹ D. H. Lawrence, *Kangaroo*, p. 198.

²² *The Boys Who Stole the Funeral*, S 110.

²³ John Carroll, 'Defeat in the Dardanelles', *Age Monthly Review*, 1, no. 7 (1981), p. 7.

²⁴ See *Don Quixote*, vol. I, p. 314, 'Let none presume to tell me that the pen is preferable to the sword . . .'.

²⁵ John Hayward, *Prose Literature Since 1939*, p. 20.

²⁶ *A History of Australian Literature*, vol. II, p. 1325.

²⁷ E. Morris Miller and Frederick T. Macartney, *Australian Literature: A Bibliography to 1938, extended to 1950* (A & R, Sydney, revised edn, 1956), p. 247.

²⁸ Idriess, *The Desert Column*, pp. vii-viii.

²⁹ *The Great War and Modern Memory*, p. 310.

³⁰ *The Desert Column*, p. vii.

³¹ Ibid., pp. 30-1. It should be noted, however, that a similar reference to the act of diary-keeping in *The Desert Column* is taken directly from the original record. See p. 36.

³² AWM collection; *The Desert Column*, p. 25.

³³ *The Desert Column*, p. 321.

³⁴ Ibid., p. 318.

³⁵ Ibid., pp. 192-3.

³⁶ Ibid., p. 55.

³⁷ Ibid., pp. 185-6.

³⁸ Ibid., p. 11.

³⁹ Ibid., p. 9.

⁴⁰ See Hilmer-Smith's Foreword to *Experiences of a "Dinki Di" R.R.C. Nurse* (Australasian Medical Publishing, Sydney, 1933); the Moberly Papers, MS 7960, La Trobe Library, Melbourne.

⁴¹ E. J. Rule, *Jacka's Mob* (A & R, Sydney, 1933), p. ix.

⁴² May Tilton, *The Grey Battalion* (A & R, Sydney, second edn, 1934), Author's Note.

⁴³ *Backs to the Wall*, p. 202.

44 See *Beowulf*, a prose translation with an introduction by David Wright (Penguin, Harmondsworth, 1957), p. 40.

45 See *Reveille*, 1 November 1934, p. 2. The other details on Mitchell come from *Reveille*, 1 March 1936, p. 8.

46 *Backs to the Wall*, pp. 103-4.

47 *Reveille*, 1 March 1936, p. 8; 1 November 1934, p. 2.

48 See advertisement for *Backs to the Wall*, *Reveille*, 1 April 1937, p. 28.

49 *Reveille*, 1 May 1937, p. 23; 1 March 1936, pp. 8-9.

50 Ibid., 1 November 1934, p. 2.

51 *Backs to the Wall*, p. 271.

52 Ibid., p. 168; 'sense of personal superiority', p. 229.

53 Bill Gammage, 'Anzac', in *Intruders in the Bush*, p. 63.

54 *Backs to the Wall*, p. 107.

55 Ibid., pp. 82, 265.

56 AWM collection; diary entry, 20 October 1914

57 *Backs to the Wall*, pp. 280-1.

58 See, for example, 'It Must Not Happen BUT!', *Reveille*, 1 September 1935, pp. 2-6.

59 H. R. Williams, *The Gallant Company: An Australian Soldier's Story of 1915–18* (A & R, Sydney, 1933), pp. 272-5.

60 Ibid., pp. 273-4.

61 Ibid., pp. 12-13.

62 Ibid., pp. 146, 271.

63 Ibid., p. 266.

64 Ibid., pp. 75, 17.

65 Ibid., p. 92; 'minced flesh and warm blood', p. 127.

66 E. J. Rule, *Jacka's Mob*, p. 105.

67 See *Reveille*, 1 May 1933, p. 2.

68 *Jacka's Mob*, pp. 61, 59, 152, 128, 164, 184, 197, 201, 110, 138.

69 Ibid., pp. 5, 6, 277.

70 Ibid., p. 51. See also p. 336 for Rule's own savage contempt for German prisoners: '. . . I can never imagine Aussies cringing like they do. I always feel I'd like to put my boot in their faces'.

71 *Backs to the Wall*, p. 122.

72 *The Gallant Company*, p. 152.

73 *The Broken Years*, p. 237.

74 *The Gallant Company*, pp. 25, 3, 215, 274.

75 *Jacka's Mob*, pp. 312, ix.

76 Major G. D. Mitchell, *Soldier in Battle* (A & R, Sydney, 1941), pp. 84-5.

77 *The Gallant Company*, p. 45.

78 See the listing in *All About Books*, 5, no. 1 (January 1933), p. 10.

79 *Reveille*, 1 November 1932, p. 31.

80 *Hell's Bells and Mademoiselles*, p. 231.

81 Ibid., pp. 10-11; 'as many illusions', p. 3.

82 Ibid., p. 16.

83 Ibid., pp. 2, 76-7, 174.

84 Ibid., p. 130.

85 See *Hell's Bells*, pp. 8-9; the reviewer of *Hell's Bells* in *Reveille* (1 November 1932, p. 5) says that Maxwell may well have been describing a second, later, fracas

in the 'Wasser' district, but that his description reads very like an account of the infamous Easter riot.

86 *Hell's Bells and Mademoiselles*, p. 7.
87 Ibid., p. 13.
88 Ibid., p. 56.
89 Ibid., p. 191.
90 Ibid., pp. 180, 253.
91 *War Letters of General Monash*, pp. 168-9, 172.
92 Monash, *The Australian Victories in France in 1918* (A & R, Sydney, 1936), p. 270. Bean's criticisms can be found in vol. VI of the *Official History*, p. 210.
93 Donald Black, *Red Dust: an Australian Trooper in Palestine* (Jonathan Cape, London, 1931), pp. 40-1.
94 Ibid., pp. 34, 36, 62-3, 208, 154, 198, 62.
95 Ibid., p. 65.
96 Ibid., p. 286.
97 Ibid., see pp. 181-8.
98 Ibid., p. 182; see C. E. Montague, *Disenchantment*, p. 176.
99 Ibid., pp. 257-8.
1 R. F. Lushington, *A Prisoner of the Turks, 1915–18* (Simpkin, Marshall, and Co., London, 1923), p. 6.
2 John Halpin, *Blood in the Mists*, pp. 122, 202-3.
3 Ibid., pp. 136, 234.
4 See pp. 259-60.
5 *A Prisoner of the Turks*, p. 29.
6 T. W. White, *Guests of the Unspeakable* (John Hamilton, London, 1928), pp. 180, 191, 76; see *Blood in the Mists*, p. 156, for Halpin's opinion of the English.

V DISSENTING VOICES

1 The poems from *The Burning Marl* to which I refer are 'Anzac' and 'The Patriot'. It should be noted that Brereton tempers his anti-war feelings with admiration for the Australian troops. 'Anzac', for instance, praises the courage and the heroic purpose of those who, led by 'other banners' than the pacifism that ruled the poet, answered 'Freedom's summoning trumpets'. For a detailed commentary on Australian poetry of the Great War, see J. T. Laird, 'Australian Poetry of the First World War: A Survey', *ALS*, 4, no. 3 (1970), pp. 241-50.
2 See Introduction to Chris Wallace-Crabbe and Peter Pierce (eds), *Clubbing of the Gunfire: 101 Australian War Poems* (MUP, Melbourne, 1984), p. 8.
3 *Official History*, vol. VI, p. 42.
4 *A Fortunate Life*, p. 256.
5 Vance Palmer, 'The Line', in *Separate Lives* (Stanley Paul, London, 1931), pp. 219, 220-1, 225-6.
6 'Two Masters' first appeared in 1923 in the Sydney University magazine, *Hermes*. It was reprinted in the *London Mercury* and also in O'Brien's *Best Stories*, 1925. (See E. Morris Miller, *Australian Literature*, p. 775.) In 1929 the story was published by Faber & Faber in its *Criterion Miscellany* series (no. 1), and also in *The Mercury Story Book* published by Longman, Green & Co.
7 See *Reveille*, 1 March 1935, pp. 8-9.

8 'Two Masters', in *The Mercury Story Book*, introduced by J. B. Priestley (Longman, Green, London, 1929), p. 184.

9 Ibid., pp. 185, 187.

10 Ibid., pp. 192-3.

11 Ibid., p. 202.

12 J. P. McKinney, *Crucible* (A & R, Sydney, 1935), p. 16.

13 Ibid., pp. 241-2.

14 Ibid., pp. 29, 160.

15 Ibid., p. 8.

16 Ibid., pp. 29-30.

17 Ibid., pp. 41-2, 77.

18 Ibid., pp. 141, 155-6.

19 Ibid., pp. 228-9; see *Saints and Soldiers*, p. 75.

20 *Crucible*, p. 253.

21 Ibid., pp. 238-9.

22 Ibid., p. 272.

23 See McQueen, 'Emu into Ostrich', pp. 86-7.

24 *Crucible*, p. 97.

25 Leslie Meller, *A Leaf of Laurel* (Faber & Faber, London, 1933), pp. 14, 28, 48, 41.

26 Ibid., pp. 59, 62.

27 Ibid., p. 50.

28 Published in, respectively, 'Corrie Denison', *Glimpses* (Scholartis Press, London, 1928), and *Three Personal Records of the War: R. H. Mottram, John Easton, Eric Partridge* (Scholartis Press, London, 1929).

29 See E. Morris Miller, *Australian Literature*, pp. 853-4.

30 Partridge, 'Frank Honywood, Private', p. 282.

31 Ibid., pp. 280, 372, 306, 341, 373-4.

32 Ibid., pp. 374-5.

33 Graves, *Goodbye to All That*, p. 183.

34 Martin Boyd, *A Single Flame* (J. M. Dent, London, 1939), p. 121.

35 Ibid.

36 'Two Masters', p. 196.

37 *A Single Flame*, p. 121.

38 'Frank Honywood, Private', pp. 369, 372.

39 Edgar Morrow, *Iron in the Fire* (A & R, Sydney, 1934), pp. 169, 204.

40 Martin Boyd, *A Difficult Young Man* (Cresset Press, London, 1955), p. 131.

41 *A Single Flame*, p. 47.

42 Ibid., p. 74.

43 Ibid., pp. 71-2. There is no evidence to suggest that Boyd's 'upper-class' parents, who in some ways were unconventional in their attitudes, agreed with the uncle's assessment of the apparently squalid nature of soldiering in the A.I.F. And it should be noted that Martin's two brothers fought in the A.I.F. and resisted promotion to commissioned rank.

44 Ibid., p. 29.

45 Ibid., p. 80.

46 Mann, *Flesh in Armour*, p. 3.

47 Ibid., p. 7.

48 *A Single Flame*, pp. 106, 156, 159, 160-1.

49 Brenda Niall, *Martin Boyd* (OUP, Melbourne, 1974), p. 3.

[50] *A Single Flame,* p. 69.
[51] Ibid., p. 88.
[52] C. E. Montague, *Disenchantment,* pp. 2-3, 6-7.
[53] *A Single Flame,* pp. 36, 103.
[54] Eric J. Leed, *No Man's Land,* pp. 81-2.
[55] *A Single Flame,* p. 123; 'rancorous references', p. 225.
[56] *Day of My Delight* (Lansdowne Press, Melbourne, 1965), p. 235.
[57] Ibid., p. 277.
[58] See Niall, *Martin Boyd,* p. 38.
[59] *Day of My Delight,* p. 72.
[60] Martin Boyd, *When Blackbirds Sing* (Abelard-Schuman, London, 1962), p. 5.
[61] Ibid., pp. 37, 126; *Day of My Delight,* p. 233.
[62] *When Blackbirds Sing,* pp. 38, 6, 9, 14, 21, 25.
[63] Ibid., p. 33.
[64] Ibid., pp. 74-5, 61; Evelyn Waugh, *Sword of Honour* (Chapman & Hall, London, 1965), p. 16.
[65] *When Blackbirds Sing,* p. 155.
[66] Ibid., see pp. 71, 85, 173, 75.
[67] Ibid., pp. 119, 137.
[68] Ibid., pp. 138, 143.
[69] Ibid., pp. 143, 6.
[70] Ibid., p. 173.
[71] Ibid., pp. 178, 184, 188.
[72] Quoted in L. T. Hergenhan, 'Novelist at War: Frederic Manning's "Her Privates We" ', *Quadrant,* 14, no. 66 (1970), p. 19.
[73] Peter Davies, Introduction to the 1943 edition of *Her Privates We,* reprinted in 1964 ed.; see also Miller, *Australian Literature,* p. 79.
[74] See, for example, L. T. Hergenhan, 'Frederick Manning: Neglected Australian Writer', *Quadrant,* 6, no. 4 (1962), pp. 5-18. Also J. M. Douglas Pringle, '*Her Privates We*: An Aesthete Goes to War', in W. S. Ramson (ed.), *The Australian Experience* (Australian National University Press, Canberra, 1974), pp. 121-40.
[75] Bourne's remarks on 'good comradeship' are illustrative:

> "I didn't think heroism was such a common thing . . . I have seen a man risking himself for another more than once: I don't say that they would all do it. It seems to be a spontaneous and irreflective action . . . At one moment a particular man may be nothing at all to you, and the next minute you will go through hell for him. No, it is not friendship. The man doesn't matter so much, it's a kind of impersonal emotion, a kind of enthusiasm, in the old sense of the word . . . We help each other. What is one man's fate to-day, may be another's to-morrow. We are all in it up to the neck together, and we know it."
> Frederic Manning, *Her Privates We* (Peter Davies, London, 1964), pp. 87-8.

(J. M. Douglas Pringle, in 'An Aesthete Goes to War', p. 140, calls this 'the best description of "mateship" ever written'.)
[76] Cyril Falls, *War Books: A Critical Guide* (Peter Davies, London, 1930), p. 292.
[77] Ibid.
[78] See Margot Strickland, *Angela Thirkell, Portrait of a Lady Novelist* (Duckworth,

London, 1977), p. ix.

79 See the remarks of her son, Lance Thirkell, quoted in Stuart Sayers, 'Young Thirkell back after 50 years to lay some ghosts', *Age*, 'Saturday Extra', 2 March 1985, p. 14.

80 *Official History*, vol. 1, p. 558.

81 Strickland, *Angela Thirkell*, pp. 47-8, 49-53.

82 Strickland indicates that Thirkell wrote the original draft of the novel – then called *What Happened on the Boat* – soon after her arrival in Australia in 1920, while the experience was still vivid in her memory. See *Angela Thirkell*, p. 53.

83 *Angela Thirkell*, pp. 88, 171.

84 See Laird, *Other Banners*, p. 186.

85 *Angela Thirkell*, p. 88.

86 Graham McInnes, *The Road to Gundagai* (Sun Books, Melbourne, 1967), p. 76.

87 See Leonie Kramer (ed.), *The Oxford History of Australian Literature* (OUP, Melbourne, 1981), p. 110.

88 Angela Thirkell, *Trooper to the Southern Cross* (Faber & Faber, London, 1934), pp. 66, 87, 104, 111, 115, 282, 129, 118-19, 214.

89 *The Oxford History of Australian Literature*, p. 110.

90 *Saints and Soldiers*, p. 87.

91 *A Handful of Ausseys*, pp. 245-6.

92 *Trooper to the Southern Cross*, p. 22.

93 Ibid., p. 139.

94 Ibid., pp. 41, 27-8.

95 Ibid., pp. 200, 37, 244, 51, 40, 59.

96 Ibid., p. 17.

97 Ibid., pp. 14-15.

98 Ibid., p. 36.

VI SONS OF ANZACS

1 *The Diaries of Evelyn Waugh*, ed. Michael Davie (Weidenfeld and Nicolson, 1976), pp. 448-9. Diary entry dated 'All Saints 1939'.

2 Scannell's poem 'The Great War' is quoted in Fussell, p. 319; Douglas's poem 'Desert Flowers' can be located in Brian Gardner's anthology *The Terrible Rain: The War Poets 1939–1945* (Methuen, London, 1966), pp. 109-10.

3 Eric Lambert, *The Twenty Thousand Thieves* (Frederick Muller, London, 1952), p. 19.

4 *My Brother Jack* (Collins, London–Sydney, 1964), p. 329.

5 See David Walker, 'The Getting of Manhood', in *Australian Popular Culture*, pp. 121, 124.

6 Lambert's biographer, Zoe O'Leary, notes that *The Twenty Thousand Thieves* sold 750 000 copies. See *The Desolate Market* (Edwards and Shaw, Sydney, 1974), p. 105. See also Walker, 'The Getting of Manhood', p. 122.

7 Heseltine, 'Australian Fiction Since 1920', in Dutton (ed.), *The Literature of Australia*, p. 221. For specific instances of ironic references to the 'bronzed Anzac' ideal see Eric Lambert, *The Veterans* (Frederick Muller, London, 1954), p. 12; Lambert, *Glory Thrown In* (Frederick Muller, London, 1959), p. 83; T. A. G.

Hungerford, *The Ridge and the River* (A & R, Sydney, 1952), p. 186; Peter Pinney, *Road in the Wilderness* (Australasian Book Society, Melbourne, 1952), p. 62; Richard Beilby, *No Medals for Aphrodite* (A & R, Sydney, 1970), p. 217; Beilby, *Gunner: A Novel of the Retreat from Crete* (A & R, London, 1977), pp. 130, 234.

8   *Iliad*, p. 383.

9   Michael McKernan, *All In! Australia During the Second World War* (Nelson, Melbourne, 1983), pp. vii-viii, 1.

10 Ibid., p. 20; see also pp. 6, 17.

11 Eric Lambert Papers, MS 10049, La Trobe Library, Melbourne. Diary entry dated 21 February 1941.

12 Ken Clift, *The Saga of a Sig* (K. C. D. Publications, Sydney, 1972), p. 1.

13 *All In!*, p. 29; see also p. 21.

14 C. E. W. Bean, *The Old A.I.F. and the New* (A & R, Sydney, 1940), p. 3; *Official History*, vol. VI, p. 1096.

15 Kenneth Slessor, *Bread and Wine: Selected Prose* (A & R, Sydney, 1970), p. 212.

16 George Johnston, *Australia at War* (A & R, Sydney, 1942), p. 164; see also pp. 4-5, 69, 115.

17 See pp. 5, 23, 52, 86, 199.

18 *Australia at War*, p. 199.

19 Quoted in Christine E. Wilkinson, An Australian Perspective on the Use of Song During the Second World War, B.A. Honours thesis, Monash University, 1979, p. 199. *Sons of the Anzacs* is the name of the 'official' film of the Australian Fighting Forces in World War Two. It included campaign footage by Damien Parer and Frank Hurley.

20 Ken Clift, *The Soldier Who Never Grew Up* (Haldane Publishing, Sydney, 1976), no page number.

21 Lawson Glassop, *We Were the Rats* (A & R, Sydney, 1945), pp. 54, 61.

22 Ibid., p. 128.

23 Henry 'Jo' Gullett, *Not As A Duty Only: An Infantryman's War* (MUP, Melbourne, 1976), pp. 21, 28.

24 John Hetherington, *The Australian Soldier: A Portrait* (F. H. Johnston, Sydney, 1943), pp. 24-5.

25 Alan Seymour, *The One Day of the Year* (Souvenir Press, London, 1967), pp. 118-19.

26 *Bulletin*, 1 May 1946, p. 13.

27 See Author's Preface, pp. vii-viii, *Rusty Bugles* (Currency Press, Sydney, 1980). See also 'The Play in the Theatre', pp. xv-xxxiv.

28 *Gunner*, p. 14.

29 See Jon Cleary, *A Very Private War* (Collins, London-Sydney, 1980), p. 63; *Gunner*, p. 3.

30 *A Very Private War*, pp. 106-7; *The Veterans*, pp. 141-2.

31 Boyd, *Day of My Delight*, p. 276.

32 Beilby, *No Medals for Aphrodite*, p. 54.

33 John Hetherington, *The Winds Are Still* (Georgian House, Melbourne, 1948), p. 262.

34 *A Very Private War*, pp. 35, 165.

35 *Gunner*, p. 234.

36 Ibid., p. 261.

37 Ibid., p. 72.

38 Lambert, *The Twenty Thousand Thieves*, p. 182.
39 Ibid., pp. 192-3.
40 Ibid., p. 301.
41 Glassop, *We Were the Rats*, p. 273.
42 Ibid., p. 96.
43 Ibid., p. 184. The self-conscious 'eloquence' of Reynolds, as illustrated by this quotation, brings to mind the observation of the *Bulletin* reviewer of *Hell's Bells and Mademoiselles*, who commented that Joe Maxwell's purple patches have 'the disastrous effect . . . of presenting the heroic narrator as a low-comedy pundit moving polsyllabically among a ribald crowd of Ginger Micks'. See *Bulletin*, 26 October 1933, p. 2.
44 *The Veterans*, pp. 51-2, 11, 137.
45 Dymphna Cusack and Florence James, *Come in Spinner* (Heinemann, London, 1951), p. 213.
46 Xavier Herbert, *Soldiers' Women* (Panther Books, St Albans, 1963).
47 Cusack and James, *Come in Spinner*, p. 307. See also Geoffrey Dutton, *Andy* (Collins, London, 1968), p. 124.
48 Jon Cleary, *The Climate of Courage* (Collins, London, 1954), p. 212.
49 Walker, 'The Getting of Manhood', p. 140.
50 Glassop, *The Rats in New Guinea*, pp. 20-1.
51 Dutton, *Andy*, p. 101.
52 Ibid., pp. 115, 46, 153.
53 *We Were the Rats*, p. 59.
54 *The Twenty Thousand Thieves*, p. 111; Hungerford, *The Ridge and the River*, p. 30; Lambert, *Glory Thrown In*, p. 22.
55 *Andy*, pp. 92-3.
56 *My Brother Jack*, p. 306.
57 *Glory Thrown In*, p. 22.
58 *Gunner*, p. 70.
59 *The Winds Are Still*, pp. 99-102.
60 *Road in the Wilderness*, pp. 69-70.
61 Lambert, *The Dark Backward* (Shakespeare Head Press, London, 1958), p. 113.
62 *The Winds Are Still*, p. 188.
63 See Roger Hunt, *The Drongoes Who Dared* (Horwitz, Sydney, 1960).
64 Cleary, *The Climate of Courage*, pp. 11-12, 66, 317.
65 *We Were the Rats*, p. 165. Reynolds, however, is unwilling to relinquish entirely his sense of intellectual superiority over the common Digger. His scholarliness is too vital an ingredient of the all-round lustre of his self-portrait for that. Thus, to boost his mates' flagging morale, he is inclined to quote them inspirational chunks of Rupert Brooke and even *Macbeth*. See p. 192.
66 Norman Bartlett, *Island Victory* (A & R, Sydney, 1955), p. 46.
67 Ibid., pp. 47, 129-30, 44, 144.
68 George Turner, *Young Man of Talent* (Cassell, London, 1959), pp. 196, 21, 78, 98, 47, 49.
69 Ibid., pp. 285-7, 212.
70 *No Medals for Aphrodite*, p. 32.
71 Ibid., pp. 22-3, 39.
72 See 'ANZAC . . . A Myth For All Mankind', pp. 14-16.

[73] *My Brother Jack*, p. 305.
[74] Ibid., p. 309.
[75] Ibid., pp. 299-301.
[76] See *Young Man of Talent*, p. 143.
[77] *My Brother Jack*, p. 50.
[78] Ibid., pp. 40, 58.
[79] *My Brother Jack*, pp. 38, 162, 171-2.
[80] Ibid., pp. 301, 338, 382.
[81] Note the observations of Archie Calverton in Johnston's *Clean Straw for Nothing* (Collins, London-Sydney, 1969), p. 194. In Australia, argues Calverton, 'The brave young adventurous Digger turns into an RSL slob, the heroic fighter-pilot becomes a nong, the lithe young athlete gets a beer-belly and fallen arches, the dedicated young actor who takes Molière around the factories settles for the advertising business'.
[82] *My Brother Jack*, pp. 50, 90.
[83] Ibid., p. 63.
[84] *Clean Straw for Nothing*, p. 51.
[85] *My Brother Jack*, p. 353.
[86] Ibid., p. 309.
[87] Ibid., pp. 333, 382; see also pp. 239, 248, 350.

VII THE SECOND A.I.F. IN *THE WAR*

[1] Anthony Powell, *The Soldier's Art* (Heinemann, London, 1966), pp. 2-3.
[2] '*Over There*' with the Australians, p. 15; *Sword of Honour*, p. 476; Wyndham Lewis, *Blasting and Bombardiering* (Caldar and Boyars, London, 1967), p. 207; *The Soldier's Art*, p. 2. See also chapter VI ('Theater of War') of *The Great War and Modern Memory*.
[3] George Eliot, *The Mill on the Floss* (Penguin Classics edn, Harmondsworth, 1985), p. 250.
[4] Walker, 'The Getting of Manhood', pp. 124-5.
[5] See Robert Hewison, *Under Siege: Literary Life in London 1939-45* (Weidenfeld and Nicolson, London, 1977), pp. 37-8, 47-8.
[6] L. W. Sutherland, *Aces and Kings* (A & R, Sydney, 1935), p. 235.
[7] David Campbell, *Flame and Shadow* (UQP, St Lucia, 1976 edn), pp. 168-9.
[8] See 'The Tomb of Lt. John Learmonth A.I.F.', in John Manifold, *Collected Verse* (UQP, St Lucia, 1978), pp. 73-5.
[9] *Gunner*, pp. 45, 52, 115; *Sword of Honour*, p. 464.
[10] Lambert, *The Twenty Thousand Thieves*, p. 19.
[11] Johnston, *Australia at War*, pp. 199-200, 189.
[12] Chester Wilmot, *Tobruk 1941: Capture-Siege-Relief* (A & R, Sydney, 1944), p. 315.
[13] Alan Moorehead, *The March to Tunis: The North African War 1940-1943* [American edition of the *African Trilogy*] (Harper & Row, New York, 1965), pp. 363-4.
[14] Barton Maugham, *Tobruk and El Alamein*, vol. 3, *Australia in the War of 1939-45, Series One: Army* (AWM, Canberra, 1966), p. 745.
[15] Moorehead, *The March to Tunis*, p. 363.

[16] Rolf Boldrewood, *Robbery Under Arms* (Dymock's Book Arcade, Sydney, 1947), p. 1.

[17] See *Meanjin*, 11, no. 4 (Summer 1952), p. 416.

[18] *The Twenty Thousand Thieves*, p. 313. The dust jacket blurb of the Muller international edition of the novel (it had been published first, in 1951 in Australia, by Newmont) calls Lambert 'a new Remarque'.

[19] Ibid., pp. 54, 219. Lambert is quoted in O'Leary, *The Desolate Market*, p. 35.

[20] Gullett quoted in *The Desolate Market*, p. 47. The extensive press reportage of the controversy can be found in the Eric Lambert Papers.

[21] *The Desolate Market*, p. 47.

[22] *The Twenty Thousand Thieves*, p. 124.

[23] Ibid., p. 212.

[24] Letter dated 27/9/51, contained in the Eric Lambert Papers.

[25] *The Twenty Thousand Thieves*, p. 125; other quotations from the novel in this paragraph: pp. 48, 211, 311-12.

[26] *Guardian*, 27 September 1951. See Eric Lambert Papers.

[27] *The Twenty Thousand Thieves*, p. 316.

[28] See Baker, *The Australian Language*, p. 269.

[29] *The Desolate Market*, pp. 90-1.

[30] Glassop, *We Were the Rats*, pp. 83, 192.

[31] Ibid., p. 128.

[32] G. H. Fearnside, *Sojourn in Tobruk* (Ure Smith, Sydney, 1944), pp. 96-9.

[33] M. L. Skinner, *WX—Corporal Smith, A Romance of the A.I.F. in Libya* (R. S. Sampson, Perth, 1941), p. 226.

[34] Ibid., pp. 21, 57, 37, 73, 84, 112-13.

[35] John Robertson, *Australia at War 1939–45* (Heinemann, Melbourne, 1981), pp. 139-40.

[36] David Forrest, *The Last Blue Sea* (Australasian Book Society, Melbourne, 1959), p. 77. Forrest—the pseudonym of David Denholm—received the inaugural Dame Mary Gilmore Award in 1959 for this novel.

[37] Hungerford, *The Ridge and the River*, p. 196.

[38] Peter Ryan, *Fear Drive My Feet* (A & R, Sydney, 1959), p. 129.

[39] Cleary, *The Climate of Courage*, p. 221.

[40] Nigel Krauth, ' "His Universe Contracted": The Australian Soldier's Experience of the New Guinea Jungle War in Fiction', *New Literature Review*, no. 12 (1983), pp. 20-1.

[41] *The Last Blue Sea*, pp. 78-9; 'no illusions': p. 92.

[42] See *The Climate of Courage*, p. 248.

[43] *The Ridge and the River*, pp. 9-10.

[44] See *The Last Blue Sea*, p. 50; also pp. 217, 47.

[45] *The Ridge and the River*, p. 5.

[46] Bartlett, *Island Victory*, p. 16.

[47] Allan Dawes, *Soldier Superb: The Australian Fights in New Guinea* (F. H. Johnston Publishing, Sydney, 1943), p. 9.

[48] *The Climate of Courage*, p. 222.

[49] Raymond Paull, *Retreat from Kokoda: The Australian Campaign in New Guinea in 1942* (William Heinemann Australia, Melbourne, 1982), p. 165.

[50] *Soldier Superb*, p. 9.

[51] *The Last Blue Sea*, pp. 227-8.

⁵² *The Ridge and the River,* pp. 112, 44; *Road in the Wilderness,* p. 20; *The Last Blue Sea,* pp. 223 (see also pp. 144, 217).

⁵³ *The Climate of Courage,* p. 232.

⁵⁴ *The Twenty Thousand Thieves,* pp. 317, 311-12; *The Ridge and the River,* p. 142.

⁵⁵ Ryan, *Fear Drive My Feet,* pp. 162, vii.

⁵⁶ Ibid., pp. 236-7; see also pp. 3, 206, 228.

⁵⁷ Barbusse, *Under Fire,* pp. 5, 329; Manning, *Her Privates We,* pp. 202, 43; *The Veterans,* p. 174.

⁵⁸ *My Brother Jack,* p. 329; see, for example, 'Spirit of Port Moresby in Black and White', *Australasian,* 18 July 1942, p. 9.

⁵⁹ *Soldier Superb,* p. 13.

⁶⁰ See 'New Guinea: The Twilight War', in *Bread and Wine,* pp. 267, 272.

⁶¹ Clement Semmler, 'War Correspondents in Australian Literature: an Outline' *ALS,* 12, no. 2 (Oct. 1985), p. 199; see also Semmler (ed.), *The War Diaries of Kenneth Slessor* (UQP, St Lucia, 1985), p. xxvi.

⁶² Osmar White, *Green Armour* (Wren Publishing paperback edn, Melbourne, 1972), pp. 207-8.

⁶³ Quoted in Graeme Kinross Smith, 'T. A. G. Hungerford', *Westerly,* no. 2 (June 1976), p. 37. See also Hungerford's remarks in *ALS,* 12, no. 2 (Oct. 1985), pp. 263-4.

⁶⁴ *The Rats in New Guinea,* p. 75; *Climate of Courage,* p. 222.

⁶⁵ *The Veterans,* p. 12; *Road in the Wilderness,* p. 61 (see also p. 65); *The Last Blue Sea,* p. 198. Peter Ryan's *Fear Drive My Feet* contains a classical example of macabre Australian military humour. Ryan recollects Australians marching past some rough graves of Japanese, from one of which a stiffened hand and forearm protruded: ' . . . they bent down one by one and shook the hand of death. "Good on you, sport," each one said gravely to the hand as he moved on towards . . . perhaps just as rough a grave of his own'. See p. 250.

⁶⁶ *The Ridge and the River,* p. 219. General Hamilton's observation is quoted in Moorehead, *Gallipoli,* p. 132.

⁶⁷ *No Medals for Aphrodite,* p. 166.

⁶⁸ See Charlotte Carr-Gregg, *Japanese Prisoners of War in Revolt: The Outbreaks at Featherston and Cowra during World War II* (UQP, St Lucia, 1978), p. 56; Peter Cowan, 'Seaforth Mackenzie's Novels', *Meanjin,* 24, no. 3 (Sept. 1965), p. 301; Donovan Clarke, 'Seaforth Mackenzie: Novelist of Alienation', *Southerly,* 25, no. 2 (1965), p. 84.

⁶⁹ Kenneth Seaforth Mackenzie, *Dead Men Rising* (A & R Classics edn, Sydney, 1975), pp. 51, 18, 116.

⁷⁰ Ibid., pp. 38-9, 40.

⁷¹ Quoted in Hewison, *Under Siege,* p. 120.

⁷² *Dead Men Rising,* pp. 35-6.

⁷³ *Andy,* p. 212.

⁷⁴ A. W. Penfold, W. C. Baylis, K. E. Crispin, *Galleghan's Greyhounds: The Story of the 2/30th A.I.F.* (2/30th Bn A.I.F. Assoc., Sydney, 1949), p. 377.

⁷⁵ Randolph Stow, *The Merry-Go-Round in the Sea,* pp. 164, 207.

⁷⁶ See *Of Love and War: The Letters and Diaries of Captain Adrian Curlewis and his family, 1939–1945,* ed. Philippa Poole (Lansdowne Press, Sydney, 1982).

⁷⁷ Quoted in Carr-Gregg, *Japanese Prisoners of War in Revolt,* p. 25.

⁷⁸ See Nevil Shute, *A Town Like Alice* (Heinemann, Melbourne, 1950), p. 129.

[79] Quoted in Lionel Wigmore, *The Japanese Thrust,* vol. IV, *Australia in the War of 1939–45, Series One: Army* (AWM, Canberra, 1957), p. 587.

[80] Ray Parkin, *Out of the Smoke: The Story of a Sail* (Hogarth, London, 1960), p. 152.

[81] See Yeats's Introduction to *The Oxford Book of Modern Verse 1892–1935* (The Clarendon Press, Oxford, 1936), p. xxxiv.

[82] 'Ek Dum', 'Naked Island and Naked Souls', *Stand-To,* June–July 1952, p. 21.

[83] See John Romeril, *The Floating World* (Currency Methuen, Sydney, 1975), pp. 84-95.

[84] Ian Sabey, *Stalag Scrapbook* (Cheshire, Melbourne, 1947), p. 8.

[85] Arthur Koestler, *Scum of the Earth* (Hutchinson, London, 1968), p. 126.

[86] Russell Braddon, *The Naked Island* (Werner Laurie, London, 1952), pp. 165-6.

[87] See Rohan Rivett, *Behind Bamboo* (Seal Books, Adelaide, 1973), p. 151; also Stan Arneil, *One Man's War* (Alternative Publishing Co-operative, Sydney, 1980), p. 3; Kenneth Harrison, *The Brave Japanese* (Rigby, Adelaide, 1966), p. 132.

[88] My inclusion of this statistic is not intended as an exculpation of the German and Italian treatment of Allied prisoners, the harshness of which is extensively documented in an appendix to the third volume of the official history, Barton Maugham's *Tobruk and El Alamein.* On the other hand, at least on the evidence of Mackenzie's *Dead Men Rising,* the Australian handling of the Japanese POWs seems to have been lenient to the point of laxity. Note that exact figures of Australian POW losses can be found in Wigmore, *The Japanese Thrust,* p. 642.

[89] Gullett, *Not As A Duty Only,* p. 127.

[90] Russell Braddon, 'Song of War', in *End of a Hate* (Cassell, London, 1958), p. 186.

[91] John McGregor, *Blood on the Rising Sun* (Bencoolen Books, Sydney, 1980), p. 223.

[92] Paul Brickhill, *The Great Escape* (Faber & Faber, London, 1951), p. 32.

[93] Norman Carter, *G-String Jesters* (Currawong Publishing, Sydney, 1966), p. 18. Another prisoner of the Japanese, George Sprod, writes how his pride (and that of his comrades) 'nose-dived' when taken into custody by men who looked like 'a mob of schoolboys on an outing'. Quoted in *Fighting Words: Australian War Writing,* ed. Carl Harrison-Ford (Lothian, Melbourne, 1986), p. 190.

[94] Douglas Valentine, *The Hotel Tacloban* (A & R, London, 1985), p. 61.

[95] W. S. Kent-Hughes, *Slaves of the Samurai* (OUP, Melbourne, 1946), pp. 165, 57, 82.

[96] Ray Parkin, *The Sword and the Blossom* (Hogarth, London, 1968), p. 199. For the views of Bean and Manning on soldierly self-interest, see *Official History,* vol. I, p. 607, and *Her Privates We,* p. 164.

[97] *Of Love and War,* p. 210.

[98] Eric Lambert, *MacDougal's Farm* (Frederick Muller, London, 1965), p. 40.

[99] Ray Parkin, *Into the Smother: A Journal of the Burma–Siam Railway* (Hogarth, London, 1963), pp. 105-6, italics mine.

VIII VIETNAM SURVIVED

[1] 'Ek Dum', 'Naked Island and Naked Souls', p. 21.

[2] See my article 'The Rise of the Prisoner-of-War Writers', *ALS,* 12, no. 2 (Oct. 1985), pp. 270-4.

3 Barney Roberts, *A Kind of Cattle* (AWM and Collins, Canberra-Sydney, 1985), p. 14.

4 *A Fortunate Life*, p. 277; for a description of bayonet fighting, see p. 260.

5 Rae Desmond Jones, 'The Photograph', in *Shadows from Wire*, p. 78.

6 Roger McDonald, 'The Last Anzac Muster', *Shadows from Wire*, p. 24.

7 See David Malouf, *Fly Away Peter* (Chatto & Windus, London, 1982), p. 103. For Malouf's remarks about the impact of the war on Australia, see *ALS*, 12, no. 2 (Oct. 1985), p. 266.

8 *Fly Away Peter*, p. 131.

9 *The Great War and Modern Memory*, p. 231.

10 Roger McDonald, *1915* (UQP, St Lucia, 1979), p. 131; *Fly Away Peter*, pp. 37-8.

11 Patrick White, *The Tree of Man* (Penguin, Harmondsworth, 1961), p. 187.

12 Ibid., p. 199.

13 Bergonzi, *Heroes' Twilight*, p. 219.

14 McDonald, *1915*, pp. 59-60.

15 *1915*, pp. 144, 110, 22, 27.

16 See *ALS*, 12, no. 2 (Oct. 1985), p. 265.

17 *1915*, p. 12.

18 D. H. Lawrence, *Kangaroo*, p. 183.

19 *1915*, pp. 417, 135, 313.

20 Veronica Brady, review of *1915*, *Westerly*, no. 4 (1979), p. 79.

21 *1915*, p. 294.

22 Ibid., p. 423.

23 John Carroll, *Token Soldiers* (Wildgrass Books, Melbourne, 1983), p. 66.

24 See Shirley Cass, et al., *We Took Their Orders and Are Dead* (Ure Smith, Sydney, 1971), p. 26.

25 Rhys Pollard, *The Cream Machine* (A & R, Sydney, 1972), p. 88. The poems by Craig Powell and Roland Robinson can also be found in Wallace-Crabbe and Pierce, *Clubbing of the Gunfire*, pp. 181-2, 179.

26 *Token Soldiers*, pp. 171-2.

27 Kenneth Cook, *The Wine of God's Anger* (Cheshire-Lansdowne, Melbourne, 1968), pp. 24-5.

28 Ibid., p. 140. See *The Twenty Thousand Thieves*, p. 302.

29 Ted Serong, 'Lost, our spirits and our standards', *Age*, 1 May 1985, p. 13.

30 See David Alexander, *When the Buffalo Fight* (Hutchinson, Melbourne, 1980), p. 9:

> They [the Australians in Vietnam] were secure in the knowledge that the Australian is superior to the man of every other nation, and while there might be more of the others, with greater wealth, they were definitely inferior. Without realizing it, two of their great strengths were the dry Australian sense of humour and the inborn independence of the Australian male, ingested with his mother's milk, that allowed him not to be over-awed by another's appearance and reputation, but to reserve judgement and base approval or rejection on visible performance.

31 William Nagle, *The Odd Angry Shot* (A & R, Sydney, 1975), pp. 10-11.

32 Ibid., pp. 40, 81, 93.

33 Ibid., p. 43.

34 For a more searching portrayal of the traumatic effect of Vietnam on ordinary Australians, see Terry Burstall, *The Soldier's Story* (UQP, St Lucia, 1986).

35 *The Odd Angry Shot*, p. 92.

36 *All Quiet on the Western Front*, p. 297.

37 Michael Frazer, *Nasho* (Aries Imprint, Melbourne, 1984), p. 42.

38 Ibid., pp. 87, 90, 274.

39 Ibid., p. 296.

40 Rowe's criticism of the American handling of the war in *Count Your Dead* landed him in official hot water. (He was working with the Defence Intelligence Agency in Washington at the time of writing the novel.) Following the furore, he resigned from the Army. See William H. Wilde, et al., *The Oxford Companion to Australian Literature* (OUP, Melbourne, 1985), p. 601.

41 See Hugh Lunn, *Vietnam: A Reporter's War* (UQP, St Lucia, 1985), p. 141; Michael Herr, *Dispatches*, p. 173.

42 See Pat Burgess, *WARCO: Australian Reporters at War* (William Heinemann Australia, Melbourne, 1986), p. 154.

43 Roger McDonald, 'Who Owns the Great War?', *Age Monthly Review*, 3, no. 9 (September 1983), p. 3.

44 Gerard Henderson, 'The Anzac Legend after *Gallipoli*', *Quadrant*, 26, no. 7 (1982), p. 62.

45 See *Age* 'Saturday Extra', 7 January 1984, p. 8. The 'experts' who selected the *Official History* were Brian Johns (Publishing Director of Penguin Books Australia), and the novelist and short story writer, Frank Moorhouse.

46 Gammage, *The Broken Years*, pp. vii, 279.

47 Adam-Smith, *The Anzacs*, p. ix.

48 Alec Hepburn, *True Australian War Tales* (Rigby, Adelaide, 1983).

49 *WARCO: Australian Reporters at War*, p. 164.

50 George Johnston, *The Australians* (Rigby, Adelaide, 1966), p. 265.

51 Lawson Glassop, 'A Walk in the Snow', in *With the Australians in Korea*, ed. Norman Bartlett (AWM, Canberra, 1954), pp. 216-17.

Index